D1283086

THE MIRAGE
OF
MODERNIZATION

THE MIRAGE
OF
MODERNIZATION

BORIS KAGARLITSKY

Translated by Renfrey Clarke

MONTHLY REVIEW PRESS
NEW YORK

Library of Congress Cataloging-in-Publication Data
Kagarlitsky, Boris, 1958–
    The mirage of modernization / by Boris Kagarlitsky ; translated by
Renfrey Clarke.
        p.   cm.
    Includes bibliographical references and index.
    ISBN 0-85345-911-8 (cloth) : $38.00. — ISBN 0-85345-912-6 (pbk.):
$18.00
    1. Economic development—Case studies. 2. Economic Development—
Social aspects. 3. Europe, Eastern—Economic policy—1989– 4. Europe,
Eastern—Social conditions—1989– I. Title.
HD87.K34 1994   94-31720
338.9—dc20   CIP

Monthly Review Press
122 West 27th Street
New York NY 10001

10 9 8 7 6 5 4 3 2 1

CONTENTS

PREFACE

I began writing this book in 1984. At that time everything in the world appeared clear and simple. Leftists believed in the revolutionary liberation of the masses, technocrats in technical progress, and bureaucrats in stability. All looked forward confidently to the future. Underdeveloped countries hoped to enter the ranks of the developed. The industrialized societies of the West regarded their high living standards and social stability as guaranteed. Communist governments were convinced that no dissidents could prevent them holding sway over half the world. The peoples subject to communist governments expected nothing but a gradual rise in living standards and a slow democratization. Anyone who thought differently was an extremist.

Since that time everything has changed. The word "stability" has gone out of fashion. The Soviet Union, which in the early 1980s appeared to be a model of stagnation and immobility, began once again to astonish the world with rapid changes and political upheavals. As in the early decades of the century, the attention of humanity was once again riveted on our country. Russia had been the first country where bourgeois modernization had miscarried, where the rulers' attempts to catch up with the flourishing West had led first to political catastrophe, and then to the collapse of capitalist society.

Such collapses began occurring regularly. One after another, developing countries tore themselves loose from the capitalist path. The Eastern bloc and its third world satellites could always be grouped together on one indubitable basis: in none of these countries—apart from Czechoslovakia and East Germany—had a process of bourgeois modernization been carried through.

The third world states that tried to imitate the Soviet experience during the 1960s and 1970s were not occupied by Soviet troops. Everything that occurred there arose out of the contradictions of these societies themselves. The ideas of the Russian Revolution appealed to the peoples of underdeveloped countries precisely because, as the German historians M. Brie and E. Boelke noted, they represented "a highly effective ideology for noncapitalist modernization."[1] Seventy years after the Revolution of 1917 it had become clear that trusting economic development to a centralized bureaucracy was a mistake. The failure of the Soviet model was not just evident in Russia. Its collapse was universal, from Romania to tropical Africa.

Regardless of the ideological clothing in which it was presented, the Communist experiment in the East was primarily an attempt to overcome underdevelopment. The gains that were made allowed the ruling elites and the populations of the Communist countries to forget where they had started from, and to compare themselves with the developed West. This forced the Soviet Union, with its numerous Eastern European, Asiatic, African, and Caribbean allies and clients to enter into a pointless, drawn-out rivalry with the West, and also gave rise to unrealizable hopes of consumer abundance. Even the bureaucracy's successes thus prepared the way for a new social crisis.

The collapse of faith in Communist ideology could hardly fail to create massive illusions concerning the possibility of joining the West. The failure of the bureaucratic experiments was followed everywhere in the 1980s and 1990s by conscious or unconscious attempts to return to the capitalist road. The banner of the epoch became privatization. Liberal ideologues held forth on "the end of history," on a final victory over socialist ideas. The politicians were more cautious than the ideologues, but they could not stay on the sidelines. Some political leaders triumphantly denounced the past, while others spoke of continuity. All, however, were united in the hope that the second attempt at capitalist modernization would be more successful than the first precisely because it would rest on the achievements of the spurned noncapitalist past.

Reality did not bear out these hopes either. Almost everywhere, the turn to capitalism did not signify merely a shift to new methods of rule and new forms of development, but was also accompanied by a return to the starting point. Years and in some cases decades of noncapitalist development were lost, and the countries in a certain sense were left even more backward than before the anticapitalist experiment began. The contradictions which the Communist regimes had failed to resolve made the emergence of modern forms of capitalism impossible as well. Once again the countries would be forced to pass through the stages of primitive accumulation and rapacious exploitation, and again—sometimes for the third time!—to destroy their traditional forms of social life.

Doing away with the consequences of the bureaucratic experiment often proved to be even more catastrophic than the experiment itself. The societies of Eastern Europe and the third world found themselves in a vicious circle. Not only Russia, but also the countries of Central Europe have finished up in practice closer to Central America than to their western neighbors. A tragic consciousness of the real state of affairs is beginning to dawn, an understanding that the countries of Eastern Europe and the former USSR are to share in the fate of the third world—that is, of the great majority of humanity.

The worldwide triumph of liberalism has turned out to mark the beginning of a new global crisis. Ideologues who only yesterday were issuing guarantees of progress and enrichment to countries that adhered to the free market have begun complaining that these countries are ill-prepared to assimilate advanced forms of the market economy. The Western world itself, far from gathering the fruits of a great historic victory, has been hit with a multitude of new problems. As the German philosopher Robert Kurz noted ironically, "if we are really about to experience 'the end of history,' then this will be a far from happy end."[2]

Both the third world and the former Eastern bloc are again facing a choice of roads. It is necessary to understand the mistakes of the past and to see the dangers of the future. The decades of previous development can either serve as the basis for new modernization, or else they can be "lost," depending on which conclusions are derived from our experience.

If we can learn useful lessons from our own past, there is a slim hope that, for the majority of humanity, development in the future will be something other than a chain of errors, failures and catastrophes.

CHAPTER 1

THE THIRD WORLD IN A LABYRINTH OF PROBLEMS

The crash of Communist ideology in Russia and Eastern Europe was invariably accompanied by calls for these countries to return to the "bosom of civilization," to become "normal." And the only models of normality, of course, were the developed countries of the West.[1]

The liberal propagandists thus effectively declared the great majority of humanity to be abnormal. This is because today's norm for the majority of people on the planet is backwardness and underdevelopment. Meanwhile, the notion of the West and the Western road as standards of successful development still prevails, and not only in Eastern Europe. Even non-European authors repeat the old European formulas. There is nothing surprising in the fact that most well-informed foreign observers failed completely to anticipate the Islamic revolution in Iran. But many Iranian politicians, both on the right and the left, proved incapable of understanding where their country was headed. After the Iranian revolution the theoreticians of modernization were forced to review many of their concepts. They began speaking of the "enormous importance of culture and mass consciousness as factors shaping social life," and of the fact that no strategy for change can be effective "if it is reduced solely to narrow economic aspects."[2] Finally it was recognized that as a result of the instability of the social and political structures in third world countries, culture was bound to become the primary force uniting people. It was impossible to explain the changes that were taking place by using a textbook on economics. Nevertheless, the theoretical riddles of the third world have not been solved. Moreover, the collapse of the Communist system and the rapid

11

transformation of the former Eastern bloc into the new periphery of the capitalist world has brought us face to face with new problems.

The crisis of the early 1980s showed how little the developing countries had achieved during the previous decades. For these countries, the events in Eastern Europe and the USSR during 1989 and 1990 created new problems. Throughout almost all the postwar period, the rivalry of the United States and the USSR had allowed the developing countries to maneuver between East and West, using Soviet military aid as a counterweight to the economic dominance of the Western powers. This became impossible after economic crisis first paralyzed Soviet foreign policy, then led to the collapse of the USSR itself and to the recognition of the "historic victory" of the West in the cold war.

Some leftists declare that in the early 1990s the cold war, in its broader historic sense, is continuing, but with the collapse of one of the two protagonists.[3] If, however, one can speak of continuing conflict, this is no longer a conflict of two world systems, embodying two incompatible models of economic and political organization. It is now a clash of rich against poor, of developed against underdeveloped, of hegemonic against dependent countries within the framework of a single world capitalist system, of which Eastern Europe, Russia, and China have, subject to certain conditions, become part.

During the 1970s the developing countries not only experienced enormous difficulties themselves, but also created unpredictable problems for their patrons, destroying the political equilibrium and placing both superpowers in embarrassing positions. In the early 1980s a left-wing British journalist could write that the third world had issued a challenge simultaneously to imperialism and capitalism and to Soviet foreign policy.[4] Ten years later, the disintegrating Soviet Union became a source of instability.

The abolition of the colonial system in the 1960s aroused wild hopes in the new states. No one was arguing that all problems would be solved, but many people assumed that the winning of political independence would lead to the solution of social and economic problems. Everywhere, the aim of development was proclaimed to be overcoming backwardness, creating a national industrial base, raising living standards, ending illiteracy, and creating a viable independent modern economy. In short, it was necessary to catch up with the European countries. The key to solving all problems was industrialization. A technocratic euphoria seized both the third world ruling circles and the intelligentsia. The Chilean sociologist L. Ratinov wrote of a genuine technological fanaticism among the middle layers of society, with factories seen as the only real symbol of progress, and a general naive confidence that industrialization would automatically lead to a more equitable distribution of income, to social improvements, and so forth.[5] In documents prepared by the United Nations, one also finds the same naive faith that industrialization could solve all problems—social progress was regarded as a natural outcome of economic growth.[6] Technocrats of both left and right joined in repeating slogans of development that today sound like demagogy or ironic jests: For wealth to be divided up, it must first of all be created.[7]

The crisis of the early 1980s showed the chosen path to be a dead end. Certainly, wealth was created. Many factories were built. Nevertheless the gap between rich and poor countries increased, dependency in many cases was strengthened, and social problems grew more acute. Political independence has not helped overcome the catastrophic gap between the center and the periphery of the world capitalist economy. Overall, this gap is even increasing.

Virtually all experts now agree that the development strategies followed by third world governments in the 1960s and 1970s ended in failure. The exceptions to this rule can be counted on one's fingers. If we leave out of account those countries which managed to raise their living standards thanks to the oil price rises of 1973 and 1974, we can speak only of South Korea and the newly industrialized countries: Taiwan, Hong Kong, and Singapore, the "tigers" of Southeast Asia.

The rapid economic growth experienced by these countries in the 1970s and 1980s aroused huge interest not only in the third world, but also in the countries of the Eastern bloc, trying to escape from the impasse in which the entire Communist world found itself by the end of the 1980s. The stream of cheap goods pouring into world markets from the newly industrialized countries even led some writers to conclude that the center, not the periphery, now has most to lose from participating in the capitalist world system.[8] East European authors who have called for close study of the examples of South Korea and the Asian tigers have stressed that these countries managed to avoid socialist experiments. And indeed, one cannot speak of socialist ideology in South Korea, where a harsh anticommunist dictatorship has held power. For two decades all the Asian tigers have succeeded in avoiding not just socialism, but also any kind of democracy. Moreover, not one of them has succeeded in avoiding a major statization of the economy. The Soviet researcher V. Mikheev, while declaring categorically that policies of nationalization and of developing the public sector are invariably ineffective and harmful to development, is simultaneously forced to acknowledge that state intervention in South Korea was "broad and stringent."[9] The South Korean miracle would hardly have been possible had certain of the methods of Stalinist industrialization not been repeated there. As the British researcher Aidan Foster-Carter noted, the state intervened in the development of the South Korean economy in the most diverse ways and at all levels. It did not simply fine-tune the economic mechanism or correct market disproportions, but governed and determined the whole process. Thus, the degree of state control over the investment funds (until recently the state owned all the largest banks) was unprecedented outside the Communist world. Meanwhile, the situation in agriculture, where the state fixed prices, invested capital, gave credits, and purchased crops, effectively transformed the whole sector into one gigantic state farm.[10]

However, one cannot help but note two fundamental differences with the Stalinist model. First, the Soviet leadership placed its stake on the maximum possible degree of isolation of the economy from international influences, on the creation of a military-industrial sector, and on the formation of an internal market controlled by the state. In South Korea what was involved was above all the expanding of exports and the conquering of external markets. Second, the Soviet Union sought the maximum possible degree of technological and financial independence from the outside world, while South Korea and the other Asian tigers remained dependent not only on foreign markets, but also on Western technological and financial centers.

Mikheev insists that there is nothing inherently evil in dependency, since before long it ensures economic and social progress. But he is forced to admit that this very progress has many flaws: "Trusting in rapid economic growth had the effect of shifting long-term and—from the point of view of current objectives—inefficient basic research onto the back burner. This is largely responsible for the phenomenon of the brain drain, in which talented scientists have seen no possibility of their rational employment within the country."[11] It is typical that in the USSR and Eastern Europe the crisis of Communist modernization also led to a sharp growth in technological and financial dependency, and then in addition to unsuccessful attempts at reorientation from the internal to the external market.

The success of South Korea on the world market in turn gave rise to numerous internal problems which undermined the foundations of the economic miracle. The wages of hired workers began rising rapidly. "Korea's wage," wrote a British researcher, "has exceeded that found in earlier industrial revolutions, including that of Japan. The real earnings of British workers are estimated to have risen by 150 percent between 1781 and 1851, but Korean manufacturing workers achieved a comparable gain in about twenty years (from 1955 to 1976)."[12] This rapid wage growth, which followed inevitably on the expansion of exports, led to a fall in the competitiveness of Korean products. Between 1988 and 1990 seventy-seven foreign firms ceased operations in South Korea, while the enterprises which they shut down found new local owners in only twelve cases. Meanwhile, South Korean firms are preferring to invest their capital not at home, but in Asian and Caribbean countries where labor power is even cheaper.

The limited democratization which has occurred in South Korean society has also played a negative role. These firms are leaving the country since they can no longer count on the authorities suppressing workers' struggles as they did earlier, before the democratic movement of 1987 altered the relations of social forces. Since then, workers have begun resorting to strikes, demonstrations, and publicity in their fight for higher wages and better working conditions.[13] Entrepreneurs who once invested in South Korea have begun showing increased interest in China, and recently in Vietnam, for the precise reason that the stable Communist regimes there are capable of defending property owners from strikes, independent trade unions, and other "horrors" of democracy. The model of development adopted by the Asian tigers excludes democracy not only because the banning of strikes and suppression of trade unions renders the country attractive to foreign investors, but also because the export-based model consciously presupposes a low cost of labor power; consequently, achieving success in external markets is possible only through restraining the growth of living standards at home. This means constant social tension; meanwhile, the more complex the country's export products become, and the more the country is linked to external markets, the more rapidly will dissatisfaction increase. Preserving equilibrium in such an unstable system is impossible without dictatorship. Any democratization, even a partial one, places the entire model under threat. In this respect the Asian miracle reproduces in a striking way the contradictions of the Communist system. The political liberalization that began in the region in the late 1980s has undermined the basis of the system to no less a degree than the reforms that occurred in Eastern Europe after the death of Stalin.

The weakness of the bourgeoisie and the strength of the bureaucracies in all the newly industrialized countries means that a perestroika oriented toward installing normal bourgeois-democratic regimes in these countries will meet with numerous problems, and events will most likely fly out of control. However, the problems of South Korea might well seem trifling beside the catastrophic difficulties which other peoples are encountering. Most of the countries of the third world, including those that have oriented toward exports and have sought conscientiously to copy the Korean model, have not succeeded in climbing out of poverty.

The failure has been almost universal. Many young states after three decades of development have finished up in worse shape than when they achieved independence. Many people in Africa and Asia now regard the onset of independence as the beginning of an even more difficult period.[14] In the field of technology, the developing countries after the 1970s lagged behind the West by a whole historical epoch. The most successful countries managed to avoid the general fate, but this served merely to increase the heterogeneity and to intensify the contradictions within the third world.

The rapid increase in oil prices enriched a few countries, for a short time creating the illusion that a miraculous solution had at last been found. But no miracle occurred. Throughout the 1950s and 1960s oil prices had been held at artificially low levels. Having won their political independence, oil producers managed to unite in the OPEC cartel and obtain more advantageous prices. In essence, what occurred was a normal change of the market conjuncture within the framework of the existing system. Nevertheless, oil was declared a weapon of the third world. At first this weapon was used quite effectively. The increased oil prices of the 1970s were retribution for the colonial exploitation of these countries' natural resources during earlier decades. But this strategy drastically worsened the position of developing countries which did not have their own oil. The world market eventually responded by lowering demand. Maintaining prices at their earlier levels became impossible, and bitter disagreements broke out between oil exporters.

The revenues from oil proved insufficient to give a major boost to the economies of such densely populated countries as Nigeria, Mexico, or Indonesia. Only small or middle-sized countries made real gains. In the early 1970s per capita incomes in Venezuela, Kuwait, and Libya were almost as high as in the West, but these countries' underdevelopment was not overcome. Earlier, backwardness had been associated with poverty, but after 1973 there appeared a whole group of wealthy states which despite their riches remained underdeveloped. They were like beggars who had suddenly received huge inheritances, and who had no idea what to do with their millions. The economies of these countries could not digest the funds they were receiving from oil exports. Their industries remained weak and technologically dependent. There was no layer of highly trained local personnel, and commercial experience was lacking. Labor resources were limited, and the social system was not ripe for change. In a number of oil-producing countries food output soon declined sharply, and foreign indebtedness began a rapid increase. The ruling elites often took to exporting capital, reinvesting their profits in industrialized countries. In this way, the wealth of the oil-exporting countries obstructed development and gave rise to parasitical tendencies. "After creating the illusion of wealth," the radical Egyptian economist Samir Amin wrote, "oil played the same role that gold had played in Spain in the seventeenth century: it delayed the serious transformations on which an authentic Arab renaissance depended."[15]

A significant proportion of national income was simply squandered. Arab sheikhs and Venezuelan oil millionaires became notorious throughout the world for their extravagance.[16] In other cases the accumulation of large amounts of capital, when combined with limited opportunities for industrialization, gave rise to political expansionism and foreign expansion. At times the interference by the oil powers in the affairs of other developing countries was regarded as a new form of economic colonialism.[17] The liberal Soviet scholar Viktor Sheinis noted that these processes can lead to the appearance of subimperialist formations, claiming the role of power centers in world politics. They rest on the monopoly ownership of important factors of production, particularly oil and other raw materials. In internal politics the first economic achievements which appear not as the result of wise policies, but as a sort of gift of fate, serve only to strengthen bureaucratism in the state apparatus, and to strengthen authoritarian regimes which ascribe any successes to themselves. As a rule, the power of subimperialist elites is exercised in repressive, antidemocratic forms. To strengthen their position, subimperialist rulers constantly engaged in conflicts with the Western powers, and more rarely with the Soviet Union. Meanwhile, the anti-imperialist (anti-American, anti-British) sentiments of the masses are also mobilized in order to strengthen the positions of groups of the new and old oligarchies.[18]

One of the first clashes between the forces of the West and a regional power which had developed a powerful military potential was the war between Great Britain and Argentina over the Malvinas Islands in 1982. Another example of subimperialist expansion was the intervention by Libya in the civil war in Chad. Throughout the 1970s and 1980s Libya was constantly on the brink of war with its neighbors and even with the United States.

Irrespective of whether the territorial claims of the subimperialist powers on their neighbors were just, these situations were always marked by the reactionary policies of the local elites, which combined domestic repression with foreign expansion. Millions of petrodollars went on the purchase of the most modern weapons in the Soviet Union, in the United States, and in other countries. The poor states of the third world were forced in turn to arm themselves. The arms race had catastrophic consequences. From the 1970s, the developing countries began to arm themselves more rapidly than the industrialized states, while the need for standardization that is inherent in military technology spurred an accelerating growth in military potential.

The use of petrodollars to finance the arms race made possible the expansionist policies of the regime of Saddam Hussein in Iraq. The growth of the military might of Iraq, and of other subimperialist powers in Latin America, Asia, and Africa, would have been impossible without the support of the West and the Soviet Union. France, Italy, West Germany, and the USSR together helped to create the Iraqi military machine. This strategy had the full support of the United States and of the Arab oil sheikhs, and above all of the Emir of Kuwait. As scholars have noted, it was thanks to this aid that the Iraqi government, even during the conflict with Iran, was able to build roads and stylish five-star hotels, while paying social benefits to the people who served as the regime's base of support. The West and the Soviet Union jointly helped create the regime which simply in order to exist required a constant crisis.[19] As often happens, the former allies turned into mortal foes. A British radical weekly remembered that it was the United States and the West that created Iraq in the capacity of a subimperialist power in order to compensate for the collapse of another subimperialist power after the Shah of Iran was overthrown. The attack by Iraq on Iran received full support from the West, but the regime of Saddam Hussein, like that of the Argentinian generals earlier, soon went out of control. After Iran, Kuwait became a victim of Iraqi aggression, and the answer was an attack by the United States and its allies on Iraq. The subimperialist was now trying to become a full-fledged regional power. It had gone into battle against those who earlier supported it. Thus the conflict over Kuwait was a clash between the imperialism of the United States and its allies on the one hand, and a rising subimperialism on the other: a struggle among thieves.[20]

Like other analogous regimes in similar situations the government of Saddam Hussein resorted to anti-imperialist demagogy, trying to present itself as an expression of the national hopes of the Arab people. But the Iraqi regime's previous policies were too well known for anyone to believe this in the West. Even some of the most radical Trotskyist grouplets noted that the Hussein regime was bourgeois and totalitarian,[21] connected by a thousand threads to capitalism and imperialism.[22]

The Iraqi government succeeded in using the patriotic sentiments of the Arab masses for its own purposes. On the Palestinian lands under Israeli occupation, newborn babies were named Saddam Hussein. A correspondent for *Le Monde,* a paper which is hard to suspect of Iraqi sympathies, reported from Algiers, "Saddam Hussein has become a hero, since whatever might be said in the Western press, which no one here disputes, he has not bowed his head and is holding out, one against all."[23]

After the American and British bombers had hurled thousands of tons of explosives at Iraq, destroying not so much military targets as bridges, factories, and residential districts, demonstrations of many thousands of people supporting Iraq began to occur throughout the Arab world. Even the Iraqi opposition, part of which had conducted an armed struggle against Hussein, did not support the Western allies. The leaders of the antigovernment grouplets, both Muslims and leftists, recognized unanimously that to fail to speak out against the war means to lose the moral right to oppose the regime.[24]

As the Arab masses awakened and their self-confidence increased, they began putting forward demands directed at the local regimes. It must be recognized that subimperialist expansion can play a progressive role in certain circumstances. A left-wing British journalist even compared Hussein to Bismarck, and his struggle for hegemony over the Arab world to the unification of Germany under Prussia in 1871.[25] But unlike Bismarck, who shattered the armies of Austria and France, Saddam Hussein could not pride himself on military victories. Huge sums spent on arms and militarization did not result in victory either in the eight-year war with Iran, or in the clash with the United States.

Of course, the very fact that in 1991 the armed forces of a small Arab country for two months held off the attacks of a coalition uniting some thirty countries, many of which were stronger militarily than Iraq, could not fail to arouse enthusiasm in the Arab world. But finally the Iraqi forces, after suffering enormous losses, were forced to quit Kuwait, and the price paid by the people of Iraq for their ruler's expansionism was that tens of thousands of peaceful citizens died under American and British bombs. Increased military power and conflicts with the West do not in themselves solve any of the problems of the third world. In Russia in the eighteenth century, modernization of the army was seen as a basis for the modernization of the whole society. But the costs of such a strategy are exorbitant. A Soviet economic journal noted: "At the same time as world military spending rose by approximately three times over fifteen years, the military outlays of developing countries increased on average by six times, and in Africa by nine times! Thus the arms debt of many developing countries became the most rapidly growing component of their foreign indebtedness."[26]

Nevertheless, the main cause of the new crisis has not been the arms race, but the failure of the entire strategy of economic growth. The countries with the greatest foreign debt were not the most backward ones, but those which had achieved a certain level of industrialization.

Around a third of the debts of the developing world were owed by the countries of Latin America. In 1985, when the debt crisis broke out, Latin America's gross debt to the West amounted to $360 billion.

It would be easy simply to blame this situation on incompetent governments. "Third world states spending money unaccountably have failed thoroughly to enrich the lives of their citizenry or to entrench just laws that would allow the citizenry to create the wealth to enrich themselves," the Canadian economist Patricia Adams instructs us. "States should live within their means, balancing their expenditures with their revenues."[27] Meanwhile, it is well known how difficult it is to achieve a balanced budget even in highly developed countries. Under conditions in which the economy suffers from a constant shortage of capital investments in both the state and private sectors, the use of credits is the only way to speed industrialization. Describing the catastrophic situation in Bolivia, a British journalist notes: "If it is possible for a country to become totally bankrupt, then this is what has happened to Bolivia." However, he continues, "did the Bolivians really display greater incompetence than the governments and bankers throughout the world who allowed the helpless South Americans to bring things to a general financial crisis?"[28] The supposed incompetence of the bankers had its rationale. As has already been explained, the growth of oil prices during the 1970s created a surplus of capital in the OPEC countries. Millions of petrodollars poured into Western banks. The West was not short of money either, the more so since during those years the governments of developed countries, employing Keynesian doctrines, preferred inflation to depression and covered their own budget deficits with the help of the printing press. An era of cheap credit opened up. The Western banks themselves encouraged the developing countries to borrow as much as possible. A proportion of the credits went to Eastern Europe. Using cheap Western loans, the government of Poland brought about a rapid growth in industrial output and a rise in living standards, while the Soviet government also actively bought up advanced technology.

By the early 1980s the situation had changed drastically. Economic recession in the West and the coming to power of neoconservative forces led to sharp cuts in state spending and a tightening of credit. Meanwhile, the prices for oil and raw materials fell. The incomes of the developing countries declined at the very point when payments to creditors were falling due. If the debts were to be paid, new loans were required. It was necessary to seek new credits to maintain the national economies at existing levels. The industrial programs that had been implemented were linked to foreign technology and increased the demand for hard currency, essential for components and spare parts. Not only was it impossible to pay off the debts, but the debts constantly reproduced themselves. As noted by an Algerian economist, indebtedness was transformed into a relationship of production, a relationship of power, a state of dependency in which the disproportionality of world economic relations was reflected with growing force and distinctness.[29]

The industrial projects for which the debts had been contracted did not yield the expected results. This was not only because these projects, which had as a rule been worked out with the help of Western firms, proved ineffective. The changed economic situation in the West led to a sharp worsening in the position of countries which had invested funds in developing export production. It was not only the case that particular states, such as Zaire, Brazil, and Mexico, found themselves on the verge of bankruptcy. The program of modernization, which had united debtors and creditors in the first place, was bankrupt!

Meanwhile, the Western financial organizations not only refused to accept their share of responsibility for the crisis, but on the contrary, made use of it to strengthen their positions in the third world. The debtor countries were urged to conduct their dealings not with separate banks, competing among themselves, but primarily with centralized organizations—the International Monetary Fund and the World Bank. The IMF in turn ceased merely to address financial problems connected with the payment of foreign debts, but now also dictated the economic policies which debtor countries should follow. What was demanded was the privatization of the state sector in favor of Western corporations, and often, the curtailment of production in precisely those sectors where the debtor countries posed a threat to Western competitors. In the early 1990s the IMF began dictating analogous policies in the countries of Eastern Europe and the republics of the former Soviet Union. When the USSR collapsed, its total debt to the West stood at around $70 billion, and annual debt service payments had reached $9.8 billion. Ukraine undertook to pay 16 percent of the debt, while the rest was to be paid mainly by Russia, which under bilateral agreements took responsibility for the debts of Turkmenia, Armenia, and Kirghizia.[30] The sums required to meet debt payments were not to be had, and the fate of the Russian economy depended on decisions of the IMF.

"Debt dependency on the West," writes Hungarian economist Peter Bihari, "has allowed the latter to involve itself directly in the mechanism of political and economic management. The representative of the IMF in Hungary was an employee of the economic section of the country's government, and a member of the central committee of the Communist Party. Access to loans was surrounded by demands for control over the economy, including the setting of prices on various products and the provision of particular supplies to certain enterprises, and by demands for specific political measures." According to Bihari, the Hungarian ruling elite fell increasingly under the influence of foreign creditors; in its own country, the elite ended up expressing alien interests. "The direct producers lost any influence over the use of their net income, being forced to hand a part of it over to the creditors. Between 1980 and 1989 the sum spent in order to service the foreign debt exceeded the sum originally borrowed; that is, the country's debt doubled as a result of interest charges. Directly or indirectly, the creditors determined the use to which a large part of accumulated income was put. In this way the Hungarian economy, irrespective of the form of property, effectively became part of the world capitalist economy."[31]

In some cases, for example in Poland, the economic recovery programs mapped out by the IMF brought a reduction in foreign indebtedness through a simultaneous fall in production and a lowering of living standards. Sometimes the debt continued to rise even after all the IMF's recommendations had been implemented. There was not a single case in which the problem was solved through these methods. As British economist Susan George notes: "Third world countries have fallen deep into debt because they have accepted, internalized, and followed the development model promoted by the World Bank, the IMF, and similar institutions."[32]

Former Colombian President Belisario Betancur compared the financial burden of Latin America with the destructive contradictions at work in Europe after World War I. He reminded his readers that the earlier situation had culminated in the crash of the world economy, and later in World War II; overcoming the Latin American debt crisis is essential for preserving peace throughout the world.[33] At the height of the debt crisis the ambassadors of the Latin American states in London had a letter published in the *Times*. If order were to be restored in national finances, the ambassadors stressed, there would have to be victims among the already impoverished population. Implementing such a program would be possible only at the price of major social upheavals, and under conditions of democracy this was almost impossible.[34] As the experience of Central America showed, any large scale conflict in the third world, even an internal political one, would result in a heightening of international tensions and of intervention by the superpowers.

In conditions of chronic social crisis one of the few types of business to flourish in the third world has been the export of narcotics. The United States spends millions of dollars waging its war on drugs, but narcotics production in Asia and Latin America continues to increase. Since the late 1980s the former Soviet Union has been added to these regions. The intervention by the United States in Panama and the overthrow of President Manuel Noriega, who was accused of links with narcobusiness, changed nothing. Narcotics dealers have become an important political force in Colombia and many other countries.

Most scholars agree that it was by no means inevitable that Colombia would be transformed into a country where narcotics became the most important product in the entire economy. The land is poorly suited to growing coca. In the 1950s and 1960s it seemed that an industrial society would quickly take shape there. Output of textiles, steel, cement, and chemical products was growing. But when the world economy went into recession in the 1970s, Colombian goods no longer found markets, indebtedness began increasing, and the country started to grow poorer. Washington strengthened Colombia's dependence on cocaine, introducing restrictive tariffs on imports from this country.[35]

The foreign debt is not, of course, the only problem blocking development. "Unbridled population growth," writes Robert MacNamara, former president of the International Bank for Reconstruction and Development, "seriously aggravates the problems of unemployment, excessive urbanization of the population, inadequate food supplies and the inequality of their distribution, and widespread poverty."[36]

The temptation is great to blame all problems on the population explosion. Most specialists agree that the period since the mid-1950s has been without precedent in demographic history. It is true that as early as the nineteenth century Malthus asserted that human beings had an innate propensity to multiply more quickly than the amount of food at their disposal would allow.[37] At that time Europe was undergoing something similar to the present population explosion. This phenomenon is typical of the transition from agrarian to industrial society.

By the beginning of the nineteenth century, annual rates of increase in different countries of Europe jumped to anything between 0.5 percent and 1.5 percent per annum, that is, to 2.5 to 7.0 times the rate that had prevailed in the centuries before. Total population of Europe therefore grew from 118 million in 1700 to 187 million in 1801 and to 321 million in 1900.[38] It is not hard to see that like the popular revolts in Britain in the eighteenth century, the French Revolution as well had a counterpoint of demographic problems.[39]

The present-day third world differs from nineteenth century Europe, however, in that demographic pressures are no longer being dissipated, but are increasing even as birth rates decline to a degree. As a world leader, Britain was able to survive its population explosion with the help of expansion and colonization. Backward and dependent, the countries of the third world face more restricted possibilities.

Overpopulation is not a new factor in the history of India or China. As early as the first millennium B.C., India had between 100 and 140 million people, almost half the population of Asia and around a third of the population of the world. But the twentieth century saw the appearance of new conditions of life unknown in traditional societies. In earlier times the familiar features of life included famines and epidemics which swallowed people in such numbers that, as a Soviet demographer put it, problems of limiting the population did not exist, even if the absolute numbers were high.[40] Unfortunately, these idyllic times have vanished into the past. Many people complain that irresponsible European medicine, brought into backward countries by the colonizers, spoiled everything; death rates fell, while birth rates remained high as couples, acting in line with long-ingrained tradition, sought to have large numbers of children as a reserve. In addition, a child in traditional society was seen as an additional worker. He or she was regarded less as a burden on the family than as a form of wealth which could be used, hired out, or even sold.[41] These attitudes persist thanks to the continuity between the old and new societies, and are reproduced under urban conditions.

The belief that population growth poses a serious problem is far from general. Libyan leader Muammar Qaddafi once declared that a period of rule by the black race was about to open up, and that black people would rule the world, since they were in an extremely backward state, and this would ensure their numerical superiority.[42] The author of the *Green Book* was prepared to bless the backwardness of Africa and perpetuate it—in the name of world domination. On this point, however, there are few who share Colonel Qaddafi's optimism.[43]

The situation is complicated by the fact that the level of labor culture in various countries is different. In China, for example, it is incomparably higher than in Africa, where making use of surplus labor resources for modern production is extremely difficult. In India, where industrialization began under the British in the nineteenth century, rapid population growth between the 1950s and 1970s wiped out almost all the economic achievements of this period. The overwhelming majority of the people have been left on the borderline of physical survival.

If economic growth was high enough to bring about some improvement in living standards, all the fruits of these successes were appropriated by privileged layers and the military-bureaucratic apparatus. In terms of their living standards, these groups made up a sort of Belgium in India, sharply divorced from the mass of half-starved people. In Brazil and Mexico during the 1960s and 1970s something similar could be observed. In the view of Soviet researchers, at the lowest levels of development economic growth is accompanied by increased inequality, and consequently, works against the poorest layers of the population.[44]

It could be said that contrary to Western theories, the interests of the poor in these countries were not served by economic growth, a situation which also existed in Britain in the time of Marx. "Under these conditions," Soviet demographers note, "the function of the population as the main productive force in society cannot be effectively realized. The chronic hunger of almost 50 percent of the poorest layers of the population lowers the quality of their labor power—their fitness for work, their level of activity. It is not by chance that the productivity of individual labor in India is extremely low, and does not meet the requirements of modern intensive production."[45]

The programs aimed at limiting the birth rate, despite their broad scope, have not had the expected results. Declining fertility is linked with rising living standards, but the demographic explosion is aggravating the poverty of most of the population. The natural consequence of overpopulation has become hunger. If European norms require that a ton of grain be grown to feed a person for a year, the norms of the third world require only 200 kilograms or one-fifth of a ton. These quantities of food exist on our planet. Contrary to Malthus, world agriculture produces enough food to solve the problem of hunger. Production is even growing a little faster than demand. In the framework of the existing social and economic structures, however, the problem is insoluble. The poor countries have been unable to meet their needs for foodstuffs themselves, and have been unable to purchase food in sufficient quantities on the world markets. In many cases, output of agricultural produce in the underdeveloped countries in the 1960s and 1970s even declined.[46]

Every year almost as many people in the developing countries die of hunger as perished throughout the whole of World War II. The crisis of agriculture and rural overpopulation have brought about a massive flight to the cities. "The social or psychological structure of life in the hinterland has collapsed," wrote the outstanding British economist of the 1970s, E.F. Schumacher; "[P]eople have become footloose and arrive to the capital city at the rate of thousand a day to squat on some empty land, against the police who come to beat them out, to build their mud hovels and look for a job. And nobody knows what to do about them."[47] Rates of urbanization outstrip population growth by two to one. In the underdeveloped countries the urban population grew between 1950 and 1975 by 554 million, and the increase was especially marked in the case of large cities.[48] The urban economy cannot digest a huge mass of new residents, since there is not enough work for all. Some specialists have termed this a false urbanization, and an Indian writer has even introduced the term *pseudo-city*.[49]

The European experience of urbanization is inapplicable here. The number of residents of shantytowns is reckoned in millions, something that in the West has not been seen even in the very worst periods. Programs of urban improvement based on European models invariably fail. The residents of the shantytowns are afraid to leave the places where they have been able at least somehow to establish themselves. If the hovels are cleared away, new ones promptly spring up. International experts who have studied the problem have come to the sad conclusion: The only means of eradicating the shantytowns, short of doing away with the reasons for their existence, is simultaneously to eradicate their inhabitants.[50]

It should not be imagined that this is a joke. Authorities obsessed with the desire for progress and order are fully capable of resolving on such a radical transformation. A final solution of this type was tried by the regime of Pol Pot in Kampuchea. When the European model of the city proves unsuitable, and there is no new one, why not liquidate the city itself along with its inhabitants? The more so since the concentration of declassed, marginal elements in the cities creates the danger of a social explosion—an explosion having nothing in common with a revolution, since the spontaneous protest of the dispossessed can be used not only by the forces of progress, but also by those of reaction.

False urbanization aggravates the crisis of the countryside. Those who come to the cities are the most educated. This creates the notion of the harmfulness of education, another symptom of Pol Potism, which has recently gained wider currency: "In the seminar on questions of education in the francophone countries of Africa, several of the participants ... argued that the village school in its present form has an adverse effect on the social and economic development of these countries, since it deprives the village of its best people and exacerbates the situation in the cities, since these people are unable to find work there, and increase urban unemployment with all the consequences that flow from it."[51]

The migration psychosis not only aggravates economic problems, but also impedes the stabilization of society and the formation of durable class structures. Even in the modern sector of the economy the growth of the industrial proletariat is proceeding extremely slowly. In India people who have been workers for many years nevertheless retain links with the countryside, and return there at the end of their working lives. A hereditary proletariat either does not exist, or forms an insignificant minority. The picture in other countries is similar.

For all the attempts by politicians to ascribe the problems to demographic explosion, it is impossible to mistake the fact that the explosion itself was born out of the structural contradictions of society: "The relatively high fertility is determined by the laws of natural or traditional modes of production, and the relatively low mortality by the laws of modern economic systems."[52] Here it is pointless to blame underdevelopment, the difficulties of the transitional epoch, or the heritage of colonialism. It might be hoped that just as Western Europe in the nineteenth century managed to solve its problems, the third world too will sooner or later escape from its dilemma. But the analogy with the industrial revolution in the West applies only within limited bounds. No one will dispute that a high level of development is preferable to backwardness, but it should be remembered that in transition periods the situation of the masses can deteriorate noticeably compared with their position in a traditional economy. From the point of view of a modern European, scientific and technical progress is indisputably a boon, but inhabitants of the third world have cause to doubt this. Among a number of primitive tribes, ethnographers have noted a relatively high level of satisfaction of food requirements along with a small expenditure of time on productive activity. In 1948, American scholars found that working four to five hours a day, Arnhem Land aborigines not only supplied themselves with food, but in its caloric value, their food met the optimum standards of the National Research Council of the United States.[53] Such data also exist for several African tribes. Hunger and poverty in developing countries are not born of primordial backwardness, but of delayed progress. Philosophers can promise us harmony on a higher level and the return of a lost paradise, but the development of production has brought about a crisis of the traditional structures, and cannot overcome this crisis. We are forced to acknowledge: Progress is not an absolute good, and backwardness is not an unmitigated evil.

How are we to escape from this impasse, and how are we to resolve the contradictions of development? During pre-perestroika times Gorbachev's adviser Yevgeny Primakov, who headed Soviet foreign intelligence during the last months of the USSR, explained all the ills of the developing countries on the basis that most of them were "either continuing or beginning their development along the path of capitalism."[54] At the time when Primakov was writing his anticapitalist tracts, we were under the sway of the theory that it was possible to leap across the intermediate stage and proceed directly from feudalism to socialism (and back again?). In fact, as the Soviet oriental scholar V. Khoros rightly noted, history does not allow any chance of a fantastic leap from archaic to highly advanced forms of production and social life.[55] We can, of course, turn to the classical Marxist concepts on which socialists based themselves in analyzing the colonial question in the early twentieth century. But there are no ready-made solutions for present-day problems here either. Marx objected constantly to attempts to turn his theory into a universal master key, reminding his readers that the historical inevitability of the road described in *Capital* was "strictly limited to the countries of Western Europe."[56] Meanwhile, he wrote repeatedly on colonial countries, mainly India. He was convinced that for backward countries capitalism would be a huge step forward. In his view, the bourgeoisie "on pain of death" would force all nations to implant the bourgeois mode of production. The practical means employed by the colonizers were often primitive and cruel, but in the final analysis the intervention of the British in India and other countries "brought about the greatest, and to speak truthfully, the only social revolution which Asia has ever experienced."[57] Driven by avaricious and often contemptible motives, the colonizers destroyed the old society, but that society was a brake on development, bearing the brand of caste discrimination and slavery, and had made even murder into a religious ritual.[58] During the period of anticolonial struggle few leftists recalled these words. Ultimately, however, it had to be recognized that, as a Tunisian scholar wrote, it was precisely the old system that had "brought our countries to decay, fetishism, and finally, to colonization," and that constituted "the main obstacle on our countries' road to progress"; if these countries wanted seriously to follow a path to socialism, it was necessary "first of all to change these very structures."[59]

Marx's sober assessment distinguishes him sharply from the vulgar critics of colonialism and the defenders of patriarchalism. Marx insisted that the work of destruction carried out by Europeans in the colonial countries was historically inevitable. Discussing the prospects for the development of the conquered countries, he showed extraordinary optimism. Destroying the Asiatic despotism which Marx hated, the British in his view were forced to lay the basis for a modern society in India. The spread of private property, for which Asiatic society "has such a hunger," would result in the establishment of a democracy of the Western type. "The free press, introduced into Asiatic society for the first time and run mainly by the offspring of mixed Indian and European marriages, is a new and powerful factor in the restructuring of this society." A new intellectual and entrepreneurial elite would appear, "possessing the knowledge indispensable for ruling the country, and familiar with Western science."[60] All this would occur simply because economic necessity would turn the colonizers into a weapon of development, and would force them to carry out the restructuring of the conquered societies. Marx had no doubt that the Asiatic countries would ultimately, albeit through following their own paths, become normal capitalist societies in which the conditions for socialist transformations would arise. Was Marx a supporter of colonialism? He considered unreservedly that the most advanced peoples of the West would have to play a leading role in establishing a new world system, and that the colonization of the East was aiding the progress of humanity. Meanwhile, unlike liberal Western progressives, Marx never forgot the price of progress. He criticized the bourgeois order primarily because the price of progress was exorbitantly high. Socialism, according to Marx, was essential above all because it would ensure that the progress of humanity went ahead with minimal sacrifices. Socialism would not only carry out different historical tasks from capitalism, but would also carry out these tasks in a different manner, using different, democratic means. "Only after the great social revolution takes possession of the achievements of the bourgeois epoch, of the world market and the modern forces of production, and places them under the general control of the most advanced peoples, will human progress cease to resemble the repellent pagan idol which refuses to drink nectar except from the skulls of the slain."[61]

Marx hoped that, under the impact of the expansion of the advanced peoples, the countries of Asia and Africa would themselves come to resemble Western Europe, though the corresponding processes would occur there after a certain delay. In fact, the whole process turned out to be far more complex. Lenin repeated Marx's error, declaring that "the East has finally embarked on the Western road."[62] As the Latin American economist T. dos Santos notes, Lenin was completely certain that the export of capital from Europe and the United States would bring about economic progress in the backward countries, and hence failed to foresee the transition to a new stage of dependency.[63] Rosa Luxemburg was the first to note that the classical

Marxist conception contained an obvious error: the penetration of the East by capitalism did not by any means signify that the Western road would be repeated there. "To ensure its own survival and continued development, capitalism requires noncapitalist forms of production as its environment," she argued; capitalism could only exist so long as it found this environment.[64]

Surveying the world capitalist system, the Latin American sociologist A. Cordova later wrote, Luxemburg was the first to discover the dialectical link between the accumulation of capital in the center and the accumulation of backwardness on the periphery.[65] The center needed the backward noncapitalist and semicapitalist countries as consumers of manufactured goods, as suppliers of cheap raw materials, and finally and perhaps most importantly, as fields for the investment of surplus capital which could not be employed in the developed countries. If backward countries had not existed, it would have been necessary to create them. Often, this is precisely what happened.

In the first stages of its development in the colonies, capitalism recreated the institution of slavery. In its own fashion, slavery in the southern states of the United States and in the West Indies helped to strengthen British industry, which was based on free labor. Western capitalism never needed the full modernization of backward countries. It needed only their partial modernization. In the 1960s Andre Gunder Frank observed that underdevelopment was born and is born anew as a result of the very historical process which gave rise to development— by the development of capitalism.[66] Dependent countries do not stand still; they modernize, but their development remains the development of underdevelopment.

Capitalism, Luxemburg argued, required noncapitalist social layers as a market for its surplus value, as a source of its means of production and as a reservoir of labor power for its system of hired labor. Natural economic forms could not fulfill all these functions.[67] In its original form the traditional economy of most backward countries, particularly in Africa, was not oriented to the production of goods for the market. In many parts of the continent this situation has persisted throughout the twentieth century despite the changes that have taken place in the world. "Even in Ghana, where commercial agriculture is more developed than in other countries of tropical Africa," a Soviet researcher noted in the late 1970s, "and where the products of urban factories have penetrated into the most remote corners, there are still regions where the sale of agricultural produce is considered reprehensible, and where there is a popular belief that if you sell part of a harvest, the gods will punish you with a poor crop the following year."[68]

Nevertheless, the traditional sector is gradually coming to interact with the modern one. Capital does not completely wipe out the old economic structures, but subordinates them to the requirements of its own reproduction. Archaic structures collapse, but only partially, and their downfall is most marked in the case of those structures that are linked to the natural economy. It is thus entirely natural that most developing countries that once met their own food requirements are now food importers.

History records two types of development. When new forms arise in a society, they are either strong enough to restructure it to their advantage and according to their model (as in seventeenth-century Britain), or else they fail to do this. In the latter case, their effect is not so much to restructure society as to bring about its decomposition. The feeble bourgeois elements in Spain played just such a role after the discovery of America. The new helps bring about the downfall of the old, but there is nothing progressive about the process that has been set in motion. Society in general, including the new social forms, enters into decline. In such a case, crisis is a normal condition of life for millions of people.

A rift inevitably appears between the modern and traditional sectors. While interaction takes place between them, they do not make up a unified economic mechanism. They have different dynamics, and their reproduction has a different logic. They complement one another, but they are not a united whole. Originally integrated, the economy and society finish up multistructured. The term "multistructured" harks back to a characterization that was used very successfully by Lenin— "various [intermingled] socioeconomic structures"—in analyzing the Russian economy after 1917, though he completely ignored this phenomenon in his earlier studies of prerevolutionary Russian society.[69]

From the point of view of Marxist theory, to say that a society is multistructured means that its basis is heterogeneous, and that its social and economic structures are atomized and disordered. All this has driven classically trained Marxists into a dead end, preventing them from categorizing multistructured societies either as capitalist or as examples of some other type of formation. According to the classical schemas, the coexistence and conflict of several structures must result in the "establishment of the economic and political hegemony of a single, more 'modern' structure."[70] But nothing of the sort takes place. In the East, wrote the Soviet sociologists V. Sheinis and M. Cheshkov, various structures "have not replaced one another, but have become intertwined."[71] V. Krylov, evidently for the first time in our country, addressed the striking fact that in conditions of demographic explosion the number of people in the traditional sector grew rapidly, while the weight of this sector in the economy underwent a sharp increase. Consequently, what is involved is not the heritage of precolonial times, but a phenomenon which has arisen in the underdeveloped world in accordance with the laws of its own development.[72]

The old is dying and the new is being born, but the old is unable to die completely. "The dead seizes hold of the living." Archaic, obsolete forms continue to develop and grow, often crowding out the new and at times becoming grafted onto it. In this symbiosis, it is difficult sometimes to say what is new and what is old. Behind the outward changes, there is a lack of real transformation. Instead we find the dying reborn—to use Spengler's wonderfully apt term, as a "pseudomorphosis."

One of the Soviet experts described the essence of this problem precisely, declaring that the old forms of culture and consciousness do not vanish, and are not simply preserved and adapted to the new conditions, but are reproduced, becoming subject to a complex restructuring.[73] This applies not only to culture, but also to the relations of production, the social structure, and to political organizations. The modern and traditional structures become like Siamese twins, incapable of existing without one another. Before us we find a transitional society in which no transition is taking place. The specific nature of the countries of the third world consists in the fact that they have become stuck in a phase of transition, and that this state has become self-reproducing, constant, and without prospects for change. The multi-structured character of backward countries has become an indispensable element of the world economic structure, and is maintained. The organization of society in these countries remains extremely heterogeneous and inorganic. This is the source of the fully justified concept of a golden precolonial age; society was then in fact healthier and more organic. There is nothing more terrifying than a society stuck in a transitional phase of its development.

Mirabeau once remarked that the road from evil to good was worse than evil itself. But where is the promised good? In this case, the reproduction of transitional forms means that history is spinning its wheels and going nowhere. Contradictory, inherently unsustainable structures continue for decades, increasing the disproportions in the economy, accumulating unsolved problems, giving rise to monstrous calamities and the impoverishment of millions. The tragedy of the third world is not the tragedy of backwardness, but the tragedy of partial modernization; in the words of Marx, it has "lost the old world without gaining the new."[74]

There is a direct link between the prosperity of the developed industrial world and the poverty of the developing countries. The normal functioning of the international capitalist economy is made possible by preserving the backwardness of the third world. However, this formula turns into an empty slogan unless we show the concrete economic mechanisms which give rise to such a situation. Marx once joked: "The method of theft is defined by the mode of production. For example, a nation with a developed system of stock-market speculation cannot be robbed in the same way as a stock-herding people."[75] To ascribe all the ills that befall the underdeveloped world to imperialist interference, in the spirit of the well-known formula "foreign devils are to blame for all the disasters of China,"[76] is far from the best approach one can take to the facts. Marx explained the backwardness of the precolonial East compared with Europe in a particularly precise fashion as the result of the conservatism resting on brutal political despotism of the Asiatic mode of production. Thus colonialism from the very first had a dual role. As the Hungarian scholar T. Szentes wrote, the burdensome heritage of colonialism does not consist in the fact that the Western powers failed to create universal literacy in Africa or to establish heavy industries there, but in the fact that the "positive impact of colonialism (the destruction of ossified social forms, the initiation of rapid development in some countries, the integration of the colonies into the world market, and so on) had negative consequences, giving rise to factors which now appear as fundamental obstacles standing in the way of development."[77]

Under conditions of dependency specific structures take shape. In the words of Dos Santos, dependency ceases to be an external factor; it becomes a domestic situation and it is "impossible to put an end to it by isolating the country from external influences, since this only creates chaos."[78] The old is destroyed more rapidly than the new can be created. People cannot enter a new life, which they are not ready for, but neither can they live in the old fashion.

Psychiatrists testify that a significant increase in the volume of information to be dealt with, and even the spread of education in a population with a low level of literacy, occasions serious psychological stress. Contact with the modern world leads to a dramatic rise in expectations, which traditional society is simply not able to satisfy. Television, radio, and the cinema strengthen the demonstration effect. "Before the twentieth century," writes the Hungarian economist I. Bognar, "there was virtually no personal contact between the populations of developed and underdeveloped countries. As a result of this, people who lived in closed communities were unfamiliar with the conditions of life of others, and found many things which others possessed to be superfluous or incomprehensible."[79] In the modern epoch the role played by consumption has changed fundamentally. Workers in traditional society themselves consumed a large part of their product, while the surplus went to maintain the elite. Workers in a modern machine-building plant cannot consume their own product in any case. The creation of a modern sector in the third world gave rise to consumer society, and led simultaneously to the spread of Western living standards. In the traditional sector a process of moral discounting took place as people marked down the value of their own way of life, of their labor, and at times even of themselves as individuals. "The old society," a Senegalese sociologist writes, "impressed on young people that they held a prestigious place in the collectivity because the founder-ancestors of the clan and all their descendants had occupied this place since time immemorial. From such a point of view all work was prestigious."[80] Now this is no more. People conclude that they are second-class human beings. It is significant that something very like this also occurred in Eastern Europe, especially in the republics of the former Soviet Union after the collapse of Communism.

The fall in production is accompanied by a rise in the prestige of consumption. A typical problem of developing countries, writes Khoros, is the awakening of material demands in circumstances where the possibilities of satisfying them are minimal.[81] Some radical thinkers see in this one of the sources of dependency, since it was Europeans who brought their way of life and standards into the colonial world. But whatever the case, annulling the new demands is now impossible without resorting to the most brutal terror, such as occurred in Cambodia under Pol Pot. This model of a solution to the crisis was precisely what Dos Santos feared. Links with the outside world were severed, and the European way of life was annihilated along with its adherents.

The isolationism of Pol Pot did not arise out of a vacuum. Trade between developed and underdeveloped countries is extremely unfavorable to the latter. The third world has not only been unable to overcome its dependency and backwardness within the framework established after World War II, but in a certain sense has suffered from the expansion of world trade and from its own economic growth. Because the underdeveloped countries specialize in areas of production with a relatively low organic composition of capital, a significant share of the value which they create accrues to the developed countries because of the tendency of the equalization of rates of profit. [82] In the countries of the third world, where production using simple labor-intensive technology predominates, profit rates have to be significantly higher than in the capital-intensive production of the West. Countries with labor-intensive technology lose from the establishment of average rates of profit, while countries with capital-intensive technology gain.[83] If the average rate of profit in the world during the 1960s was 12.7 percent, in the third world it was 17.9 percent. By the end of the 1970s the gap had widened. The world profit rate is showing a tendency to even out, or else the gap would be still more marked. The competition between blocs of capital that is causing the gap to narrow works against the underdeveloped countries, which cannot market all their goods at prices corresponding to their value. As producers of raw materials and intermediate products, they are in a worse position than the producers of finished goods.

The demand for raw materials is dependent on the demand for finished goods. An increase in the prices of raw materials leads to rises in the prices of industrial products. This is followed by a fall in the demand for industrial products. This rebounds on the countries of the third world where it means, in turn, falling or static prices for raw materials. The inflationary processes that gathered strength in the West following the 1973 rise in oil prices also dealt a blow to the underdeveloped countries, whose reserves of hard currency were limited. The crisis of 1979 to 1984 brought an abrupt fall in demand for raw materials and showed how weak the positions of the backward countries in reality were. Even resource-rich states were shaken. An Italian journalist wrote with malicious delight that the financial game which the Arab sheikhs had cynically played with raw materials prices after the oil shock and until recently, had turned against them.[84]

The major gains from the rise in oil prices were not made by the developing countries, but by the Western firms trading in oil on the world market, something which was not hidden from public opinion in Western countries. Millions of petrodollars accumulated in Western banks, and from there were sent as credits mainly to oil-poor countries of the third world, laying the basis for the subsequent debt crisis and for new financial dependency. The apparent success of the third world in the 1970s merely worsened the state of affairs in the countries of the poor South, and so played into the hands of the rich North. The attempt by Iraq in 1990 to repeat the shock of 1973, using political and military means, ended in total failure. Despite an abrupt leap in prices as a result of the war in the Persian Gulf, the market quickly stabilized.

The greater the shortage of a raw material, the greater the chances for particular countries of holding out under crisis conditions, but here as well the damage is dealt mainly to other underdeveloped countries which require that raw material. The gap between the center and the periphery does not close automatically once market relations are brought to bear on it. A situation arises in which the countries of the center receive all the benefits from the variations in supply and demand on the world market, while in times of economic downturn shifting the weight of the crisis onto the periphery. The Brazilian economist Celso Furtado once observed that the stability of capitalist society in the West and the high standard of living in the industrialized countries would be impossible to maintain without the exploitation of the third world. If by development was understood a transition to the European model, the countries of the third world would never succeed in developing.[85] For all its seemingly paradoxical nature, Furtado's observation is thoroughly convincing. If the third world indirectly finances the West, who is to pay for the prospering of the third world? Turning all the underdeveloped countries into highly developed European-type societies under present historical conditions would quickly lead to the exhaustion of world resources and environmental catastrophe. Consequently, the way of life established under the conditions of industrial capitalism is meant only for a minority, since any attempt to extend it to all humanity would inevitably bring about the crash of the entire system.[86]

In the final analysis, it is the position of the developing countries on the periphery of the world economy that determines most of the difficulties they face. The French socialists in a collective study argue that the states of the third world are united only by one common feature: external dependency.[87] Experience shows convincingly that it is impossible to solve the problems of the underdeveloped countries within the framework of dependent development. A vicious circle is formed: underdevelopment nourishes and reproduces dependency, while the latter deepens underdevelopment. A Colombian economist states categorically: "Underdevelopment is not a stage."[88] The term backwardness is misleading. The poor countries do not simply lag behind the West, as Marx and Lenin suggested; they are doomed to follow a completely different path. Scholars are more and more coming to the conclusion that dependency is an expression of a specific type of development, governed by its own laws. On the basis of dependency, a new type of society has arisen, expressing itself in a distinct fashion.[89] The pattern of development of this society cannot be a repetition of what has gone before, a reproduction of the Western experience with a delay of several decades, or for that matter, of centuries. Although the comparison between the impoverishment of this society and the prosperity of the advanced West constantly arouses the temptation to remake everything in the Western manner, this almost never succeeds. No one gets to repeat the history of another. But the question of another road, of new variants of development, of nations that have not been able to become part of the world capitalist center having their own choice, remains tragically open.

CHAPTER 2

THE ILLUSIONS
OF NATIONAL INDEPENDENCE

How is economic independence to be achieved? Liberal theoreticians contend that everything is simple: growth rates need only be speeded up, while at the same time creating private property, a free market, and other bases of civilization. Socialists and social democrats argue that breaking the vicious circle of backwardness and dependency requires "relations of a new type between Europe and the Third World."[1] If the backward countries cannot solve their problems on a unilateral basis, a general perestroika is required. A resolution of the Thirteenth Congress of the Socialist International in November 1976 declared that success could be attained "only through radical and decisive international measures and under the influence of new feelings of solidarity throughout the entire human community."[2] During the 1970s the Italian Communists advanced the slogan of a struggle for the planned administration of the world economy, which would allow profound changes in the structure of the economy and society, indispensable for the creation of a new international order.[3] During the same years Willy Brandt's independent commission declared: "Genuine progress can only be achieved within a national framework if it is guaranteed on an international level." Otherwise it would be impossible to avoid worldwide economic collapse, with consequent chaos and human suffering.[4] In the late 1980s, under the influence of the new realism which had triumphed in left parties, such radical slogans were not discarded but simply forgotten.

Discussion of a new world economic order died away, since the Western social democrats, who had participated enthusiastically in theoretical debates on the question, turned out to be incapable of taking practical steps. The most radical critics of the West argued that imperialism had blocked the process of change, while others noted that the governments of developing countries themselves "have not utilized their collective potential to bargain for a more just system, and instead have capitulated individually."[5] Liberal scholars, stating that attempts to create a new international economic order had failed, declared that the existing, old order was the only one possible.

The growth of right-wing forces in the West, followed by the collapse of the Eastern bloc, by the transformation of the USSR under Gorbachev into a junior partner of the United States, and then by the Soviet Union's disintegration, might seem to have rendered the question of world economic reform untimely—at least until the crisis of capitalism itself places the existing structures of the world economy in doubt. Meanwhile, the worst forecasts of the pessimists who have warned of impending worldwide social chaos have begun to be realized. At the same time as leaders of left parties have preferred to use the word *reform* more sparingly, and have ceased altogether to utter the terrifying and old-fashioned word *revolution*, the necessity for comprehensive change has everywhere begun to be felt with unprecedented force. The main economic contradictions which gave rise to the demand for worldwide reform have not disappeared. As the American scholar W. Langley notes, "[O]ne can only conclude that these problems cannot be dealt with politically within the confines of the liberal order."[6]

The idea of worldwide reform is not so far removed from the old Marxist idea of world revolution. Despite its reformist cover this slogan, if taken seriously, assumes genuinely revolutionary changes in the life of humanity. From the very beginning, however, many people have reacted skeptically to the idea of comprehensive change. A Soviet reviewer accused the Brandt Commission of exaggerating the role of the external sphere.[7] This view is shared by many leftists in the West and in the third world itself. K. Griffin, for example, considers that there is no point in hoping for international reform: there is little reason to believe that underdevelopment can be banished through efforts to change the world. This must be achieved, he argues, through changes to the politics and economics of the country concerned— something which has been done, with well-known results, through the revolution in China.[8]

Of course, the results of the Chinese Revolution can scarcely be regarded as totally clear and indisputable. But in any case, the slogan of relying on one's own strength is highly attractive to the people of the third world. These populations cannot wait passively for global changes that depend on events in Europe, but must promptly undertake some action or other in order to effect change here and now. For supporters of world reform every national revolution, if it is not part of a broad international process, appears as a partial reformist change which solves none of the main contradictions of the epoch. But for the people of the country involved this might be a question of life or death.

During the second half of the 1960s a wave of nationalizations swept across huge areas of the world. Western firms that had controlled extractive industries in former colonial countries lost their positions. In the course of the 1960s and 1970s most foreign concessions passed into the hands of the liberated countries either through expropriation or through gradual purchase. Between 1956 and 1972 foreign monopolies in these countries were deprived of property worth $10 billion. In the period from 1970 to 1976 some 914 acts of nationalization of third world affiliates of transnational corporations were carried out. At times these measures were proclaimed as socialist, but even authors who spoke for the Soviet regime recognized that the class negation of capitalism was something quite alien to the nationalists.[9] It was not by chance that in many countries local large-scale capital gave (or threatened to give) practical support to government moves to limit the activity of foreign firms.[10]

No one thought of establishing a new system of social and economic relations. Once the country's economic policies had been made more independent, all that was necessary was to transfer control over the use of national resources to the local leadership. Only an insignificant proportion of foreign property was expropriated without compensation. In most cases the young states were forced to pay huge sums in compensation. This harmed their financial position and forced them to resort to borrowing. Grotesque situations arose. After nationalizing the property of British firms, the Sudan was forced to apply to Britain for a loan in order to pay compensation. Only the form of dependency was changed. The place of the old raw-materials monopolies of the 1960s was taken in the 1970s by new transnational corporations which consciously exploited differences in the prices of labor power and the degree of organization of labor power in various regions and countries.[11]

A large proportion of capital investment was now directed into manufacturing industry. Corporations took on a supranational, cosmopolitan character. Their links with a particular base country grew weaker, though they did not cut their ties with the states of the capitalist center, counting on them for help in the event of crisis. The assault by transnational business on the third world from the late 1970s was so successful that many people came to regard what happened as a fatal necessity. An Algerian economist asked, "Are progressive regimes not throwing themselves one after the other into the embraces of the transnationals, like lovers who have long answered all entreaties with categorical refusals, only in the end to surrender themselves with even greater passion, verging on madness?"[12]

A conflict with such a firm can be altogether too expensive, both in the direct and figurative senses. The technological character of the enterprises set up by transnational corporations prevents them from being expropriated without compensation. The transnationals "disperse the production of various components of finished goods between the base countries and the developing states. There is scarcely a single daughter enterprise in the developing countries in which the whole productive-technical cycle is concentrated. Either the most demanding and technologically complex components are produced by the parent enterprises in the base country, or experts in installation work are brought in only from that country, or the main markets in which the product is sold are located there. The share of the developing countries consists mainly of the production of simple parts, and assembly."[13]

Nationalizing one or even several enterprises of a transnational corporation in a particular country does not make it possible to successfully exploit the possibilities which these enterprises offer for national development. Indirect methods of control are not especially successful either. If a company finds these controls too burdensome, it can easily transfer production to another country. Only in the extremely rare cases in which transnationals have invested a substantial share of their assets in the economy of a single country are they liable to be transformed, to use the phrase of V.P. Lukin, into "hostages of their own interests."[14]

Official Soviet commentators during the Brezhnev era described the antinational thrust of the activity of the transnationals, together with their deformed character that was said to be undermining and destabilizing the world economy.[15] As early as the 1970s, scholars oriented toward liberal ideas criticized this approach. Viktor Sheinis once declared that in Soviet commentaries social and political processes took on the character of scenes from the puppet theater. Soviet scholars should not, he maintained, argue that international campaigns violated the natural course of events, since it could scarcely be said that any writer possessed "a knowledge of the norm which distinguishes the 'natural' from the 'unnatural'." While the class nature of the transnationals should not be forgotten, he continued, it was necessary to recognize that in many countries they represented one of the motor forces of development.[16]

These questions, which were discussed heatedly by Eastern European scholars during the early 1980s, took on a new meaning when the ruling circles in the very same Eastern Europe and Russia became increasingly inclined to see the hegemony of transnational firms as the sole solution to the region's problems, and the high road to the restructuring of its economies. Defenders of the transnational firms argued that these companies helped backward countries create a modern sector, supplying finance and new technology. A Marxist might add that the rise of transnational corporations reflects the objective tendency for capital and production to become internationalized. But there are other ways in which countries can participate in the world economy apart from becoming subordinated to transnational corporations.

Western companies agree to invest capital only in those sectors of the economy which they find essential to their operations. Very often, the perspectives of these firms are at odds with the liberated countries' own plans for economic development.[17] The firms' interests can even be in conflict with the interests of the industrialized countries of the center, since international monopolies that export capital and transfer whole branches of industry to the developing world aggravate the structural contradictions of the West. The experience with transnational corporations in the territory of the former USSR showed that the numerous subsidiaries and joint ventures which they established did virtually nothing to assist economic growth. Despite their feverish activity, they were unable to stop or even to slow the collapse of the Soviet economy. Later, however, they managed to benefit from this collapse, exporting resources which were in short supply in Russia and which they had obtained for trivial prices, and exploiting their highly qualified workforce.

The industrial powers of the West possessed qualified workers, a powerful technological and scientific potential, and a developed apparatus of economic regulation that was capable of exercising relatively effective control over the activity of transnationals in their territory. For backward countries, this task was much more difficult. As foreign capital seized key positions in the most important economic sectors, national institutions were increasingly losing control over the economy. The country's fate now depended on external, conjunctural factors. In Brazil by the early 1980s, transnational corporations had come to control all of automobile manufacturing, 80 percent of the pharmaceutical industry, 70 percent of electronics, 59 percent of machine building, and 50 percent of the chemical industry. Can development of the modern sector according to this pattern be considered a guarantee of independence?

Transnational firms urge their own model on the third world. The main capital investments are directed into a small number of countries which are already relatively far advanced along the road to industrialization; these include various countries of Southeast Asia and Latin America, especially Mexico and Brazil. The firms are attracted here by a relatively educated labor force which is also cheap. With qualified labor power available, modern technology can be used; meanwhile, unit labor costs remain low.[18] The conditions for investment are considered especially favorable in cases where the country is ruled by a dictatorial regime; the workers are not united in political organizations; there are no free trade unions; there are vicious antistrike laws; taxation is minimal; there are few or no health and safety controls or environmental regulations, and there are no restrictions on the right to repatriate profits. It was precisely because of their political regimes that China and Vietnam, along with a number of "progressive" dictatorships, began to attract the transnationals during the 1980s. Not only do Communist methods of control over the population fail to hinder the activity of international capital; under certain conditions they are even favorable to it.

During an initial phase the influx of foreign capital investment speeds economic growth. In Latin America people spoke of the Brazilian miracle. The Soviet scholar I. Sheremet'ev recognizes that the activity of the transnationals provided "much of the impulse for the 'economic spurt' seen in Mexico, with relatively rapid development of its economic, mainly industrial potential."[19] It was only toward the end of the 1970s that the other side of the coin began to appear.

As has already been noted, the success of South Korea became possible thanks precisely to the ability of its ruling circles to implement an independent policy of development. A quite different situation arose in countries whose economies were effectively under the control of transnational corporations. During the period from 1965 to 1973 deliveries of industrial goods from the developing countries to the West increased substantially. According to the *Economist* (London), exports of the products of manufacturing industry continued to grow by an average of more than 10 percent a year in real terms during the economically difficult 1970s. Even against a background of recession the poor countries increased their exports of industrial products by almost 7 percent a year.[20]

During the 1980s, however, the rate at which exports were growing slowed noticeably. In the model of development that had been adopted, production for export was the most modern sector, and had the effect of shaping the structure as a whole. Internal development was dictated by the trends of the world market. The huge internal market was sacrificed. Export products retained their competitiveness mainly thanks to their cheapness, or more precisely, thanks to the miserly wages paid to their producers. Although the earnings of workers employed by the transnational corporations were higher than the national average, it should be remembered that the work in these enterprises was more difficult and the cost of reproducing labor power was significantly higher. A European type of personality was being created, with demands resembling European ones, while the wages of workers in this sector were even further out of line with the real value of their labor power than for workers employed in locally owned enterprises.[21]

Often, locally owned enterprises are closely linked to the transnational firms and are indirectly exploited by them. The most paradoxical outcome of the transnationalization of the economy is the relative weakening of the local bourgeois layers, the breaking up of the labor market, and the creation of conditions in which capitalist relations (and consequently the system as a whole) become extremely unstable, and the growth of entrepreneurship from below is blocked.

The export orientation is not always associated with foreign capital. But whatever the case, what is involved here is *pseudoindustrialization*, which does not create the conditions for organic growth of the economy. When economic growth of this type occurs, living standards rise only by insignificant amounts, or fail to rise at all. The increase in exports makes it possible to speed up the accumulation of capital, creating the illusion of success. But the capital is not concentrated in the branches which are vital for the country's development. The American economist P. Burkett has called this *externally oriented accumulation.*[22]

Development continues to be accompanied by the impoverishment of the masses. Internal demand fails to increase, and in the final analysis the increase in production turns out to be less than was originally foreseen. The buying power of the population may even decline. Economists speak of growth without development,[23] and of social crises against a background of economic expansion.[24] As a French scholar has justly remarked, "to produce the same things with the help of lower-paid workers or with worse conditions of labor represents a step backwards in social terms."[25] Even in the countries of Southeast Asia, the rapid growth of the export sector has been accompanied by a slowing of the rate of increase of employment in the rest of industry. An increase in social tensions is inevitable. In order to avoid an explosion, the authorities are constantly forced to strengthen their repressive apparatus.

But even military dictatorships are not always able to hold down the growing social pressures. The crisis of the 1980s also showed the economic weakness of this model. Western observers noted with alarm that the Brazilian miracle was turning into a nightmare.[26] A weak national economy had been unable to develop immunity against international economic diseases of which the transnationals and the export sector had objectively served as the carriers. Celso Furtado observed that Brazil could advance a long way along the road of industrialization "without losing the basic features of underdevelopment: a huge gap between the productive forces of the city and the countryside; the majority of the population living on the brink of physical exhaustion; a growing number of urban dwellers without permanent work, and so on."[27] The growth of industry has not only failed to ensure independence, but in the apt words of Soviet scholars, has served to tighten the economic structures of the liberated countries to match the new demands of neocolonial exploitation.[28]

The democratization in Brazil was linked to the economic failures of the military regime, which was oriented toward transnational capital. But the revived constitutional order was equally unable to achieve stability in a country on the brink of social chaos. Thefts became commonplace, and hunger and violence became features of everyday life. Crowds of hungry people stormed food stores. Debts increased to the point where this wealthy country was on the verge of bankruptcy. It became quite clear that unless the economic model was changed democracy would not survive. The question of reforms became vital for ensuring development in conditions of freedom. A financial crisis also arose in Mexico, as a result of which the transnationals began feverish efforts to transfer the funds of their subsidiaries abroad through private banks, trying to avoid losses from the devaluation of the Mexican currency.

In Mexico, unlike the situation in Brazil, a powerful state sector acted as a stabilizing force. The state sector in Mexico employed around 700,000 people, more than the subsidiaries of foreign firms. Nationalization of the banks saved the country from bankruptcy. In Brazil the weaker state sector was unable to fulfil such a role, but if it had been abolished, as some economists had advocated during the boom period of the 1970s, the position would have been still worse.

The new economic upturn which began in the mid-1980s was accompanied by a strengthening of the positions of transnational capital in the newly industrialized countries. This time the Western firms, which were collaborating closely with the IMF and the World Bank, were not satisfied with establishing their own enterprises, but set out to take control of the state companies whose viability had been proven by the preceding events. Through selling off the state sector, the governments of Mexico, Brazil and Colombia hoped to obtain additional funds with which to pay off their foreign debts. At first it appeared that impressive gains had been achieved through this method; in 1990–1991 alone Mexico's foreign debt shrank by 22 percent, and it proved possible to reduce indebtedness almost by half compared with 1985, when the debt crisis had burst into the open. The neoliberal experts claimed total success, noting with satisfaction that "the country no longer needs to borrow on the foreign market."[29]

In reality, the situation was much less favorable. The new capital investments did not lead to substantial economic growth. The dependency of the peripheral countries on the center was strengthened, as was the exploitation to which they were subject. Unemployment rose sharply. Latin American trade unions declared that policies of this kind would lead to the liquidation of national economies, and to the annihilation of the working class.[30] In Peru 700,000 jobs were lost as a result of privatization, and in Mexico, 130,000 in a single year in the oil industry alone.[31] The failures of the 1980s convinced many Latin Americans that the road to economic independence lay in economic integration. An intergovernmental conference in Quito in 1984 called for the economy of the entire continent to be organized as a single unit, and Peruvian President Alan García, who in the mid-1980s was seeking to act as one of the leaders of the movement for a new world economic order, stressed that integration was the true road to democracy and socialism.[32]

In the 1990s, confronting problems of indebtedness and dependency, the governments of Eastern Europe also began talking of integration. The fall of the Communist regimes had been accompanied by the severing of the established links among the countries of the Soviet bloc and by the abolition of the Council for Mutual Economic Assistance. As early as 1992, Polish President Lech Walesa was obliged to speak of the need for a new union of the countries of Eastern and Central Europe. The French economist Catherine Samary stresses that without integration the countries of the former Communist bloc will be unable to defend their interests against the dictates of the IMF and the World Bank.[33]

Controlling the activity of the transnationals is inconceivable without regional planning. But regional integration in itself solves none of the problems. The Brazilian economist Roy Mauro Marini emphasizes that integration is pointless unless the international organizations themselves are democratized, and the interests of the majority of the population of the developing countries are represented in them.[34] Unless serious social and economic reforms are carried through, integration will perpetuate economic backwardness and one-sided development. Acting in a one-sided manner, meanwhile, the countries of the third world cannot advance a comprehensive alternative to the transnationals. This does not mean, however, that nothing can be done. Sheremet'ev notes that Mexico has been led by its experience to an important conclusion: "Foreign capital must not be allowed to reach the 'critical mass' at which it is able to destroy or seriously destabilize the model of development which is adopted. It is also clear that the only way in which this danger can be averted is through a strategy of national development which ensures, in the most complete manner possible, the use of internal possibilities and reserves."[35]

To the strategy of export-led pseudoindustrialization pursued by international capital, third world countries have often counterposed a strategy of import-substitution industrialization with backing from the state sector. Western scholars acknowledge that in many parts of the world private entrepreneurs are unable to ensure the indispensable degree of economic growth.[36] Most experts agree that in this case the function of accumulation cannot be fulfilled by anyone except the state.[37] Dependency results not just from the presence of foreign economic interests, but also from the lack of local economic bodies capable of decisive actions.[38] Bodies of this kind are established by governments in a centralized way.

The industrialization of the West proceeded on the basis of private enterprise and the free market, but in the third world this is impossible. The free market was ideally suited to the conditions of the European economy during the period of classical capitalism, but is not at all appropriate to carrying out the tasks faced by developing countries in the twentieth century. Max Weber showed that the formation of the Western entrepreneurial bourgeoisie took place in specific circumstances that can hardly be recreated. Profit-oriented private enterprises, Weber noted, "have existed in *all* of the cultured countries of the world, so far as we can judge from the surviving records of their economic life." Such enterprises "existed in ancient China, India, Babylon, and Egypt; they were present in the Mediterranean states of antiquity; they remained throughout the Middle Ages, and have continued into the modern epoch." Nevertheless, capitalist entrepreneurship with its specific culture and its traditions of productive accumulation and of the rational organization of labor appeared only relatively recently, in a particular setting; this culture and these traditions, according to Weber, are features specifically of Western capitalism.[39] As the experience of Japan has shown, the achievements of Western bourgeois civilization can be adopted, but cannot be mechanically reproduced. Still less is it possible to create a class of owner-entrepreneurs by decree, proclaiming freedom of trade, or as in Eastern Europe in the 1990s, distributing the national wealth.

The failure of the capitalist experiments of the 1950s and 1960s led third world economists and political leaders to conclude that the tasks of development, and in particular the tasks of scientific and technical progress could not be solved through the movements of the market alone; they demanded "the active intervention of the state, both on the national and international levels."[40] The state had to assume responsibility both for the tasks of accumulation, and for a series of tasks of administration and planning. But the active participation of the state in economic life creates other problems. And above all one has to ask: what kind of state is involved?

The failures of the state sector in developing countries are as well known as the predatory behavior of transnational corporations and the incompetence of local entrepreneurs. If left-wing scholars complain of the injustice of the world economic order and of the poverty that accompanies capitalism in the third world, liberal experts cite hundreds of grotesque instances of the inefficiency of the state and of the corruptibility of its officials.

The mixed economy has been seen by reformist ideologues in the third world as a miraculous way of avoiding the bureaucratization of the state sector. Senegalese leaders, for example, declared that the nationalized sector could develop successfully only if it were possible to ensure "a rise in the quality of administration, which remains relatively low."[41] But even the most capable managers, when forced to deal with a bureaucracy at once absurd and aggressive, quickly found other avenues for their talents or began to concern themselves solely with their own careers and their personal enrichment. Solving one problem, the nationalized sector gave rise to others. New disproportions appeared in the economy. In most countries the state sector was not self-financing, and became a burden on the entire society. In order to speed the accumulation of capital, the authorities restricted consumption by the population and resorted to borrowing.

In this way, the national strategy of development came more and more to resemble the neocolonialist one. Sacrifices were demanded from the masses in the name of progress, while external dependency remained. Import-substitution industrialization reduced imports of foreign goods, but not of foreign technology. Often, the state acted just like the transnationals. "New technological processes," notes a Colombian scholar, "are based mainly on imported raw materials, and are introduced without any changes to suit local conditions."[42] In Mexico, with its developed state sector and relatively advanced scientific level, the picture is the same: 80 percent of the technology employed by national industry is of foreign origin.

An identical process took place in the third world states that oriented themselves toward the Soviet Union. The USSR concluded agreements with third world countries on terms that were more advantageous for them than those offered by the transnationals. The interest rates on Soviet credits remained unchanged over many years, while the rates on loans from Western banks were increased. Officially, it was given out that Soviet aid to developing countries was directed above all toward satisfying internal demand.[43] But the ability of the USSR to provide aid in the 1970s, and especially in the 1980s, was extremely limited. By 1983 our country already rated eighth among the world's twenty largest debtor states. The Soviet bloc was laying out only 0.01 percent of its gross national product on aid to developing countries, while the corresponding figure for the Western countries was 0.08 percent.[44] The more Soviet society lagged behind the West, the less effective its aid became. By the end of the 1980s, the Soviet government could offer its third world clients only outmoded technology.

The Soviet Union concentrated its assistance on a small number of regimes that were its most reliable allies. This aid could be paid off either by adopting the Soviet model, or through collaborating with Moscow's military and political plans. As a counterweight to the capitalist world system, a Communist world system was created. The relationship between the center and periphery was identical, though the form was less harsh.

Even within the Soviet Union, disproportions remained between the highly developed North and the backward South. To a considerable extent, the development of industry in the republics of Central Asia went ahead through the resettling of Russian workers and technical staff, who produced goods mainly for Russia, Ukraine, and Belarus. The indigenous population remained in the countryside, contributing to hidden unemployment or swelling the ranks of the bureaucracy. Despite the growth of the cities, society retained its tribal and clan structure, something which was reflected in the apparatus of power. The collapse of the Soviet Union in 1991 was accompanied by the exodus of a considerable number of Russians, Koreans, Germans, Armenians, and Tatars, and by the breaking of economic ties between the southern republics on one hand, and Russia and Ukraine on the other. In the newly independent republics, the same problems arose as in the countries of the third world.

China, which in the 1950s had adopted the Soviet economic model, but which did not join the Soviet world system, has so far achieved considerably more than the countries of the Soviet bloc. Cuba and Vietnam, the USSR's most faithful allies in the third world, could not boast of huge successes. Some problems were solved, but dependency on the center was not overcome; all that was achieved was to exchange one center for another. After declaring in the 1970s that collaboration with the USSR was the cornerstone of Vietnam's entire national development program, the Vietnamese leaders soon became convinced that their country's desire for economic independence and modernization would not be met in this fashion.

The Soviet economic journal EKO (no. 1, 1984, p. 152) offered these telling statistics: Vietnamese-Soviet trade saw a rise in imports from the USSR from 67 billion rubles in 1965 to 232 billion in 1976, skyrocketing to 725 billion in 1981. During the same period, Vietnamese exports to the Soviet Union totaled 28 billion rubles in 1965, 64 billion in 1976, and 167 billion in 1981. In correlation, Vietnam's trade deficit came to 39 billion rubles in 1965, 168 billion in 1976, and 558 billion in 1981.

Receiving expensive machinery and equipment, the Vietnamese paid for it with cheap consumer products, an exchange which conformed totally to the traditional pattern of center vs. periphery. Thanks to the Soviet-type system of distribution, the lower ranks of society suffered somewhat less from poverty, while the Soviet brother could not guarantee the elite a standard of living as high as that of ruling groups in countries which had taken the capitalist road.

By the end of the 1980s the Soviet Union was collaborating with forty-seven African countries, helping to carry out 348 projects and 300 preliminary studies. For the African countries involved, the results of this collaboration included not just industrial plants (often with obsolete and polluting technology), but also huge debts to Moscow. The largest debtors included Ethiopia, owing 2.86 billion rubles, Algeria

(2.519 billion), Angola (2.028 billion), Egypt (1.707 billion), and Libya (1.707 billion). Among the USSR's debtors were not only countries which had proclaimed their noncapitalist orientation, but also countries from the pro-imperialist camp, both the very poorest and the relatively rich. They were united solely by the fact that at one period or another of their history they had been military and political partners of the USSR.

In the late 1980s, by which time the political situation in our country had changed radically, liberal newspapers in the USSR began to argue publicly for the ending of aid to poor countries. Soviet assistance to Moscow's traditional third world allies, including Cuba and Ethiopia, was sharply reduced. Liberal economists maintained that it was necessary to orient solely to countries which had real prospects of paying.[45] However, finding credit-worthy clients in the third world was no easy task. Great hopes were held of Nigeria, relatively wealthy and true to the capitalist path. This was a country that paid its creditors in hard currency. Soviet experts had begun the construction of a metallurgical complex at Abeokuta in Nigeria back in the Brezhnev era, in 1980. But when in 1990 the Soviet government, which had itself become one of the world's greatest debtors, sought prompt payment of the sums owing, the Nigerians explained that they could not pay and wanted a postponement of four to five years.

While complaining about the insolvency of the few trade partners who still wanted to buy Soviet technology and products, the Russian liberal economists did not even think to ask whether it made sense to build huge industrial installations in developing countries, or which types of production were really necessary for development rather than for satisfying the ambitions of third world rulers. When it helped implement projects which were clearly doomed to failure or which were ill-suited to solving the real problems of the societies involved, the Soviet government, like its new senior partners in the United States and Western Europe, merely aggravated the crisis.

Marx in his time wrote that if a machine is imported "to a country possessing iron and coal, you will be unable to prevent this country from itself producing such machines."[46] This is no longer valid. The production of machines is controlled by those who control the technology. Without the necessary technology neither iron nor coal will be used for industrial purposes. To have control over technology means ultimately to have control over the process of industrialization. As a Latin American author wrote, a country cannot be economically independent if it is unable "to make independent decisions on questions of technology, and to develop the main elements of technical knowledge on an autonomous basis."[47] In practice, "every wave of import substitution has required the importing of ever more complex techniques for the production of the goods which are no longer imported. The process has thus seen dependency on imports of consumer goods replaced by dependency on imports of capital, of the equipment needed for implementing technical knowledge."[48] Everywhere, the advanced technology and the financial resources obtained in the form of state loans have been used inefficiently.

For some reason, the experience with hydropower stations was especially unfortunate. The Aswan Dam, built in Egypt with Soviet help, was not only the largest electrical generating installation in Africa, but also became a symbol of irrational management. Egyptian President Gamal Abdel Nasser and Soviet leader Nikita Khrushchev built themselves a monument for future centuries, but the country's economy did not benefit. From the very beginning, the gigantic structure on the Nile was a source of problems for Egypt. The degree of salinity of cultivated lands increased, and the silt which used to fertilize the land every year now gathered on the bottom of Lake Nasser. Fish began to disappear from the Nile delta.[49]

Alexandria was threatened by the depletion of the Nile Delta, on which the city was built. Previously the river had annually washed down and deposited huge quantities of silt and sand, but now the process was reversing. Using the dam's productive potential to the full proved impossible. The Egyptians were forced to invite Soviet, French, and American experts to try to remedy the situation.

In the early 1980s a correspondent for *Time* magazine reported from Latin America: "Many projects have turned into bottomless pits, swallowing financial resources as a result of poor planning and incompetent management. The Chingas hydropower station in Colombia should have cost $300 million, but instead cost a billion."[50] An analogous situation arose with the Itaipu hydropower station on the Brazil-Paraguay border. The governments of developing countries preferred to invest funds in grandiose Pharaonic projects.[51] Venezuela poured huge sums into five-year industrialization plans, not one of which was fulfilled. The Arab countries, both the oil-rich and the poor, set out to amaze the world with mighty industrial monuments suited mainly to glorifying the memory of the rulers.

Most of the state projects were aimed at duplicating the 1930s Soviet model of industrialization. Funds were invested in heavy industry and electricity generation, irrespective of need. This drew criticisms even from Soviet experts. At a conference in the Moscow Institute of Oriental Studies, it was stated that the basis for industrialization was the establishing of "large-scale machine production in general; in other words, industrialization in principle can begin with any economic sector, not excluding agriculture ... depending on the concrete conditions of the place and time."[52] These concrete conditions were ignored by the national governments, at times to an even greater degree than by the colonizers in earlier years.

What was the cause of these oversights? A centralized bureaucratic system simply cannot avoid them. In almost all developing countries, the Algerian economist M. Bacha writes, "the bases are lacking for democratic bodies able to substitute their authority for rule by the oligarchy (whether military or familial) which creates and controls all institutions. These institutions remain true citadels of incompetence and mediocrity, in which nothing remains of democracy but the appearance." Workers lack the opportunity to express their views. Even leaving out of account the fact that in conditions of general poverty such regimes are forced to outlay huge resources on the apparatus of repression, the absence of democracy is "linked to the (pathological?) inefficiency of capital investment."[53]

The state sector is dominated by large-scale, capital-intensive enterprises which cannot pay off their original cost for many years. These enterprises are required to fulfill not just productive tasks, but social ones as well. It is clear that no one apart from the state can create such expensive enterprises in the third world. But when the state is primarily an uncontrolled and despotic bureaucracy, there is no way of determining whether the decision to build such a plant reflects the country's real long-term interests, or whether it stems from simple incompetence or the satisfying of bureaucratic ambitions. The centers of industrialization in the third world have the same relationship to their hinterlands as the developed countries have to the underdeveloped. The dichotomy of the center and periphery is reproduced within the developing world itself, with the prosperity of the new industrial regions achieved at the expense of perpetuating the backwardness of the periphery. Society is rendered more and more heterogeneous. The gap between the modern and traditional sectors grows ever wider.

As a result of the narrowness of the internal market, import-substitution industrialization quickly exhausts its potential. The traditional sector cannot consume industrial products in large quantities. Since colonial times it has provided industry with cheap raw materials, but the reverse linkage has remained extremely weak. If its growth is to be sustained, industry must be reoriented toward external markets—that is, it must return to an export model.

Import-substitution industrialization causes just as much ecological damage as the activity of transnational firms. Poor countries do not have the resources to restore the environment. Initially, they refused altogether to take these problems seriously. Asked what he dreamt of seeing in his country in thirty years' time, a Ugandan government minister answered: "Smog."[54] Environmental crises seemed to him a comparatively cheap price to pay for industrialization. Things have now changed; a study of the quality of the air in large Indian cities has shown that the level of pollution there is twenty-five times (!) higher than in the cities of Western Europe or the United States. Scientists report that the cutting of forests has reached levels close to catastrophic, destroying the ecological balance not only on a regional, but also on a global scale. The disappearance of forests leads to desertification. This in turn increases dependency on food imports and the demand for foreign currency. Such methods offer no way out of the vicious circle of dependency and crisis. "Unlike analogous crises in the past, the environmental crisis has the symptomatic feature that the possibility of escaping from it in the present technical-productive and socio-economic conditions is questionable."[55]

However paradoxical it might seem, industrialization also brings with it a dramatic increase in unemployment. By organizing the mass production of goods, new enterprises create unfavorable conditions for small producers, often reducing them to ruin. This does not mean that industrial production is always more efficient; large enterprises are simply better equipped to survive. Backed by the state or by big capital, they can allow themselves to work at a loss. Small production and handicrafts are limited by the physical conditions of survival of the worker. Jobless workers who receive unemployment benefits are in a relatively better position than petty proprietors. It was not by chance that in Latin America, which is relatively far advanced along the road to industrialization, around 30 percent of the workforce in the mid-1980s were unemployed, or did not have full-time work.[56]

The distinguished Polish economist M. Kalecki noted that the problem of unemployment in underdeveloped countries differs fundamentally from the corresponding problem in a capitalist economy. Even Kalecki, however, suggested that it might be solved through the creation of large industrial complexes. According to this point of view, all the problems can be reduced to a lack of investment and the main task confronting developing countries is to bring about a sharp increase in capital investment.[57] This has turned out to be fundamentally untrue. Without experiencing an investment drought, Brazil in the late 1970s encountered a severe crisis. Scientific and technical progress was making industrial equipment increasingly complex and expensive; the results included an ever greater investment barrier blocking the path to establishing new enterprises, and an increasing shortage of trained personnel. Even though a third of the potential labor force was underused, labor costs were constantly increasing.

In the West, the development of modern labor-saving technology required almost two hundred years. Europe in the period of the industrial revolution also experienced a mass influx of people to the cities, the destruction of the traditional rural economy, and even something like a demographic explosion. However, the machine technology of that time was still relatively simple, cheap, and labor-intensive. This allowed the rapid absorption of idle labor power into industry. Now the reserve army of labor is far greater, and the possibilities of employing it incomparably less.

Even the term "reserve army of labor" is hardly applicable to the third world unemployed. It is quite impossible to use these surplus labor resources in industry. Modern labor-saving technology not only deals a blow to the traditional sector, but with each turn in the spiral of technical progress, creates additional unemployment in the modern sector. In the traditional sector, meanwhile, the cheapness of manual labor means that the profitability of machinery may be placed in doubt. As in China, the use not only of modern machines but even of draft animals may become unprofitable.[58]

An analogous situation has also come about in agriculture as a result of the green revolution. Technology imported from the West and the USSR has turned out to be unsuitable for many countries of the South. "It is becoming more and more obvious that the direct transfer to the developing countries of agricultural methods used in milder climatic zones can have adverse effects on the environment, including an increase in the problem of erosion. At times even the use of a common plough has negative consequences."[59]

It was indispensable to forge a compromise between modern and traditional methods that would allow the traditional sector to be reorganized from within. The French scholar G. Etienne wrote that third world agriculture required a new mode of production, distinct from the traditional agrarian organization. It would be a mistake, however, to "go to the other extreme, creating large mechanized enterprises of the European or North American type."[60] This is true for industry as well.

It is becoming more and more obvious that the growth of the modern sector should not be forced, but that it is necessary to try to close the gap between the modern and traditional sectors. From the early 1970s appeals have been made for the process of development to be placed on a totally new basis, involving the use of methods that would succeed better in satisfying human needs.[61] In the first place work would have to be carried out to create an intermediate sector of the economy, able to provide work for the majority of the people and gradually to take the place of the traditional sector. People who are linked to the old forms of production cannot be abruptly incorporated into the modern economy.

This new approach to development was set forward in E.F. Schumacher's widely read and exceptionally well-written book *Small Is Beautiful*.[62] As Schumacher wrote, "[I]f people cannot adapt themselves to the methods, then the methods must be adapted to the people."[63]

Schumacher had a great deal to say about intermediate technology, which in his words by "making use of the best of modern knowledge and experience, is conducive to decentralization, compatible with the laws of ecology, is gentle in its use of scarce resources, and designed to serve the human person instead of making him the servant of machines. I have named it intermediate technology to signify that it is vastly superior to the primitive technology of bygone ages, but at the same time much simpler, cheaper and freer than the super-technology of the rich. One can also call it self-help technology, or democratic or people's technology. . . ."[64]

Once traditional productive methods have been improved with the help of modern science, their efficiency can be increased dramatically. Economic growth and import substitution do not by any means have to be accompanied by the building of large industrial complexes, or by the concentration of production in large cities. It is better to take the road of creating a mass of small enterprises serving the internal market. The inhabitants of remote districts need to receive work where they are; this prevents an exodus to large cities. Since the equipment is simple and cheap, and lengthy training is not required for its use, it does not present a psychological barrier to people from the traditional sector; meanwhile, the goods produced are cheap and accessible to all. Equipment of this kind can be developed and produced in the third world, thus removing the problem of technological dependency. This technology is also environmentally safe. Most importantly, such methods will lead to the gradual modernization of the traditional sector itself, to improvements in the tools of its labor, to raising the level of labor culture, and broadening the internal market. After the gap between the old and new elements of the economy has been closed, a new stage of modernization can begin.

Even before Schumacher, the idea of a new technology was advanced in a general way by Herbert Marcuse. His concept was simply not taken seriously. Even in the late 1970s, Leszek Kolakowski in his *Main Currents of Marxism* poured scorn on such fantasies.[65] In the 1980s the fantasy became a reality. Windmills or water mills, improved using modern methods and equipped with minicomputers, can be used to obtain electricity. More and more devices using solar energy are beginning to appear. Sailing ships are again putting out to sea, though their sails are very different from those of old, and much simpler to handle. There is renewed interest in airships, which at times are seen as the transport of the future.[66] Interest in the new technology has been shown mainly in the West, in the Scandinavian countries and in Holland. But people in the third world are turning to it more and more often.

Research centers have appeared in India and other countries. In Nigeria an authority has been established to encourage the use of solar energy; this has been transformed into a large research center, with its own plant producing industrial equipment and everyday utensils. In Mali a regional West African solar energy center is being set up.[67]

Soviet authors who accused Schumacher of aiming to perpetuate the backwardness of the third world were forced to admit that in the third world itself, a certain degree of attention was being paid to his ideas.[68] Small-scale industry was no longer perceived as something of secondary importance. The revolutionary government of Nicaragua stressed that its plans for developing the country's technological potential were not linked to the establishing of large heavy industries, though the raw materials for such industries exist and were being studied. The main thrust of technological innovation was within the traditional branches of the economy, and the primary task was to raise the profitability of the existing industrial and agricultural enterprises. Taking account of their specific national conditions of production, the Nicaraguans declared, they were setting out to create their own technology, suited to their particular needs.[69] In Mexico during the 1980s the United Socialist Party adopted in its programmatic documents the slogans of a "new development" aimed at creating a genuine popular economy.[70] In China during the 1980s more attention began to be paid to small industry in the villages and regional centers.

Nevertheless, intermediate technology will not solve a single problem unless socioeconomic and political reforms are carried out. Intermediate technology can be used just as inefficiently as industrial technology. In China during the period of the Great Leap Forward, it was resolved to increase the output of pig iron through the use of small-scale metallurgy. What was involved was an attempt to restore age-old traditional methods. This scheme was a catastrophic failure, leading to chaos on the railways, which were overburdened with shipments of iron ore. In any case, implementing such a project in a centralized manner, binding people's communes everywhere to obligatory targets, meant reducing it to an absurdity. Developing small-scale industry requires decentralization and democratic local self-management. People have to have an interest in the results of their work. Neither the traditional forms of private property, nor concentrating the means of production in the hands of the government will help to develop this sector. Such enterprises have to be either municipal or collective. "Generally speaking," wrote G. Dauncey, one of the propagandists of the alternative economy, "the greater the element of local ownership in an economy, the greater the stability in that economy, and the greater the commitment of local people."[71]

The development of the intermediate sector is impossible without a certain level of industrialization. But from this point on, the priorities are different. The task of industrialization is not to reproduce the Western or Soviet structure of production as precisely and quickly as possible, building the greatest possible number of industrial plants, but to produce equipment for the intermediate sector and products for the people who work in it.

The nationalized sector of industry could become the moving force and major support for such transformations. But this is inconceivable so long as control over investment and the administration of the economy are in the hands of bureaucratic, bourgeois or transnational elites. The functioning of state enterprises depends directly on the type of regime that holds power in a country, on its social nature, and on the structure of power that it has set in place. Only in an authentically democratic state, where the masses are able to take part in government, can the state sector become a real locomotive of development. The organization of production in the intermediate sector requires collectivist methods which in many ways resemble the patriarchal collectivism of traditional society, but which are distinct from any of the forms of totalitarian collectivism. What is involved is not a strengthening of patriarchal values, but their gradual transformation from within. It is here that everyday practice has to provide an answer to the interminable and fruitless arguments between Westernizers and "children of the soil" which began in nineteenth-century Russia, and which in one variant or another have been repeated in all developing countries.

As the Soviet orientalist A.V. Gordon remarked aptly, returning to traditions does not in the least signify renouncing the struggle for progress: "Looking on the traditional culture as an obstacle to development means denying its capacity for development, that is, in the final analysis denying obvious facts associated with the historical destinies of the bearers of this culture."[72] The question is: on which elements of the old culture should one's stake be placed? Khoros considers that without the kind of borrowings that he calls the synthesis of tradition and modernity, progress is impossible. "It might be supposed," he continues, "that from the point of view of mobilizing mass consciousness and simultaneously softening its negative manifestations, the ideal is an ideological program and strategy of development aimed at a more or less organic synthesis of modern structures with progressive elements of the national sociocultural heritage, that is, at actively incorporating traditions into the process of development."[73]

In the 1930s the Mexican President Lazaro Cárdenas established self-governing peasant communes, the *ejidos*. These were an important element of his modernization program. For all their shortcomings, the *ejidos* provided the peasants with a measure of defence during the process of agricultural and industrial revolution in Mexico, reduced social tensions, and stabilized society.[74]

The reformist regimes in Senegal and Tanzania also tried to organize a system of peasant communes, which according to local ideologues differed both from the Soviet collective farms and from Western-style cooperatives.[75] The government put its stake on local peasant self-management. In Tanzania renewing the *ujamaa* commune became the center of government policy and ideology. Analogous measures were also put into practice in Madagascar.

At least on the ideological level, all these regimes recognized the role of popular education. Tanzania achieved a higher level of literacy than most countries of black Africa, and Senegal in the early 1980s was assigning as much as 30 percent of its budget to education and culture. What was involved here was serious work, not the noisy and ineffective campaigns of struggle against illiteracy conducted by some radical regimes. Avoiding the industrial psychosis, these governments in a number of cases were even able to make choices in favor of nature. In Kenya, for example, a factory on the banks of Lake Nakuru, home to a large population of flamingos, was shut down when it was discovered to be polluting the water. The readiness to learn from the mistakes of others has often only been verbal. "The mistake of the Russians," wrote Senghor, "was that they failed to take account of the role of the peasantry in agriculture."[76] The Tanzanian leadership also declared that agriculture had to be assigned a central place in development plans.[77] In practice, however, the mistakes of others have unfailingly been repeated. The reformist regimes in Africa managed to ensure society relative stability and respect for human rights. Analyzing the experience of Tanzania, the well-known economist Immanuel Wallerstein notes that the reforms that have been carried out could be justified even if they fall far short of their ostensible objectives.[78] Nevertheless, one cannot speak of success in this case. The most radical of the attempts at reform, the *ujamaa* program in Tanzania, has not justified the hopes placed in it. Many scholars recognize that despite its drawbacks, the collectivism of *ujamaa* represents a correct approach to development, but realizing its potential is impossible without the defeat of bureaucratism, which remains "the main obstacle to putting this theory into practice."[79] In Senegal, despite the declarations of the government, in 1987 a total of 93 percent of the population above the age of six years had never been to school. The foreign debt stood at 69 percent of gross national product, which between 1980 and 1987 grew on average by only 0.1 percent a year. Unemployment had reached threatening dimensions.

As late as 1978 Willy Brandt was calling on progressive groups in the third world to create their own independent forms of social democracy.[80] Initially it seemed that after the failure of the radical experiments in the third world, the time of the moderate reformers had arrived. Official Soviet authors wrote uneasily about the growing degree of penetration of the developing countries by the ideas of democratic socialism, something which in their view was fraught with great dangers.[81] In Latin America, governments which had come to power at the beginning of the 1980s spoke of their adherence to social democratic values. Even in Africa there were attempts to create a regional Socialist International. Soon, however, it became clear that the forces hiding beneath the social democratic slogans had little in common with the European social democrats. The government of Tunisia, which declared itself to be social democratic, was forced to substantiate its statements by legalizing the opposition and holding elections; voter lists were falsified, the contents of ballot boxes were discarded, and the government juggled openly with the results. In Senegal the ruling Socialist Party allowed opposition currents to operate openly, democratized its internal life, and called for the establishing of good relations with other parties including the Communists.[82] The socialists in Senegal managed to create a stable parliamentary regime— a rare achievement in African conditions. Supporters of this model argue that such a variant of development is less fragile by virtue of its flexibility.[83] But to speak of the triumph of democracy in Senegal is at best premature. When the Socialist Party candidate, President Abou

Diouf, was re-elected for a second term in 1988 with 73 percent of the votes, the opposition accused the authorities of rigging the elections. The government's answer was repression. "The multiparty system in Senegal is very superficial and limited," says Amadou Guiro, the leader of a left-wing opposition group. "Political parties exist, operate and have their press, but not one of them has access to the mass media. Moreover, the electoral law makes it easy to falsify elections in the interests of the regime in power."[84]

Kenya retained a one-party system until 1992. Here the individual rights of citizens are observed more scrupulously than in many other African states.[85] Nevertheless, the situation in Kenya has not borne any close resemblance to democracy. In Tanzania, despite the lack of political freedoms, a system of local self-government has been established. Western writers recognize that thanks to this the workers and peasants have not merely been made to listen to appeals and promises, but have had some real possibility of determining their own fate. Meanwhile, political discussion has been carried on without any particular restrictions, and on a high theoretical level.[86] Madagascar has seen the establishment of something in between pluralism and a one-party system. The only parties permitted have been those endorsing the Charter of the Malagasy Revolution.[87]

Following a period of enthusiasm for progressive transformations, the reformist regimes moved to the right, and in response to the demands of the International Monetary Fund began carrying out privatization, establishing favorable conditions for the activity of transnational corporations and international banks.

The greatest successes enjoyed by any of the African states proclaiming a socialist orientation are reckoned to have been achieved in Zimbabwe. The Mugabe government, which came to power in Zimbabwe following a war of national liberation lasting many years, has declared itself to be Marxist, but it has never gone further in this direction than uttering ideological rhetoric. "Certainly," write the British scholars Colin Stoneman and Lionel Cliffe, "there has been precious little attempt so far to transform the socio-economic structure or to change the terms of the country's involvement with the world economy, in directions that would suggest a transition to socialism and that are differentiated from a more Africanist-oriented path of capitalist development after the decades of racist capitalism."[88]

The model tested out in Zimbabwe has lain at the basis of government policy in Namibia since the winning of independence by this, the last African colony. Like the Zimbabwean insurgents, the leaders of the South-West African People's Organization (SWAPO) came to power after spending many years fighting for their independence, and stressed their realism and moderation. While repeating revolutionary slogans, they simultaneously insisted that they were always ready to recognize the necessities—of compromise, pragmatism, gradualism—in order ultimately to achieve the brave new society for which they have endured so much for so long.[89]

The secret of Zimbabwe's success lay mainly in the fact that from the very first this country had been one of the most developed in the region. As new problems arose, the regime gave increasing proof of its conservatism. By the early 1990s, having finally forgotten their socialist rhetoric, the Zimbabwean leaders in practice accepted the strategy urged on them by the International Monetary Fund. "Today Zimbabwe is heading down an ultra-capitalist road mapped out by a 'home-grown' Structural Adjustment Program," South African economists relate. "... Traveling along this road we are beginning to come across the wreckage of lives and misappropriated capital so familiar to economies under the thumb of international capital. At one level, the finished products of transnational corporations are squeezing out local firms (in the process drawing away scarce foreign currency that should instead be utilized for retooling plants and equipment). At another level, vast amounts of food production are being abandoned in favor of well-irrigated tobacco for export, as tens of thousands starve during the country's worst drought in memory."[90]

The real social democratic model was developed in countries where a developed democracy, strong trade unions, and a dynamic and balanced capitalist economy have all traditionally existed. In other words, social democracy is a recipe for the wealthy, an ideology of income redistribution that can only be applied where there is no problem ensuring that production goes ahead.[91]

The forces of the left in the third world, if they really want to improve the lives of the population and to change society, are *doomed to radicalism.* In the developing countries new ideological currents are emerging and proclaiming socialism as their goal. For the time being they are weak, but the growth of a hereditary working class will inevitably enhance their prospects.[92] In the absence of a certain level of development, the existence of a left alternative is also inconceivable. But this alternative will only become indispensable and genuine when socialists understand that what is involved cannot and must not be a continuation and acceleration of the former pattern of development through new methods.

Samir Amin has written that a strategy of alternative development is in the interests of the peoples of the third world, that it is possible and even objectively necessary, but that at present there is no serious political force proclaiming such a course. Unless left-wing parties adopt such a strategy in the immediate future, they will lose any influence they possess, while the program will be implemented in any case, through spontaneous methods in the course of a popular revolt.[93]

In actual fact a spontaneous revolt is capable only of destroying the old world, not of creating a new one. Successful social and political transformations can only come about through creative work, in which the concept of balanced development becomes a matter of first priority. While not rejecting the building of industry, it is necessary to reject the kind of models of industrialization that lead to the destruction of nature and of the human personality.[94]

The countries of the third world have the opportunity to make use of the results of scientific progress, while avoiding many of its costs. Without repeating all the zigzags of the path followed by Europe, it is possible to use the experience of Europe in formulating a distinctive course of development. But the concepts of an alternative, ecologically friendly, humanist economy will remain utopian dreams so long as they are seen as an alternative to class struggle and to social transformations. The only chance of really achieving a different course of development is through working people winning it in struggle.

CHAPTER 3

THE ZIGZAGS OF POLITICAL MODERNIZATION

The institutions of political power have always exerted a huge influence on society. In the third world this influence is becoming decisive. This is not only because the government often assumes the functions of planning and accumulating capital, but also for the reason that in a diverse society divided into a multitude of groups, castes, sects, nationalities, and tribes, it is the state that welds the country into a united whole. No one disputes the role of political power; it is recognized by all scholars and all parties. But what will this state be like? Which forces will it serve? Which strategy of modernization will it select?

The aim of social modernization has always been to form an orderly, homogeneous social structure, to overcome the gaps between sectors, to form broad modern classes, and to develop the political and cultural institutions that are typical of highly developed societies.[1] In the conceptions of early ideologues of modernization the idea of industrial society was closely linked with democracy on the Western model. Parliamentarianism and civil liberties were considered indispensable political elements of modernization, conditions of its success.

Industrial societies without democracy existed in Eastern Europe, but already in the 1960s their example was showing that at a particular stage the lack of freedom acted as a brake on development. The crisis in Eastern Europe provided evidence of a clear link between the maturation of modern, highly developed forces of production and the need for civil rights. In Czechoslovakia in 1968 the contradiction between a highly developed economy and a totalitarian structure of power spurred attempts to carry out democratic reforms from above. The defeat of the Czechoslovak reformers marked the beginning of two decades of stagnation and economic crisis, to be followed by fresh political earthquakes.

Meanwhile, the ideologues of modernization in third world countries were feeling less and less sympathy for parliamentarianism and democracy. The well-known sociologist F.H. Cardoso observed in 1978 that initial suggestions concerning the political consequences of economic growth and the inevitability of democratization clearly do not correspond to the actual development of political history, in which at every step we encounter military coups and the spread of authoritarian regimes. This unforeseen turn of events makes everything which is now occurring in the majority of Latin American countries seem like an epidemic of political pathology. "There are no more then three or four out of more than twenty countries which can by any stretch of imagination be called democratic."[2]

During the second half of the 1980s, constitutional regimes were restored in most of the countries of Latin America. After sweeping through Latin America, the democratic wave moved on to Africa. But by the beginning of the 1990s the euphoria aroused by the fall of military dictatorships had everywhere been replaced by uncertainty and alarm.

In some third world societies, despite all the forecasts, democracy not only survived but even managed a degree of stability. India, Malaysia, and Sri Lanka remained faithful to British parliamentarianism, though parliamentary democracy was often combined with interethnic violence, repression, and even civil war. Scholars are unanimous in recognizing that Indian society has succeeded brilliantly in mastering the institutions of parliamentary democracy. At first glance it seems that the further a society has advanced along the road to modernization, the greater its readiness for democracy. But why, then, did parliamentarianism collapse or decay in a number of the most advanced countries of the third world, while the much less advanced society of India made a splendid success of it?

One has the impression at times that the third world bourgeoisie rejects bourgeois democracy. In most cases its democratic traditions are decidedly suspect. But as a rule, the bearer of the capitalist orientation in the third world is not the bourgeoisie, while the social base for anticapitalist regimes is not provided by the proletariat. Both of these classes are weakly developed, lack strong political organizations, and are socially unconsolidated. The technocratic middle layers play a far more important role. It is they that select one or another ideology and practical model, depending on their concrete historical experience.

The goal of technocracy has never been capitalism, much less socialism. Its goal has been modernization, the construction of an industrial society. What constitutes an industrial society is a separate question. The choice of a model and of ideological formulas has often seemed like a question of tactics. When the colonizers departed from the young states, they left behind elites educated in the spirit of Western technocratic thinking. Respect for the democratic principles of European civilization, it seemed, would become an essential part of their ideology and world view. But from the very beginning, it was to be no more than a part.

In Latin America, the ousting of the Spaniards was almost everywhere accompanied by the proclaiming of republican constitutions, drafted under the influence of the French Revolution. These constitutions did not prevent civil wars, the rule of semifeudal oligarchies, or the installing of military dictatorships. Following the departure of the British and French from Asia and Africa, parliaments were elected almost everywhere, and almost everywhere these parliaments were soon dissolved. Western scholars recognize that in Kenya and Tanzania, the traces of British political and administrative institutions and traditions have not disappeared.[3] Sometimes these traditions have even taken on a sort of second life. But not one of these countries could be called a parliamentary democracy. Among the young states, India, Sri Lanka, and Malaysia remain the only significant exceptions.

The fact that they are exceptions is not accidental. These were among the earliest British colonies, and here the formation of local Europeanized elites began back in the nineteenth century. Marx was entirely correct in pointing to the huge role played by democratic freedoms in laying the foundations for Indian statehood even while the colonizers remained. In this respect his forecasts were borne out. As early as the beginning of this century, the old British colonies had seen the formation of a broad layer of people who had acquired not only the external signs of European thinking, but also a liberal political culture. The principles of liberalism had been assimilated by the local elite long before any theory of modernization saw the light of day. British traditions of justice influenced not only those who collaborated with the colonizers, but also those who fought against them. In a sense, these traditions served as an ideological support for the local nationalist elite in its anticolonial struggles. "This educated middle-class elite which provided all the leaders of the National Movement," the Indian scholar Achin Vanaik writes, "came to oppose British rule in the name of the most advanced bourgeois democracy, represented by Britain itself."[4]

Everywhere, European education has played an enormous role in the ideological development of the countries of the third world. The main theories and political myths which prevailed here after World War II arose in Europe and were disseminated in the dependent countries thanks to the European system of instruction. In his remarkable study of nationalism, Benedict Anderson writes of "the unique role played by colonial school-systems in promoting colonial nationalisms."[5] A similar picture can be discerned not just in French Indochina, in British Burma, or in tropical Africa, but also in countries which were never colonized. Samir Amin writes that when Turkey proclaimed itself a republic in the 1920s, its main borrowings from the West were the principles of military and state organization and "its nationalist ideology, nationalist precisely in the very European sense of the word, through affirmation of the 'Turkish'—Turanian—nation and renunciation of the multinational character of the Ottoman Empire."[6]

The paradox of the political situation in colonial India was that British rule in many respects was the heir of precolonial Asiatic despotism. Over the centuries India had lived under the rule of diverse conquerors, and the British in a sense continued this tradition. In many ways the power structures of the British colonial administration in India duplicated the structures of the empire of the Great Moguls, to which the country was accustomed. The British rested on traditional local rulers, supporting and strengthening their power.[7] The anticolonial movement was inspired by the liberal ideas of the West. In other words, British rule at the local level often embodied an Asiatic political culture, while the independence movement, on the other hand, was European in character. The struggle for independence was begun by liberals, who simply blamed their rulers for not being genuinely British.[8] In 1906

one of the leaders of the Indian National Congress, calling for liberation from British rule, declared that the free citizens of the British
Empire in India could no longer remain beneath the yoke of despotism.[9] The struggle of the Indian bourgeoisie to free their country from
colonial bondage was at the same time a struggle for liberal European-
ization, waged against the remnants of Asianism embodied in the
British administration and its semifeudal allies.

A parliamentarist political culture was acquired by increasingly
broad social layers, and was assimilated ever more deeply. In Indian
elections, which were held from 1892, only an insignificant proportion
of the population at first had the right to vote. The franchise was
gradually widened, and by 1935 had been extended to approximately
20 percent of the population. In Sri Lanka, such elections were held
on the basis of universal suffrage from 1931. By the time independence
was declared, Indians had come to make up the overwhelming majority
of functionaries at the lower and middle levels of the state apparatus,
and half of the upper echelon known as the Civil Service. Lenin in his
time described this latter stratum as a staff of supremely well-paid
supreme bureaucrats. An analogous situation also developed over time
in the officer corps of the Anglo-Indian colonial army.[10] Traditions that
were instilled during the time of Queen Victoria remain alive to this
day. As a correspondent for the London *Times* writes, "The Indian
army, the fourth largest in the world, conducts its parade-ground drill
in exactly the same manner as would a British sergeant, only giving this
manner even greater stress." What is involved here is not just the
parade-ground drill, uniforms, and military rituals that have been
preserved with striking meticulousness. Non-participation by the army
in politics is also a tradition inherited from British times.[11]

Sociological surveys in the 1970s and early 1980s showed that the
behavior of Indian voters was strikingly similar to that of British ones.
In Japan only 15 percent of voters identify themselves with a political
party, and in the United States, 35 percent; in Britain and India, by
contrast, the figure is 70 percent. To the question of whether ordinary
people can influence the actions of governments, 39 percent of those
polled in Britain and India answered positively; in Japan this was 26
percent, in West Germany 25 percent, and in the United States 57
percent. What is striking here is not just the relatively high degree of
interest shown by Indians in parliamentary politics, but above all the

obvious correspondence between the results of the Indian survey and the British one.[12]

To explain this, it is far from enough to refer to British traditions. The American scholars Samuel Bowles and Herbert Gintis write: "A highly democratic culture will not coexist for long with highly undemocratic rules. By contrast, where the rules support the culture, which in turn is consistent with the perpetuation of the rules, an institutional equilibrium may be said to exist."[13] It is sufficient to turn to the experience of Pakistan and Bangladesh, which were also parts of British India, to see what happens when such equilibrium is lacking. As Vanaik notes, in India the national bourgeoisie and middle layers established during the colonial epoch acted as a stabilizing force for democratic capitalism. In Pakistan and Bangladesh, which were among the most backward regions of British India, the national bourgeoisie was extremely weak, and the only modern, well-organized forces were the bureaucracy and the army. The predictable result was military-bureaucratic dictatorship. The experience of Pakistan, Vanaik concludes, confirms the formula: No bourgeoisie, no bourgeois democracy.[14]

The comparison between India and Pakistan is instructive in another sense as well. The lack of a developed national bourgeoisie did not prevent Pakistan and Bangladesh from developing along the capitalist road, but it made democratic capitalism impossible. This lesson is of no small significance for people in Eastern Europe who dream of the triumph of Western democracy. Meanwhile, the national bourgeoisie in India would not have been able to strengthen and preserve its ruling position if it had not created a corresponding type of state system, if it had not defended its interests with the help of a powerful state sector, protectionist policies, and a relatively closed model of the market economy. In other words, to establish a liberal democracy in India the ruling circles were obliged not just to renounce traditional liberal economic precepts, but to implement policies that were the direct opposite of these doctrines. Economic liberalism was sacrificed to political democracy.

Since the second half of the 1980s the Indian model has been in obvious crisis. Communal clashes, growing corruption and political instability have all become aspects of everyday life. Outbursts of violence have been put down through the use of government repression. "Perhaps one-third of our armed forces are already deployed for the protection of Indians from other Indians, rather than for defending the nation as a whole," the progressive weekly *Mainstream* observed. "That in itself holds grave dangers to the democracy we pride in."[15]

The Indian National Congress Party, which has ruled the country throughout almost the entire period of its independence, is in crisis. The traditional party of the national bourgeoisie has lost its ability to rule the country. In November 1990 *Newsweek* published an article in which the Indian journalist Pranay Gupte called for the parliamentary system inherited from the colonizers to be replaced by presidential rule. "The system created after the winning of independence has exhausted its potential, and cannot cope with the new problems of a more complex and populous country," he wrote. "The present Westminster parliamentary model has degenerated into a circus, in which the shrillest voices often determine the future of national politics." A new presidential system would be called upon to strengthen order in the country and to make it more governable. The author of the article pointed out who would benefit most from this order. Political reform and the introduction of a strong regime would win the trust of foreign capital, and would allow Indian entrepreneurs to obtain credits on the international capital markets.[16] The national bourgeoisie's liberal government would have to give way to authoritarianism reflecting the interests and demands of the transnational corporations. This would provide the crisis with a certain type of solution, though not one in the interests of most Indians.

One cannot speak of democracy in India during the 1980s and 1990s as having collapsed. "Every conceivable kind of conflict has taken place," Vanaik writes, "short of revolutionary crisis and attempted seizure of power, at one end of the spectrum, or a military coup d'etat, at the other." Taking all this into account, one is forced to recognize that the stability of the Indian state has been "quite exceptional."[17]

It cannot be said that democracy in India works badly. If a system withstands such stresses, one might consider that it works extremely well. The crisis of political institutions is inseparable from the changes occurring within Indian society itself. The point is not just that parliament and the government are coping ever more badly with a multitude of problems, but also that the national bourgeoisie is on the whole losing the ability to consolidate and stabilize society, and to organize development. If the role of the national bourgeoisie as the leading democratic force has been exhausted, the question arises of a new political hegemony, of who will lead development during the next stage.

Following the assassination of Indira Gandhi in 1984, when her son Rajiv inherited the leadership of the party and the post of prime minister, politicians of a new type came to predominate within the ruling circles. As described by Tariq Ali, these were "urban university-graduates, with technocratic bent," who were carried away with "computer-predictions and television electoral campaigns."[18] This new technocracy, which had arisen within the framework of the Indian National Congress and the state administration, was unable to consolidate its power. The ruling party suffered defeat in the elections, and was replaced by a heterogeneous and unstable opposition coalition. The assassination of Rajiv Gandhi in 1991—just when it seemed that problems among the victors would allow him to hope for a return to power—deepened the political crisis still further. The success of the Congress Party at the elections following the latest murder of the latest leader had become a sort of tradition of the Indian parliamentary system, which was incapable either of conquering violence or of reconstructing itself.

Indian society has proven its devotion to democracy, but what will Indian democracy be like in the next stage? Which forces will unite the country, and who will be able to ensure a new hegemony that guarantees the stability and effectiveness of democratic institutions? The technocrats? The transnational corporations and their local representatives? The middle classes? Or the left forces, the workers movement, the most organized and qualified layers of the working class? "The Left," wrote *Mainstream*, "must explain to the people that the present political crisis is an expression of the crisis of development."[19] In order to save democracy, it would be necessary to change the model of development.

In the conditions of a heterogeneous, multistructured society, culture, including political culture, acts as an important unifying, integrating factor. It is thus not surprising that democracy, which in India grows from deep historical and psychological roots, continues to be viable there. In other countries, which spent much briefer periods under the colonial yoke, the ruling circles have proven to be not less Europeanized, but less democratic. The formation of Europeanized national elites took place there during a different epoch.[20] From Europe and the United States, these colonies imported a different culture—no longer liberal, as during Victorian and Edwardian times, but technocratic. Similar processes also occurred under North American influence in the independent countries of Latin America, though in less intensive fashion. At first the contradiction between the two cultures seemed inconsequential, since the former did not in the least reject technical progress and industrialization, while the latter did not initially reject democracy. Gradually, however, the incompatibility between technocratism and democracy in the third world became more and more apparent.

In the words of an African journalist, the local elites that took over from the colonialists retained the antidemocratic structure of the colonial state. Where the departing Europeans had tried to introduce parliamentary rule, the local leaders quickly did away with such innovations, restoring colonial methods. Like the colonialists before them, the new leaders were certain that Africans were "not ready for democracy."[21]

The Western model of the parliamentary system could not work ideally in the third world simply because it had come into being under completely different historical conditions. A heterogeneous, multistructured society gives birth to a political and social context radically different from the European one. As sociologists note, "within any system, its 'own' specific process of class formation goes ahead, a particular feature of which is the coexistence of old and new class structures."[22] This means that a single bourgeoisie and a single working class do not take shape. At different levels several varieties of bourgeoisie and proletariat emerge, and conduct extremely diverse forms of class struggle between themselves. Traditional and semitraditional layers, for their part, give birth to their own conflicts and contradictions.

Some theorists see in the multistructured formation of these societies a sort of historical advantage: the heterogeneity of society strengthens the alternative character of development. Each of the numerous classes nurtures its own historical project. From this, Cheshkov and Sheinis even draw the conclusion that the future of such a society is defined not by the level of development attained by the forces of production, but by the particular group which manages to come out ahead in the political struggle. However, they themselves acknowledge the extreme instability of the alternatives.[23] Most of the supposed social projects are based on extremely narrow social foundations, thanks to which a change of paths can occur very easily. In other words, what is involved is not a historic choice, but only zigzags in a general political course. Narrow social groups and minuscule classes cannot avoid using violence as they try to impose their particular projects on the rest of society. Regardless of which project is chosen, the means used are similar, as a result of which the alternative projects turn out to be suspiciously similar as well.

Ultimately, it is the means which determine the end. The result of the historical process depends more on the methods which are chosen than on the slogans that are proclaimed. In a sense, the historic goal is no more than a projection of the means which are employed. Meanwhile, only a depressingly monotonous arsenal of methods exists. The majority of groups which enter social struggles in the third world are totally unfitted to implement a historical project. They content themselves with a utopia, whether this is a return to the past, a rapid transition to socialism, or assimilation into the Western world. Attempts to realize such utopias clearly cannot be successful. The multi-structured nature of these societies thus gives rise not so much to an increased range of alternatives for development, as to extreme social and political instability.

Acute crises arise at every step, and the entire social structure comes under unbelievable stress. Who can act as the savior of democracy? The bourgeoisie? The bourgeoisie, however, is weak and lacks liberal traditions. The patriarchal elements at the base of society lack the necessary level of political culture. The traditional elites at times make use of democratic institutions, but in a thoroughly eccentric fashion. In Lebanon the semifeudal ruling layers transformed parliamentary parties into tools of internecine struggle. One example is the Progressive Socialist Party. Soviet scholars note that "in reality, the great majority of its adherents are Druse peasants dependent in feudal and clientelist fashion on the Jumblats, one of the most powerful of the aristocratic clans. When Kemal Jumblat became head of the clan, he founded his own party."[24]

The proletariat is just as heterogeneous and divided as the bourgeoisie. In the view of political scientists, the diversity and organizational atomization of the left forces in the third world constitutes a "natural and permanent tendency" since "the various cohorts of workers, forming and taking on a mass character at different stages of industrialization, differ significantly from one another and from their predecessors in their social position, world view, historical experience, social psychology and so forth, and thus gravitate toward the 'appeals' of different political organizations, including revolutionary ones."[25] In this connection, an Argentinian sociologist speaks of the almost universal incapacity of the main classes to achieve social hegemony.[26] Neither the bourgeoisie, nor the working class, nor the peasantry is able on its own to become a force directing development.

During the 1970s Western sociologists hoped that the urban middle layers, the bureaucracy and technocracy, would act as a prop for democracy in developing societies. It was held that only these groups, possessing education, links to the state, and a relatively privileged social position, would be able to claim hegemony in political life. The unity of the bureaucratic apparatus and the technical structures, the similar education which these people had received and their similar way of life made them a particularly dynamic and compact social mass, a type of example for society as a whole. History seemed to have designated them for the role of social integrator. Western scholars wrote that in the third world the middle layers would play a truly providential role, supporting the democratization of national institutions, the stability and continuity of these institutions, and the successive transformation of the social structure.[27] But despite these expectations, the middle layers did not become the guardians of political freedom. Almost everywhere in the third world, the gravediggers of democracy were members of the Europeanized groups: the army, the bureaucracy, the middle layers— and at times, it must be said, the radical left-wing intelligentsia. All of them regarded democracy as an obstacle to modernization, as an ineffective political system incapable of coping with periodic crises. Western political scientists also gradually leaned toward this view, speaking of a dictatorship of development as the optimal political form for backward countries, declaring that under conditions of modernization democratic institutions were not very appropriate,[28] and maintaining that it was necessary to recognize the practical impossibility both of democratic and of noncoercive solutions.[29] In this way, the search for a democratic variant of development was removed from the agenda.

Democracy is labeled a luxury for the rich. Explaining why the

Brazilian armed forces in the 1960s took and abolished civil liberties, Latin American sociologists wrote that a country seeking to achieve productive successes, to catch up with the West, "cannot allow itself the luxury of preserving democratic liberties, of recognizing the right of the exploited to protest, since this would impede the economic growth which is required for security and order."[30]

The main task of technocratic modernization, as summed up by a Soviet scholar, is "to 'integrate' society, to grant integrity to the social organism 'from above'."[31] The weapon of integration is the state, and the method is coercion. The supreme principle governing the trans- formations is no longer freedom, but order. Modernization provides third world technocrats with a historical slogan and a justification. Their actions appear more necessary than ever before. Technocratic ideology in the West did not have so cruel a basis. Extreme need justifies both extreme forms of authority and extreme ideas. Technocracy acquires a heroic spirit and revolutionary slogans. The myth of the orderly world that inspires it appears directly as a myth of progress. Any actions are justified by the need to carry out the objective tasks of development. Of course, dictators who claim to act out of objective necessity always impose on society their own subjective understanding of this necessity. As the French sociologist J. Comblin wrote, in the course of events goals lose their meaning, and the same words come to denote different things. Methods change as well; new factors emerge, new means of action, new formulas, or simply new conditions.[32]

The third world repeated, a century later, a more terrifying version of the rapture about a machine civilization that had been dominant in Europe in the late nineteenth century and in the Stalinist Soviet Union. Nietzsche provides an extreme expression of this mood in his call for the new individual to be educated on the model and in the likeness of the machine, and for society to be organized along the lines of machine production: "The machine itself teaches the human masses to cooper- ate, demanding operations in which each has to perform only one function: it provides a model of party organization, and of the waging of war.... Its overall effect is to teach the use of centralization."[33]

To value order above liberty means to despise the human individual. As Comblin notes, if the nation is to achieve great ends, then from now on it must regulate itself in the same way as the material world; what is involved is the application of a definite sum of forces for the attainment of a particular goal. Human beings as independent factors are not valued. The rationalist utopia is imposed forcefully. Under such an approach, the Soviet historian G. Vodolazov wrote, "the problem becomes exceedingly simple. All the 'subtleties' and complexities of transitional stages and measures are banished. Crude, straight lines are drawn through the solution of the problem, and these lines then acquire the actual form of barbed wire, prisons, concentration camps and so on."[34]

Technocracy began its ascent in the third world during the struggle against the traditional elites and the colonialists. In undemocratic rule the struggle allowed those with an uncommon will to power to take leading roles. Marx wrote that the exercise of power may become relatively independent of society and classes during periods when none of the contending sides has gained the upper hand.[35] In multistructured societies which have become stuck in the phase of transition, the role played by power expands to become a permanent and autonomous social factor. The bureaucratic-technocratic bloc is organized on the basis of state institutions and, not least, of the organs of repression. The concept of order and the concept of power become inseparable. An ideological chain reaction begins. "Power can sustain itself, that is, maintain its essence," wrote Heidegger, referring to Nietzsche, "only if it is capable of excelling and exceeding, or we might say, of prevailing over every degree of power achieved earlier, and thus over itself. If power stops at one or another degree of might, it is transformed into impotence."[36]

Wherever a regime rests primarily on coercion, force becomes its justification, its law, and its ideal. The more difficult it is to ensure the hegemony of the rulers and the willing assent of the ruled in a multistructured society, the more power becomes the goal of the ruling group. The meaning of their ideology changes. Initially they fought for power in the name of the country's liberation and rebirth. If they are now to hold on to power, the project of modernization must at all costs be carried through to its end. Nietzsche hoped that the will to power would give birth to a superman, but it is giving birth to a super-mediocrity, compensating with the help of violence for moral bankruptcy. The less real faith remains, the greater the need for an ideological cover. Heidegger noted that a regime in such cases appeals constantly to its philosophy and appears extremely ideologized, but in fact philosophy as learning and as cultural education disappears.[37]

The decay of the original meaning of ideology is accompanied by the semblance of ideological expansion. The less the old ideals mean, the more they are talked about. The degeneration of the modernizer grouplets at times extends so far that they lose even the appearance of progressive aims, and the reactionary essence of their power can no longer be concealed. In place of the order of industrial society, the order of the graveyard takes over. So it was in Kampuchea under Pol Pot. However, Pol Potism is only the final stretch of the road which many technocratic modernizers are taking or may take. If we turn to the experience of Stalin's Russia, of Kemal's Turkey, or of the regimes which arose in Eastern Europe following the collapse of the Communist governments, we see the same picture everywhere. For a technocratic utopia, human beings are an excessive hindrance. Humans, linked to traditional production and to the old culture, prejudices, and beliefs, cannot be enlisted immediately into the splendid new order. Coercion by the state arouses resistance, if not in the form of open revolt, then in that of passive protest. From this stems the need for more harsh and determined measures.

The transformations carried through by the authorities are presented to the masses not as policies reflecting particular social interests, but as work for the good of the whole people, since the regime's ideology cannot be other than nationalist. In conditions of dependent development, the liberation of the workers is also often perceived in the categories of national renewal. The leaders of the official trade unions in Mexico declared that for them, national liberation is to a significant degree the essence of social revolution.[38] Leopold Senghor, one of the founders of African social democracy, wrote: "The social problem today is not so much the class struggle within the nation, as the global war between the 'propertied' nations (including the Soviet Union) and the proletarian nations (including the People's Republic of China). We belong among these poor nations."[39]

The concept of negritude allowed Senghor, using the French language and European traditions, to call for the renewal of national culture. Thanks to negritude, educated Senegalese felt themselves to be not just black French, but Franco-Africans. The French socialist J.-P. Biondi observed correctly that just as "there is no genuine independence without economic development," so also "there is no integrated development without cultural self-affirmation."[40] However, the slogan of national distinctiveness in conjunction with authoritarian politics always led to an aggressive rejection of dialogue with other nationalities. Nationalism is closely linked with an inferiority complex. Academician D. Likhachev, who takes a sympathetic attitude to the idea of a national ideal (at least where the Russian nation is concerned), recognizes that "Nationalism is a manifestation of a nation's weakness, not of its strength. The nations that become infected with nationalism are mainly weak ones trying to preserve themselves with the help of nationalist sentiments and ideology."[41] The left version of nationalism is hidden by slogans about international workers' solidarity. Stalin, who despite his Georgian origins was in Lenin's view a typical Great Russian chauvinist,[42] never spoke openly of his nationalism. Mao was more candid: in 1938 he called for the purging from party ideology of ideas of non-Chinese origin and foreign stereotypes, and demanded that Marxism be Sinified.[43]

African experience has shown that on the soil of chauvinist hostility to European ideas a black racism arises. A South African radical student organization declares: "Whites have to be excluded from all matters bearing on the struggle for our aims." The result of such policies has been a split in the liberation movement.[44]

The triumph of nationalism leads not to the promised national democracy, but to dictatorship. In Haiti black racism has been directed not against whites, but against people of mixed race. Thirty years after the proclamation of the concept of negritude, Senghor remarked despairingly: "Distrust of European values has rapidly been transformed into contempt for them, and it should be said, into racism. We thought and stated that we blacks were the salt of the earth, the bearers of fantastic revelations that could not be proclaimed by anyone apart from us."[45]

The enemies might turn out to be neighboring peoples belonging to the same oppressed race. When Nigeria encountered economic difficulties in 1983, President Shehu Shagari, who prided himself on teaching democracy to all Africa, banished from his country almost three million foreign workers, chiefly citizens of Ghana. Those banished were forbidden even to take their savings with them. The government radio carried broadcasts in an eminently fascist spirit: "At a time when our nation is on the road to moral revolution, we can no longer watch patiently while these foreigners defile our beloved national values."[46] According to journalists, the foreign workers were distinguished by their labor discipline, said to be superior to that of Nigerians corrupted by petrodollars. The measures adopted by Shagari merely deepened the crisis. His government fell, but not long before this occurred the president traveled to India and there delivered an inflammatory speech denouncing South African apartheid and racism.

In Latin America nationalism usually takes the form of anticommunism, but even when progressive and anti-imperialist, it still displays conservative features. In the view of Dos Santos, the ideological hegemony of nationalism has meant that even where a modern proletariat has taken shape, it has often proved unable to organize itself independently.[47] Left-wing nationalism is capable of retarding social progress to an even greater degree than the right-wing variant. To reject the democratic traditions of the Western world means also to reject the basic principles of socialist ideology. Gen. Juan Velasco Alvarado, who headed the left-wing military regime in Peru between 1968 and 1975, noted correctly that it was in the West that "the basic values of modern revolutionary thought arose, since not one of these currents of revolutionary thought arose in Africa or Asia. I repeat that they arose in the West, and in this sense they undoubtedly have close historical links with such a concept as Western civilization."[48] None other than Lenin wrote that socialism represents a struggle for the same European ideals.[49]

Wherever democratic values, human rights, and the freedom of the individual are repudiated, where people are forced to conform to an absolute unity, where the government identifies itself with the nation, and where antigovernment elements are declared to be antipopular and unpatriotic, minorities—whether political, social, ethnic, or religious—are oppressed.

The answer to state nationalism is antistate nationalism and minority separatism. The Sikhs, whose founder Guru Nanak taught his followers to stand above religious discord, have been drawn into a bloody struggle against Hindus. Peace-loving Buddhists in Burma and Sri Lanka are at loggerheads with members of other religious communities. Following the collapse of the Soviet system a wave of nationalist hysteria swept across Eastern Europe and the republics of the former USSR, causing destructive wars, massacres, and the flight of large numbers of "citizens of non-indigenous nationality."

In many third world countries, especially in Africa, nations have not been consolidated. An insignificant section of the people, a ruling tribe or sect speak in the name of the nation. Tribalist concepts are propagated as a national ideology, while representatives of the ruling tribe, using nationalism as a cover, never miss an opportunity to accuse their opponents of tribalism. "Denunciations of imperialism and references to the intrigues of the imperialists," a Soviet author acknowledges, "and often, as well, hostility to neighboring states, serve as a sort of emotional safety-valve for relieving the dissatisfaction aroused among the masses by the internal difficulties of national development following the attainment of independence." While focusing on an out of reach adversary (Western capitalism or Soviet Communism), the nationalists prefer to remain silent about local problems. For both the rulers and the ruled, a sober understanding of the situation is replaced by formulas promising magical solutions. The ideology "becomes simplified; its authors resort to a set of truisms; analysis of the reasons behind this or that problem is replaced by calls for the condemnation of imperialists, tribalists, 'malign individuals' and so forth." These primitive formulas "as a rule are unproven, but through constant repetition they become rooted in the consciousness of the masses to the point where they are regarded as self-evident."[50]

Theodor Adorno stressed that this principle generally lies at the heart of propaganda. The more underdeveloped a country, and the more weakly defined its national culture, the more aggressive and authoritarian is its nationalism. On the psychological plane, nationalism not only fails to assist in overcoming backwardness, but aggravates it.

As early as the 1920s the Turkish revolution, the first in the third world to proclaim nationalist slogans and to announce the replacement of a traditional Asiatic monarchy with a modern European republic, showed what such promises are worth. The reforms carried out by Mustafa Kemal Atatürk, the Turkish historian A. Ender notes, "were implemented in circumstances in which the masses were denied any possibility of expressing their will, the workers' movement was suppressed, and the Kurdish national movement had been shattered." All of the Kemalists' progressive transformations went ahead against a background of total repression.[51] There is no contradiction in this. The ideology of the revolutionaries held that the nation was embodied in the national state, and that the interests of the people were present in their totality in the interests of the nation. At least in the eyes of its supporters, state despotism thus became modern, progressive, and even democratic.

The failure of the first attempts to impose technocratic regulation on society within a framework of democracy left the modernizers no alternative to military dictatorship. The technocrats see the military stabilizer as their last hope, arguing that amid the general chaos only armies "are imbued with the ideology of national salvation and have sufficient power to 'stabilize' society."[52] The army represents a sort of ideal for the technocratic modernizers, combining modernity and order, knowledge and discipline. Here is to be found something like a model of the future social system. In the words of an American writer, the army acts as the final arbiter on which the realization of the technocratic project depends.[53]

Modernizing the army and the bureaucracy has always been easier than changing society. Hence the first (and sometimes also the last) modernization has been the modernization of coercion. In many countries by the end of the 1970s regimes had arisen which, in the apt words of Latin America sociologists, represented the union of the soldier and the technocrat.[54] Examples of this type can be found in almost all regions of the third world—in Turkey, Brazil, the Philippines, South Korea, Iran, Taiwan, Uruguay, Chile, Argentina, Bolivia, Zaire, and so forth. The orientation to the Western model of the industrial system is strengthened here through the rejection of the Western model of civil society, while the ruthless denial of freedoms is justified by the need to defend the "free" world.

The military-technocratic bloc is without the liberal illusions of previous modernizers, and its ideologues regard European democratic traditions as harmful vestiges of the past. The Chilean dictator Pinochet described the Western parliamentary system as "dissoluteness concealing a vacuum of power" and as "the lack of an organic state," while the Shah of Iran observed a lack of discipline in the West.[55]

The policies of the new dictators at first seemed extremely effective; economic growth rates increased, and Western corporations eagerly invested funds in development. By the 1980s, however, almost all such regimes with the possible exception of that in Taiwan were in profound crisis. Iran provides an especially striking example. Nowhere was the technocratic experiment pursued with such determination and competence as in Iran, or with such initial success. Nowhere did it end in such a complete and catastrophic failure. The technocratic revolution in Iran began with the ousting from power of the constitutional government of Mossadeq. This government was anti-Western, or more precisely, anti-British, which later allowed some Soviet writers to label it as progressive. Mossadeq's brave defence of the constitutional system, which aroused the sympathy of European liberal opinion, helped strengthen this myth. In fact, Mossadeq's government was extremely conservative. At its base were small national entrepreneurs and usurer capitalists who had already shown their complete incapacity to create a genuine bourgeois society. Mossadeq was also supported by semi-feudal landowners, by large merchants, by the clerical hierarchy, and by right-wing nationalist and chauvinist-minded members of the middle classes.[56] Oil nationalization provoked a conflict with the British, thus redirecting internal dissatisfaction outward and providing a substitute for domestic reforms. Even scholars sympathetic to Mossadeq note that he was seeking to divert attention from social problems.[57] The nationalization itself was poorly prepared, and led to a sharp decline in the economy. By the time the Shah drove Mossadeq from power, Iran was in a state of economic chaos; the government was deliberately attacking workers' living standards, and suppressing the democratic movement.

Initially, the Shah's coup of 1953 might have been viewed as a victory by progressive forces within the ruling elite. As Soviet orientalists recognized, what was involved was not just "the replacing of a formally constitutional monarchy by a Bonapartist monarchy," but the development of a bourgeois social revolution. The Shah "in a sense 'smothered' the class to which he himself belonged. But he did this not in order to abolish that class, but merely in order to overcome its resistance, to drag it 'kicking and screaming' into capitalism."[58] The oil industry remained under state control, the share of the nationalized sector in industry and construction rose steadily, a modern health care system was established, and women received equal rights. Agrarian reform undermined the position of the old landed aristocracy, creating new relations of production in the countryside. Capitalist and cooperative farms arose where there had been semifeudal estates. The Shah's regime claimed to be revolutionary; its white revolution was said to be putting an end to the feudal order that used to prevail in the country.[59] In some instances ideologues of the white revolution even used Marxist terminology. The Shah stressed that his policies were based on the scientific dialectic.[60] For its part, the Iranian Tudeh (Communist) Party during the 1960s gave the Shah's regime increasing support.[61]

The rise in oil prices provided additional funds for industrial development. In Asia, Iran's economic growth rates second only to Japan's and, at times, even outstripped Japan. In some years the growth of industrial output reached 20 percent, while the state electrical generating plants were increasing their output by 30 percent. Iran was viewed both as an example of the successful development of capitalism and as an effective model of the planned economy. As late as 1977, that is, a year before the beginning of the revolution, a British author hailed the successes of the Shah, who, he maintained, knew "the strengths and shortcomings of his own people better than anyone," and who was said to have "a fair idea" of what Iran needed in the future.[62]

In Iran the foundations had been laid for a modern economy. However, this had been done without the participation of the popular masses or, to a significant degree, the bourgeoisie either. Development was proceeding under the exclusive direction of a technocratic elite, which rested on a repressive military apparatus. A Soviet orientalist compared the growth of modern capitalist structures in Iran to the building of a skyscraper. "Unlike the classical form, which resembles the tip of a cone resting on a broad base of private enterprise capitalism and petty commodity production built up over centuries, the Iranian state-monopoly capitalism that took shape had the form of a narrow skyscraper without any solid foundation in the form of relatively broad, modern private capitalist and petty bourgeois social structures. This also doomed the completed building to instability, despite the sensational indices for the growth of national income and the outward lustre of the country's intensively advertised economic 'prosperity'."[63]

The social relations that had been implanted from above proved less viable that those that had grown up from below, while the technocrats failed to predict the outcome of their policy of transformations. In the course of agrarian reform a significant sector of the peasantry was forced off the land. The urban marginal layers grew dramatically.

Marginal, declassed elements are not necessarily jobless, impoverished, and living on casual earnings. These are people whose links with their class have been broken, and who have not forged new social bonds; people whose social positions are extremely unstable, and whose way of life is uncertain; no longer a peasant, but not yet an experienced worker; already an urban resident, while retaining a rural psychology. A marginal is a person whose internal make-up does not correspond to his or her new station in life. During the process of modernization, a Soviet orientalist writes, "the ill-adjustment of these 'neoproletarians' to the new historical conditions has become fully apparent."[64] The main purpose of the social and cultural programs in the Shah's Iran was to reduce tensions by preparing people for the "shock of rapid change."[65] But the pace of the transformations, which were destroying established human bonds and patterns of life even among industrial workers, aroused irritation and dissatisfaction.[66] What grew up was not a proletarian but a traditionalist consciousness, since the established proletariat was overwhelmed by new arrivals from the villages. Dissatisfaction grew even more rapidly among the traditional and semitraditional layers.

The marginal urban layers became the main opposition force, although they were incapable of advancing any progressive alternative. The breaking of traditional bonds, and feelings of disorientation and powerlessness, was combined with recollections of the good old days when people's material prosperity might have been less, but their social position was more definite and secure. The urge to return to the past creates the conditions in which a reactionary utopia can ripen. A genuine return to the past is, of course, impossible. As Erich Fromm once wrote, unless the entire industrial system and all the means of production are destroyed, reducing society to the pre-industrial level, people would remain individuals, completely cut off from the natural world.[66] Restoring traditional values is unthinkable, since there is no possibility of restoring the traditional nonindividualist personality. In Kampuchea, Pol Pot followed the road of direct annihilation of the new productive forces, creating a medieval base for his neo-archaic superstructure. In Iran, salvation lay in Islam. Under conditions of savage repression the mosque was the only place where it was possible to criticize the regime freely; also the bonds of religion were the only surviving real ties. Such bonds provided the illusion of stability; they could not restore or replace lost patriarchal relations between people, but they could create the appearance of harmony. Consequently, the significance and prestige of religion in the process of modernization was increased, not diminished, by modernization. Some writers have been astonished by the survival of an extremely reactionary variant of Islam in Iran despite prolonged contacts with Europe. "In Iran," writes a German scholar, "unlike the situation in the countries of Sunni Islam, there has been no Islamic modernism."[68] Precisely because Shi'i Islam in Iran had escaped reform, precisely because it was clearly at odds with the conditions of the modern world and the new reality, it became a vital necessity to masses of people who had been dragged forcibly into this reality.

The failure of a Westernizing project leaves no opportunities for a reformist variant of traditional religion. A return to old religious forms has not only occurred in Iran; the same process has been observed in other countries, involving not only Islam, but also Buddhism and Hinduism. The less the reactionary utopia of the Ayatollah Khomeini and other leaders of the Iranian clergy had in common with modern ideas, the more attractive this utopia became.

Modernization destroyed the social and historical bases of traditional Islam, but gave it a second wind; the more these bases are destroyed, the greater the adherence of the masses to the superstructure. Society can do away with old forms of social consciousness only when the new ones are in place and stable. Until the period of transition draws to a close, the old ideology not only fails to die, but stirs increasingly into activity, becoming a factor in the social organization of the declassed masses. But since the transition is drawn out, the new, modern ideas and institutions suffer defeat in the struggle. This is one of the secrets of the Islamic renewal.

The regime of the Shah was unable to replace the traditional structures with modern ones. The further the country proceeded along the road of modernization, the greater was the resistance, and the more ruthless the Shah's dictatorship became. The politics of reform turned out to have close links to the politics of repression.[69] Ritter notes correctly that every new step of the white revolution required "qualitatively new political enforcement," particularly new police measures.[70] Initially, the Shah and those around him honestly believed that modernization would create the conditions for a transition to a more liberal regime; they even promised to introduce elements of worker self-management into industry. But for the Shah, modernization had to be carried through first; then would come the time for democracy. Meanwhile, the few freedoms which Iranians had enjoyed prior to the early

1970s were abolished. The white revolution, Ritter continues, did not give birth to a political democracy which might have been supplemented by an economic democracy. Instead, strikes were brutally suppressed, and opposition was regarded as treason against the homeland.[71] The regime began to be totalitarian, which threatened modernization. Despite modernization's economic successes, its ineffectiveness created the need for dictatorial methods to suppress traditionalist moods. Despite modernization's social failures, its effectiveness gave birth to modern individuals with new needs, requiring at least elementary freedoms. To deal with these free individuals, who posed a new and unexpected obstacle to the technocratic scenario, for modernization additional repression was required. The regime found itself between two fires. The newly created social relations could not develop under conditions of terrorist dictatorship.

Demand in the modern sector outstripped prosperity. "A Samoyed who consumes seal fat and pickled fish," Marx wrote, "is not poor, since in his secluded society all have the same requirements. But in a progressive state, in which over some ten years total productive output per capita has increased by a third, a worker who earns as much as ten years earlier is no longer on the same level of prosperity, but has become poorer by a third."[72] Economic growth itself became a socially destabilizing factor. The revolution of expectations also affected the traditional sector, where there were even fewer opportunities for people to improve their lives. In Brazil, and later even in Poland, analogous processes could be observed. When economic growth slackens or stops, expectations continue to grow. An intoxication with the economic miracle is followed by an explosion of dissatisfaction. In this respect the Iranian situation is not unique; it is even characteristic of the third world.

However paradoxical it might seem, cultural progress is a factor destabilizing underdeveloped societies and impeding their democratization. The very term *cultural progress* arouses a certain protest: can there really be progress in cultural matters? Obviously, one can hardly say that the culture of Victorian England was more progressive than the culture of the Elizabethan era, especially if we compare Shakespeare's theater with that of the nineteenth century. Medieval Iranian culture appears more refined than that of the present day. However, we are not concerned here with the culture of the elite, but with mass culture. If millions of people learn to read and write, grow used to listening to the radio, and receive news of the outside world, this is incontestably cultural progress.

Ending the cultural gap between the elite and the masses—or at any rate, that section of the masses which is linked to the modern sector—is an objective necessity. In the East the possessor of written culture also used to be the holder of power, since "literacy was regarded as a distinguishing attribute of people privy to authority."[73] Among the Incas, a knowledge of hieroglyphs was an exclusive mark of the ruler and of a narrow circle of the most privileged dignitaries. The ending of a cultural monopoly quickly undermines the authority of traditional elites and of traditional forms of power. Cultural equality strengthens the demand for the redistribution of wealth and for the reordering of social relations. To workers, it becomes clear that "we" are in no way worse than "they." Europe experienced a similar conflict when the advent of the printing press at the end of the fifteenth century created a new situation, in which the rapid dissemination of knowledge weakened the existing systems of moral and political authority, and this in turn forced the rulers to use harsher methods. "Manuscripts," wrote Ivan Illich and Barry Sanders, "had been so rare and precious that authorities could often suppress the work of an author by literally seizing *all* the copies, burning them and extirpating the text. Not so books. Even with the small edition of two hundred or a thousand copies—typical for the first generation of print—it was never possible to confiscate an entire run. Printed books called for the exercise of censorship through an *Index of Forbidden Books*.[74] The printing press not only made inevitable the appearance in all countries of the institution of censorship, but also coincided with the founding of the Inquisition, and with witch-hunts and repressions against heretics. Medieval states did not possess developed repressive apparatuses. It was the beginning of the modern enlightenment that impelled governments to set up such services. Hobbes argues that "in societies based on inequality, especially stormy outbursts of social strife are the consequence of preliminary formation and of a definite consciousness of equality of claims."[75]

As knowledge becomes widespread, social tensions grow dramatically. The rulers can no longer keep the people in darkness, but they will do their best to keep them in subjugation. The more the objective conditions for democracy ripen, the less liberal the rulers become. Iran could be a constitutional monarchy in the 1950s, when only small groups of the privileged layers—the products of European-style education—took part in political life. Mossadeq could allow himself liberalism. But the modernizing Shah could not afford to be a liberal. Technocracy demanded a monarchic despotism to maintain itself in power and continue its program of change. For the same reason, the Shi'i clergy who took over from the Shah (and who rapidly took on various technocratic features) could not rule the country except with the help of terror. The Shah's moderate opponents thought it would be possible to continue the policies of modernization without repression. They did not understand their own country's historical situation and cultural peculiarities. After being driven from power by the forces of Islam, the moderate President Abolhasan Bani-Sadr complained that the Ayatollah Ruhollah Khomeini had "developed his political line on the basis of my theories."[75] In precisely the same fashion, Trotsky complained that Stalin had "robbed" him. Both argued, however, that their stolen original projects had never included the widespread use of repression; their projects had not only been stolen, but also perverted. Sadly, the victors had not so much perverted the ideas of the vanquished, as carried them to their necessary, logical conclusions.

The enthusiasm of the modernizers for enlightenment forces them to forget the problems which enlightenment creates for society. Programs to do away with illiteracy involve very broad layers of the population. This poses a threat to the power of the minority ruling group, even if it is a modernizing or enlightening minority. Unless illiteracy is ended, neither a homogeneous society nor modern production is possible. But it is not by chance that in the history of Soviet Russia and in that of many other countries, a cultural turning point, a period of rapid transition to mass literacy, has coincided with massive repressions. What is dangerous to the authorities is not literacy as such, but the explosion of mass education. Recent history confirms this. Whether the privileged groups have been capitalists, patriarchal masters, or bureaucrats, whether they have been considered progressive or conservative, and whether they have cited Marxism-Leninism or the ideals of the free world, the danger to which they are subject has grown. They have simply had no way out except repression. Alongside the teacher there has always been the policeman, and sometimes the hangman as well. The cultural turning point is either the moment when the danger of totalitarianism is at its greatest in not-yet-totalitarian society, or the time of the worst orgies of repression under a totalitarian system. After the turning point has been passed, the conflict which it has created does not disappear, but becomes less acute. India, with its liberal tradition of gradual change, is apparently emerging from the danger zone, while Iran has experienced catastrophe.

Under conditions of cultural rupture, the only possible resort of Iran's technocratic elite was to repression; the strategy that had been adopted simply did not permit other options. But the failure of these methods was just as inevitable. An anti-Shah bloc began to form, uniting progressive and reactionary forces that were suffering alike from the repression. From a theoretical point of view the bloc was unnatural, but in practice it proved extremely effective. The successful struggle waged by the Shah against the left and democratic forces served only to bring the religious opposition to the forefront. The religious opposition's ceremonies, processions and plays with themes like the martyrdom of Imam Hussein by tyrants, were understood to refer to contemporary tyranny, but could not be suppressed.[77]

Unlike the democratic parties and groups of the new type, the religious movement had no need of new organizational structures; they were intimately associated with the way of life of the traditional and semitraditional layers. Unless this way of life and these layers themselves were totally eradicated, the religious opposition could not be destroyed either. The Shah was not defeated because he was reactionary; compared to Mossadeq and Khomeini he was progressive. But his technocratic conception of modernization was unsustainable. Development without democracy led to catastrophe.

The collapse of the Shah's regime in 1978 and 1979 aroused heated discussion throughout the world. Most writers interpreted the events as one more proof of the unsuitability of Western models for the third world. "This revolution showed that social and economic structures developed in the West rarely take root in other countries," wrote the Englishman B. Mey. "The collapse of the Iranian model of development, based on imitation of the West, reminds one of other, less impressive failures that are occurring in Third World countries as a result of incompatible cultures. One has the impression that few people yet understand this lesson."[78]

Other scholars see the Iranian lesson in analogous terms: "We are concerned here with the most momentous cultural conflict in world history." In present-day conditions cultural opposition is more important than the armed struggle that leads to the liberation of colonies.[79] The experience of Iran, according to *Le Monde diplomatique*, testifies to the rejection by the whole nation of "a model of social and economic development imposed from outside."[80] Ritter went even further, declaring that from the very beginning the white revolution was undertaken by forces alien to Iran.[81]

In reality, it was not armed struggle that brought about the liberation of the colonies. In the history of the young states, wars of independence were the exception rather than the rule. The Shah and his officials were not foreigners. The technocratic model was imposed on Iran from above, but not from outside. A cultural conflict certainly took place, but why did the people of Iran reject Western influences, which the people of India used to renew their own traditions?

Antipopular regimes in the third world have been established by representatives of the Europeanized part of society. But the rise of anti-Western, anti-European ideas has also been influenced by Europe. The ideology of struggle against colonialism was formulated either among people who had been educated in the metropolis, or among the corresponding local strata. The most extreme forms of anti-Western totalitarian nationalism bear the obvious marks of their European origins.

The Ayatollah Khomeini lived for many years in Paris, and took in a great deal from Europeanized Iranian emigres such as Bani-Sadr. In the words of the Polish commentator W. Gurnicky, Pol Pot and his associates were typical products of European fears and French education. "They spent too many years in France, and became too deeply imbued with the Cartesian-pragmatic way of thinking."[82] Consequently, the problem is not in the mythical unfitness of Western culture for the third world, but in the bankruptcy of technocratic ideology and practice—that is, of an ideology which ceased long ago to be the exclusive property of the West.

CHAPTER 4

THE NEO-ARCHAIC STATE

The clearer the unsuitability of Western models for the third world became, the greater was the attractiveness of the Soviet experience. For the leaders of the former colonies, socialist orientation signified a break with the unfulfilled hopes of the capitalist West and with the principles of liberal democracy.[1] For countries at a low level of development the construction of socialism, as a Western economist noted accurately, is "an inappropriate ideology, applied in an inappropriate place and at an inappropriate time."[2] But states which had absolutely no claims to a socialist orientation also tried to copy the Soviet experience. The countries of the Communist bloc put before the third world their own model of noncapitalist, state modernization.[3]

Pro-Soviet and pro-American regimes in Africa created similar structures. Progressive regimes collaborated with transnational corporations, and pro-imperialist governments carried out nationalizations. Changes of government altered little. Soviet authors wrote that "a change of political regimes does not bring with it the privatization of state property or substantial changes in the relationships with the local exploiter classes."[4] The models of development adopted in revolutionary Congo and pro-Western Zaire differed little from one another.

In Angola, despite revolutionary transformations, foreign capital—Italian, French, and even Brazilian—dominated the oil industry. Very similar methods of rule were employed in the regions controlled by the pro-Soviet government and in those held by pro-Western insurgents. Western correspondents who had been in the territories occupied by the anticommunist rebels of Jonas Savimbi wrote of "iron discipline in the spirit of the Chinese cultural revolution."[5] The government in Luanda enjoyed the support of the USSR, but help also came from

Nigeria and the Scandinavian countries, while the insurgents received support from the United States, North Korea, China, and Romania. Savimbi at one time had called himself a Marxist-Leninist, but still he appealed for help to the West and to the Republic of South Africa. The South Africans secretly obtained weapons in Bulgaria for delivery to the anticommunist rebels, while U.S. business executives preferred to deal with the Marxist government in Luanda. Of the transnational corporations operating in Angola, the oil monopolies prospered, and also international banks including Chase Manhattan, Citibank, and others, and also Boeing, Lockheed, and General Electric. Cuban internationalist fighters provided reliable protection for the property of Western monopolies. Foreign business interests were wary of Savimbi, suspecting that if he were victorious "he would be the worst socialist of the lot."[6] This confused picture is easily clarified if one accepts that the conflict in Angola is rooted not only in class but also in ethnic antagonisms. Savimbi has based his power on the tribe of the Ovimbundu, while the government is linked with the mulatto caste.[7]

The same regimes pass readily from the anti-imperialist to the pro-Western camp, and vice versa. In Somalia during the 1970s the regime of Siad Barre studiously copied the Soviet ideology and institutions, then in the 1980s became one of the main props of U.S. support in Africa. In 1977 Barre declared that his guiding concept was scientific socialism.[8] Friends of the USSR in Africa welcomed this as a historic step.[9] A short time later the same Barre provided bases to the American fleet, without changing his internal policies. Guinea was the first African country to establish friendly relations with the Soviet Union. It nevertheless became "Moscow's first failure in Africa,"[10] when President Sekou Toure preferred collaboration with France to anti-imperialist solidarity with the USSR. In Surinam the armed forces, on seizing power, promptly expelled a Cuban diplomat from the country and arrested one of their own government functionaries for having pro-Cuban sympathies. Then followed a period of friendship with Cuba and the USSR. Local dictator Desi Bouterse declared himself a follower of Marxism-Leninism. The 'supporter of Cuba' whom he once had arrested has now become the minister for mobilization of the masses, reported *Time* in May 1983.[11] In autumn the same year, following the U.S. invasion of Grenada, Bouterse expelled Cuban diplomats from Surinam and drew closer to the United States.

The former colonies tried to repeat the industrialization successes of the USSR. But already in 1960 the American economist Simon Kuznets warned that even the pre-industrial level of the developed countries was several times higher than the present level of most underdeveloped countries.[12] In the 1930s, at the time of Stalin's modernization project the Soviet economy already possessed a significant industrial potential. Russia had never been a colony. As Andre Gunder Frank correctly noted, a condition of the economic spurt by the Soviet Union and Japan was that they had not participated in the world capitalist system in the capacity of satellites.[13] Russia avoided a demographic explosion, and possessed abundant resources, but despite this Stalinist modernization exacted a catastrophic price from the peoples of the USSR. This price included not only the millions of victims of repression, but also the collapse of agriculture, the exhaustion of natural resources and the squandering of funds. The sacrifices of the people and the price of progress aroused little anguish in the followers of Stalin and Mao. In the words of a British scholar, the ideology of modernization forces people to think "in the categories of final goals."[14] Nevertheless, none of the radical dictators achieved results comparable to those in the USSR and China.

Marx once noted that the answer to the question as to which new mode of production will take the place of the old depends on the character of this old mode of production.[15] The extremely disordered character of the base and the widespread presence of traditional and semitraditional structures have excluded any possibility of success through borrowing either the Western or the Soviet model.

A condition of the successes registered in Russia, in China, and to a degree in Vietnam and Cuba was a genuine popular revolution. There had been many peasant uprisings in these countries, but only when the working class participated did these uprisings achieve any revolutionary character. In the states of the Afro-Asian world that have tried to imitate the Soviet and Chinese path, there is no massive, organized workers' movement. As scholars from the Institute of Oriental Studies in Moscow recognized, it was only countries that were among the most backward in economic respects that borrowed the Soviet model.[16] The technocratic minority, represented mainly by state functionaries and military officers, was unable to base itself on significant modern layers. National entrepreneurs were lacking, and foreign investment was insignificant. In such countries the Stalinist road not only seemed ideal, but appeared to be the only possible way forward.

The French Marxist Y. Craipeau characterized the rulers of Algeria as "technobureaucrats."[17] In contrast to more developed countries, technocrats here were involved less in the management of modern production, and more in administrative and military matters. To a significant degree their thinking was determined more by the structures of bureaucratic consciousness than by technological and productive structures.[18] If in Algeria one can speak of technobureaucracy, in more backward countries even this would be too flattering. Here it would be more correct to speak of military-bureaucratic modernism. Even in developed countries the technocratic structures have a dangerous tendency to degenerate into bureaucratic ones; in the most backward countries, there is no particular difference between these structures. Their modernizing layers are backward even in comparison with other countries of the third world, and assimilate both European ideas and national traditions in their most primitive forms. An African writer has spoken bitterly of rulers devoid of political culture and of any culture at all.[19]

Here there have been neither revolutionary uprisings nor democratic elections bringing radical governments to power. But in order to legitimize themselves ideologically, new regimes have to claim to be revolutionary. The revolutionary origins of power have, as it were, taken the place of a popular mandate. But the revolution has merely been simulated. The population has been forcibly organized to take part in acts of universal approval prepared by the authorities themselves. The unity of the party and the people has been expressed in ritualistic form, through general prayers or the repetition of magical slogans. "The auditorium chants, applauds, with little understanding of why," wrote a Congolese journalist. "The people do not believe in their own ovations, since our lofty verbiage does not seem to them totally convincing." The newspaper in which these lines appeared was of course banned, and its writers were declared to be troublemakers who had slandered the exultant populace.[20]

Since the time of the French revolution the degeneration of revolutionary regimes has been accompanied by mass rituals supposed to prove that despite appearances, the revolution is alive. In paradoxical fashion, the Afro-Asian pseudorevolutions of the 1960s and 1970s began with the kind of spectacles with which the genuine revolutions ended. The government would implement various extremist measures directed against local bourgeois elements, in a sense punishing them for their previous ineffectiveness. The helpless bourgeois strata did not represent a danger to the new authorities. Nevertheless the regime would declare uncompromising struggle against them, nationalizing everything right down to the level of retail trade. Such measures drew criticism even from Soviet scholars: "Hasty, ill-considered nationalizations, and the economically unjustified construction of industrial plants, lead to the appearance of unprofitable, loss-making enterprises which form a dead weight on the national economy. Hence the task is not to do away with the private sector in the shortest time possible, but to find a correct relationship between the state and private sectors, and to ensure the efficiency of publicly-owned enterprises and of the economic system as a whole."[21]

In reality, extremist antibourgeois measures are by no means pointless. They help to simulate a class struggle. Such policies are reminiscent of the Russian war communism of 1918 to 1921. After consolidating themselves, the new authorities correct their course and adopt a tolerant attitude to local and transnational capital. If at first they staged a simulated revolution, now they simulate development. The centralized state sector is sufficiently strong to create problems for private capital through its constant interference in market relations, but is too weak to replace private capital. In all of the countries which have oriented toward the Stalinist model, the state sector has had low indices of profitability.[22] A lack of experience of state regulation, together with shortages of funds and of competent personnel, has meant that the economic links between the city and the countryside have been severed, difficulties have arisen in the areas of supply and sale, and production has withered.[23] Development then becomes paralyzed. A few high prestige industrial projects are capable at best of distracting attention from the economic stagnation which prevails in the country. The multistructured character of the economy persists.

Just as economic development is simulated, so too is cultural development. An eloquent example is that of Benin, where from time to time campaigns to do away with illiteracy were launched; each lasted no more than sixty days, beginning and ending simultaneously in all the villages of the region. Meanwhile, the education system was in a deplorable state. Hundreds of classes had no teachers at all, and in 1979 only 40 per cent of schools were receiving their basic material and technical requirements.[24] In South Yemen also not one of numerous campaigns achieved its planned result. Most of the people who were drawn into the campaigns remained illiterate.

The functions of an educational institution are taken on by the army. There is nothing radical about this; in Iran under the Shah the army also played the role of teacher of the rural population.[25] The soldiers did not cope with this task as well as professional pedagogues. Moreover, their literacy classes were always accompanied by ideological instruction. The result often turned out to be the reverse of what was expected. People not only failed to assimilate the government slogans, but began to see education itself as something alien and hostile. This was what happened in Afghanistan following the seizure of power in April 1978 by the People's Democratic Party headed by Nur Mohammad Taraki and Hafizullah Amin. As the Pakistani journalist Raja Anwar observed, the reforms were implemented by urbanized young men, being totally unfamiliar with the dynamics of the tribal society they were trying to change. Their actions and manners were perceived by the rural population as outrageous. "The basic teaching materials used by the literacy program were no more than superficial propaganda, where 'A' stood for Amin, and 'T' stood for Taraki."[26]

In simulating development, the authorities push society backwards. The results achieved by the regime of Mengistu Haile Mariam in Ethiopia provide an illustration. By 1984 the country owed the Soviet Union $3 billion and the people were still starving. "Now more than ever," wrote *Libération* (Paris) in the mid-1980s, "Ethiopia can be called one of the poorest countries in the world. The annual per capita income is no more than $130."[27] Even sympathetic observers recognized that appalling poverty reigned in the country, the streets of Addis Ababa were full of starving beggars, mainly refugees, and prostitution, as before, was widespread.[28] The famines in 1965–1966 and 1972–1974 were perceived in Ethiopia as proof of the incompetence of the imperial regime to solve the food problem. In 1984, ten years after the military seized power, an even more terrible famine occurred. The failure of the entire development program became obvious. Even the government was forced to recognize that the main reason for the hunger was not drought, but the government's agrarian policy, which destroyed the peasants' way of life and lowered food production without bringing about real reforms.[29]

In South Yemen after many years of rule by the radical military, average life expectancy, the level of literacy, and the numbers of medical personnel in relation to the population remained among the lowest in the world. Despite substantial Soviet aid, industry was practically nonexistent.[30] Social changes were not proceeding more quickly here than in the most conservative Arab countries. In the view of Western experts, the society of South Yemen remains more traditional than many others in the Arab world.[31] The modernization of life in Aden, the capital of the republic, has been reflected among other ways by the growth of crime and alcoholism. The bureaucracy has acquired huge privileges; despite an acute housing crisis, high-placed officials provide themselves with two houses, and bribery has become the norm. In 1975 the government responded to pro-Western attitudes by adopting a law forbidding contacts with foreigners.

In Algeria, despite income from oil, the foreign debt rose catastrophically during the 1980s. The government was forced to recognize that the economic norm had become bad management and indifference to developments.[32] The state, which was supposedly a model of noncapitalist orientation, continued the work of French colonialism in destroying the traditional society. By the end of the 1970s unemployment in the cities had reached 11 percent, even though many people simply could not allow themselves to be without work and took on any jobs, on any terms, in order to survive.[33] The burgeoning state apparatus appropriated the lion's share of the results of economic growth. The departure of the French left vacant a substantial area of housing space, but urban housing was insufficient, and shantytowns arose.[34] It is not surprising that after two decades of revolutionary rule in Algeria, the country began to see a rise of Islamic fundamentalism similar to that in Iran under the Shah.

In a book on third world revolutions the Trotskyist Michael Löwy sets out to explain the increasing problems of bad leadership. In his view, the failure of the transformations in Algeria resulted from the fact that the liberation movement had "no proletarian-socialist leadership, and this led inevitably to the interruption and channelling of the revolutionary process by petty-bourgeois and bourgeois reformist strata entrenched in the revolutionary army."[35]

Unfortunately, in Russia, where the leadership in 1917 was incontestably socialist and to a significant degree proletarian, the revolution also failed to achieve its goals. In Angola and Mozambique, revolutionaries came to power who had been through the school of guerrilla warfare, and who based themselves on Marxist theory; nevertheless, they consistently repeated all the errors of their petty bourgeois predecessors. With independence both countries received incomparably more competent and cultured governments than Ethiopia or South Yemen. The regimes enjoyed broad mass support. Nevertheless, the decolonization of Angola ended in failure. "This country, which was exploited by the Portuguese, and which with its diamonds, gold, oil, fisheries and agriculture is potentially among the richest in Africa, is now living on foreign aid. Oil output has fallen substantially, the mines are closed, and the countryside is abandoned. Luanda is surrounded by hovels, and of the 'African Rio de Janeiro' only the ghost remains: long queues outside the few shops that remain open, multitudes of job-seekers, unfinished buildings, smuggling and corruption. The cooperatives work badly, and transport and distribution even worse."[36] The authorities have had to resort to the forced mobilization of the masses to perform so-called voluntary work. The government's policies, which do not reflect the basic needs of the population, and which contradict its traditions and way of life, have come to be based increasingly on noneconomic compulsion. As if to console the revolutionaries, Soviet scholars wrote that compulsion was acting as the principal means of creating modern productive forces, though it also suffered from social and moral drawbacks.[37]

Leaders have sought to make up for their economic failures through foreign aid. One of the first to turn to the USSR for help was Sekou Toure in Guinea. Even the Africans were struck by the Khrushchev leadership's eccentricity, which was well known to Soviet economic planners. "The ignorance of conditions on the continent and the inappropriateness of the aid that was offered," a French journalist wrote later, "created situations that were in the spirit of King Ubu, and which became a caricature of the Soviet presence in the Third World. An example was the unloading of snow-clearing machines in the airport in Conakry."[38] Sekou Toure and those like him received the aid they deserved. During the 1970s the quality of Soviet aid improved significantly, but it was still not used effectively.[39] The collaboration by

African countries with the United States, China, and Western Europe was no more successful. The example of Somalia is noteworthy. Under the Barre regime this country, which received assistance in turn from the Soviet Union, the United States, and the Arab oil sheikhs, turned into a "graveyard of foreign aid."[40] By the end of Barre's rule the country lay in ruins, and the people were destitute.[41]

The copying of Soviet economic methods was often combined with anticommunist ideology. The Burmese leadership based its policies on Buddhist religious principles. This resource-rich Asian country made its guiding law a universal equality of poverty.[42] The black market became the only dynamic sector of the economy. Western journalists wrote that the government was leading the country confidently along the road to the past. A foreigner who visited Burma remarked that there one can gain an exact impression of what the world was like seventy years ago.[43] In 1972, following decades of development, living standards were lower than before World War II. Industrialization had collapsed. The potential of agriculture, forestry, and fisheries was virtually untapped. Exports of rice had fallen. The financial position was dismal. Of its own will, Burma had isolated itself from the outside world, but this did not save the country from the effects of the world economic crisis. The bureaucratic apparatus could not cope with growing problems. After 1972 the most secluded economy in Asia lost its hermetic qualities. The Burmese leadership began increasingly to orient toward cooperation with foreign capital.

The situation was no better in the Arab world. Analyzing the experience of Syria and Iraq, Samir Amin showed that attempts to copy the Stalinist industrialization policies of the 1930s brought about a fall in agricultural output and a strengthening of technological dependency. If a relatively closed economy with its own technological base had been created in the Soviet Union, the experience had not been duplicated. The ability of national industry to satisfy local demand even decreased. The radical regimes were not able to ensure independent development; they merely created more favorable conditions for the penetration of their countries by transnational corporations. The noncapitalist road which they had chosen was simply a shorter route to a new stage of dependent peripheral capitalism.[44] Thanks to partial modernization, the demand for foreign technology and capital had been strengthened. In the view of Amin, Egypt's shift under President Anwar Sadat to an open door policy toward foreign capital resulted naturally from previous policies; it was not treachery, not a rejection of the national strategy of development, but its logical result. In the final accounting, the actions of the pro-Soviet third world radicals objectively served the interests of the transnational corporations. In a sense, they managed this even better than the openly pro-Western groupings, since they created repressive states able to keep the people in subjection. Amin's argument explains why the desertion from the pro-Communist camp in the third world began long before perestroika and the collapse of the USSR. Unlike Mao, third world leaders in the 1960s and 1970s were unable to develop their own original version of Stalinism. As in Russia, the ruling elites exploited society with the help of their monopoly control over the nationalized sector of the economy and the organs of the state. M. Cheshkov described this new structure as "etacratic" (state-ruled) and its ruling layer as the "etacracy." The distinguishing features of the system were the indissoluble connection between the superstructure and the base, and the concentration of all state power and property within the bounds of a single social organism. Power in this case acts "as the decisive factor of reproduction."[45] In the words of Marx, "the state is counterposed directly to the direct producer."[46] There can be no question of democracy in such circumstances, since the monopoly on power of the ruling group would be broken.[47]

Because of its monopoly of power, the state bureaucracy is no longer simply a weapon of the ruling class, but a replacement for it. The apparatus "represents the direct organized essence of this class."[48] But if in China, for example, the bureaucratic apparatus succeeded in reordering the social structures, in the third world no one has achieved this. The main advantage enjoyed by the etacracy is its ability to expropriate the entire surplus product and to concentrate it in the hands of the state; under the conditions which apply in a multi-structured state this is impossible. Destroying the old structures with the help of terror does not always succeed either. The demographic explosion and the slight value placed on human life mean that even terror has little effect. The ideal system of order becomes that of the concentration camp, but this order is short-lived; it is replaced by the order of the graveyard.

A technocratic dictatorship arises in different circumstances from a traditional despotic state. It has different goals, and its social origins are different. All this occurs, however, in countries with lengthy traditions of authoritarian rule. Scholars have recognized that a characteristic feature of third world countries is a situation in which archaic forms are directly "woven into the structure as it takes shape, becoming an organic part of it. In this way they are in a sense reborn, acquiring new functions and broadening their influence."[49] The new despotism becomes more and more like the old. The return to archaic models of power can be observed almost everywhere in third world countries with authoritarian regimes. Modernizing rule degenerates into patriarchal bureaucratism or into senseless tyranny. The bureaucratic organizations have only weak links to modern production, and thus are poorly defended against the influence of old relationships and traditions. Even a very modern bureaucratic structure, according to some sociologists, can establish working relations with the traditional structure of power much more easily than a modern enterprise can relate to traditional forms of production. Traditional forms can readily be included in a bureaucratic system; the importance of family, clan, and tribal ties in the politics of the third world testifies to this.[50]

A bureaucratic apparatus cannot succeed in checking on the competence of all of its members; the criteria for this do not exist. One can judge the efficiency of a machine, but not of a particular screw. Bureaucratic structures are therefore relatively open for people whose cultural level is even lower than is required under the accepted rules. A bureaucracy is comparatively defenseless against incompetence. "In many Third World societies we see bureaucratic structures directed at all levels by people who have acquired only in part, or not at all, the type of consciousness which is indispensable for bureaucracy."[51] The rapid growth of the apparatus which takes place in backward countries that imitate the Soviet model brings with it a lowering of the average cultural level of the functionaries. The new generation combines superficially assimilated bureaucratic stereotypes with archaic habits of thought.

The nonrevolutionary origins of the regime are just as important a factor as the country's general backwardness. In most cases the apparatus of power has not acquired a finished, highly developed form, and as Soviet scholars acknowledged, retains a military or semimilitary character. Meanwhile, the claim of the sole ruling party to exercise vanguard functions in all areas of public life has not been borne out by the party's actual role.[52] The American sociologist A. Wilder notes that although the Communist regimes were incontestably modernizing in character, their political organization could not be described other than as "neotraditionalist."[53] Both Bukharin and Deng Xiaoping accused Stalin and Mao of military-feudal methods. Many people saw Stalin as a Byzantine emperor or eastern despot. Nevertheless Stalin, like Mao, was neither of these; resemblance does not signify identity. In the third world, on the other hand, we do indeed see identity. Between the structures of the new system and the traditional despotism there is not only a clear link, but also a direct continuity; this could not exist in Russia or China thanks to the revolution. The etacracy acts as the heir of the archaic form of social organization which Marx termed the Asiatic mode of production. Analogous structures also existed in Africa. A Soviet historian described them as a polito-system. "In its mature form the latter represented a system of places, each of which was associated with the right to receive a particular share of the surplus product; the number of these places, meanwhile, was always limited. It is not enough to say that every member of the ruling class was included in this system. Properly speaking, it was only the holding by a person of a particular post in the polito-system that made him or her a member of the ruling class. If deprived of this post, the person involved was automatically excluded from the ruling class."[54] The shift from a polito-system to etacracy is extremely simple. All that occurs is a broadening and consolidation, and a partial restoration of the archaic polito-system undermined by the colonial-capitalist order. The modernizers create a neo-archaic state.

The past might in its way be better than the present, and a return to the past does not necessarily signify regression. What we are presented with here, however, is not a dialogue with history, but a falling out of history. Archaic forms are not bad in themselves; they are bad when they are present in the new conditions. The obstacle to development is not in fact the past, but the present, with its monstrous combination of the archaic with the modern. Much worse than the conservatism of traditional societies is the pseudotransformation in which archaic forms change, acquiring a new aspect. This is transformation without renewal—pseudomorphosis.

The historic task is to make use of the traditions and experience of the old society to serve the new. But what is happening is the opposite:

modern slogans are being subordinated to conservative structures inherited from the past. The elements of tradition that are emerging triumphant are precisely the ones that need to be overcome.

The idea that the aim of progress is to bring about a return to the lost values of the past, to a lost harmony, is far from new. But these primordial, "eternal principles of genuine human existence" must be restored on a new level. To return to the past is impossible. The triumph of reaction will bring stagnation and decline, and in some cases the rise of unnatural new forms, but will never bring back the past, since it is impossible to restore the old productive base, the old technology. Even Pol Pot's Kampuchea, where the modern technical base was totally destroyed, remained a modern society so long as people were still alive whose thinking was not medieval. Pol Pot understood perfectly that the superstructure and the base had to correspond to one another, and in the name of strengthening the state structure, proceeded to obliterate the cities, destroy the factories, and abolish money. However, people are also part of the forces of production, and to liquidate all the bearers of modern consciousness was a task beyond the powers even of Pol Pot.

Neo-archaic structures hinder progress, not so much by bringing back the past as by conserving and perpetuating the most repellent features of the present. The Islam of Khomeini was not the Islam of the seventh century. Neo-archaic forms issue from the new epoch, from the decay or disintegration of modern structures. The neo-archaic state is the natural result, the characteristic continuation, of technocratic modernization which has ended up in a blind alley.

Only a fundamental overturn that sweeps away the authoritarian-bureaucratic system, the old and new oligarchies, and also obsolete conceptions of development, can offer the hope of salvation. A neo-archaic regime cannot do this. To combine stability and dynamism is not within its capacities. The words uttered by an Egyptian Communist in relation to the Nasser dictatorship can be applied to all neo-archaic regimes: from the dictatorship's very first day, its political organizations were transformed "into bureaucratic institutions, alien to genuine social activism and including bureaucrats who were ruled by considerations of prestige and who strove to win additional privileges."[55] The etacracy in the third world becomes rotten and parasitic before it can even set about fulfilling the historic mission it has set itself. What the neo-archaic state creates is not a copy of the Soviet or Chinese social and political structures, but a caricature of them; it reproduces the shortcomings of its model, without duplicating the achievements.[56] If the party in the Soviet Union took on the task of providing leadership, while the state apparatus assumed the executive and technical functions, in the neo-archaic system no such division of functions takes place. The party itself becomes the state. In most countries the planned intermingling of the party and state apparatuses has been incorporated in the constitution. In Guinea under Sekou Toure the party leadership was simultaneously the legislative assembly, the chamber of commerce, and the people's court. Within the party, departments of police, state security, agriculture, and so forth were established. Syria and a number of other countries legislated the leading role of the party in their constitutions even before this was done in the Soviet Union.

Despite its supercentralization of authority, the etacracy has turned out to be extremely unstable. Society has retained its heterogeneous structure, and the economy its multistructured character, while the state has become the prisoner of social contradictions. The ruling bloc in a neo-archaic regime is not formed on a class basis, since the etacracy is incapable of becoming a self-reproducing class, but on a group, tribal, or clan basis. This gives the contradictions an irrational character. The party is unable to consolidate itself, and its power does not become stabilized. Even if power becomes concentrated in the hands of members of one tribe or sect, new groupings quickly arise, based not on political but on personal or family ties. In Afghanistan just such a role was played by the Khalk and Parcham factions, which tried periodically to wipe one another out. In Syria the seizure of power by the Arab Socialist Renewal (Ba'ath) party was followed by a three-year intraparty struggle involving the use of some nonpeaceful forms.[57] Under President Hafez Assad a degree of unity has been achieved; at the base of this, according to a French journalist, lies "a compromise between various clans."[58] The fact that they coexist peacefully does not mean they have been reconciled. "The problem confronting Assad," reported *The Observer* (London) in July 1984, "is that over many years leading officers have created feudal fiefdoms for themselves in the armed forces. Their interests extend far beyond the military field, affecting politics and commerce. The system of private domains is based on the existence of special subdivisions, each of which keeps an eye on others, and of numerous intelligence and state security ser-vices."[59] As soon as Assad's health deteriorated, his political position began to suffer as well. "The clans began to make their existence known, and to organize themselves."[60]

In South Yemen the one-party state was officially counterposed to tribal loyalties. But as Western journalists have testified, although the representatives of the ruling elite feel that maintaining such ties con-tradicts their ideology, there are times when they see their tribes as ready-made props for their own power, to be used for their personal advancement.[61]

Even in the Soviet republics of Central Asia, clan and tribal ties continued to play an enormous role in political life; as the Soviet system lost its dynamism in the 1970s, these influences even increased.[62] By the beginning of perestroika the bureaucracies of most of the Islamic Soviet republics were split into clan and ethnic groupings. Following the collapse of the Soviet Union, these rivalries led, in a number of cases, to bloody armed conflicts. In 1992 a vicious civil war broke out in Tadzhikistan. Even compared with the other armed conflicts that have flared up in the territory of the former USSR, this war has been distinguished by its brutality. "The lack of discipline of the fighters, the treachery and irresponsibility of their commanders, and the multitude of small groups have created chaos and anarchy, and are leading to unthinkable acts of savagery," repeated the liberal weekly *Novoe Vremia* (Moscow). "Tadzhiks are fighting Tadzhiks, clan against clan. The poor who are without power are fighting those who are outraged at having lost it, and people who want to live according to the laws of an Islamic state are fighting those who find the laws of a socialist state more familiar and comprehensible...."[63]

Power in Tadzhikistan lay traditionally with people from Leninabad, the most developed region of the republic. Here, emissaries sent to proselytize for Islam were met with stones. Trying to maintain their position, the Leninabad group united with Uzbeks and with migrants from the backward Kulyab region to wage a general struggle against natives of the Garma region. The Islamic elements in turn received support from part of the local pro-Western intelligentsia and from the leadership of Russia. In their efforts to throw off the old Leninabad nomenklatura the supporters of a Western orientation were ready to unite with ideologues of an Islamic state, while officers of the Russian army in the various localities and the republic's Russian-speaking population gave their preference to the Kulyab faction.[64]

The instability of the neo-archaic system forces it to resort to additional means in order to consolidate itself. Wherever such a regime has come to power, ideology has been transformed into religion, and the party-state has become the party-church. Pseudosocialism has become pseudoreligion; theory has become magic, and the leader a prophet. The possession of a particular doctrine, "expressing itself through the mastering of a set of verbal formulae," supposedly serves to "guarantee pragmatic achievements in the most diverse fields of activity."[65] In a despotic state, there is no need for law. Saddam Hussein's Iraq serves as a classic example. "The law is at best secondary," an Arab journalist wrote, "and just as citizens cannot avoid punishment and torture, so they cannot deal with the endless decrees and resolutions that every day pour down on their heads."[66]

The law is replaced by ideology, offering the masses miraculous solutions to all their problems. "In essence, the set of these methods that is presented in various countries, however different the countries might be, is not especially diverse."[67] The neo-archaic state might use Western and Soviet political terminology, but both become elements in verbal conjuring. The word takes on the character of an invocation and even a talisman. In China during the 1960s, according to eyewitness reports, functionaries of the youth movement tried to touch foreigners with the little red book of quotations from the works of Chairman Mao, in order to effect a magical transfer of the power which this book possessed. "It was suggested that this would have a direct influence on the infidel, which was how people unacquainted with the 'ideas of the chairman' were perceived. The chairman in turn was believed to possess not just exaggerated human powers, but also superhuman ones."[68] In China, such displays of ideological cultism have been rare, but for neo-archaic regimes they have been everyday practice, and have even been prescribed in official orders.

The right to be privy to the magical secrets of ideology is gained exclusively through joining the party-church. The relations between party members and nonmembers, and between party functionaries and rank-and-file members take on the character of relations between initiates and non-initiates, between priests and the laity. According to the theological teachings of European Catholicism, the church knows the true desires and interests of the laity much better than they do themselves. Any attempt at taking an independent decision is fatal. "The medieval church saw attempts by lay people to create for themselves an independent conception of the world and of God, or of ways and means of salvation, as a fully developed syndrome of Satanic madness, for the curbing of which any measures were appropriate." The members of the lay population were thus regarded as less than totally human, and "because of the defectiveness of their nature, as deserving only of supervision."[69] The reasoning of the party-church is identical. The party-church claims to be the bearer of the progressive impulses of the nation, and hence will not allow the nation to freely express its will. Any utterance at variance with the ideas of the party-church, any sign of disagreement with it, places in doubt not the competence of the leadership, but the reliability of whoever is dissatisfied. If people disagree with the party, if even the entire nation is opposed to it, this does not by any means signify that the party is wrong, because the party is truth itself. On the contrary, the nation is wrong, since it has failed to understand its fundamental interests.

The ideology of party infallibility is taken to the absurd. The magical figure of the charismatic leader, the fuhrer-prophet and symbol of the party, "becomes the incarnation not just of the world outlook, but also of the unity of the collective. Preserving and defending the symbol is perceived as one of the most important tasks of the collective, and any violation of the symbol is seen as an infringement on the social being, its moderation and stability." The symbol is defended through various prohibitions. It is surrounded by love and fear. Repressive compulsion is augmented by "an effective 'moral terror', inspired within a framework of mythological and religious consciousness."[70] For the neo-archaic system, the cult of the personality of the ruler is even more important than for classical Stalinism and Maoism. Stalin's relation to the masses was that of a national patriarch, a supreme high priest, but even at the pinnacle of his authority, he did not go as far as his imitators in the third world. For all the scope of the Stalinist cult, there was never a total and absolute religious identification of the party with the leader, which was shown not only by Khrushchev's posthumous unmasking of Stalin in 1956, but also by the comparatively painless change of leadership three years earlier. In Soviet ideology, Stalin had always formally been assigned the second place after Lenin. A neo-archaic ruler, on the other hand, not only lays claim to god-like honors, but also aims to take the place of God. The death of the god means the collapse of the party-church and party-state.

The personality cult has deep roots. In archaic political systems the structure of distribution of the surplus product within the ruling class coincided with the structure of the state apparatus. The peak of the pyramid "is the place from which the surplus product flows throughout the political system, its central point of distribution. The individual who occupies this place is the supreme distributor of surplus product among all the members of the possessing class as a whole."[71] For the neo-archaic state, the replication of this model is ideal. "In traditional society, the ruler is simultaneously a political and religious leader, the person responsible for the economic and social life of the clan," we read in an African newspaper of the 1970s. "Instructions from the ruler are not discussed, but are fulfilled."[72] The holder of such power is invariably idolized. The image of the great leader was formed over centuries. Modernization has merely enriched this image, giving it new features.

The ruling leader invariably possessed the attributes of a hero-conqueror, a titan, a giant. The president of Iraq is "the valiant hero Saddam Hussein, flying to victory."[73] In Togo the slogan "Immortal Eyadema!" was proclaimed. "Money is being collected in the country to erect a monument to him. Everywhere portraits can be seen of Guiassingbe Eyadema with angel's wings behind his shoulders. Slogans hang on the walls of houses and on fences: 'Thank you, Eyadema, for the year of the peasant.' 'Agriculture—the main concern of our leader.' Eyadema is the 'beloved leader,' the 'national provider,' the 'father of the nation.'"[74] In Guinea Sekou Toure was called the father of the revolution and the supreme leader.[75]

General Mobutu Sese Seko in Zaire went furthest of all. The official ideology was proclaimed a religion, the party was declared a church, and the president "was elevated to the dignity of a prophet."[76] The churches were closed, or were used for the new cult; in place of the icons, there appeared portraits of the leader. His name resounded in hymns, in place of the name of Jesus. The new religion received the name Mobutism. The president compared himself with Christ, declaring that the party was taking his ideas to the people just as the church had taken the gospels to the masses. The cult of the leader in Zaire reached such dimensions that even the role of the party-church was placed in doubt: "The people and the leader are one, and even speak as one person."[77] When such an approach is taken, the party risks looking like an unnecessary intermediary.

European influences are declared to be fatal. At times even European names and clothing have been forbidden. While interested in European industrial technology, the neo-archaic state tries to eradicate all traces of European liberalism from the public consciousness. The Catholic church, which resists the ideological monopoly of the party-state, is persecuted. The more incoherent and helpless the official doctrine, the greater the need for repression. In Guinea in 1970 the Archbishop of Conakry was arrested and charged with participating in a conspiracy aimed at subverting the existing authorities. In Zaire in 1973 the Catholic church was accused of carrying out subversive acts and preparing counterrevolution through its religious education of the young.[78] In Congo, an incessant anti-Catholic propaganda campaign was waged. Even the emperor of Ethiopia was described in Congo as an agent of the Vatican.

Since the leader of the people must be a great thinker, theoretical works are compiled on the basis of Soviet and Chinese textbooks, revealing the long-awaited truth to suffering humanity. As an example, one can cite the *Green Book* of Libyan dictator Muammar Qaddafi. His tract has been published in Libya in the main world languages. *Le Monde* reports that a World Center for the Study of the Green Book operates in Libya. "This organization, located in Tripoli and with enormous funds at its disposal, holds symposiums on the 'thought' of Colonel Qaddafi in foreign countries (!)"[79] "A woman is a human being," asserts the Libyan leader. "A man is also a human being. This is an indubitable and uncontested truth." However, the author considers a more precise definition to be essential. "Nevertheless," he writes, "a man is a man, and a woman is a woman. Why is this? Why does humanity not consist solely of men or solely of women, instead consisting of both?"[80] Indeed, why? After lengthy reflection Qaddafi concludes that the simultaneous existence of men and women is to be explained by "natural necessity." Then we read: "A woman is an individual of the female sex. A man is an individual of the male sex. By virtue of this a woman, as a gynecologist states, 'experiences menstruation, that is, regular sickness in the form of monthly flows of blood. This phenomenon is not characteristic of the male organism. If this does not occur, the woman has become pregnant.... A man, however, is free of all this.' Such is the view of a medical specialist."[81]

For a leader, there is no difference between an exploit and a crime. It is enough to recall Emperor Bokassa I of Central Africa, or Ugandan dictator Idi Amin. In the late 1970s both dictators received recognition from the international community. Idi Amin was elected president of the Organization of African Unity. When Bokassa, who was dissatisfied with being president-for-life, followed the example of Napoleon and declared himself emperor, he invited to his coronation state dignitaries from the whole world. None of the heads of state who were invited refused to attend.[82]

The seizure of power in Uganda and the Central African Republic by mindless dictators became possible thanks to the failure of modernization. Bokassa and Amin were by no means foreign to European ideas. Bokassa imitated Napoleon, creating a guard regiment wearing (in Africa!) fur hats. As soldiers, both rulers had links to the modernization of their societies. In Uganda everything began with unsuccessful attempts by the initially left-wing government of Milton Obote to win economic independence. Control over the commanding heights in the main sectors of the economy did not in itself ensure greater economic independence, much less socialism. The government, as even sympathetic writers acknowledged, could not devise a strategy of structural transformations answering the main needs of the people.[83] Amin continued Obote's industrial policies, but supplemented them with terror. The same logic, in the final analysis, guided the Shah of Iran, the Brazilian generals, and the Algerian technobureaucrats.

Amin was an anti-Semite, but in Uganda there was a shortage of Jews. His persecution of Asian traders recalled the anti-Jewish pogroms in Nazi Germany. The funds seized from foreigners were supposed to go to finance development, and the African petty bourgeoisie hoped to gain from the removal of competitors. But instead of the expected prosperity, chaos ruled in the country. The repressions hindered economic growth. Murdered corpses lay everywhere. Uganda, in the words of eyewitnesses, was in a state of total desolation.[84]

Intervention by the French in the Central African Republic and by the Tanzanians in Uganda put an end to the power of the most odious dictators of modern-day Africa, but could not put an end to the conditions that had created them. This is shown by the subsequent fate of Obote, who on returning to power took to heart the lessons of his rival, and tried to make massive repression his main strategy for the renewal of Uganda. The chaos continued until 1986, when the next coup took place. The victors promised to restore democracy, but were in no hurry to carry out their pledge. A neo-archaic state cannot exist without large-scale repression. The ruling minority is extremely unstable. Despite the simulated popular support, these regimes are isolated. The main problem they face, as Soviet scholars recognized, is "a lack of politically reliable cadres."[85] Repression is not secret and serves as part of the propaganda.[86] The authorities speak of the struggle against world imperialism and internal reaction, but repression is aimed at the working class, national minorities, the liberal intelligentsia, and the forces of the left, since these are the social groups least receptive to the official propaganda.

In many countries discrimination against national and religious minorities is officially sanctioned. In Burma during the years when the neo-archaic regime was flourishing, Article 153 of the constitution limited the right of non-Burmese to use their native language, retain their customs, culture, traditions, religious beliefs, and so forth, since these rights could pose a threat to the existing order, "the basis of the entire Burmese union."[87] In Ethiopia the armed forces continued the national policies of the imperial regime.[88]

The working class was recognized only verbally as a revolutionary force. The president of Congo declared that the Congolese working class remained "the principal revolutionary force in the country," but that, at the same time, it was not exerting "its decisive influence on the course of the revolution."[89] During the 1970s the industrial proletariat in tropical Africa was less than 4 percent of the total number of workers, while in Algeria the figure was around 7 percent. Wherever the workers tried seriously to defend their interests, they were quickly put in their place. Leading proponents of African socialism accused the industrial proletariat of seeking special privileges. "Attitudes differed, but African leaders were agreed that socialism did not involve working class control of production: some because they said the working class was minute (and in this they were often factually correct) or because they claimed that the workers were selfish."[90]

A neo-archaic regime does not recognize independent organizations of workers. Free trade unions which have arisen under the influence of the Western workers' movement are abolished or placed under the control of the state. Since wages in industry are higher than in the traditional sector, workers are called on to make sacrifices. In the name of overall development they are subjected to discipline and oriented not toward consuming but toward productive activity.[91] The Ethiopian military, for example, declared that the trade unions should not concern themselves with wages and working conditions, but should "aid the economic development of Ethiopia."[92] The efforts by the authorities to strengthen discipline and restrain the real wages of workers in the modern sector have impeded its normal development. The funds obtained from additional exploitation of workers went to finance absurd pharaonic projects. According to Samir Amin, all the efforts of workers served only to feed the growing "appetites of the new bureaucracy."[93]

Although in Russia in the 1930s workers' incomes remained low, they were nevertheless significantly higher than the real incomes of peasants. Workers enjoyed various advantages: Stalin's conscious policy was to keep the prices of many goods in the cities low, while the costs of this practice were paid by the countryside. Whatever we might think of such measures, they achieved the goal of stimulating the labor of industrializing workers. The neo-archaic state, on the other hand, applies every possible pressure to the working class, seeing in this class the bearer of harmful European traditions. There cannot be mutual trust between the workers and the authorities, since, unlike the situation in Russia and China, the origins of the state power owe nothing to workers' revolution.

The example of Ethiopia is one of the most tragic. During the 1970s a wave of mass uprisings against the imperial regime turned into something like a revolution. Power, however, was seized by the armed forces headed by Colonel Mengistu. After giving short shrift to the emperor, they did everything in their power to crush the popular movement as well. The abolition of the empire, according to I. Afeverki, one of the leaders of the left, "created a vacuum which the armed forces, as the only organized force, were able to fill." Initially, some left groups hoped "to form a tactical alliance with the military regime," but the military clique "decided once and for all to wipe out all the democratic forces in Ethiopia, in order to consolidate itself firmly in power."[94] The antimonarchical coup blocked the development of the revolution. The military-bureaucratic regime, which had declared itself Marxist-Leninist, began a massive campaign of terror against the workers and left organizations.[95] The leftists described the new authorities as a fascist regime.[96] The first victim of the repression was the People's Revolutionary Party. Some 18,000 of its activists were killed or imprisoned. "This was the most terrible period of the 'revolution'," wrote *Libération*. "Every morning on the streets of Addis Ababa dozens of corpses would be found, victims of the 'red terror'."[97] Socialists, ultraleftists and deviationists were all shot. On May 1, 1977, about a thousand university and school students taking part in a protest demonstration were massacred. A purge was conducted within the army itself. Among those who were shot was Gen. Tafere Banete, who for a time had held the post of head of the government.

In the words of Craipeau, the rule of the armed forces was marked by "a series of bloody coups."[98] Following the rout of the People's Revolutionary Party and the Socialist Movement, the authorities turned on the Confederation of Ethiopian Trade Unions (CETU). In September 1975 the CETU published a document supporting freedom of speech, the press, and trade union activity. These demands had been formulated by the union of teachers, but had the support of substantial groups within the working class. When a number of workers were arrested for distributing a document of the CETU, strikes began occurring in the factories.[99] These actions were ruthlessly suppressed. The authorities declared that the workers' actions had been "provoked by reactionary elements."[100] The government dissolved the trade unions, accusing them of pursuing mercenary goals, and of posing "a direct threat to order and security." Under a 1975 law all trade unions were compelled to "undergo reorganization."[101]

The 1984 drought was used as a means of disciplining the rebellious population. Regions that were considered unreliable were denied food aid. Under the pretext of fighting hunger, local populations were deported. Thousands of people perished. In the words of a British journalist, this was to a significant degree a "political famine."[102]

Despite the brutal repression, the resistance of the left-wing forces was not broken. The main center of guerrilla warfare was Eritrea, where a significant part of the country's modern production and most of its industrial proletariat were concentrated. In 1974 there were already almost five times as many workers here as in all of the rest of Ethiopia. The Marxist Eritrean People's Liberation Front, which simultaneously expressed both national and social protest, mounted successful armed actions. After Eritrea, other provinces rose in revolt. Soviet aid dried up.

Trying to save his regime, Mengistu in the late 1980s sharply changed his ideological orientation. The Workers Party of Ethiopia was renamed the Party of Democratic Unity, the ideology of Marxism-Leninism was denounced, and the leadership declared that it sought to encourage private enterprise and foreign investment. "In the space of a single night the monuments to the founders of scientific socialism were demolished," reported *Izvestiia*. "Of the hammer and sickle, only fragments remained."[103] Nevertheless, the crisis of the regime continued. In May 1991 President Mengistu fled from a country convulsed by revolt.

It was not only in Ethiopia that the armed forces and technobureaucracy combined socialist slogans with repression against organizations of workers and the left. In Egypt, President Nasser threw Communists in prison. The same happened in Sudan, Iraq, and Syria. In Angola the government imposed prison terms of as much as eight years for participation in strikes, which were described as "crimes against production."[104] In Congo an attempt to found a Communist party was crushed. In Iraq during the 1970s, thousands of people, including Communists, nationalists, democrats, and members of the religious opposition, fell victim to widespread arrests, tortures, and executions. Kurds who were struggling for their national rights were subjected to vicious persecution.

The government of Syria has also acted unhesitatingly to suppress discontent. People of the most diverse views have been subject to repression, from liberals and leftists to Islamic fundamentalists. Prisoners are held for years without trial or investigation. Under the state of emergency laws, families are denied the right to protest against the detentions. Sometimes they appeal to the local governor, but frequently they do not, fearing punishment. The state security service can be merciless: in 1980 a special team burst into the Tadtur prison and killed some 600 to 1,000 prisoners, evidently in reprisal for an attempt on the life of the president.[105] Following a revolt in 1982 by the Islamic Brotherhood in Hamah, around 20,000 people were killed there.

"Anyone who says 'no' to President Assad quickly loses his head," boasted one of the regime's officials.[106]

In Surinam the Bouterse government dealt harshly with trade union activists and radical leftists who initially had welcomed the formation of the revolutionary regime. Surinam, to use the phrase of one of the dictator's surviving opponents, has been transformed into "a country of mutes."[107] Guinea under Sekou Toure presented a no-less-frightening picture: Amnesty International confessed itself incapable of establishing even approximately the number of people who had been imprisoned. Unlike Amin and Bokassa, Sekou Toure "organized his repressive apparatus with meticulous efficiency, systematically disposing of everyone who might be dangerous to him. Beginning in 1958, when Guinea became independent, President Sekou Toure unmasked no fewer than fourteen 'conspiracies against the revolution,' sending large numbers of people to concentration camps. The best-known of these was the Boiro camp near Conakry, where thousands of people 'disappeared' without trace."[108] The prisoners were subjected to appalling humiliations and tortures. The terror was unleashed primarily against former fellow-travellers among the leftists. In 1961 a teachers' conspiracy, reminiscent of the Stalinist doctors' plot, was uncovered. In 1967 a Chinese-style cultural revolution was launched.

When Guinea won its independence, Sekou Toure declared to President de Gaulle: "We would rather be free in poverty than wealthy in bondage."[109] The new regime gave the people poverty and bondage simultaneously. The entire population was recruited into a single party, which with a degree of irony was called "Democratic." One-third of Guinea's population of six million people fled abroad. On the eve of the 1984 military coup the situation in all areas of life was catastrophic. Summing up the results of twenty years of Sekou Toure's rule, a military officer stated: "The hopes of a more just and decent society vanished, swept away by a cruel and bloody dictatorship."[110]

The lessons of history forced third world radicals to make a more sober assessment of neo-archaic regimes operating under a "revolutionary" banner. The 1952 coup d'etat in Egypt, which brought Nasser to power and began a whole series of simulated revolutions, is no longer regarded as a heroic exploit. An Egyptian Communist recognizes that the new authorities "did not believe in the organized people, and did not want their [popular] organizations to play an independent role."

The Nasser era was not a period of progressive change, but a time when the rights and freedoms of the people were suppressed. "The regime, it is true, tried to mobilize the masses within the narrow framework it had itself set up." But without success. In the final accounting, Nasserism "halted and destroyed the national democratic revolution in Egypt."[111]

The most enduring support found by the neo-archaic dictators was among left-wing intellectuals in the West. Intellectuals in London or Paris did not want such regimes in their own countries, but they often considered such rulers suitable for Ethiopians. People who were sincerely worried about the fate of two or three dissidents in Czechoslovakia reacted calmly to the disappearance of thousands of people in Syria and Iraq. It is difficult to avoid the thought that these responses hid a profound, and profoundly racist, contempt for the people of the developing countries.

The fall of the Sekou Toure regime dealt a heavy blow to the neo-archaic mythos. The ease with which the oldest and most stable dictatorship in Africa was overthrown provided a pointer to the fate of other regimes. Neo-archaic despotism could not carry out irreversible changes. Stalin and Mao succeeded in transforming social structures. Not one of the neo-archaic leaders managed this.

The armed forces president of Guinea remarked in November 1984 that although Sekou Toure killed large numbers of people, this had not been his greatest crime. Toure had killed hope, had crushed the initiative of the population, and had left the new authorities with "a desolate country, with its social fabric destroyed and its citizens passive. For us today the main thing is to bring about a change of consciousness, so that Guineans can once again set to work, so that they can reveal their spirit of enterprise, and begin to strive for their own betterment and that of their country."[112]

As Samir Amin predicted, once the Moscow-educated Guinean military came to power, they turned to the international corporations.[113] But the turn to the West did not occur in every case. Where a "revolutionary" ideology had not worked, the state-church needed a more organic religion. Such artificial inventions as Mobutism or borrowings from Soviet textbooks were unsatisfactory as a basis for the official faith. It is therefore not surprising that many neo-archaic regimes set out on the road of Islamization. Twentieth-century pseudoreligions cannot compete with Islam, which has a tradition extending back more than a thousand years. The source of social organization is expressed more clearly in Islam than in other religions. The Qur'an, the Islamic holy book, and the Shariat, the code of Islamic law, regulate not only the behavior of the individual in the family and society, but also his or her personal, economic, and social life. In the eyes of believers, Islam is not simply a religion, but also a way of life.

The Islamic revolution in Iran drew attention to processes which had begun in the East significantly earlier. In Algeria, Sudan, Guinea, and Libya Islamization began in the absence of any political overturn. In Algeria revolutionary slogans were gradually forced out by Islamic ones, government measures were provided with a religious basis, and the position of the Christian minority deteriorated. The Nimeiri regime in Sudan, trying to avoid its own collapse, Islamized the constitution and the laws.

By the early 1990s the majority of neo-archaic regimes had either collapsed, or were in acute crises that were forcing them to carry out political reforms. In Bourkina Faso the regime of Thomas Sankara was ousted by a military coup, while in South Yemen the bureaucratic clans were pursuing a bloody civil war among themselves. Both groups declared their loyalty to Marxist-Leninist ideology, but in the early 1990s declared its main task to be securing unification with monarchist and feudal North Yemen. In Burma strikes and demonstrations led to the fall of the government. The development of a popular revolution was interrupted by a new military coup d'etat, after which a military regime of the classical type took power. The military dictatorships in Somalia and Ethiopia, which for many years had fought a bloody war, collapsed almost simultaneously in 1991. First Barre fled, then Mengistu.

In Africa, democratic slogans were triumphant. Free elections were held in Benin. In Angola and Mozambique, the governments held talks with the insurgents. Neither the ruling regimes, nor the opposition groups who were financed by the South African apartheid government had been able during the 1970s and 1980s to offer the people any prospect of democracy. Nevertheless, the need for compromise had made the creation of a multiparty system essential. Despite the corruption and bureaucratization of their regimes, the ruling parties in Angola and Mozambique had retained certain links with the masses.

Thanks to this the presidential elections in Angola in 1992 ended in victory for incumbent President Eduardo Dos Santos. The government of Mozambique proclaimed in law the right of citizens to choose their place of residence, and promised that in future it would not deport unemployed workers to the countryside as it had done in 1983. Strikes were permitted. After a persistent struggle by Mozambican journalists, the constitution now included a lengthy article on press freedom. The constitution abolished the monopoly of the party and the state on printing, creating the possibility of setting up independent publications. A left-wing American journalist called it one of "the most progressive" constitutions in Africa.[114] Elections in 1994 ended in a grudging acceptance of Frelimo's victory by the leaders of the opposition guerrilla forces.

All the same, one could hardly speak of a triumph of democracy. A balance of fear rarely provides a basis for freedom. More often, it serves as a threshold for chaos and a new dictatorship. After the overthrow of Barre and Mengistu, the victors set to struggling among themselves. In Somalia a civil war began, leading to intervention by the United States.

Neotraditionalist and Islamic fundamentalist grouplets quickly filled the political vacuum. When a shift to a multiparty system began in Algeria following disorders in 1988, the main political force to emerge was neither the left, nor liberal Westernizers, but fundamentalists from the Islamic Salvation Front. The technocrats had to resort to force in order to maintain themselves in power. A state of emergency was declared, and in place of the short-lived liberalization came another turn of the screw. For all the open violation of democratic freedoms in Algeria, liberal circles in the West welcomed the steps which the Algerian authorities had taken in supposedly saving the country from the threat of Islamic fundamentalism. This was despite the fact that it was the techno-bureaucratic regime which began the process of Islamization during the 1970s.

The Islamization of neo-archaic regimes allows us to understand better the riddle of the Iranian revolution. If in more backward countries the degeneration of the modernizer state has proceeded gradually, in Iran the same result was achieved through revolutionary means. The Shah's effective technocracy ensured that the transition to a neo-archaic state took the form of a national catastrophe.

Unlike the African and Asian neo-archaic regimes, the new authorities in Iran had no need to simulate revolution, because the country was living through a genuine social earthquake. The Ayatollah Khomeini's regime in Teheran had no need to cloak itself in progressive and socialist slogans. It was able to justify itself as a movement against the Shah. Khomeini's Iran was the first state openly to declare a neo-archaic ideology. Iran witnessed the simultaneous unfolding of a democratic revolution of the modern layers and a reactionary uprising by the traditionalist clergy. Both movements appealed to Islamic tradition, though each understood it differently. Both movements were struggling against the same government, and often rested on the same mass following. The people's traditional way of life was destroyed before modern structures were set in place. "The slogan 'Death to the Shah'," wrote a Soviet orientalist, "temporarily united in one movement the leaders of nomadic tribes, separatists from various national districts, the Islamic clergy, and Marxist parties and organizations whose roots in Iran had not been torn out even after long years of vicious persecution. No other slogan could have directed into a single channel groups which were so diverse and which were even counterposed on the basis of interests, ideology, and program. No other slogan could have created a movement of such unprecedented size."[115] To draw a dividing line between right-wing and left-wing opposition was in practice not at all simple. The banners of the left were democracy and socialism, and those of the right, tradition and Islam. But the main socialist organization in Iran, the Mojahedeen, tried to speak to the masses in the language of the Qur'an, though after the establishment of a theocratic regime it reverted to Marxist terminology.[116] The clerics for their part used progressive slogans.

Chaos and instability in the social structure preordains that the class struggle will have a chaotic nature as well, that the ideological principles of rival parties will be blurred, and that their social bases will be unreliable. The contradictions of industrial society are superimposed on the conflicts of the modernization period. The essence of the Iranian tragedy lies in the fact that the participation of the progressive and democratic forces was an indispensable condition for the triumph of reaction. The opposition received a significant part of its dynamism from the leftists. Observers acknowledge that it was the leftists who "played the leading role in accelerating developments, in mobilizing the masses to seize power in the capital and other cities." But in the

space of only one or two days "power effectively passed to the supporters of the religious forces, who were more organized and united, and
who had at their disposal the clear and broadly ramified structure of
the clerical hierarchy, which had the unconditional support of the
masses of the country's faithful."[117] Participating in the demonstrations
against the Shah, the Marxists and democrats were not only preparing
their own downfall and the defeat of their ideals, they were also
doomed to play an important, if not decisive, role in the process that
was unfolding. To abstain from participating in the struggle against the
Shah was impossible, if only for moral reasons. At the time of the
Iranian revolution of 1909, Karl Kautsky wrote that "in a democratic
movement supported by all the working strata of the country, there are
always reactionary tendencies." This is a thought which is not only
applicable to Iran; Kautsky was in fact pointing to one of the causes of
the downfall and totalitarian degeneration of many revolutionary
regimes. "But this," Kautsky continued, "is not a reason to stand aside
from the struggle. It is simply a reason to work in the democratic
movement against these reactionary tendencies."[118] In order to win the
leadership of the movement, the leftists needed to counterpose to
Khomeini's slogans their own historic project, arising out of the real
conditions and possibilities that existed in the country.[119] They had no
such project. Their aim of carrying through a rapid transition to
socialism would, if they had seized power, have led inevitably to the rise
of a local variety of Stalinism. In ideological terms, the goal of making
such a transition was shared both by the members of the Tudeh
People's Party and by the leaders of another large left group, the
Fedayeen Communist Union.[120] The Stalinist groups entered a tactical
alliance with the Islamic clergy to whom they were spiritually close.[121]

When Khomeini was still in Paris he had called for "the establishment of a theocratic form of rule in which secular and spiritual
authority would be indivisible. In these circumstances the form of a
parliamentary republic would be deprived of its content, since the
parliament elected by the people would not exercise power, but would
be a consultative organ obliged to fulfil unquestioningly the instructions it received from the decision-making group."[122] Even more than
by Khomeini's ideas, the clergy were guided by their own political
instincts. To the organs of local self-government and workers' councils
that had arisen spontaneously during the mass demonstrations and

revolts, the clergy counterposed revolutionary committees and squads of Islamic revolutionary guards set up under clerical control. The leftists were too late in grasping the real significance of these measures.

In the summer of 1979 the Supreme Tribunal issued a decree shutting down opposition newspapers and banning democratic parties and organizations. Then followed an Islamic purge of institutions of higher education. A decision was made that the choice of people for jobs in the state apparatus "would be guided in the first instance by the piety of the candidate, and not by considerations of professional aptitude."[123] The liberals confined themselves to demonstrating in the streets. Some of them tried to retain their posts at the cost of making concessions. The leader of the moderates, Bani-Sadr, won a reputation as a person with a boundless capacity for surrender.[124] This failed to help. In June 1981 Khomeini removed him from the post of president. It was only with the help of the Mojahedeen that Bani-Sadr managed to save his life and flee the country.

At a time when the left-wing forces had gone over to armed resistance, the Stalinists of the Tudeh Party continued to support the regime. The Stalinists characterized Bani-Sadr and the liberal leaders as linked to imperialism, and the Mojahedeen and other left groups as "revolutionary in words," but in terms of deeds "lining up with the blackest reaction," and as people with whom the People's Party had "nothing in common."[125] The Tudeh leaders continued to support "the anti-imperialist course of Khomeini" and to stress their "loyal attitude to the regime"[126] even when rank-and-file members of the party were already being thrown in jail. At the Twenty-sixth Congress of the Communist Party of the Soviet Union, when Khomeini's repression was at its height, Brezhnev declared that Iran was on the road to "freedom and prosperity."[127] Soon after this the Tudeh leaders were arrested on slanderous charges of spying for the USSR, and most of them were shot. The Shi'i clergy had no intention of sharing power with anyone. An anti-Soviet campaign began in the press. Soviet diplomats were expelled, and Moscow was criticized equally with Washington. By an irony of fate, the court proceedings against the Iranian Stalinists, involving absurd confessions and self-indictments by the accused, clearly recalled the Moscow trials of 1937.

The leftists struggled heroically, but they had already lost contact with the masses.[128] The propaganda machine created by Khomeini's followers established total control over the population. Opponents of the government were physically liquidated. The war with Iraq created an atmosphere of national hysteria. The authorities reported proudly to foreign correspondents that ten-year-old children had been sent to the front. Some of the boys were so eager to die in the "holy war" that according to official sources, they falsified their birth certificates in order to appear older.[129]

The clergy exercised absolute power, and could implement any social or economic project they chose, but they had no distinctive, original project. As the *Financial Times* noted, for a long time the Iranian leadership could not decide which ideology would determine the development of the economy.[130] The new leadership was capable of experimenting with Soviet and Western economic models alike. Initially the ayatollahs were inclined to the Soviet path. Completely intolerable conditions were imposed on the conduct of private business. In July 1979 the Union of Proprietors of Civil Construction Enterprises adopted a resolution by 598 votes against 2 calling on the government to "nationalize their enterprises without compensation."[131] This was, in fact, followed by a wave of nationalizations. The government declared the goal of creating a closed economy and of limiting imports. The state established control over fifty business corporations, banks, and insurance companies, and reduced the country's economic links with the West. Soon, however, it became clear that the clergy was incapable of running a state-owned economy. Functionaries who were reliable in religious terms, and who had an exquisite knowledge of sacred texts, fared poorly in trying to organize production.

The only area in which some successes were registered was the defence industry. During the conflict with Iraq, 90 percent of essential small arms were produced in Iran, including excellent copies of the American M-16 rifle and the Israeli Uzi machine pistol, as well as 75 percent of munitions. Assembly plants were built for Japanese off-road vehicles and for trainer helicopters.[132] Civilian production, meanwhile, went into total collapse. Social planning was practically nonexistent, having been replaced by charity combined with terror. Poverty, unemployment, corruption and speculation continued to plague society. As early as the autumn of 1979 experts remarked on "the inactivity of nationalized enterprises and of the banking system."[133] Four years later an Italian journalist stated: "The economy is at a standstill. Nothing is being produced in the factories, and the position is the same in agriculture."[134]

After unsuccessful experiments with the Soviet model the ruling groups began increasingly to orient toward Western methods. Before 1979 was out the *New York Times* noted with satisfaction that the Khomeini government was not holding fast to doctrinaire socialist attitudes.[135] The nationalizations had initially been justified by citing quotations from Islamic religious texts. When a review of economic policy became necessary, it was unexpectedly remembered that nationalization was linked with Marxist ideology, and contradicted the Qur'an. "A free, unrestricted capitalism appeared to them to be better suited to an Islamic republic," the *Financial Times* observed ironically.[136] The changes to economic policy became particularly evident in the summer of 1984. The turn to capitalism was accompanied by the rejection of further nationalizations. By the beginning of the 1990s new steps were being taken in the direction of capitalism. State-owned vehicle plants began to be denationalized. This might at first glance have seemed like a concession to the feeble and intimidated bourgeoisie, but in essence it reflected shifts in the thinking of Islamic circles and of the section of the middle layers that supported them.[137]

A Soviet historian noted correctly that Khomeini's economic policies combined the rationalism and irrationality of the middle layers. A theocratic regime cannot rest on the clergy alone. It needs the active collaboration of the middle layers. If the Shah rested on the technocratic elite, Khomeini relied on the far more backward mass of middle-class Iranians. "As a result, it became possible for the 'middle layers' to express everything that flowed from their reasoning and their prejudices, and in such a form that the one was inseparable from the other."[138] The vacillations between attempts at nationalizing the economy and capitalist entrepreneurship did not signify shifts in the regime's social base, but merely changes of tactics. Despite the shifts of course, the social base itself remained stable. The new technocratic layers and the clergy grew closer. Economics and management began to be taught in the seminaries, while managers began learning texts from the Qur'an by heart. The need to solve economic problems brought a rapid technocratization of the clergy. The new regime formed on this basis could have been called "techno-theocratic."[139]

The catastrophic outcome of the Iranian revolution was interpreted by rightists as further proof that any revolution leads inevitably to totalitarianism. Khomeinism, however, was not only the child of the Shah's policies (prior to the "white revolution" Iran had no strong technocratic opposition), but also in a peculiar sense their continuation. Pol Pot and Khomeini were no less smitten by the idea of an orderly society than were the modernizers, despite using different methods. The neo-archaic regime receives its initial ideological impulse, and a significant part of its social base, from technocratic modernization. In this sense the reaction is not so much the negation of the work of the technocrats as its culmination.

It is only possible to learn something from the Iranian experience if one finally understands the tragic consequences of development in the absence of democracy. It is naive to argue that there can be no democratic road in the third world. The instability of technocratic and neo-archaic structures constantly creates the possibility of a democratic opening. The vacillations of the middle layers and the heterogeneity of society make possible the formation of broad tactical and strategic blocs. Despite the failure of the majority of programs for industrial development, the size of the modern proletariat has grown, and so in consequence has the social base of the left.

The fall of military regimes in the countries of Latin America, the collapse of neo-archaic political systems in most of the countries of Africa, and the crisis of other dictatorships show that the need for democracy exists. The real question is different: how can democracy be made viable?

CHAPTER 5

THE REVOLUTIONARY
MODEL: I

To be a leftist in the third world has always meant to be a revolutionary. The poverty and lack of rights of working people have been so appalling, and the short-sightedness, cruelty, and incompetence of the ruling groups have been so obvious, that no honest person could speak seriously of gradual progress or class collaboration. At times, liberals from the developing countries have proven to be more left-wing than Western European social democrats. The word *revolution* has acquired a thoroughly concrete, tangible meaning. For third world revolutionaries China, and later Cuba, have served as actually existing models. Both countries lived through a people's war and anticapitalist transformations. In both countries the revolutionary regime defended itself in a conflict with the United States. The Cubans learned a great deal from the Chinese. Che Guevara admitted this openly, recalling that China had experienced a revolution "similar to that in Cuba."[1] In both countries the actions of the new authorities included examples of both moderation and extremism. For some time both countries served as ideals for progressive youth in the third world. In both countries, the Communist Party retained power despite the shocks of 1989.[2]

China is now perceived rather as a reformist model, attractive not so much to third world states as to Eastern European countries in which the shift to the market along the lines dictated by the International Monetary Fund has brought economic catastrophe.[3] The slogan of Chinese leaders since Mao has not been revolution, but reform. Such a reform, however, would hardly have been possible without revolution.

Maoist China knew both a heroic period and a period of decline. As in every backward country, the proletarian party quickly became bureaucratized after the seizure of power. A new oligarchy controlling state property took shape.[4] Democratic tendencies were crushed, and the working class was excluded from the direct exercise of power. Widespread terror and persecution of dissidents within the Communist Party marked the culmination of the shift from a revolutionary to a totalitarian regime. But when Deng Xiaoping came to power the ruling circles not only renounced terror, but set out on the road of structural reform. At first this struck foreign observers as totally incredible.[5] Nevertheless, deep and irreversible changes were underway in Chinese society.

Centralized bureaucratic planning in the countryside was completely abolished, and the people's communes into which peasants had been herded by force were dissolved or transformed. The land, in turn, was handed over to individual households and cooperatives. From the mid-1980s, the reform had a serious impact on the management of industry. A serious approach was taken toward the forming of small enterprises. The tasks of the planning organs were restricted. Instructions from the center played the decisive role only in the production of the sixty most important industrial commodities (coal, oil, cement, and steel) and the top ten agricultural products. Enterprises became independent in most questions of finance, of labor organization, price formation, and profit distribution. The planners began relying less on directives, preferring instead economic methods such as control over prices, taxes, discounts, and subsidies. Bureaucratic centralism was gradually replaced by "planning regulation in coordination with the market."[6] The omnipotence of party leaders became a thing of the past. As Western observers noted, "the question of power at the level of the enterprises was resolved to the advantage of the managers."[7] The Chinese government proclaimed the goal of creating a market economy of a noncapitalist type.[8]

As the reforms continued, China became more and more part of the world capitalist economy. Some regions of the country were opened to foreign investment. Western firms, especially transnational corporations, responded avidly to the appeals of the Chinese Communist government and began investing capital in China.[9] Between 1979 and 1983, 188 joint venture companies were formed. By the beginning of 1984 the total sum of foreign investments had reached $15 billion.[10] The growth of foreign entrepreneurship in China continued during the second half of the 1980s and early 1990s, slowing only a little as a result of the 1989–1990 political crisis. The petty private and cooperative sectors acquired considerable freedom. The state issued more than five million licenses for the opening of small stalls, workshops, and food outlets. The use by private enterprises of hired labor was permitted, within certain limits.[11] The outlines of a mixed economy began to appear. In 1983 investment by foreign firms amounted to only 1.3 percent of total capital investment in the national economy, and the share of the local private sector was several times smaller. However, the state bureaucracy was quickly reorienting and learning how to profit from the new situation. Functionaries no longer restricted the business activities of foreigners, but instead served these interests.

The Chinese leaders declared that the country needed a comprehensive reform of the economic structure, promising that the success of this effort would, in twenty-five years, transform China into "a state with a high level of civilization and democracy."[12] According to the government, the decentralization of power and the broadening of the rights of managers, moves which were accompanied by cuts in the party apparatus and its cadre, represented only the first step. The next task was "to create real guarantees of participation by manual and white-collar employees in the democratic management of enterprises."[13] At first the liberalization of the political system was quite genuine. People recalled the slogan of the early revolutionary period: "Let a hundred flowers bloom, let a hundred schools contend!" The everyday propaganda was changed as well. "The main elements in ideological work were declared to be the theses 'the emancipation of consciousness', 'maintaining a realistic approach', and 'practice as the sole criterion for truth'."[14] Writers and scholars who had suffered during the years of the cultural revolution were allowed to return to their posts. After two decades of cultural isolation, Chinese students again began studying abroad, and books that had earlier been forbidden were published in Chinese.

Interest in China rose throughout the world. If Beijing in the early 1970s had been the mecca of radicals, ten years later it was the focal point of reformers. Once again many people saw in China a fruitful experiment, deserving imitation.[15] During the 1970s, Chinese reformers had secretly admired the Hungarian "road." In the late 1980s, the Hungarian scholar D. Barac wrote enthusiastically about the "unprecedented dynamism" of reform in China.[16] Westerners assessed the reform policies more skeptically: "It will be a long time yet before this country becomes not just a potential, but a real international force," wrote a German journalist.[17]

Though all agreed that the reforms were a success, the evaluation of the changes depended, naturally, on the position of the observer.[18] Some Western analysts wrote of a Chinese Thermidor, and of persecutions against Jacobins—that is, against the Gang of Four and orthodox Maoist-Stalinists.[19] Others saw in Deng's policies "a mixture of elements of the socialist and capitalist modes of production."[20] The *Economist* (London) saw a return to peasant capitalism.[21] Meanwhile Ernest Mandel suggested that what was involved was a change of tactics that affected neither the essence of the regime nor its strategic goals: the new leaders were said to be persisting with the Maoist project, but relying on effective material stimuli, not on political mobilization, propaganda, or coercion.[22]

To radical writers, the main sin of the Chinese leadership remains its use of foreign capital, though these same critics have often acknowledged that China cannot maintain its present rates of growth at a high technological level without developing links with the West.[23] In 1982, only 5 percent of output of the means of production in China met the world standards of the 1970s, so Western technology was virtually indispensable. However, national industry lacked the funds for large-scale imports of modern equipment. Foreign entrepreneurs immediately declared their willingness to invest money in the Chinese economy. The Hong Kong scholar Leung Wangyue wrote: "China with its 1.03 billion population is now offering one of the world's lowest-paid labor forces to international capital, against the backdrop of a relatively stable government very much in control of the population and of trade unions."[24]

The Communist regimes of Southeast Asia also became attractive to Western and Japanese firms when they began to implement reforms on the Chinese model. The rapid growth of foreign investment in Vietnam caused many experts to speak of a quick repetition of the South Korean miracle. More than $1 billion was invested in Vietnam between 1986 and 1990. Shell, British Petroleum, and the French firm Total have shown interest in regional oil deposits, and entrepreneurs from Singapore, Thailand, Hong Kong, and Taiwan became active in many branches of the economy. (American pressure has thwarted the activity of South Korean firms.) A Finnish company was reconstructing the Hanoi water supply, and Australia signed a trade agreement. Japanese firms, which earlier were restrained by the American embargo, were sending hundreds of missions to Vietnam, and observers noted that when Washington's last fears abate, Japanese business activity here would probably exceed that of the Europeans. Hanoi's official representatives declared proudly that they had so many offers that before long they would be unable to assist all the companies interested in Vietnam.[25]

Policies of liberalization have also been developing successfully in Laos. A Japanese newspaper observed that reforms, launched in 1988, quickly filled the markets of Vientiane with consumer goods. Meanwhile foreign entrepreneurs, mainly from Thailand, rapidly took up positions that had remained vacant since 1975.[26]

International firms were attracted not only by cheap labor power and the weakness of trade unions, but also by the exceptional dependency of Chinese (or Vietnamese) workers on the authorities. In the words of the American scholar A. Walder, the Chinese bureaucracy managed to create a "new tradition of labor relations," based on the total dependency of the worker, not only on the state, but also on the job supervisor, the workshop head, and the enterprise management.[27] The position was similar in other Communist countries, but to a lesser degree. In the European areas of the USSR, which have low birth rates and persistent shortages of labor power, the personal dependency of workers vanished everywhere in the 1970s and 1980s, except perhaps in Moscow and Leningrad. But in China, during the early stages of reform, it was still very powerful.

The defenselessness of workers encouraged the transfer to China of capital not just from Western countries, but also from the authoritarian states of Southeast Asia. "As a result," Leung Wangyue notes, "attempts to organize or strengthen workers' rights and trade unions in foreign-owned plants in some other parts of Asia have been seriously undermined, particularly in other Asian export processing zones where capital is most footloose."[28] Only a small part of the foreign capital was really invested in developing modern technology. In the second half of the 1980s only 10 percent of the foreign enterprises specialized in this sphere. The main investments were in light industry, tourism, and property. No more than 15 percent of foreign capital was invested in machine-building.

During the decade of reform, the psychology and ideology of the ruling circles changed. A new generation of party leaders arose. "In their rush to a new future," remarks the American journalist Orville Schell, in general sympathetic to the reforms, "they brushed aside China's socialist past, as if this aspect of their country's persona was a bothersome, somewhat embarrassing detail they now wished everyone would forget. What interested them was managing and using the exciting new financial instruments of bankruptcy and stocks and bonds to create maximum productive power. In this sense they were the true heirs of Deng Xiaoping's pragmatism."[29]

The pragmatism, which had become the ideology of the ruling layer, could not fail to make a strong impact on the life and culture of Chinese society. To argue that there was no opposition to reform in China is to ignore the facts. Here as everywhere, the failure of the first half-hearted changes aroused an obvious urge to return to the old methods.[30] This was completely natural for the statocracy, the class-apparatus that based its power not on juridically guaranteed property, but on the monopoly appropriation of the administrative-control functions of the state. Any measures that really brought the country closer to socialism meant the partial expropriation of the ruling oligarchy. The development of capitalist relations, ultimately presuming the juridical consolidation of property in the hands of the ruling circles, was much more acceptable than socialist experiments. But for the bureaucracy, this variant as well was fraught with serious risks. The Chinese leadership was thus forced to act with extreme caution, avoiding hasty steps. De-Maoization in China was carried through more decisively than de-Stalinization in the USSR, though Mao himself was not subjected to such severe criticism. China's position in 1976 and 1977 was worse than that of the Soviet Union in the years from 1953 to 1956. In the USSR at that time there was no economic crisis. Despite his economic failures, Mao had a long series of achievements to his credit, but by 1976 the negative results of his policies clearly outweighed the positive ones. In terms of economic growth, China ranked among the most dynamic of the developing states, standing alongside such countries as Brazil, Colombia, Peru, the Philippines, and Malaysia, but the growth was extremely unstable, and technological progress was slow.

The regime's international ambitions clearly exceeded its possibilities. The Chinese leadership placed its stake on primitive rationalization under the slogan "a technical revolution from below."[32] A Japanese economist points to the remarkable fact that China managed to eliminate hunger despite a growth in population of 300 million people between 1957 and 1977.[33] Meanwhile the productivity of labor in the countryside rose only a little, and without serious reforms, it would have been impossible to maintain even that little growth. As broad layers of the bureaucracy realized this, the position of the reformers grew stronger, and their ideas began to arouse interest even among conservative functionaries.

When changes began in 1976, the Chinese economy was on the brink of catastrophe. While this crisis strengthened the reformers in the power struggle, it rendered reforms more difficult. Western experts warned, correctly, that any radical restructuring of institutions would create new problems.[34] The expanding of the rights of enterprises was accompanied by economic disorganization. "A fierce struggle began between enterprises over raw materials, fuel and energy. Prices for the means of production 'leapt', and established economic links began to collapse.... Chaos and anarchy grew increasingly apparent."[35] Most of the initial measures had the opposite of the desired effect; inflation, the black market, and corruption all increased.

Conservative local bureaucrats sabotaged the new policies. The government recognized that the party contained a large number of officials still tempted to return to the past.[36] The conservatives cited problems, trying to show that despite the inefficiency of centralized planning and administration, their abolition, in a country as huge as China, would lead to chaos.[37] Not without reason, many of the reformers shared these fears. In 1981 the changes were curtailed.

When reforms from above are stalled and the old system has already decayed, the pressure from below grows dramatically stronger. The authorities risk losing control over the processes that are in motion. A serious threat hung over the Chinese bureaucracy. The crisis sharpened the contradictions within the ruling circles to such an extent that the struggle taking place there began to affect the mood of the population. As a Soviet historian acknowledged, as early as 1976 clashes were occurring, not only between members of the apparatus, but also among the masses. Participation by the lower orders of society in political affairs, even in the most limited way, created the preconditions for deeper changes: "The crisis of Maoism entered an explosive stage; the situation could only be saved through radical methods, including even the serious revision of some of Mao's postulates."[38]

While the great helmsman was still alive, antigovernment demonstrations took place on Tienanmen Square in Beijing. The ostensible cause was attacks in one of the newspapers on the late Zhou Enlai, but the real grievances were more important. The demonstrators stuck posters on the monument to the heroes of the revolution, declaring that China's leaders had forgotten the revolutionary ideals. The authorities did not deny that the action was directed against Chairman Mao.[39] Despite massive repression, the disturbances continued. In 1975 and 1976 strikes took place throughout the country, along with rice revolts and even armed clashes. At first the authorities tried to conceal what was happening, but later they had to admit that the reports of these events, appearing in the Western press, were true.[40]

The crisis of the reforms in 1980 and 1981 brought fresh antigovernment demonstrations. Uncoordinated but repeated strikes, slowdowns, and demonstrations revealed the worker dissatisfaction with low wages, poor working conditions, and layoffs. Underground publications reported continuous efforts to create independent trade unions.[41] Newspapers noted that, under the influence of the Polish revolution of 1981, this slogan was becoming increasingly popular. Workers were calling for trade unions independent of the party and state.[42] They also began advancing more radical demands. The underground journal *Voice of Democracy*, which had its roots in the worker milieu, reported triumphantly on the events in Poland. The journal's editors stressed that the Chinese authorities had to recognize "the right of the population to publish unofficial journals and newspapers."[43] As early as 1977 and 1978 such *samizdat* publications were distributed relatively widely. The journals *Analyses, February Flower,* and *The Wall* appeared, along with wall posters calling for democratization. Young dissidents, Craipeau notes, "were not satisfied with criticisms of the Gang of Four; they questioned the bureaucratic system and demanded democracy, calling for a Western-style democratic system or still worse, like the young worker... [who] unmasked the bureaucratic class and spoke out for genuine socialism. This situation was unacceptable to all factions of the bureaucratic class."[44]

The dissidents were almost all workers. It is true that these workers would have been intellectuals had it not been for the Cultural Revolution.[45] But this created an even greater threat to the authorities, since close bonds arose between the workers and the intelligentsia. By frightening the ruling elite, the mass protests would have strengthened the conservative tendencies within it. One might, therefore, have expected that the reforms would be reversed, or else that the authorities would lose control of the process of change. In fact, neither happened; instead, the reforms continued to deepen. After a two-year pause, a new stage of economic reconstruction began.

In the course of thirty years, China had passed through all stages, from revolutionary extremism to bureaucratic conservatism, and then to liberal-technocratic reforms. Because of the speed of this process some stages were superimposed on others, and various phases of development were combined. To paraphrase the remarks of Engels on Cromwell, it might be said that Mao was at once both the Lenin and the Stalin of the Chinese revolution (and also its Trotsky). Deng Xiaoping was not only the leader of de-Maoization, but had also been among the makers of the Maoist revolution.

Stalin died just eight years after the victory over Germany, while throughout the entire period after 1958 Mao could not boast of major successes. On the other hand, after Deng and the party old guard had lost their positions, they were not physically annihilated, and the power of their leader Zhou Enlai was untouched. Mao often refrained from pursuing the intraparty struggle to its final conclusion, and in addition, he quite consciously saved a number of revisionists from destruction, hoping that they might still prove useful. In the late 1960s and early 1970s, when the regime as a whole was conservative-authoritarian, it still retained certain features of revolutionary extremism. The speed and disorderliness of the movement destabilized the elite, and facilitated the transition to the reforms. The terror of the Cultural Revolution disorganized the upper echelons of society far more than its lower orders. The revolutionary shock which the country had experienced in the 1940s was still influencing the psychology of the Chinese, making both the elite and the masses more dynamic.

The reforms represented a reaction to the degeneration of the revolutionary regime. If the original revolutionary impulse had died away completely, the new elite would, after a few oscillations to the right and left, have found an optimum solution without much trouble. It would either have shifted to a conservative course, or else, after finally destroying the economy, would, as in the USSR, have set about privatizing whatever property was left intact. In China everything happened quite differently. The combination of instability at the top and pressure from below demanded experimental reform.

Craipeau noted correctly that the Deng group could not have consolidated itself in power if it had not enjoyed the unconditional support of the population.[46] Reforms from above became possible only thanks to pressure from below. Despite their mass character, the popular demonstrations did not pose a real threat to the existence of the regime. The bureaucracy controlled the situation, and in historical terms was irreplaceable; the country lacked the social and political forces capable of creating a new society. The protesting masses could not put forward a real alternative. After using the opposition for its own ends, the reformist wing of the elite tried to rid itself of its inconvenient allies. By the early 1980s the dissidents had once again been driven into clandestinity.[47] A campaign was launched against "spiritual contamination," understood to include Western ideological influences and free thought in general. "A motley collection of bourgeois ideas is being introduced into our philosophy and other social sciences. This has become a real fashion among theoreticians. Such pernicious ideas are a source of contamination in the theoretical field of the social sciences, a situation which has far-reaching consequences." The official press came down especially hard on scholars who under the guise of teaching Marxism were putting forward ideas of bourgeois liberalization, and also on young people who "subject to the influence of a series of ideas of bourgeois liberalization," were trying to evade their social obligations, and were "taking the road of the so-called 'liberation of the individual'."[48]

Even while suppressing dissidents, Deng continued to implement the most profound reforms from above in the history of the twentieth century. To go further within the political framework of leadership-controlled change would simply have been impossible without undermining the position of the ruling stratum itself. American journalists correctly observed that "what the leadership of Deng Xiaoping is doing is in many respects more revolutionary that what Mao Zedong did. This is an attempt, while avoiding bloodshed, to dismantle a large part of the Stalinist economic mechanism created by Mao and the party over thirty years."[49] The success of the Chinese reforms appears even more striking against the background of the economic catastrophe in Russia and Eastern Europe. Deng himself characterized the reforms of 1979–1984 as "a great revolution, radically altering the backward economic aspect of the country," and leading to "numerous changes in productive relations and the superstructure." Unlike the experiments of Stalin and Mao, the events in China in the 1980s amount to "a revolution not in relation to human beings, but in relation to the system." In this way, Deng concludes, "reform also represents revolution."[50]

It is impossible to deny the political wisdom of the Chinese rulers. If we compare Deng to Khrushchev, it is obvious how much more perspicacious and experienced the first was than the second. This cannot be explained simply as the result of intellectual superiority. Deng Xiaoping was the product of a different historical and cultural tradition; his statecraft did not emerge from a vacuum, but was based on China's long political history. If Indian and to some degree European culture, to quote the apt words of a Soviet philosopher, are characterized by "an obvious bias toward ontological searches for the secret of being, the main consideration for Chinese culture has been solving the problems of social ethics and political administration."[51] In Chinese political thought the notion of regulating society is completely traditional, but it is viewed on the level of a philosophical generalization. Confucian philosophy, which has held sway in China for many centuries, is notable for its ethical pragmatism. Even in the twentieth century, this tradition has, in the general view, been the main influence determining the political culture of state officials.[52]

Because of the use of Confucian terminology, Marxist and other European texts translated into Chinese have acquired some features of the ancient social wisdom. New ideas have enjoyed most success in determining people's thinking when it has been possible to express them "in the symbols of traditional culture."[53] As Sun Yatsen observed, "What is newest for Europe is not new for China."[54] The ideas and propositions of Western technocracy, in China, have been recast in the Confucian spirit. The ideology of modernization in China has had a far more profound effect than in other countries. Thanks to Confucian and, to some extent, Marxist influences, current political tasks have had to be brought into conformity with moral values and historical tradition.

One of the central ideas of Confucianism is that of rational changes, implemented by an enlightened authoritarian regime. For the reformist opposition that was taking shape even while Mao was alive, the study of Confucius provided ready-made ideological arguments. For this reason, the campaign to criticize Confucius that was organized in the early 1970s had a direct political point, and was aimed at supporters of technocratic reforms. However, the efforts of Mao to eradicate Confucianism from the Chinese consciousness with the help of a brief campaign of brainwashing was doomed to failure.

In prerevolutionary China, Confucian tradition was well-known and widely studied, but failed to work, since it did not aid in the working out of an ideology of reform, or in the rethinking or organic assimilation of Western theories. Historians recognize that although the Chinese legal system was permeated with Confucian ideas, the repetition of philosophic formulas was an empty ritual, and that, "for all the good intentions of the Confucianists," the wise precepts "played the role of a cover for what in reality was lawlessness."[55] As a result of the revolution, which dealt a fundamental shock to the whole edifice of Chinese society, the ruling bureaucracy acquired a certain dynamism. The Marxism which was grafted onto it allowed it to overcome the rationalist formalism of Confucianism without resorting to particularly primitive variants of technocratic ideology.

This applies as well to the lower orders of Chinese society. "The passive, taciturn Chinese masses, accustomed to suffering, were transformed spiritually thanks to their participation in guerrilla warfare," writes the British sinologist D. Robinson.[56] The old models of behavior and the old psychology were not replaced fully by new ones, but the traditions of submissiveness and subordination were rethought. Everything that conduced to effective action aimed at transforming the lives of the population was moved to the forefront, though even in times of armed struggle or cultural revolution the initiative for change came from above. The synthesis of revolutionary dynamism with Confucian values was the main distinguishing feature of Maoism, though the great helmsman set himself completely different goals. The revolution could not lead a backward country to socialism, but it helped bring about modernization. It did not give rise to fundamentally new methods and models for the exercise of power, but it renewed and refashioned traditional ones. In other words, the sources of the ideology of modernization in China were not Western ideas or traditional culture as such, but a revolutionary synthesis of both. Traditionalism, when renewed by revolution, became modernism.

The post-Maoist reforms in China can be seen as a deviation from revolutionary principles, as a liberalization, as a return to realism, and as the overcoming of errors. All these explanations are correct in their own way, but the central truth is that Deng's reformism was a continuation and culmination of Mao's policies, and the natural outcome of the revolution. The reformist restructuring testified to the fact that the revolutionary impulse was still alive.

Toward the end of the decade, China's dynamic development encountered a new crisis. The successful reforms finished up in massacres on the same Tienanmen Square on which Deng's rise to power had begun. The reforms had not only failed to create a socialist economy with specific Chinese features, but on the contrary, were increasingly forcing the country to live by the laws of developed capitalism. The new middle layers and the technocracy that had consolidated itself in the course of the transformations were inclined to the traditional scheme of modernization and to classical models of market ideology, but the more China came to resemble other backward developing countries, the worse things became. Deng's agrarian policies, which had been considered his greatest achievement, began unexpectedly to stumble. The reliance on small private farms justified itself so long as production could be increased through more intensive labor. But it soon became clear that without the use of new machinery and technology further progress was impossible. The peasants did not have the necessary funds. State purchases of the main types of agricultural produce at fixed prices could not ensure stable supplies of foodstuffs to the cities. The peasants preferred to produce more profitable goods. As growing grain and cotton became less and less profitable, the peasants began to use their resources for other ends. They raised more profitable crops such as tobacco and fruits, invested money in trade, and perhaps most frequently of all, simply spent their earnings: they built houses, and purchased consumer goods. Despite the decline in peasant investments in agriculture in 1984, production that year reached a very high level. In 1985 output of grain and cotton, the most important food and industrial crops, fell sharply, as they had done during the period of the Great Leap Forward. The level of 1985 has still not been regained. If in the early 1980s China had been an exporter of grain, now it has become a major importer.[57]

As a result of the setbacks suffered by their agricultural policies, the authorities were forced, as in Russia before collectivization, to strengthen their administrative pressure on the peasantry. They compelled the rural population to supply grain in quantities specified by the state. The peasants, in turn, resisted with all the means at their disposal, including murdering tax collectors. The country's financial position deteriorated. As the Hong Kong economist Yang Hai notes, the economic boom of the preceding decade had in fact been financed to a significant extent by huge internal and foreign loans.[58] Galloping inflation, overheating of the economy, the rapid growth of urban unemployment, and the new exacerbation of the food supply problem marked the end of the era of "wise reforms." Millions of people came out onto the streets of Beijing, demanding freedom and social justice. The government answered with massive repressions. A return to Stalinist orthodoxy in politics was the only means of defending technocratic pragmatism in the economy.

Even before the events on Tienanmen Square, the Deng Xiaoping regime brutally crushed the opposition in Tibet. The American R.D. Schwarz, who was an eyewitness to events in the late 1980s, wrote: "Hundreds of Tibetans were arrested, beaten, tortured in prison, then released several months later with no charges. Accounts from released prisoners indicate that torture was used during interrogation sessions primarily to intimidate and create an atmosphere of fear—not to extract confessions or gain information." The reformist regime's pragmatism was also apparent in the repressions. "Unlike in past, there is no attempt to legitimate repression through ideology—or to use ideology as an instrument of social control."[59]

On the night of the June 3, 1989, the same type of cynical repression was used against demonstrators on Tienanmen Square. The massacre carried out by Deng's forces shocked the world. Western corporations, however, unhesitatingly continued their collaboration with the Chinese government; foreign capital investments in the economy increased by 4.1 percent in 1989, while the international position of the Chinese state remained substantially unchanged.[60]

The events in Tienanmen Square vindicated the observers who had warned that what was happening in China under Deng was not democratization, but only a transition to a less ideologized form of military regime.[61] The market reforms continued, while the democratic opposition was crushed. Meanwhile, Chinese society during the years of reform became more complex, and more capable of recognizing its interests. On the agenda today is the question of new reforms—of reforms won by the popular movement, of a democratic revolution which would also open up new possibilities of progress toward socialism in China.

The repression undermined the people's trust in the ruling hierarchy, and discredited the ideas of market socialism proclaimed by the government. But subsequent events in Russia, and the chaos and economic collapse of the countries that took the path of liberal reform, could not fail to influence public opinion in China. In the words of the Chinese dissident Liu Binyan, "[T]he people are now giving the Communist government another chance."[62] In this situation, Liu concludes, the hope remains that there will be a new stage of democratic transformations, headed by reformist elements within the Communist Party itself.[63]

The Chinese drama possesses some features in common with the dialectic of revolution and reform in the developing countries. In third world societies revolution often precedes a period of reforms, rather than crowning it. Successful reforms can help to consolidate and stabilize the conquests of the revolution. Where the regime that arises out of the revolution proves incapable of transforming itself, degeneration and crisis ensue.

The experience of Cuba ultimately confirms this lesson. Cuba served for many years as a revolutionary model for a whole continent. The Cuban revolutionaries sought to make their country a laboratory where new forms of struggle were developed, and regarded their victory as the beginning of a radical restructuring of the entire third world. In 1959 Che Guevara argued that the revolution in Cuba was only the first step in the Latin American revolution.[64] The country's leaders declared their adherence to the principles of political freedom, and promised not to obstruct the development of private enterprise within the context established by the new laws. Initially, their words and deeds were not at variance. The government was dominated by moderate professionals, and elections were promised within two years. As an American author observed, the program of the original Castroism "was democratic, anti-dictatorial and anti-Communist."[65]

The Cuban revolution revealed the profound crisis of the Latin American Communist parties, showing the worthlessness of their political methods, and their inability to assess the local situation correctly. The Popular Socialist Party—the Cuban Communists—following the instructions and dogmas of its brother parties in power, ended up on the political sidelines, isolated from the events that were taking place.[66] The victory in Cuba was won through the methods of armed struggle, while the orthodox Latin American Communist parties had never supported guerrilla warfare. The leader of the Uruguayan Communists, Rodney Arismendi, admitted honestly that for his party the Cuban revolution had been a theoretical scandal.[67] Meanwhile, the Cuban revolutionaries were quickly transformed into arrant dogmatists. How did this degeneration take place? How did it happen, that after beginning their struggle in the name of new revolutionary ideas, the Cuban leaders finished up as ordinary Communist bureaucrats?

The original basis for the new revolutionary model was provided by Che Guevara in his writings. A number of ideologues, including such natives of the industrialized countries as Régis Debray and Andre Gunder Frank, then tried to set this model on a more solid theoretical footing. However, it was Guevara's ideas and actions that had the decisive influence on radical leftists in Latin America and throughout the world. In essence, Guevara's theories can be summed up in the well-known formula: "It is not always necessary to wait until all the conditions for a revolution ripen; a focus of insurrection can create these conditions."[68] In other words, even a country which is not ready for a socialist revolution can achieve this end if the appropriate political organization exists. As an Argentinian follower of Guevara explains, "Revolution is possible anywhere, if the revolutionary will capable of making it is present."[69]

Despite Che's Marxist language, his formula was repeatedly and justly disputed by Marxists. The important thing is not so much what Che says, as what he forgets to say. Before us is an example of a particular approach to revolutionary action, according to which a struggle can be launched without waiting for the corresponding socioeconomic and political project to be worked out.

For Che Guevara armed action (guerrilla warfare) and socioeconomic change represent not a means and an end, but two equally important stages in the revolutionary process. At first glance it seems logical that under conditions of authoritarian rule revolutionary struggle should prepare the way for social change. But in Che's theories each of these concepts occupies the rightful place of the other. The technical problem of guerrilla war—which arises, among other preconditions, only thanks to particular social processes—is moved to the forefront, replacing the problem of the mass movement. The essence of the first stage of a revolution never consists, anywhere, of armed action. The main development during this first stage is the formation of a massive social bloc calling for change. Whether this is accompanied by an armed uprising is a question of tactics. The struggle can take various forms, but its key element is nevertheless the development by the revolutionary vanguard of its historic project, capable of effectively mobilizing the masses.

Che Guevara maintained that armed action is capable of fulfilling not only military, but also sociopolitical and even cultural functions. Political questions are reduced to technical military ones. Debray recognizes that in the organizations established by left radicals in order to conduct guerrilla warfare, "the military training of cadres predominates over political instruction."[70] The seizure of power becomes the main strategic goal (in this respect the radical left ideologues of the 1950s and 1960s remained close to Leninist tradition), and the destruction of the old system becomes a more important task than the constructive implementation of one's own program. "The task was to take power," Che Guevara states. He acknowledges that it was only when the Cuban insurgents were on the verge of military victory that they took "the first steps" toward working out "the theory and doctrine of the revolution."[71]

During the uprising social and economic slogans were advanced, but these were no more than slogans. "Throughout all this period the banner of the struggle was agrarian reform. In principle it is possible either to indicate or not to indicate the tasks and limits of the reform, or else simply to refer to the legal right of the peasants to own the land they work."[72] A strategy for agrarian reform is not elaborated and is not discussed. When the radicals take power, they conceive of agrarian reform simply as redistribution of the land, failing to work out a strategy for the development of agriculture on a new basis. The reform can therefore have woeful results, or no results at all. In Cuba a significant sector of the peasants did not receive land. Soviet experts considered that dividing the latifundia into small plots was undesirable, and would have weakened the economy of revolutionary Cuba.[73] If this view was correct, then Castro's original plans were unrealistic, and if it was incorrect, Castro simply hoodwinked the peasants. Che Guevara was right after a fashion in the particulars of his theories, but tragically wrong on the main issues. It is possible to win a battle without mobilizing the masses, and in particular circumstances to mobilize the masses without putting forward a realistic program. But to win a revolution in this way is impossible. The more unjust the system, the greater the impatience of the revolutionaries. But when the system collapses, they are liable to find themselves in an extremely ambiguous position.

Gramsci wrote that revolutionaries who lack a precisely formulated program are merely working "for someone else's uncle," and "represent the ferment of a revolt which is certain to be monopolized by the most reactionary elements, while the latter with the help of the 'technicians' will ultimately prevail over all the rest." As evidence, Gramsci cited the experience of nineteenth-century Italy. The same occurred in Iran in 1978, and in Latin America. Yet another example is the fate of the dissidents and of activists in the democratic movements in Eastern Europe. In such situations, Gramsci continues, revolutionaries often turn into mercenaries, going over to the side of whoever is strongest, pays best, and so forth.[74]

When they launched their struggle, Castro, Guevara, and their group did not even pose the question of whether the productive forces in the country had matured sufficiently for socialism, or of what should be the strategy for revolutionary transformation. They believed that the crisis of capitalist development would automatically create the conditions for socialism. Castro did not burden himself unduly with ideological constructs; he had a guerrilla war to organize. Very soon, however, this approach was given a foundation in theory. The main work was performed by Andre Gunder Frank. Through his research into Latin American economic history, Frank showed that the cause of backwardness lay not in the survival of precapitalist formations, and not in the continuing domination of the countryside by semifeudal property relations, but in the dependent character of capitalist development. It was impossible to achieve economic independence and to overcome backwardness on the basis of the capitalist path. It was not feudalism that needed to be destroyed, but capitalism, Frank concluded.[75]

The link between dependency and backwardness was well known to Rosa Luxemburg. Frank merely repeated and simplified her arguments, showing once again with modern materials that in the third world the capitalist model does not work (or more precisely, that it "works" in favor of the industrialized countries and to the detriment of underdeveloped ones), while backwardness cannot be overcome by imitating Western models.[76] Socialism, in Frank's view, makes it possible to overcome backwardness, but what happens to a socialist project in conditions of underdevelopment?

The dependent nature of capitalist development is apparent, among other ways, in the survival of precapitalist property relations. To replace these relations with socialist ones is impossible without passing through a stage of transition. Russia and China have shown what happens when attempts are made to build socialism in backward countries and to accomplish various great leaps. The more the tasks taken on by the revolution exceed its powers, the more quickly the revolution degenerates. As in eighteenth century France, revolutionary extremism prepares the way for Thermidor and Bonapartist reaction. Frank repudiated "revisionism and reformism" of orthodox communist theory,[77] and spoke out against Stalinism and Maoism. But the strategy of the revolutionary spurt proclaimed by the radicals of the 1960s led ultimately to the same results. Representative democracy was condemned as antipopular. Socialists, Frank declared, had to make a choice: either to continue operating within the system of democratic institutions or to be outside it "with the people making the revolution."[78] In practice, counterposing the people to democracy means rejecting popular revolution. The mass movement does not always take on a democratic form right from the beginning, because, in the absence of institutions of representative democracy, capable of expressing the will of the people, the masses inevitably become objects of manipulation.

The crisis of the liberal state in Latin America has made the prospects of reform increasingly doubtful, and the formula of people's war more and more attractive. The long road through the institutions of the democratic system seems too difficult; the injustices are so gross that any slowing of the pace seems immoral, and appeals to moderation appear like treachery. Constitutional bourgeois governments have been unable to achieve modernization, while the social elite has been

inclined to authoritarianism. By the mid-1970s elected civilian governments existed in a number of countries of the region, but these
countries in most cases were far from being models of democracy.
Apart from tiny Costa Rica, the most stable constitutional regime was
the one in Mexico. Here there had not been a military coup d'etat for
some decades. Nevertheless election results were falsified, and the
facade of a liberal state with constitutional guarantees and a multiparty
system concealed one-party rule. The Institutional Revolutionary Party
held a total monopoly of power, and in essence had become inseparable from the state. The trade unions and major public organizations
were subordinated to the ruling party, in which no internal discussions
took place until 1988. Party members who were loyal to the leadership
were given jobs within the state apparatus. This was all very similar to
the Soviet *nomenklatura* system.

The American political scientist Gary Wynia notes that although
Mexico with its "unusual blend of democratic rules with corporativist
and authoritarian practices" represents a unique case, similar tendencies can be observed in other Latin American countries. For example,
"Venezuela remains more competitive than Mexico, though more and
more its competitors have come to resemble one another."[79] The same
could be said of Colombia, where the alternation in power of the
Liberal and Conservative parties has been supplemented by repression
in rural districts and by the transformation of illegal drug interests into
a major political force.

Against such a background, appeals for the mounting of a struggle
to bring about change within the existing constitution have appeared
unconvincing, to put it mildly. The success of the Cuban Revolution
gave birth during the 1960s to a mass of illusions, which undermined
the positions of moderate leftists. As a result there were more than a
few attempts to duplicate the Cuban experiment. Although they invariably failed, their lack of success was invariably explained as the result
of errors and of inadequate preparation. After all, Castro's first attempt
at an insurrection had not succeeded either.

In 1965, Che Guevara had declared that the whole continent would
be engulfed in revolution within five years.[80] The radical leftists explained that the proletariat had been forced to take the reformist road
in Europe since the state there is well-armed, and the progressive forces
had been unable therefore to begin revolutionary warfare. In the third

world, by contrast, there was no other option, since "the violence of the exploiter classes against the masses grows more vicious by the day." For all its viciousness, however, the state was unstable.[81] The weaknesses of the Latin American political system were seen as the system's particular advantage.

Che Guevara believed that an organization of revolutionaries could bring about an overturn in Latin America that would accelerate social development. In most countries the conscious factor played a diametrically different role. Armed action weakened the constitutional state, but this state was replaced not by the revolutionary power of the people, but by military-technocratic regimes. One of Che's Argentinian followers, P. Giussiani, acknowledged that a substantial sector of the population supported the state terrorism employed in order to put an end to guerrilla terror. The overall result was to reinforce "precisely those conditions that it was essential to change."[82] The insurgents helped the dictators come to power. As a British journalist noted, the right has more to gain from the presence of guerrillas than have the democratic center or the left.[83] In many cases, selfless revolutionaries "worked," objectively, for reaction.

The main argument against the ideology of the radical leftists was not the failure of armed action, and not the death of Che Guevara in Bolivia in 1967, but the failure of the attempts to build socialism in Cuba. The French sociologist A. Touraine described Latin American radicals as people "struggling for power which they will never exercise, since they will never become positive heroes."[84] Their tragedy consists not in their inability to take power, but in the fact that having taken it, they do not know what to do with it.

Stalinist groups in Latin America have never been able to seize power themselves. But they have often managed to exploit the victories of others. The radical leftists, by contrast, have at times taken power, but have finished up dependent on the Stalinists, whom they earlier despised for their inability to struggle. Even historians sympathetic to Castro recognize that he had no theory or ideology capable of serving as a basis for action.[85] The Stalinists lacked the revolutionary will for armed struggle, but they had a clear grasp of how to use power. They had a ready-made model. Their weak links with the masses were not an obstacle, since honest and determined revolutionaries were unintentionally working for them. When society finds itself in an impasse, power often passes not to the strongest or most popular party, but to the people who have the best idea of what needs to be done—to the people who have their own project, genuine even if crude, and who, in the words of Gramsci, possess a high level of strategic preparation. In this respect the Stalinists have always been stronger than the radical leftists.

The American scholar A. Silverman wrote that the changes in Cuba took place in a context marked by an acute contradiction "between revolutionary will and historical constraint."[86] Such a contradiction is present in all revolutions, but in Cuba the revolutionary will was not backed up by theoretical consciousness. Every revolution seeks to exceed the bounds of its direct historic tasks and to run ahead, but the Cuban Revolution, like a number of other third world revolutions, in general failed to recognize its historical tasks.

The victorious guerrillas could not manage the economy. Moral stimuli were intended to become the major form of incentives for workers in the new society.[87] The attempts to base economic life on revolutionary ethics had even worse consequences in Cuba than in China. The attempts to create artificial moral stimuli were in themselves evidence that workers' interest in their labor was declining. Castro and his followers had no new ideas to offer in the field of labor organization. They tried to begin at the end, as if hoping that the revolutionary ethic would by itself create the conditions for its own existence. Substantiating incompetent economic decisions with the help of "dialectics," they were guided by the same logic that produced the theory of the *foco*. (This theory is discussed in Chapter 6, below.)

Western and Soviet scholars agree that in the field of planning, the Cuban revolutionaries immediately made serious errors.[88] By 1961 the degree of utilization of productive capacity on the "island of freedom" stood at 54 percent. Ill-conceived industrial projects not only failed to advance the economy, but also depleted the country's resources and raised its dependency on exports. Most of the new enterprises turned out to be unprofitable. Soviet experts recognized that the nationalizations were extremely inefficient, since the state had not prepared "a real basis for the management of industry."[90] There was no strategy for developing the state sector. The Cuban dissident M. Sales described this period as a time of "catastrophic economic defeats."[90] In the words of Silverman, who is sympathetic to Castro, the consequences of the revolutionary experiment included "the spontaneous growth of the private sector and a corresponding rise of the black market; the exposure of corruption at the highest levels of the army and trade unions; the persistent growth of bureaucracy."[91]

The Castro government became increasingly dependent on Soviet aid. Stalinist tendencies grew stronger within the Cuban leadership. Even Che Guevara began quoting Stalin. The authorities warmed to the idea of replacing their unworkable revolutionary model with something more reliable. The choice was made in favor of tested Soviet methods. The final break was made after the defeat of the Prague spring. Repressions began to be carried out, and as usual, not even active participants in the revolution were spared.[92] Many of them finished up together with counterrevolutionaries in the Pinar del Rio concentration camp. The private sector was banned, the economy was subjected to bureaucratic control, and the remnants of workers' democracy were eliminated.

Leftists have often been inclined to lay the blame for what occurred on the Soviet Union, under whose influence Cuba deviated from the correct path. However, the decisive influence on the development of events in Cuba during the 1960s was not the policies of the Soviet Union but those of the United States. It was the position the United States adopted toward the "island of freedom" which determined the role the Soviet Union would play in Cuban life.

A.I. Alekseev, the first Soviet representative on the island, acknowledges that in 1959 "few of us knew what was happening in Cuba or what type of revolution it was, or who Fidel Castro was." The new authorities were in no hurry to strike up a friendship with the Russians. They did not even give Alekseev a visa for six months. When he arrived he was struck by the raging anticommunism and anti-Sovietism on the pages of the main organs of mass information; moreover, these declarations were often made by political figures who sided with the revolution.[93] Castro and his associates took every opportunity to differentiate themselves from the USSR, and in March 1959 Castro made a special trip to the United States, trying to induce American leaders to take a more benevolent attitude to his regime.

But in 1960, Washington's unyielding course forced Cuba to seek closer relations with Moscow. The British scholar Edward Crankshaw writes that "if anyone was thrown by unjustified actions into the embraces of Moscow, and denied any other choice, that person was Fidel Castro."[94]

In essence, Alekseev says the same. By cutting off oil supplies, the U.S. administration forced the Cubans to buy oil from the USSR, and then to nationalize the oil refineries in order to make indispensable technical changes to them. When President Eisenhower reduced purchases of Cuban sugar, the Castro government responded by nationalizing U.S. property. Earlier, in March 1960, the French ship *Le Coubre*, which had arrived in the port of Havana with a cargo of Belgian weapons and ammunition, was blown up by agents of American intelligence. "The blowing up of the ship *Le Coubre*, the refusal of Britain, under U.S. pressure, to supply promised aircraft and other types of armaments, and the unwillingness of the United States to solve the growing problems by peaceful means all served to exacerbate an already difficult situation. I can testify that prior to the sabotage of the ship, the question of military aid was not raised in our discussions with Cuban leaders, including in the discussions between Fidel Castro and Mikoyan." But after 1960, Alekseev continues, Castro "had no other choice."[95]

Nevertheless, the situation would have been completely different had power really lain in the hands of the popular masses. The Cuban emigrant Samuel Farber notes that while Castro enjoyed the broad support of the masses, the people were never allowed to take part in discussion or in the making of decisions. After the insurgents had taken power they remained a narrow, closed group, using the popularity of their leaders to manipulate public opinion. In this sense Castro was acting in full agreement with the principles of classical populism. "For at least two years Castro never offered, even to his most ardent followers, any specific program or long-range perspective explaining where he intended to go politically. His method was to make sudden decisions and then to present them to the people as *faits accomplis*."[96] Methods which had been successful when used by an armed group in the struggle for power had catastrophic consequences when they became a norm of political life for a whole society. Soviet aid could not compensate for the regime's inherent flaws. Experts who had come from the USSR noted that despite all their efforts, the island's economy was "characterized by fluctuating rates of growth not only in particular years, but also over five-year periods."[97] Castro could achieve successes in the fields of health care, education, and employment, and could reform the social structure—that is, he could carry out a series of the tasks of social modernization. This would have been impossible without the revolutionary shocks of 1959. The achievements of other Latin American states were more modest. But the Cuban economy could function effectively thanks only to the huge aid it received every day from the USSR. In a sense, Castro created the most dependent economy in Latin America. Cuba redistributed what it did not produce and was not capable of producing. In 1983 *Newsweek* stated gleefully that many of the people who had looked on the "island of freedom" as a model "now see an isolated Soviet dependency unable to pay its own food bills."[98] The crisis and collapse of the Soviet Union could not fail to have an effect on Cuba. The halting of aid brought an abrupt fall in living standards, and the economy was soon on the brink of catastrophe. History's verdict on the revolution, and Cuba's longer-term ability to play any role in Latin America, will depend on the way Cuba emerges from this crisis.[99]

The Cuban Revolution has shown once again the result of attempts to build socialism in a single backward country and "in the conditions of a hostile environment."[100] Nevertheless, the main dangers are concealed within the revolutionary process itself. The collapse of a radical utopia opens the way either for military dictatorship, or for Stalinist realism.

CHAPTER 6

THE REVOLUTIONARY MODEL: II

The failures of the revolutionaries of the 1960s did not mean the end of the movement. Ten years after Batista's overthrow in Cuba, changes began taking place in Peru. Here, events unfolded according to a totally new scenario. Everything began with the failure of armed action. The Peruvian army in 1965 and 1966 easily crushed a guerrilla struggle, but among the officers this war "not only failed to arouse feelings of hatred toward the guerrillas, but helped... shift their thinking to the left."[1] The army became infected with the ideology of those it had conquered. When Gen. Juan Velasco Alvarado seized power on October 3, 1968, the Italian scholar R. Einaudi observes, it was clear from the very beginning that this was no ordinary military coup. The officers knew that "the country was in need not of a coup d'etat, but of a revolution."[2] They promised that the revolution would create "a new socialist model, combining the desire for justice and equality with clear respect for human liberty."[3] Then followed the nationalization of North American firms, and the beginnings of agrarian reform. Two years later a number of state enterprises were placed under the control of the workers. Latin American sociologists note that the Peruvian military unhesitatingly "decided to demonstrate to the whole world the possibility of an intermediate model which would put an end to capitalist exploitation, but which simultaneously would not allow the victory of communist collectivism on the Soviet model. In other words, they called for a society of participation, in which all citizens would exert an influence on the economic, political, social, and cultural life of the country."[4] Or, as the officers themselves said, they were trying to create in Peru "social democracy with full participation."[5]

The left parties found themselves in an ambiguous position. As the sociologist Guillermo Rochabrun remarks, they constantly criticized the regime which was implementing changes without them. In fact, the main efforts of the leftists were aimed at distinguishing themselves from the military government, but both the leftists and the officers were guided by one and the same paradigm: developing the country along the lines of the industrialized societies.[6]

The Peruvian officers believed in the same ideals as the Cuban revolutionaries of the 1950s, but they constantly stressed their adherence to the traditions of Western civilization and their own uniqueness. "The Peruvian revolution is thus something original, unique, different from existing models and independent in its ideology."[7] External influences were in fact very significant, but the unwillingness to acknowledge them was readily explicable. The officers were seeking to make people conscious of the differences which marked Peru off from Eastern Europe and Cuba, which at this time was undergoing Stalinization. Unlike the 1968 Prague Spring, the Peruvian model was not based on a theoretical project, but had formed spontaneously out of a series of attempts at revolution. The Peruvian model was assessed in various ways. Castro declared that the Peruvian military had succeeded in carrying out a genuine revolution. Many people argued the opposite. Andre Gunder Frank maintained that after crushing the guerrilla forces, the army was incapable of carrying out "genuinely progressive and popular reforms."[8] The development of events spoke in favor of Frank's arguments rather than those of Castro. Participation by the masses in the changes that took place was minimal, and the changes themselves were superficial. Nevertheless, the military's actions clearly went beyond the bounds of ordinary reforms, acquiring, in Einaudi's words, "many features of revolution: the destruction of a political system, administrative reorganization, reform of land ownership and irrigation rights, nationalization of the most important foreign enterprises, diplomatic recognition of the Soviet Union—these were only some of the innovations."[9]

Workers' control in industry was supposed to ensure that the whole collective would share in profits and in management. But neither Peruvian industry nor the working class were ready for industrial democracy. The participation by workers in management remained limited and formal. Workers did not have a majority in the production councils. The heads of self-managed enterprises effectively transformed themselves into petty proprietors. Sharp conflicts arose in the modern plants, and the managements began coming under pressure from below. In cases where the workers really tried to make use of the rights they had received, their collectives were not simply weakened by the lack of unity on the basis of a general, democratically formed will, but were torn apart by contradictions.

The social sector did not come to dominate the economy, and despite the attempts to democratize management, bureaucracy proliferated. "The urge to decide everything from above led to an accumulation of 'minor problems' which a mass popular movement would quickly and effectively have solved on the spot. Attempts to create state mechanisms to solve such problems led to bureaucratization, especially since the old state apparatus was retained. People increasingly lost faith in the ability of the government to lead the revolution forward."[10]

The agrarian reform was more successful. Redistribution of the land was accompanied by the creation of a system of education in the countryside and by the forming of peasant organizations. By the middle of 1973 around 90 percent of all arable land in Peru had been expropriated and handed over to the peasants. Nevertheless, the military lacked a clear understanding of the long-term strategic tasks of the reform. The changes were accompanied by the destruction of the traditional models of land use, leading to a decline in production. Attempts to mobilize the peasant masses were unsuccessful, and organizations created from above failed to win the peasant's trust.

In 1974 and 1975 the regime entered into crisis. Until 1974 economic growth rates had been satisfactory, creating a sense of well-being in the military. The position then deteriorated sharply. Annual inflation reached 25 percent. Lacking a strategy of development, the authorities did not know how to overcome the growing difficulties. As in Cuba, the temptation grew stronger to retrieve the situation with the help of well-tried Soviet formulas. In July 1974 all of the national newspapers were nationalized, and the press was subordinated to the control of the authorities. Formally speaking, the newspapers were to be handed over to workers' organizations, but these promises were not fulfilled. The Italian Marxist G. Pascuino correctly suspected that a system of rule by "a single institutionalized party" was beginning to be established in Peru.[11] The Cubanization of Peru was underway.

The Stalinist Communist Party of Peru was the only left organization actively collaborating with the armed forces. Relations with the United States became increasingly tense, while links with Cuba and the Soviet Union grew closer. The famous Peruvian writer Mario Vargas Llosa sees one of the reasons for Cubanization in the fact that "the Peruvian army began to buy its armaments, its aircraft and tanks, not in the West but in the Soviet Union, Czechoslovakia and East Germany. And after these weapons came Cuban military advisers."[12] It was these advisers, in Vargas Llosa's view, that presented the main danger. In any case, groups inclined toward the Cuban model were forming within the army.[13] Dissatisfaction also increased among the workers and in the armed forces themselves. Purges in the army leadership could not avert new disagreements. To restore unity was now impossible. Under pressure from the opposition, headed by naval officers, General Velasco quit the post of president in 1975—to the great relief of Peruvian leftists. Elections in 1978 to a constituent assembly showed that the population were disillusioned. Velasco's supporters received only six positions, like the Communists. Other leftists received eighteen positions. A majority was won by the center and right.

After 1978 everything that had been established began quickly to be dismantled. Nevertheless, the revolution provided the basis for important political shifts whose true significance only became clear toward the middle of the 1980s. The nationalist and reformist American Popular Revolutionary Alliance (APRA), which had invariably found itself in opposition to the armed forces, turned sharply to the left, and Marxist currents that had grown stronger during the 1970s discussed the possibilities and purpose of reforms.[14] The terrorist organization *Sendero Luminoso*, which had expanded its activity in 1979 and 1980, failed to win support among the radical intelligentsia. Activists of the reformist left parties were among its victims.

The bourgeois government of Fernando Belaunde Terry, which came to power in 1980, was unable to solve any of Peru's problems. According to expert assessments, the country became poorer by a quarter during his five years in power. The bureaucracy grew to such an extent that it swallowed two-thirds of the state budget. A new shift to the left seemed inevitable. This time there was little talk of a quick dash toward socialism. Peruvian political scientists note that a striking similarity existed between the programs of the Marxist United Left coalition and of APRA, and that "there was nothing in them that might not have been found in a plan adopted by the armed forces in the years from 1971 to 1975."[15] Most of the tasks that had been posed but not carried out by the revolution of 1968 were now meant to be solved through reformist means under conditions of representative democracy.

Debray often used the expression "a bet with history." It could be said that during the 1960s the left radicals lost their bet. Alternative roads for the development of the revolution all seemed dead ends— either restoration or Cubanization. The resort to violence had not justified itself, and the strategic impotence of the radicals had been evident at all stages of the struggle. But more moderate forces had not scored successes during this period either. The Chilean revolution had tried to implement socialist measures, using methods that were constitutional and, to a degree, reformist. The debacle of this revolution and the resulting death of President Salvador Allende exerted a powerful influence on the strategy of leftists both in the West and in the third world. It is true that the conclusions drawn were quite diverse. In the West the experience of Chile was seen as an argument in favor of moderation. The Chilean events provided an impulse for the Italian Communists to develop their strategy of historic compromise. The party came to the conclusion that a prolonged period of reformist work was needed in order to avoid "a schism in the country that could lead to events like those in Chile."[16] In Latin America, by contrast, Allende's defeat was perceived as an argument against reformism. The idea of armed action, which had been discredited in the late 1960s, again became popular. The ideology of revolutionary radicalism appeared to receive its second wind. After 1973 the argument was heard more and more often that for any liberation struggle on the continent "armed struggle was indispensable."[17] Even Communists took the position that armed struggle represented the main road of the revolution.[18] Allende's downfall overshadowed that of Che. The savagery of the Chilean junta pushed concern over the Cuban repression into the background. General Pinochet's butchery helped restore Castro's good name.

The resurgence of calls for armed struggle was a return to the level of thinking of the early 1960s. Vargas Llosa spoke of this with irritation. "In Western Europe, a healthy re-evaluation of values is occurring among left-wing intellectuals," he noted. Meanwhile, Latin American radicals were responding to events with primitive reflex actions, "like Pavlov's dog." Vargas Llosa complained that as a result he had "lost all illusions."[19] The Peruvian writer could not himself suggest anything except half-hearted reforms in the spirit of European social democracy. Later, disappointed with this as well, he turned to neo-liberalism, and even became the candidate of the right wing in the presidential elections.

In criticizing the radicals, Vargas Llosa failed to understand that in the third world, reformism must inevitably take on a revolutionary form. Radicalism arises out of objective circumstances. The leader of the Guatemalan socialists declared: "In order to achieve the most insignificant reform in Central America, a revolution is needed."[20] In one degree or another, this applies to almost the entire third world.

At the basis of radical ideas lie desires which in their essence are reformist. Analyzing early statements by the young Castro, Craipeau noted that his actual ideal was "serious reform, not revolution."[21] However, this type of reformism remained unconscious. In 1968 one of the Latin American leftists openly confessed that revolutionaries had not given a clear answer to the question of "how to make a qualitative definition of the changes for which we are striving, and of the direction in which we want to move."[22] The Argentinian sociologist A. Mercer Vega argues that in Latin America in general, "there is nothing resembling a revolutionary tradition in the socialist sense of the word," and that the phenomenon of guerrilla warfare simply confirms this. "There are serious reasons to think that socialist labels are being attached to policies and methods that are internally contradictory, since the forces that are struggling for power are concerned less with doctrine than with the effectiveness of their actions."[23] The radical and socialist approaches are interconnected, but are not identical. The measure of effectiveness for radicals, unlike socialists, is not the fulfillment of a strategic program, but the seizure of power.

As early as the 1920s, the outstanding Peruvian Marxist José Carlos Mariátegui wrote that the Latin American bourgeoisie remained semi-feudal, and incapable of ensuring social progress: "The bold, enterprising character, the striving to create, and the powers of the organizer that are characteristic of a real capitalist, are almost unknown among us."[24] Half a century later, Dos Santos observed that the traditional elites of most Latin American countries did not possess the historical capacity for renewal.[25] The middle-class masses are excluded from power either by old oligarchies or by the technocratic elite. The liberal traditions and culture which the middle layers established back in the nineteenth century clearly contradicted the authoritarianism of the ruling groups. The left intelligentsia and the technocrats were born of one and the same social layer, but moved in diametrically different directions. The contradiction within the middle layers between the elite and the lower orders is growing more acute as the middle layers expand and become more developed. The elite is moving to the right, and the lower orders to the left. Rodney Arismendi considered this "an important factor in the Latin American revolution."[26]

Latin America traditionally outstripped other regions of the third world not only in its level of economic development, but also in its cultural preconditions. Western culture here is not alien. A number of countries, including Argentina, Uruguay, Chile, and Brazil, have already crossed the threshold of industrial society, though without overcoming their dependency on the states of the center and on transnational capital. Radical leftists point to the exhaustion of the possibilities of capitalist development and to its antinational character. This was quite obvious back in the 1960s. Since then there has not been a single capitalist society on the continent that has escaped a crash, and not one that has managed to solve the problem of backwardness. Despite the broad publicity given to the successes of development, the gap between the center and the periphery even increased during the course of the 1980s. The attempts at modernization within the framework of capitalism proved ineffective. As a Soviet author noted correctly, the social price of such modernization is excessively high. "The people are not able to bear the socioeconomic and political pressure that weighs on them over a period of ten, fifteen, or twenty years."[27] Dependent capitalism is in an impasse. Unless economic relationships are changed, backwardness cannot be overcome.

To compensate for the instability of the model of capitalist modernization, military force and other repressive measures are employed. The fight against authoritarian regimes implies a struggle for changes in the model of development. This struggle cannot be successful without the participation of broad masses of the population. The ruling circles defend dependent capitalism, while the mass movement counterposes to it an anticapitalist and socialist ideology. The incompetence of the old elites and the authoritarianism of the new lead to the radicalization of the most dynamic and democratic layers of the population. Whether or not the country has ripened for socialism, it has ripened for revolution, and this revolution is natural and legitimate. The task of carrying through the revolutionary transformation resides with the working masses and the left intelligentsia. Inherent in both is an elemental striving for the socialist ideal.

Although capitalism no longer works, socialism is still impossible. Every revolution goes beyond the bounds of its direct historic tasks, but the more serious this running ahead, the worse the actual historical tasks of the revolution are carried out, and the less are its results. This not only destabilizes the revolutionary process, but also gives birth to false consciousness, and in the final analysis plays into the hands of the new oligarchy that is taking shape—an oligarchy of exploiters of the revolution. A discrepancy arises between the real content of the historical process and the ideology of its participants. The objective need for socialist ideology and for reforms that exceed the bounds of the capitalist model give rise to the illusion that the revolution becomes socialist from its first day, or at any rate, that it is able to ensure "a continuous progress toward socialism, though one marked by stages."[28] The transitional stages are depicted as very short. If they are mentioned at all, it is only for the purposes of stressing the need for their "close linkage."[29]

Latin American leftists are scarcely exaggerating when they assert that any attempt to bring about revolutionary changes on the continent "cannot fail to place in question the very bases of the capitalist system."[30] But this is not yet a guarantee of the triumph of socialism. It was not by chance that in Havana in 1982 the participants in a theoretical conference of Latin American leftists clearly tried to avoid the question of the degree of readiness of the productive forces for socialism.

Nothing good has come of attempts to build socialism on the basis of backwardness. But to postpone socialist transformations until better times is impossible. The crisis of dependent capitalism inevitably places before society the question of alternative paths of development. Without such elements of socialism as democratic planning, the participation of workers in the management of state enterprises, the expansion of social property, and cooperation in agriculture, an alternative model of development is impossible. And the more effectively such methods are applied, the more successful development will be. Many left ideologues have had a distinctly peculiar understanding of Lenin's remark that the main question in any revolution is the question of power. They imagine that solving the question of power allows one to solve all the other problems as well. Once power is "in our hands" and "the people are with us," then "the revolution cannot survive unless it advances toward socialism."[31] In this connection, it is worth recalling the words of Engels: "The worst fate that can befall the leader of an extreme party is to be forced to take power at a time when the movement still has not matured sufficiently for the class which it represents to exercise hegemony, and when the measures needed to ensure this hegemony still cannot be implemented. What such a leader is able to do depends not on his will, but on the level which the contradictions between the various classes have reached, and on the degree of development of the material conditions of life, of the relations of production and exchange, which invariably also defines the degree of development of class contradictions. Moreover, what this leader must do, and what his party demands of him, again depends neither on the leader himself, nor on the degree of development of the class struggle or on the conditions to which this struggle gives birth. It is connected with the doctrines and demands which the leader has advanced earlier, which once again flow not from the given relationship of social classes, and not from the given, more or less fortuitous state of the conditions of production and exchange, but which are the fruit of his more or less profound understanding of the general results of the social and political movement. He is thus inevitably faced with an insoluble dilemma. What he is able to do contradicts all his previous actions, his principles, and the direct interests of his party. Meanwhile, what he must do is unrealizable. In short, he is forced to represent not his own party, and not his own class, but that class for whose rule the movement has matured sufficiently at a particular moment. In the interests of the movement itself, he must defend the interests of a class which is alien to him, and must divert his own class with phrases, promises, and assurances that the interests of another class are his own. Anyone who once falls into this position is irretrievably lost."[32]

The degeneration of the Castro regime provides a superb illustration of Engels's thoughts. The more resolutely leftists strive to carry the revolution through to the end, the more they are working for people alien to them. The formation of a new oligarchy is the natural result of these efforts. The position is aggravated by the cult, which is traditional in Latin America, of the strong national state and the tough popular leader—statism and caudillism. For many people in Latin America socialism appears as "a state monopoly serving the broad masses," or as "a monopolistic system of state production."[33]

The collapse of capitalism is always fraught with the return of various precapitalist structures, especially if these structures were not completely destroyed earlier. The process may include the rise of repellent forms which represent a step backward even in relation to capitalism (Marx noted this possibility even in his early draft writings on communism). The more backward a country, the greater the likelihood that this will be the case. After the numerous attempts at revolution during the 1960s and 1970s, many leftists were forced to state: "There is a real danger that under existing conditions a revolution will make the position of the working masses even worse; it is enough to recall the examples of Iran and Kampuchea."[34]

"At best, in such circumstances," writes a British Marxist, Nigel Harris, "the rebels could achieve only temporary amelioration, even if they persuaded themselves that this was a fundamental triumph. Too often, the victory provided no more than the prelude to a more fundamental defeat. The workers of Karachi and elsewhere defeated Mr. Bhutto, but General Zia inherited power. The mass of Iranians overthrew the Shah, but one section of the Ayatollahs inherited. The mass of Vietnamese battled, but at the end, it was the Party which remained supreme."[35]

The contradictions of the revolutionary process in the third world could not fail to affect the development of the Sandinista movement in Nicaragua. According to historians, the Sandinistas at first were completely lacking in a clear program, and "acted under the influence of their emotions, according to the commands of their hearts and consciences. This was a spontaneous reaction to the difficult lives of the people, crushed beneath the weight of the pro-imperialist dictatorship. The young heroes dreamt of kindling the fire of a popular guerrilla movement, but to do this turned out to be far from simple."[36] Armed struggle in the *foci* had been carried on unsuccessfully since the early 1960s. As early as 1958, following the example of the Cuban insurgents, a group of opponents of the Somoza dictatorship organized the First Army of Liberation of Nicaragua on the territory of neighboring Honduras. This formation was crushed, like the group around E.L. Farfan that had been operating from the territory of Costa Rica. Between 1960 and 1962 fighters of the Sandinista National Liberation Front (FSLN) succeeded in gaining a foothold on Nicaraguan territory and in establishing a guerrilla concentration, a *foco*. However, this did not have the expected results. It turned out that the presence of a foco in itself had no effect on the development of the revolutionary process.

The history of Nicaragua showed the real meaning of the struggle in and through the foco. The idea of a foco of guerrilla war had been known long before Che Guevara, as had the concept of the ripening of the preconditions for revolution in the course of the struggle. As early as 1939 Mao spoke of armed struggle by a vanguard which would become "a factor accelerating the onset of the revolutionary upsurge in the country." He even used similar figures of speech. The whole theory of the foco is implicit in the Maoist slogan "A single spark can start a prairie fire."[37] Mao understood perfectly the real political significance of guerrilla warfare. In the special region that had been seized through his efforts, he devoted most of his attention to organizational work. This was because he appreciated that what comes into being in the foco is not a peasant war, and still less a revolution, but an organization capable of seizing power.

If an organization is viable, it can wait for years for its hour to come round—that is, until the old regime begins to fall apart from the effects of its own internal crisis. Then the political force that has grown up in the foco can fill the vacuum of power. This was how Pol Pot seized control of Kampuchea, and this was how the anticolonial movements achieved victory in Algeria, Angola, and Mozambique.

The Sandinistas succeeded in creating links between the actions of the guerrillas and the spontaneous movement of the masses. But before this came fifteen years of unsuccessful struggle, of constant failures and of political ineffectiveness. The revolutionary situation in the country came about quite independently of the actions of the guerrillas. From 1969 to 1979 the country experienced a period of rapid economic development. Industrialization and urbanization proceeded so rapidly that they outstripped the average indices for Central America. Gross domestic product almost doubled. All this was accompanied by a sharpening of the contradictions to be found in most developing countries. So long as the growth in output continued at a rapid pace, it was possible in one way or another to soften social tensions, but in 1978 and 1979 the economic growth was replaced by decline. All the contradictions emerged at once. Production fell by 7.2 percent, and later by 25 percent. Unemployment reached levels between 40 and 50 percent of the economically active population. Strikes and peasant revolts began breaking out. The Somoza government failed to take effective anticrisis measures, preferring to strengthen the repressive apparatus; this represented "a simpler course and one which, moreover, brought large profits to a broad circle of people, from arms traders to local bureaucrats."[38]

The national bourgeoisie proved incapable of bringing about changes. The motley Democratic Union for Liberation, uniting liberal and left organizations, did not present a real alternative. The Communist and Socialist parties did not possess any serious influence among the masses; the Socialists were distinguished by having even more Stalinist views than the Communists. Neither of these currents played a significant role in the struggle against the dictatorship, at times trying to conduct a dialogue with Somoza and at other times to play the role of a legal opposition.[39] The Sandinista Front turned out to be the only organization capable of heading a movement that had arisen spontaneously. Its strength lay not in a considered political strategy, but in its resolve to fight. More than this was not required at the time. The political vacuum had been filled.

By the late 1970s the Sandinistas were no longer the naive idealists who fifteen years earlier had tried to repeat the experience of Castro. In 1975 the leaders of the front had published a serious self-criticism, citing "a lack of analysis and research into the concrete historical reality of Nicaragua," "sectarianism," and "militarism and adventurism."[40] The dominant position in the leadership was held by the *tercerista* faction. If at first the Sandinistas' views had differed little from those of the young Castro, after the period from 1975 to 1977 new elements appeared in Sandinista ideology. Cuba was no longer the ideal. The Nicaraguan revolutionaries began to think seriously about how to stop the regime degenerating after the victory. Alongside the armed struggle, more attention began to be paid to political work, including preparations for a union with the opposition bourgeoisie.[41] The program became not only more moderate, but also more concrete. As observers noted, the Sandinistas drew lessons both from the errors of the Cuban Revolution and from the failures of the Allende government in Chile.[42] Political mobilization of the masses, direct democracy, and the creation of a new revolutionary army had to be combined with ideological pluralism, constitutional freedoms, and a mixed economy. The Sandinistas stressed that they did not intend to jump across stages.[43]

The program of agrarian reform was carried out using land confiscated from the Somoza family and its close collaborators, and also uncultivated land from the *latifundia*. The state sector of industry was also created on the basis of confiscated Somocista property and through the construction of new enterprises. An effort was made to avoid touching foreign property except in cases of extreme need. The Sandinistas also managed to avoid the industrial psychosis. After taking power, the Sandinistas did not set out to build gigantic plants and to force the pace of economic growth through artificial methods.

Local entrepreneurs received substantial credits from the government. After taking power, the Sandinistas hoped to divide the bourgeoisie and isolate the right-wing elements by pursuing a policy of social partnership. As Latin American sociologists acknowledged, the Nicaraguan bourgeoisie "lost its hat, but not its head."[44] At first this tactic proved fruitful. Even the right-wing newspaper *La Prensa* declared in 1978 that entrepreneurs and the prospective revolutionary regime had concerns in common.[45] But the policies of the Sandinista Front, which consisted of several factions, could not be consistent. The German journalist R. Gauger wrote: "From time to time the FSLN flings itself on the bourgeoisie with a ferocity that is in contradiction to the front's whole tactical course. These cases are relatively rare, but they create an impression of uncertainty, of a lack of ideas, and give rise to spontaneous reactions which have a powerful influence on the front's relations with the bourgeoisie. At one point the Sandinistas characterize the bourgeoisie as a mortal enemy, and at another as a comrade in arms and an ally." The weakness and confusion of the bourgeoisie itself at first left the Sandinistas with "a good deal of room for maneuver, so that it proved possible to survive these contradictions."[46] The economic situation began to improve. During the early years of Sandinista rule, from 1979 to 1983, unemployment fell from 35 percent to 16 percent. Infant mortality decreased from 12 percent to 9 percent, and illiteracy from 60 percent (in rural areas, 68 percent) to 12 percent. The London *Times*, which was not noted for sympathy to the revolutionaries, acknowledged that although at the time when the dictator fell the country had been in a frightful state, thanks to the efforts of the Sandinistas the difficulties had been partly relieved.[47] The revolution was supposed to allow the Nicaraguan leftists to proceed much further along the social democratic road than had the European social democrats. As one of the Sandinistas declared, the socialized sector in Nicaragua would "in its size, though not its relative importance, be comparable to those in many countries of Western Europe." In the final analysis, however, everything depended on how "the question of the effective political organization of society" was resolved.[48]

Sandinista ideologists repeated more than once that their revolutionary model differed from that of Cuba, insisting that "the revolution here is not communist."[49] The Communist Party was seen as an opposition force. It was accused of attempting to bind the country to a course in contradiction to the principles of the revolution, and of using its influence in the trade unions to conduct "systematic sabotage."[50] The party was not banned, but some of its activists were subjected to persecution.

The policies of the Sandinistas during these first years received the support of Western leftists ranging from social democrats to revolutionary Marxists. The moderation and commitment to democracy of the Sandinista Front promised to become a model for progressive forces in the third world, an example worthy of imitation. It was this which posed a serious threat both to the interests of North American capital and to local oligarchies in Latin America and throughout the third world. If Nicaragua had become a second Cuba, or if another dictatorship had appeared there, this would not have been especially dangerous to the ruling circles in the United States. But the successfully functioning revolutionary-reformist regime in Nicaragua represented a real challenge to the entire system of dependent capitalism. Hence the coming to power of the conservative administration of Ronald Reagan was accompanied by a rejection of the initial neutrality with regard to the Sandinistas. The counterrevolutionaries received money and weapons with which to begin a war against Nicaragua.

If Washington's policy with relation to Cuba in 1959 and 1960 can be explained as the result of political errors and of a failure to understand what was happening, this cannot be said of U.S. policy with regard to Nicaragua. Western journalists acknowledged that the military actions against the Sandinistas were organized in order to "force the authorities in the country to postpone elections."[51] As a British observer noted, the Nicaraguans quickly came to suspect that the United States was simply pushing them where they themselves did not intend to go.[52] The Reagan administration was clearly trying to force the Nicaraguan leadership to take the Cuban path.

At first everything proceeded according to Washington's scenario. The Nicaraguans turned for aid to the countries of the Eastern bloc and Cuba. A state of siege was imposed, and democratic rights were restricted. The opposition press began to be subjected to censorship, though the main bourgeois daily *La Prensa* was not banned, perhaps because it was published by the Chamorro family, members of which were also in charge of the pro-Sandinista papers *Barricada* and *Nuevo Diario*. The independent trade unions were not outlawed, though they were subjected to harassment.

In the provinces, the position of oppositionists became especially difficult. Local Sandinista Defence Committees collaborated with the Interior Ministry headed by Tomás Borge in intimidating people who expressed dissatisfaction. Sandinistas themselves described Borge's apparatus as the "ministry of repression."[53] In the early 1980s the Interior Ministry grew into a real political force. The number of its personnel increased substantially, and Borge became the main champion of the hard line. Stalinist groups inside and outside the FSLN, resting on the growing military-repressive bureaucracy, quickly consolidated their positions in the political structures of the republic.

The tougher the measures employed, the greater the ranks of the dissatisfied. The church, the entrepreneurs, and sections of the working class and peasantry went over to the opposition. The regime's international isolation increased. Western social democrats and constitutional governments in Latin America criticized Nicaragua. The revolutionary leadership came to depend more and more on the support of the military-repressive apparatus within the country and on Soviet and Cuban aid. The ideology of the front, and the psychology of its leaders, began to change. As Gauger wrote, the FSLN was in fact the leading force within the popular movement, but it began gradually to claim to be the sole possessor of the truth. The process of Cubanization became self-reproducing. "The disappearance of unpleasant news from the FSLN mass media has meant that anyone who wants objective information turns to the bourgeois press, to the newspaper *La Prensa*, to the bourgeois radio stations, or to the left-wing newspaper *El Pueblo*. The political education of the masses, conducted with the help of endless ceremonious and salutatory orations, showed the lack of confidence of leaders afraid that they would be incapable of fulfilling their own promises." As Gauger noted, the government was becoming increasingly inclined to seek bureaucratic solutions, and was departing ever further from its "proclaimed goal of a free and just society."[54]

An analogous process was occurring on the Caribbean island of Grenada, where the revolutionary New Jewel Movement came to power almost simultaneously with the Sandinistas. A British researcher wrote that the aggressive policies of the United States were "rendering the social experiment in Nicaragua and on Grenada far more difficult. One American official summed up the U.S. role in the region very accurately: 'We're like an elephant in the living room. Even if we don't move, ignoring us is impossible.' But of course, the elephant has never been totally immobile, and after the Nicaraguan revolution it began to stir dramatically."[55] In the society of tiny Grenada all the processes went ahead more quickly than in Nicaragua, and had a completely catastrophic outcome.

The anglophone territories of the Caribbean have never had much in common with Latin America. Not only the local ruling classes, but most of the population as well have been oriented to British traditions. After decolonization, close links remained with the former metropolis. The constitutions were drawn up on the British model, in a number of cases including a vice-regal governor-general. Grenada remained a member of the British Commonwealth, but the political situation that developed here was markedly different from that on the neighboring islands. In most Caribbean countries an influential social democratic party arose. Several of these parties, for example in Jamaica, have even succeeded in winning and holding power for certain periods. Even Guyanese leader Forbes Burnham, a dictator and embezzler who seized power with the help of the United States, permitted a legal opposition to exist in his country.[56] On Grenada, however, the dictatorship of Sir Eric Gairy exercised power from the first days of independence. Corruption, arbitrariness, and the systematic violation of human rights were the rule in the country. "This mechanism was based on the broad use of police terror and repression both against opposition organizations, and against particular individuals."[57]

Attempts to create a legal opposition party—the Jewel Movement—were ruthlessly crushed. Since the parliamentary road was closed, the leftists were compelled to answer violence with violence. The Jewel party fused with the Marxist People's Assembly movement to form the New Jewel Movement, led by Maurice Bishop. The choice in favor of armed struggle was an involuntary one. As the opposition leaders declared, very few people on Grenada thought that the corrupt Gairy regime would hand over power at elections.[58] Armed struggle, on the other hand, brought quick and easy success. In 1979 the regime fell, and Gairy fled to the United States. "After him," wrote a British conservative journalist, "the moderate Marxist Maurice Bishop undoubtedly seemed more attractive, despite his forcible seizure of power and the fact that the new government did not legitimize itself with the help of elections."[59]

Free education and health care were introduced, social welfare was improved, and strikes were permitted. The state sector was expanded mainly through new construction. Bishop, like the Sandinistas, oriented toward a mixed economy, avoiding ill-thought-out nationalizations. Representatives of the bourgeoisie were brought into the government, and within the bounds foreseen by the national plan, foreign capital was sought in order to serve the needs of development. Although the party's program called for nationalization of the banks, Bishop did not make haste with this. The government's main tasks were to increase tourism and to carry out agrarian reform. The revolutionaries were concerned that the growth of the modern sector should not lead to the destruction of traditional ties in the countryside, to the collapse of the rural economy, and to mass flight to the towns. Tourism had to be developed in a gradual and orderly fashion, maintaining close links with local production.

To many people, Bishop seemed excessively moderate. A British journalist wrote that in the words of Bishop's London friends, he was less like a Marxist than "a sort of social democrat."[60] In reality, Bishop was one of the few third world revolutionaries to have mastered not just Marxist terminology, but also Marxist theory. The new regime's moderation was based on a clear understanding of the historic tasks of the revolution. "Calm and cautious where most other third world revolutionary regimes have been demagogic, and determinedly abstaining from the repression that has marked many other transitions, the New Jewel Movement has set an example to the English-speaking Caribbean," a British scholar notes.[61] The fact that Bishop succeeded in achieving a good deal was due precisely to his adherence to Western democratic traditions. Even writers unsympathetic to Marxism recognized that the new government of Grenada brought together half the talented people on the island.[62]

The revolution went ahead, but many people on the island remained unchanged, reported the London *Observer*.[63] Grenada remained a British dominion, while the radical prime minister maintained close contacts with the British Governor-General Sir Paul Scoon, his former teacher. Although liberal state institutions were not fully restored after the fall of Gairy, nothing indicated that the government intended to break with British legal traditions. As Fred Halliday noted in *New Left Review*, pluralism in Grenada, as in Nicaragua, was limited, but real. In Halliday's view, this was the revolution's main "ideological attraction."[64]

Pluralism on Grenada was still more limited than in Nicaragua, since there was no legal opposition. The New Jewel Movement contained various factions. According to Western observers, they included both left centrists and "extreme supporters of Moscow or Havana."[65] But they were all united in a single party organization whose membership never exceeded three hundred people from among the island's population of 110,000. Bishop was very proud of having repealed a law forbidding the use of loudspeakers during pre-election campaigns, but what significance could this have if free elections were not held? The masses participated in deciding local questions, but direct democracy could not replace traditional representative institutions. Beneath the cover of direct democracy, the totalitarian threat was ripening.

Although Bishop dreamed of a genuine democracy of participation, this goal remained unattainably remote. The organs of self-government became bureaucratized, and were transformed into tools for the manipulation of the masses.[66] Both the left democrats and the Stalinists were minorities within the ruling party. The radical majority, which was incapable of formulating its own project, could incline in one direction or the other. Bishop and his closest associates shared many of the illusions of the left radicals, and underestimated representative democracy.[67] American interference played a role here as well. When Grenada appealed for military aid to Canada, Britain, and the United States, it was refused. Fearing that mercenaries hired by Gairy would land on the island, the government turned to Cuba. Later, many people were to argue about how many Cubans were on Grenada and how they were armed. However, the instrument of Cubanization was the Grenadan People's Revolutionary Army (PRA) itself. The training and control were mainly in the hands of Cubans, about forty of whom had been sent to Grenada as instructors. Some military aid was provided by small groups of experts from East Germany, North Korea, Libya, and the Soviet Union, but the main model for Grenada was the Insurrectionary Armed Forces, the Cuban army.[68] A people's militia was also formed on the Cuban model, but here the influence of the Stalinists was weaker. When supporters of Cuba seized power, they preferred to disarm the militia members.

The military structure, formed on the Cuban model, inevitably became a factor of Cubanization, having an impact on all of the country's social and political life. Some people suggested that Fidel Castro did not want Central America to repeat certain of his mistakes.[69] However, Castro did not heed Bishop's requests, and did nothing to rein in his followers on Grenada. After Bishop returned from Cuba in 1983, these followers staged a coup. The leader of the party and his supporters were denounced as "friends of imperialism" and "counterrevolutionary elements" who were unwilling to observe "democratic centralism." The island's new rulers declared their intention of transforming the New Jewel Movement "from a heterogeneous grouping of radicals and nationalists into a disciplined vanguard party, founded on Marxism-Leninism."[70]

The Grenadan masses met the coup with open resistance. A crowd freed Bishop and carried him on their shoulders. The armed forces opened fire. Bishop was again arrested, then shot together with two of his ministers and a trade union leader. Then followed the landing by American marines and the final downfall of the revolution. The American invasion did not meet with serious resistance. Those who fought back were mainly Cubans; the Grenadans were unwilling to die for "the murderers of Maurice." "If Bishop had not been killed," says Kendrick Radix, a former New Jewel Movement leader, "there would have been serious resistance. But the people who killed Bishop killed the revolu-tion as well."[71] This was not so much a military defeat as an ideological and psychological one. In 1984 the leftists on Grenada failed to win even a single seat in parliamentary elections—a catastrophic result even taking into account the fact that the expression of the popular will was not completely free. "Bishop himself was elevated onto a pedestal," notes a British journalist, "but the achievements of his regime in the fields of health care, education, and water supply now appear less attractive since together with these progressive measures came machine-guns, Cubans, murder, and a brief war."[72]

Castro described the murder of Bishop as a crime, by which he was profoundly outraged. "We refrained totally from interfering in the internal affairs of the Grenadans," he stressed, adding that the Cubans "could not have left Grenada under any pretext."[73] This provided the basis for a Western journalist to argue that the coup on Grenada had been approved by the Soviet Union, but not by Cuba.[74] The Soviet leadership made no comment, leaving the Cubans to justify themselves.

Whatever he might have wished, Castro could not deny that the putschists had been friends of Cuba. "Castro's expressions of shock and dismay at his Marxist protégé's execution were apparently genuine," an American journalist acknowledges. But for all that, "Cuba had been trying to strengthen its hold of Grenada by replacing Bishop. The plotters were Grenadan army leader General Hudson Austin and Deputy Prime Minister Bernard Coard—both found to have strong links with Cuba."[75]

In 1982 the Cuban commentator J. Luna wrote that, as Grenada showed, a revolution could "be born, survive, and develop" even in a small country.[76] Life proved the opposite. An isolated country is inca-pable of making a victorious revolution, if only for the reason that it will not succeed in hitting the brakes and going over to a reformist course in time to stabilize the progressive successes of the new regime. Even if this condition is fulfilled, the partial success of the revolution is possible only on a regional level; reformism, like revolution, in one country ultimately encounters the same external limitations. Rejecting the traditional forms of liberal democracy in the name of direct mass participation in government is a fatal illusion. Direct democracy is indispensable, but it will inevitably degenerate into totalitarian manip-ulation of the masses if the country lacks a parliament and political freedoms. After Grenada, all the major currents of the Latin American left more or less recognized this. The Working People's Alliance of Guyana was reported to have dropped the slogan of people's power from its program, and to declare its adherence to, in the words of the *Guardian* (London), "good old pluralist democracy."[77] By the end of the 1980s, as the noted historian Kiva Maidanik observes, all the left parties of the region recognized representative democracy "as an inalienable strategic value of popular and left culture."[78]

The events on Grenada could not fail to have an influence in Nicaragua. The first reaction, naturally, was to prepare to resist an invasion. Weapons were distributed to militia members, air-raid shelters were built in the cities, and stockpiles of fuel and foodstuffs were established. But the invasion did not happen. Analyzing the events that had led to the overthrow of Bishop, the Nicaraguan leaders saw in them a lesson for themselves. Grenada showed the Nicaraguans the vulnerable side of their own revolution. "The best safeguard against intervention is freedom," wrote *La Prensa*.[79] The Sandinistas found it unpleasant to recognize the correctness of the opposition, but many of them were inclined to the same conclusion. The attacks on opponents of the regime were replaced by calls for the opening of "civilized" dialogue. The newspapers stated that the country would not take the path of bureaucratic socialism, and that its leaders knew and understood the dangers of bureaucratization.[80] Censorship was relaxed, and the position of the opposition parties improved. Nicaragua's practical achievements in the field of human rights since 1979 have been so great that Nicaragua was hardly mentioned in the Amnesty International reports on this region. All the cases listed by Amnesty International have been promptly dealt with.[81]

Civilized dialogue with the bourgeois parties and the church yielded very little, but responsibility for this did not lie with the revolutionary government. In April 1984 it was announced that elections would soon be held. Observers were invited from the Scandinavian countries, France, and Spain, in order to guarantee that the elections would be free. Not one of the opposition parties was excluded from the election campaign. Daniel Ortega was nominated as the FSLN's candidate for the post of president. This was a serious defeat for supporters of the hard line, who had put their stake on Tomás Borge.[82]

The process of democratization did not go ahead without opposition. Armed actions by the counterrevolutionaries continued, and economic pressure on the country in 1985 was even intensified. Nevertheless, when Reagan imposed an embargo on trade with Nicaragua, he was in conflict with public opinion in the United States itself, since it was clear that in Nicaragua his actions could only serve as justification for the abolition of freedoms.[83] Every report of democratization in Nicaragua was received with extreme displeasure in the White House. On the other hand, the architects of U.S. policy in the region knew that their anti-Nicaraguan actions were appreciably strengthening the positions of the pro-Cuban elements within the Sandinistas. Paradoxically, the U.S. administration and the supporters of a hard line in Nicaragua were playing into one another's hands. The Spanish Social Democratic government, by contrast, maintained constant contacts with the Sandinistas, trying to convince them to hold elections as soon as possible.[84] At the same time, the Social Democratic governments in Europe, together with the Latin American democratic regimes that had united in the Contadora group, tried to exert a restraining influence on the United States. Economic help from Mexico and a number of Western countries also played a significant role. According to the press, the Sandinistas were prevented from exploiting this situation by immaturity and internal disagreements.[85]

Although the decision on elections was totally in line with the front's original program, approved even by Fidel Castro, it aroused a furious reaction from the pro-Cuban faction, which even tried to organize a protest demonstration under the slogan "The people have already chosen, the people have already voted." In the words of a Spanish journalist, these developments revealed acute disagreements within the FSLN leadership, "affecting not only the electoral process, but also the election itself."[86] Since the collapse of the revolution on Grenada it had been clear that the only way to save the revolution was through democratization. The Reagan administration did everything possible to undermine the elections. According to reports in the Western press, the U.S. embassy "placed pressure on various parties, trying to get them to boycott the elections."[87] The leader of the Nicaraguan liberals admitted that he had taken the decision to withdraw his candidacy following a meeting with the U.S. ambassador. Washington would clearly have preferred to see Cuban-style one-party elections in Nicaragua. This attempt did not succeed. Although the main opposition organization, the Nicaraguan Democratic Coordinator (CDN), did not take part in the elections, the liberals and conservatives put forward candidates.

The right-wing opposition received about 20 percent of the votes; of these, about half went to the liberals, whose leader had withdrawn from the elections. "This is a lot of votes," wrote a correspondent for *Le Monde.* "It shows that the liberals and conservatives (the traditional parties of the nineteenth century) are still able to attract people. It is now clear that, despite the difficult conditions which the government created in the election campaign, the CDN could have counted on real successes. It could have won the votes of all the dissatisfied elements, from waverers to convinced opponents of Sandinismo. It let slip its chance to influence Nicaragua's political evolution. The future will show whether the leaders of the CDN, which has clearly ceased to be unified on questions of strategy, were right to follow the recommendations of their 'friends' from the United States."[88] The liberals became the leading party of the opposition. Meanwhile the Sandinistas, who received 65 percent of the votes, were clearly disappointed, since they had hoped for more. For the Stalinist groups that stood separately from the FSLN, the elections finished in a complete rout.

These were not completely free elections. The Sandinista Defence Committees intimidated voters. Liberal leader Virgilio Godoy complained that people were given to understand that their choice of candidate would be known, and that punishment would inevitably follow if they failed to vote the right way. The Sandinistas themselves recognized that "The same criteria cannot be applied here as in a country with a lengthy democratic tradition. Here there is only a small portion of democracy."[89]

But the voting was not a farce either. *La Prensa* was virtually uncensored, and the government's opponents were able to inform the people of their ideas. Even critics of Sandinismo recognize that the elections of 1984 were not falsified.[90] Having won the elections, Ortega declared that national dialogue with the church and the opposition would continue, that the freedoms gained in the course of the pre-election campaign would be preserved, and that counterrevolutionaries who laid down their arms would receive amnesty. "To treat these words as pure propaganda, providing cover for a Soviet-type regime, means to ignore obvious facts," wrote the Madrid newspaper *El País.* The

Sandinistas obviously possessed "the political will to seek an original path."[91]

The elections did not mean the final defeat of the hard line. Less than a year later this faction was able to take its revenge and win a state of emergency under the pretext of increasing activity by the contras. "Tomás Borge, a strong and uncompromising man, won the battle," the Spanish journal *Cambio 16* wrote in November 1985, "and the hard line regained the positions it had temporarily lost in connection with last year's elections."[92] The situation thus remained extremely contradictory, and the struggle between the various tendencies in the revolutionary camp continued, having become a long-term factor in Nicaraguan politics.

The ideological heterogeneity of the left-wing camp has objective roots. Under the conditions of a multistructured economy and social crisis, when there cannot be complete unity among the workers even on major questions of the struggle, it is difficult to expect unanimity among the forces of the left. Under these conditions the success of the democratic current depends on the ability of the country's working class to mount independent actions. As Latin American sociologists have recognized, the independent organizations of the industrial proletariat in Nicaragua were weak, and the political influence of the working class was insignificant. It was essential to integrate the workers into the system of real economic and political power.[93] A wave of strikes in 1981 showed that establishing relations between the Sandinista leadership and the working class would not be simple. Although the authorities tried to explain the strikes as the result of subversive activity by Communists and agents of the United States, the real causes of the conflict lay deeper. As Gauger notes, a substantial sector of the proletariat was "not prepared to sacrifice its 'privileges' for the sake of reconstruction."[94] It does not follow that the workers were displaying egoism. The point is simply that the reconstruction of the economy was not linked to a broadening of the rights of workers in the modern sector. The Sandinistas' original program called for ensuring "the participation by workers in the management of enterprises and other nationalized property."[95] In practice, this was not fulfilled. Organs of workers' democracy capable of deciding questions of production and of the distribution of the surplus were not established either on the level of the enterprise or of society. The self-organization of the workers in the course of the revolutionary process is impossible without free trade unions. Nor is it conceivable in the absence of democratic workplace bodies possessing rights which, although limited, are nevertheless real.[96]

Even during the mass struggle against Somoza, there was almost no coordination between the Nicaraguan workers' organizations and the Sandinistas. Of course, the moderation of industrial workers in the third world is relative; by Western standards, even their moderate demands seem radical. But within the framework of the revolutionary bloc, there is a growing temptation to subordinate moderate urban workers to more revolutionary layers. During the 1960s some Western theoreticians even declared that since "the working class is no longer the poorest and most oppressed sector of humanity," the working class can no longer "be regarded as a dangerous class."[97] According to this theory, the real danger to the existing system is posed by the declassed masses of the oppressed.

The proletariat is in fact a dangerous class not because it is poorer than all others (this was not even the case in nineteenth-century Europe), but because its sociopolitical position allows it to become the bearer of a historical alternative. Meanwhile, the masses of the oppressed (the radical ideologues do not define them more precisely than this) are more inclined to acts of destruction than of transformation.

Advancing guerrilla warfare to the primary position serves a definite social end. Mao and Che Guevara understood this perfectly. Mao wrote that the revolutionary struggle "takes the form of a peasant guerrilla war," while the movement of the masses develops in the countryside— "this support base of the revolution." From Mao, Che Guevara borrowed the idea of a prolonged struggle in the countryside preceding the decisive defeat of the regime. Mao, however, understood the role of the political organization much more profoundly, stressing that "advancing the armed struggle to center stage does not mean that the remaining forms of struggle can be renounced."[98] The working class played a far greater role in the Chinese than in the Cuban revolution. In a certain sense the foco theory represented a step backward by comparison with the Maoist doctrine of people's war.

The peasants and the urban poor are not only the most oppressed sectors of the population, but also the least educated and organized.

They become dependent on the leadership of the movement much more readily than the workers. Here the left radical strategy is obviously close to the thinking not only of Lenin, but also of Stalin. Revolutionary struggle through the foco acted as a substitute for the spontaneous movement of the masses themselves. As an Argentinian sociologist notes, "the guerrilla wars that have taken place until now have not rested on the workers and peasants, or have rested on them only in a minor degree, having been initiated by urban intellectuals."[99]

When the political center of a movement shifts to the countryside, the movement becomes more radical, but less constructive. Authoritarian tendencies grow markedly stronger, and the greater the number of participants, the less democratic the organization. The cultural abyss between the elite of the movement and the ranks excludes any possibility of controlling the actions of the leaders. The outward democratism and sincerity of the leaders, ready to eat from the same pot as "simple people," merely strengthens their ability to manipulate the masses. The armed struggle creates a specific psychology which even in the view of a Communist historian gives rise to "spontaneous outbursts of authoritarianism."[100]

Military actions can only be effective if strict discipline is observed. Che Guevara was sure that discipline had to have an educational character.[101] This presumed that the rank-and-file fighters were trained in the spirit of the leaders' ideas. Irrespective of Che's intentions, such an organization created people who unquestioningly carried out any orders from the leadership—not only military orders, but also political ones.[102] Where military means prevail over political ones, and the armed struggle is more important than the social movement, there is no room left for democracy.

The liberated region, as Debray insisted, should become a prototype and model of the future state, and its rulers serve as examples for future state functionaries.[103] Unfortunately, Debray was correct. The wider the struggle, the greater the likelihood that tendencies that are antipopular in their essence will appear within it. With the victory of the revolution and the seizure of power, these tendencies acquire new possibilities for their development. External pressure results in the whole country being transformed into a sort of besieged fortress, while the revolutionary party becomes increasingly militarized.

People who are struggling against dictatorship have the right to resort to violence. Leftists do not in any way demand violence for its own sake, but armed resistance in various instances is "an inevitable perspective arising out of the established system of rule."[104] Rejecting armed struggle in many cases amounts to rejecting struggle itself. Clashes with the forces of order and participation in armed struggle radicalize even moderate-minded people. The transformation of moderate reformists into determined radicals is a natural tendency. Foreign interference in the affairs of small countries, the U.S. presence in the third world, and the crisis of dependent capitalism and technocracy will create new revolutionary situations in underdeveloped countries. But it is precisely for this reason that the role in this struggle of independent organizations of the working class is so important: that is, of organizations which are difficult to manipulate, which can become strongholds of democratic traditions, and which at times are simply the last refuge of good sense.

The demand for independent workers' organizations, the British Marxist Nigel Harris notes, "rose almost everywhere," but without great success. "Any such organization needed independence, but it also needed politics. For it was the politics which failed in the revolts of the seventies."[105] The point here is not that armed struggle should be rejected where it is necessary, but that armed actions should be assigned the place which they deserve. The base of the movement can only be the city, and guerrilla warfare is admissible only as an instrument of political struggle. The experience of Eastern Europe, Spain, Argentina, and even Chile, shows that even under conditions of dictatorship it is possible to achieve success through peaceful methods. Criticism through weapons cannot replace the weapons of criticism.

The experience of the Philippines testifies to the limited possibilities of armed struggle. In the early 1980s this country was gripped by an acute political crisis. The military-technocratic regime of Ferdinand Marcos was incapable of controlling the situation. "The main organizational tendencies within the Filipino left," wrote the radical sociologist Alex Magno, "placed no strategic significance on the urban arena of open political engagement and considered it subsidiary to the armed revolutionary resistance in the countryside."[106] Confronting the Marcos government was the Communist Party of the Philippines, independent of Moscow and Beijing, and linked in the cities to the mass radical organization the National Democratic Front (NDF). No fewer than ten million Filipinos supported the NDF. The party's military wing, the New People's Army (NPA), was conducting a successful guerrilla war. "The NPA has its own dynamic, its own timetable and its own political strategy, to a substantial degree independent of all others," wrote a British journalist in 1985. "It has not existed for as long as the Marcos regime, but over the past decade it has become a real force. It cannot yet decide the outcome of events in the Philippines, but it has found a strong base for itself in the fertile rural regions where it conducts armed propaganda, and its position can only improve."[107]

Many observers feared that the Philippines might become an Asiatic Cuba.[108] The guerrillas won the sympathy of a significant sector of the intelligentsia and even of many Catholic priests, who participated actively in the struggle. In 1983 and 1984 the economic situation in the country deteriorated sharply. The program of modernization being pursued by Marcos suffered an acute setback. After the murder on August 21, 1983, of the prominent opposition figure Benigno Aquino, the people came out into the streets. The mass movement began to pose a serious threat to the regime. Nevertheless, the left forces were unable to make use of the favorable situation. As Magno acknowledged, their strategy, which was oriented to guerrilla warfare, was preventing them from taking advantage of the new situation in the cities. The strikes by workers and demonstrations by students could not extend into a struggle for power, since the leftists were unable to present the masses with a unifying program. Even when the weaknesses of the old political line became obvious, the leftists developed no strategic initiative.[109] The revolutionaries yielded their hegemony over the democratic movement to liberals. When the Marcos regime fell in February 1986, the leftists were a secondary force. The right-wing generals, who had joined the movement at the last moment, played an important role in ousting Marcos. As a result they were able to dictate conditions to the new president, Corazón Aquino (the widow of the murdered politician), and later to install their protégé Fidel Ramos as president.

The experience of the twentieth century has shown convincingly that under the conditions of the multistructured economy, operating according to the laws of combined and uneven development, there is no reason to hold out hopes of gradual evolution or to believe in the effectiveness of parliamentary democracy. Radical democratic movements inevitably present a threat to the very existence of capitalism in the "backward" countries, and consequently pose the question of a socialist alternative. However, the same backwardness which makes successful capitalist development impossible leads to the degeneration of the revolutions, to their Cubanization. The success of the permanent revolution in which revolutionary Marxists believe is just as improbable as the gradual process prophesied by the liberals. The unevenness of development does not disappear following the seizure of power by socialists.

The calls for the creation of a more competent or more democratic revolutionary leadership, which, in the words of the Brazilian sociologist Michael Löwy, would counterbalance "the 'natural' tendencies towards bureaucratism that arise of scarcity and backwardness,"[110] are mere verbiage. At a particular stage, a revolution in a backward country, whatever its leadership, inevitably encounters a crisis which forces it to choose between making a reformist retreat and rejecting democracy. In this case the elimination of democratic rights, and the bolshevization or Cubanization of the regime, appear to be the only way of saving the social gains of the revolution, and the only guarantee against an odious capitalist restoration. But the experience of Eastern Europe has shown that the bureaucratic degeneration of the state is not only an exorbitant price to pay for noncapitalist development, but that it cannot ultimately prevent the restoration of capitalist property relations. Moreover, after a prolonged period of Communist dictatorship the original revolutionary ideas are compromised, the supporters of socialism are demoralized, and the new bourgeois layers that are lunging for power are even more aggressive and irresponsible than their predecessors who were overthrown by the revolution. In such circumstances a planned, conscious, reformist retreat is far from representing the worst strategy for the revolution. This remains true even if, in the course of this retreat, the leftists risk losing power, as happened in Nicaragua in February 1990.

To many people, the decision by the FSLN leadership to hold new elections despite the continuing civil war came as a surprise. If at the end of the 1970s there were few people either inside or outside Nicaragua who doubted the front's commitment to democracy, by 1990 almost no one doubted that the Sandinista regime had finally made its choice in favor of the Cuban model. Fortunately for the Sandinistas, the experience of three decades of Castroism was now available for scrutiny, while the collapse of the Communist system in Eastern Europe served as another useful lesson.[111]

An even greater surprise for foreign observers, and also for many Nicaraguans, was the defeat of the Sandinistas in the elections. They were confronted by an ill-assorted and unworkable coalition, the Nicaraguan Opposition Union (UNO). The opposition's pre-election campaign was funded from the United States, but the pro-Moscow Communists nevertheless joined in actively. The opposition bloc had appeared totally incapable of winning the elections. However, the election was not so much won by the opposition, as lost by the Sandinistas. Western journalists noted that many supporters of the FSLN stayed away from the polling booths or even voted against the front, in order to express their dissatisfaction with its policies. "It is curious that many of them spoke out publicly, pleading almost in religious terms for forgiveness (Nicaraguans called this repentance) and declaring that despite having voted for UNO, they nevertheless supported the FSLN."[112]

The elections in Nicaragua aroused stormy discussion throughout the world, especially in the United States, where solidarity with revolutionary Nicaragua had long been a principal unifying slogan for large numbers of socialist groups. Some people spoke of war-weariness in the population, while others blamed the Sandinistas for a lack of revolutionary spirit, declaring that "unilateral political concessions to external and internal elites opened space and provided historically unprecedented opportunities for the revival of counterrevolutionary politics."[113] Many recalled that the Sandinistas had undermined the fighting capacity of the mass organizations, subordinating them to the front and alienating a significant sector of the population.[114]

Liberal commentators pointed to numerous signs of the degeneration of the regime, to corruption, authoritarianism, and inefficiency. "After what we have been learning about the economies of the East European bloc, can anyone seriously continue to assert that only U.S. aggression prevented advisors from East Germany, the Soviet Union, Bulgaria, Cuba, and other countries, who dominated Sandinista thinking, from achieving success in Nicaragua?" Paul Berman asked on the pages of the journal *Dissent*, adding that ordinary Nicaraguans during the years of the revolution had had more than enough cause "to fear the Sandinista regime."[115]

The results of the FSLN's economic policies were not, in fact, especially bad, and the failures in this area were not the result of Soviet-type planning but of vacillations between centralized planning and market measures. During the first five years of the revolution the Sandinistas managed to stabilize production and to ensure a steady rise in national income. Consumption per head of population rose by approximately 25 percent, while incomes were more evenly distributed than earlier. But from 1984 the situation began to deteriorate steadily. Unwilling to copy the Soviet model, but without a clear alternative strategy, the Sandinistas in conditions of civil war totally lost control over the economic situation. In 1987 and 1988 production began to decline. Inflation rose from 24 percent in 1980 to an astronomical 33,602 percent in 1988.[116] If, at the start of the revolution, high inflation might have been endured as the price of economic growth, in the conditions of decline of 1987 and 1988 it signified the collapse of the financial system. It is not surprising that neoliberal theories of financial stabilization began to seem attractive not only to many ordinary voters, but also to many functionaries of the Sandinista administration itself.

Most writers on Nicaragua characterized the defeat of the Sandinistas at the elections as a catastrophe. For the Sandinistas, however, losing the elections was a much better outcome than the final degeneration of the regime. The Sandinistas could not emerge victorious from a conflict with the United States. But they achieved more than any of the recent revolutions in Latin America. Not only was democracy established in the country; the relationship of social forces was transformed. The changes introduced during the years of the revolution were in essence irreversible. The government of Violeta Chamorro, which came to power in 1990, was unable to restore the prerevolutionary order. The attempts to eliminate the gains of the revolution met not only with resistance from the masses; the right-wing forces in Nicaragua, as in Eastern Europe, encountered insurmountable material resistance from the new social reality that had come into being during the years when anticapitalist forces had been in power. Lacking the support of the people, the rightists could not overcome this reality. The Sandinistas remained the country's largest political party, the trade unions were ready to rebuff the government, and after the FSLN's ouster from power the mass organizations of workers became even more dynamic.

For the first time in the history of the twentieth century, revolutionaries who had seized power by the armed road left power after losing elections. This in itself testified to a real turning point both in the consciousness of society itself, and also in the worldview of revolutionary socialists. The right of the people to review their decision is one of the bases of democracy, and for socialists to respect this principle is a guarantee that they will enjoy the trust of voters in the future. From the point of view of the bolshevist-jacobin tradition, according to which the main point of political struggle is to seize and hold power, the shift into opposition after ten years at the helm of the state really does seem like a catastrophe. But it is possible to register real successes even while in opposition. In many cases it is more advantageous to hand over power, while remaining true to one's ideas and to the interests of one's social base, than to hold onto power with the help of authoritarianism or opportunism.

However limited the opportunities open to an opposition party might be, such a party also enjoys advantages. Under democratic conditions power can never be taken totally, and it is never totally lost. There are always possibilities of ruling from below, or of pursuing reform in regions where a progressive majority exists in the organs of self-government.[117]

The Sandinistas, who retain enormous influence within Nicaraguan society, now have to understand this as well. Daniel Ortega has declared that despite their defeat at the elections, the Sandinistas are capable of ruling from below.[118] Paradoxically, this defeat has created favorable opportunities for the revival of the FSLN as a political party. Heated discussions have begun within the front, accompanied by sharp criticism of former policies and of the existing leadership.[119] Now distinguishing themselves clearly from the party, the mass popular organizations and trade unions have acquired an indispensable dynamism. The defeat in the elections not only failed to undermine the position of the Sandinista front within society, but on the contrary, by preventing its degeneration into a state party on the Soviet (or Mexican) model, created the conditions for the FSLN to transform itself into a modern radical force, capable of playing a decisive role in the country's subsequent development. It now remains for the Sandinistas to find their new path, to free themselves from the authoritarian traditions of the 1980s, and to avoid the temptations of the new realism (which is, in fact, nothing but the old, habitual opportunism). The experience of Nicaragua has shown that the movement toward socialism is not a direct road, but a complex process in which heroic revolutionary breakthroughs alternate with difficult periods of stabilization. But where the crisis of the revolutionary project is accompanied by a strengthening of democratic institutions, we can hope that even our failures and retreats will serve as the threshold for new victories.

CHAPTER 7

EASTERN EUROPE:
ANOTHER ROAD
TO THE THIRD WORLD

For Eastern Europe, the year 1989 was a turning point. One Communist regime collapsed like a house of cards, and then another, and another. . . . Soviet perestroika, which had begun with moderate reforms in 1985, turned into an uncontrollable process. When Mikhail Gorbachev was elected general secretary of the Communist Party of the Soviet Union, people had expected that his giant country would turn to democratic socialism, or to Western values. But what happened in Russia and Eastern Europe was not a transformation, but a catastrophe.

After semifree elections were held for the Congress of People's Deputies of the USSR in 1989, this body turned into something resembling a parliament. Communist demagogy was replaced by the irresponsible appeals of populist leaders. New parties began to arise. Independent newspapers, as a rule ultrareactionary and of very low quality, appeared like toadstools. In short, all the elements of Western-style democracy seemed to be present. The only problem was that none of it worked. The parties had no influence on the outcome of elections; the parliament did not determine the content of legislation; and the judiciary could not function normally because of the contradictory nature of the laws.

In the summer of 1989 coal miners, disappointed by the babbling of the deputies and outraged by a sharp fall in their wages, went on strike throughout the Soviet Union. In Poland, a wave of strikes forced the government of General Jaruzelski to hold elections, which resulted in the triumph of the opposition. The distribution of seats in the Polish parliament, the Sejm, was agreed upon beforehand through a roundtable conference, with the official Polish United Workers Party (PUWP) reserving most of the positions for itself and its allies. But in free elections for the Senate, candidates of the Solidarnosc opposition won all the seats but one. The allies of the PUWP joined with the victors. For the first time in forty years a noncommunist government was formed in Poland.

In Hungary the Communist regime gradually disintegrated. Under the leadership of Janos Kadar in the 1960s and 1970s, Hungary had become a laboratory of reform, and a model for party reformers in neighboring countries. Now the model collapsed. By the mid-1980s economic growth had slowed, and the debt to Western banks had multiplied. Discontent grew stronger, and the opposition movement became active. The ruling Hungarian Socialist Workers Party suffered a split. The reformist wing formed the Hungarian Socialist Party, and proclaimed social democratic policies. Seeking to demonstrate their complete and final break with Communist tradition, the leaders of the Hungarian Socialist Party constantly reminded their listeners that their party did not "reject the idea of private property, not even its dominance."[1] The majority of members of the Communist Party did not go with the reformers, remaining true to the old party and its old name.

In 1989 the Hungarian leadership accelerated the shift to a multiparty system, fearing that with Soviet perestroika in obvious crisis, the conservatives might try to stage a comeback.[2] As in Poland, the government was forced to sit down at the conference table with the opposition. The outcome of the round table talks in Budapest were even more advantageous for the opposition than in Poland, although the former dissidents in Hungary were far weaker and less united than Solidarnosc.[3] Free elections were called, in which the government was obviously doomed to defeat.

The events in Poland and Hungary set loose an avalanche in neighboring countries. The mass flight of citizens from East Germany caused an acute political crisis there. Under the slogan "We Want to Remain!" thousands of people demonstrated on the streets of Leipzig, Dresden, and Berlin. The party apparatus was paralyzed, and the aged leader Erich Honecker went into retirement. Within less than a year the German Democratic Republic, which had been formed after World War II in the Soviet occupation zone, ceased to exist. After East Germany, demonstrations began in Czechoslovakia. In three weeks it was all over, and the people were celebrating the victory of the velvet revolution. In Bulgaria the party elite itself got rid of the corrupt and unpopular Todor Zhivkov, proclaiming a transition to democracy.

In Yugoslavia as well, the Communist regime collapsed. As later in the Soviet Union, the collapse of the party was followed by the disintegration of the federation. Over the two years from 1988 to 1990, the split in the Yugoslav League of Communists became irreversible. The Slovenes and Serbs expressed more and more diverse views on the mechanisms of the state, with one side insisting firmly on the principle of general agreement in the making of decisions at the federal level, and the other arguing in favor of a majority vote. An almost inconceivable combination of nationalist sentiments, demands for the democratic transformation of Yugoslav society, and the revival of centralist and neobolshevik ideas made the League of Communists ungovernable.[4] At the Fourteenth Extraordinary Congress in January 1990, a united organization of Yugoslav Communists on the scale of the country as a whole ceased to exist. The entire traditional system of links between the republics collapsed along with it, and each of the republics set out along its own path. Two years later the country was engulfed in a bloody civil war. Croatian, Serbian, and Islamic militias divided off their respective spheres of influence. Thousands and thousands of people fled from their lifelong homes, saving themselves from the fighting.

The Romanian dictator Nicolae Ceausescu hoped to maintain himself in power with the help of a powerful repressive apparatus. Massive demonstrations in Timisoara and Bucharest ended in bloodshed, but the regime fell. The dictator and his wife Elena were shot. Only isolated Albania managed to hold out against the wave of 1989, but not for long. In December 1990 the government was forced to proclaim a multiparty system and simultaneously to introduce a state of emergency, in order somehow to stabilize the situation. Before two years were up, power had passed to the democratic opposition.

What is so striking is the ease with which it was possible to overthrow regimes which had held power for decades, and which did not shrink from the use of force. Only the Ceausescu dictatorship in Romania risked putting up armed resistance to the insurgent population. But there as well, it was not the street demonstrations that decided the outcome of the struggle. In virtually all cases the acts of protest led to quick cadre reshuffles at the top, and to palace revolutions. If in Poland and Hungary direct deals were struck between the opposition and the government, in Czechoslovakia and East Germany a section of the hierarchy of the old regime actively supported the demands for change, and got rid of their conservative rivals. In Bulgaria and Albania the reforms were headed by a younger section of the party oligarchy, while in Romania a split took place between the Ceausescu clan and its opponents within the apparatus. The army and police not only refrained from trying to crush the popular protests, but on the contrary, played a decisive role in bringing about the victory of the uprising. In the Soviet Union (including Estonia, Latvia, and Lithuania), the bureaucratic apparatus directed perestroika, and the most prominent leaders of the opposition came, as a rule, from the bureaucratic milieu. It is enough to recall Lithuanian Prime Minister Kazimiera Prunskiene, Georgian President Eduard Shevardnadze, and the leaders of the Democratic Russia bloc Boris Yeltsin, Gennady Burbulis, Yegor Gaidar, Nikolai Travkin, Yuri Afanasiev and Gavriil Popov. All of these individuals could boast of lengthy party membership and honored positions in the old system. Not one of them had been an oppositionist, much less a dissident, before the beginning of perestroika.

Representatives of the bureaucratic elite played an active role in implementing economic reforms and in shaping the new political system. There is nothing accidental about the fact that Vaclav Klaus, who headed the Czechoslovak Civic Forum in October 1990, President Ion Iliescu in Romania, and the leaders of the liberal opposition in Russia belonged to the old elite. The East German Christian Democracy was part of the political system, taking part in the dispensing of privileges and even in the governing of the country. The Hungarian Democratic Forum united in its ranks people who were by no means dissidents.

By mid-1991 former dissidents had everywhere been forced out of positions of real power. Only in Poland were a few opposition veterans to be found in leading state posts. In the united Germany the leftists who had played a decisive role in deposing Honecker immediately found themselves beyond the pale of political life. The academician Andrei Sakharov was the only noted Soviet dissident to play an important, albeit symbolic role in the ranks of the new liberal elite. With his death, any continuity between the old opposition and the new political leaders disappeared. In Hungary the dissidents did not gain power either. In Czechoslovakia and Bulgaria dissidents were quickly forced out of key posts.

Everywhere, free or partly free elections took place. Even in Hungary, where liberal reforms had a history of more than twenty years, the Hungarian Socialist Party did not achieve any particular successes. A few radical left intellectuals joined the Socialist Party along with members of the old *nomenklatura*, but this was clearly not enough to free the party from the taint of the old regime. The traditionalists of the Hungarian Socialist Workers Party failed to win a single seat. The main struggle was played out between the two largest right-wing currents. Most of the dissidents joined the Free Democrats, but power ended up in the hands of the Hungarian Democratic Forum, consisting mainly of people who had been associated with the Kadar government. The victory of this grouping was guaranteed not by its members' past services, but by their ability to exploit the political inexperience and nationalist prejudices of the population. Western observers note that the Hungarian Democratic Forum sought persistently to arouse nationalist sentiments. Its election posters depicted "the victory sign against a backdrop of the Hungarian flag; the withdrawal of Soviet troops and the relegation of the statue of Stalin, the works of Marx and Mao to the dustbin of history."5 Encouraging anticommunist and nationalist moods in every possible way, the dissidents and reformers themselves became the victims of these moods.

The Communists were also easily banished from power in the two most developed Yugoslav republics, Slovenia and Croatia. The victims campaigned mainly around slogans of national sovereignty, relegating social and economic questions to second place. Serbia and Montenegro, on the other hand, remained under the influence of the traditional Communist Party apparatus. In practice, however, the difference between the republics was not especially great; nationalist regimes were installed in both Serbia and Croatia.

In Czechoslovakia and East Germany the former Communist parties, headed by their reformist wings, managed a degree of success, but the outcome of the elections was a foregone conclusion. Despite the relatively large number of votes in East Germany for the Party of Democratic Socialism (PDS), which arose out of the fragments of the former ruling Communist party (SED), the main struggle was between the Social Democrats and Christian Democrats. In the pre-election campaigning the tone was set by West German politicians, and the perspective of reunification with the West predetermined the result. The elections were won by the Christian Democrats, who in the past had been loyal participants in the political system of the German Democratic Republic; now they were seen as representatives of the Christian Democratic government in Bonn. The radical leftists were effectively banished from the political scene, attracting only 4.5 percent of the votes. The subsequent reunification of Germany strengthened the shift to the right. Although the PDS retained third place in the former East Germany, its share of the vote fell from 15.2 to 9.9 percent. Together with the "left list" of Western radicals, the PDS drew only 2.4 percent of votes in the united Germany. The left grouplets that continued to champion the tradition of the November revolution could not manage even this much. In the spring of 1990, explaining to journalists the reasons for the failure of the New Forum and other such groups, a Berliner noted: "To sympathize with them is one thing, but to vote for them is something quite different."[6]

In Czechoslovakia the opposition, which had campaigned under the banner of the Civic Forum (in Slovakia, as "The Public Against Violence"), won an overwhelming majority of the seats in parliament. But it was still not clear who had won the elections, since the Civic Forum included all the opposition currents from the right to the extreme left, including Communist reformers expelled from the Communist Party of Czechoslovakia.

In Romania the Communist Party was declared illegal. Later the ban was lifted, but the party disintegrated, and did not take part in the elections. The Front for National Salvation, which had ruled the country since the overthrow of Ceausescu, then became the haven both for a substantial section of the old *nomenklatura*, and for the young technocrats. The opposition accused the front of being the totalitarian Communist Party in a new guise. The various opposition programs represented a mix of ultrareactionary programs and of nostalgic recollections of the country's far-from-democratic past. Leading opposition politicians returned from exile, and at times showed themselves to have little familiarity with the lives of the people. Elections, which were acknowledged by international observers to have been completely honest (at least in the large industrial cities), resulted in a triumph for the Front for National Salvation. Its candidate Ion Iliescu became president, receiving 86.5 percent of the votes.

On the basis of the votes they attracted, the Front for National Salvation in Romania and the Civic Forum in Czechoslovakia could be considered the main victors in the Eastern European elections of 1990 and 1991. But these organizations, which represented broad and contradictory coalitions, lacked both a clear strategy and a common ideology. They could not provide their countries with stable governments, and their rise to power was merely a harbinger of new political crises. The pre-election campaigns of the Civic Forum and the Front for National Salvation, despite the diverse views of the supporters of these organizations, were conducted primarily on the basis of left-centrist slogans: combining democracy and social justice; caution in the implementation of economic reforms; and a third path between capitalism and Communism. But after these groups came to power, both turned sharply to the right, to the accompaniment of fierce internal struggles.

The Democratic Russia bloc which achieved a majority in the Russian Federation was a similarly unstable coalition, though worse organized. Its rise to power in the largest cities of Russia was followed promptly by administrative paralysis and furious clashes between former collaborators. Like the citizens of Prague, the Muscovites who elected "democrats" were not so much voting in their favor as voting against Communists. The existence of a united electoral bloc made it possible to conceal for a time the irreconcilable contradictions within the ranks of the new majority, and most importantly, opened the way for numerous behind-the-scenes maneuvers both before and after the elections. The policies that were implemented were determined not by the will of electors, voting for a particular program, but by apparatus intrigues and by the relationship of forces in clandestine deals between people and groups. As in other countries, the democratic leftists who had played a key role in the mass protests were forced onto the sidelines. The moderately left-wing pre-election program was replaced by neoliberal slogans.

The political nature of the Czechoslovak Civic Forum was initially defined by its presidential candidate Vaclav Havel, speaking of a third path and of the ills of Western society. In an interview with an Italian journal in the summer of 1990, Havel argued that both East and West, for all their differences, were experiencing a common crisis. He stated that for a long time he had considered himself "a sort of" socialist, going on to say: "I remain one even now, though I no longer use the word to define my position."[7]

In fact, the levers of power did not remain in the hands of sentimental dreamers trying to stand above the problems of capitalism and socialism, but in the hands of bureaucrats and politicians. Havel was required as a general symbol of the Civic Forum at a time when all the groups opposed to the Communist Party needed to be unified. Once the Communists had been excluded from power, the center stage came to be occupied by people quite different from Havel, including some members of the old *nomenklatura*. Heading up this new trend was finance minister Vaclav Klaus, who had joined the opposition two weeks before the regime fell. The socialist groups, Left Alternative and Obroda, were expelled from the Civic Forum. The socialist Petr Uhl, a veteran Czechoslovak oppositionist who had spent a considerable part of his life in Communist prisons, complained that he and his group had been expelled from the Civic Forum by people "whom I never knew."[8]

Unlike the situation in Czechoslovakia, a country with firm democratic traditions, the political struggle in Romania was accompanied by violence and repression. The opposition did not respect the results of the elections, and the government did not respect the rights of the opposition. In June 1990, students were provoked by the opposition into holding a demonstration in Bucharest calling for the freshly elected leadership to be excluded from power. The police were unreliable. The Front for National Salvation summoned thousands of miners into the capital to disperse the demonstration. Many students were brutally beaten. Trying to manipulate the workers' movement and use it against the liberal opposition, the leaders of the Front for National Salvation promised to avoid mass unemployment and to exercise restraint in matters of privatization. But in the autumn of 1990, when the first wave of opposition protests had been crushed, the Front abruptly changed course. Prices were raised sharply, and the government of Prime Minister Petr Roman declared its intention to privatize 50 percent of the economy over three years. In this respect Romania's neocommunist leaders proved, unexpectedly, to be more radical than many orthodox liberals. The minister in charge of reforms, A. Severin, clearly defined the new course when he declared that the authorities needed people "who have no vestige of socialist solutions in their minds."[9] The turn to the right brought about a split in the front and a fierce struggle between the liberal Prime Minister Roman and President Iliescu, who held more moderate views. The former allies turned into bitter enemies. In 1992 Iliescu was again elected president. During his pre-election campaign he promised to defend the worker and peasant masses from the horrors of speedy privatization.[10] But after winning the elections, he again moved closer to the rightists.

In Bulgaria, as related by the journal *East European Reporter*, the elections of June 1990 proved a shock to those who had thought that the opposition would finish on top, since Bulgaria turned out to be the first country of the Eastern bloc where the Communists were returned to power with a majority.[11] The success of the Communists, now renamed the Bulgarian Socialist Party (BSP), was less than solid. The party had only a slender parliamentary majority, with 211 seats out of 400. But more important, the party remained torn by political contradictions. Declaring itself the defender of the working people, the BSP began implementing the same policies as the liberal groups that had come to power in other countries. The only difference was that the government of Bulgaria, paralysed by internal dissension, was incapable of implementing even these policies consistently and competently. The Lukanov government formed by the BSP was forced to resign after only two months, yielding its place to a new government formed by the same Lukanov from members of the BSP. This in turn was soon replaced by a cabinet centered on the neutral Prime Minister Dimitar Popov. The Bulgarian sociologists Dimitrina Petrova and Krasimir Kanev noted that the socialists handed over power to the liberals with a certain relief.[12] The liberalization of prices during the winter of 1991 brought catastrophic rises in the cost of living. As in Russia, inflation and the impoverishment of the population were of no help in solving the problem of material shortages. According to economists, the social minimum needed to guarantee a normal human existence stood at 621 *lev* per person, at a time when the minimum wage was only 435 *lev*. The main burden fell upon the workers. Nevertheless, the BSP leaders still gave firm support to the government's policies, declaring publicly that there was no alternative.[13]

The opposition Union of Democratic Forces (SDS) of Bulgaria, strikingly similar to analogous coalitions in other countries, was not distinguished either by its political homogeneity or its competence. The leaders of the SDS were unable to suggest an alternative program, instead issuing proclamations full of anticommunist demagogy and appeals to the population not to trust the government. The difficulties of the opposition were heightened by political scandals. SDS chairperson Petar Beron was accused of having collaborated with the security forces of the old regime, and was forced to quit politics.[14]

Beron's resignation did not put an end to the political crisis in the SDS. A vicious factional struggle led to a split. The leading posts in the SDS were seized by the Group of 39, made up of neoliberal politicians who had not taken part in the democratic opposition. These figures accused the former dissidents and the leaders of the old pre-Communist era parties of having pro-Communist sympathies, and even of having collaborated with the state security organs. A far-reaching purge began within the SDS ranks. As Dimitrina Petrova noted in 1992, of all the people who had assembled in 1989 in order to form the SDS, only one remained in the parliamentary caucus. All the rest had gradually been forced out of parliamentary politics.[15]

In 1991 new elections brought the SDS its long-awaited parliamentary majority. The left-centrist organizations that had been established at the last moment by former dissidents and the moderate wing of the SDS suffered a crushing defeat. The new government began pursuing a tough right-wing liberal course. Among the first steps taken by the new cabinet was to expropriate the property of the opposition trade unions and of the Bulgarian Socialist Party. Loyalty tests and purges were begun in the state apparatus. Laws were introduced which limited the independence of the judiciary, and restricted the rights of national minorities.[16] The economy continued its precipitate decline. By the autumn of 1992 the SDS government was forced to resign amid catastrophic crisis and universal discontent.

Events in Albania developed much as they had done in Bulgaria. The Communist Party, which immediately renamed itself the Socialist Party, lost the first free elections, but quickly handed over power to the opposition. The economic and social crisis continued irrespective of which group held power.

In Mongolia as well, the Bulgarian scenario was repeated to a significant degree. The Mongolian People's Revolutionary Party changed its leadership and distanced itself from the Communist past. Its leaders declared that the party had "never posed its goal as the building of Communism."[17] In elections for the Great People's *Khural* the Mongolian People's Revolutionary Party retained a majority, but shared power (and responsibility) with the anticommunist opposition, in which liberal currents predominated.

It could be said that a shift to the right and the triumph of neoliberalism formed a general tendency in Eastern Europe, though it should be remembered that only in Hungary and East Germany was a neoliberal program put openly before the voters. In East Germany, this was the price that was imposed for unification with the West.

Throughout Eastern Europe, and in Russia as well, a powerful liberal wave arose. A demarcation took place within the democratic camp. Those who were dissatisfied with liberal ideology were forced into opposition. New political parties and groups, which had sprung up everywhere like toadstools vied with one another to show their fidelity to the principles of liberal capitalism and to dissociate themselves at any cost not just from Communism, but from anything that smelled even remotely of socialism. The ideas of Milton Friedman, F.A. von Hayek, and other economists of the monetarist school who proclaimed the omnipotence of the free market and private property were presented to the public as self-evident truths. The well-known Russian economist Tatyana Koryagina stated, without any particular satisfaction, that after the events of 1989 the same scientists who had faithfully served the administrative-bureaucratic system began zealously preaching capitalism.[18]

Despite the ideological triumph of liberalism in Eastern Europe in 1989 and 1990, its prospects from the outset were by no means unclouded. An unprecedented historical problem appeared before the liberal ideologues: how to build capitalism without a bourgeoisie? If in the West, capitalist property relations had arisen from below over the course of centuries, liberals in the former Communist countries were promising a transition to the highest forms of modern capitalism, even though their countries lacked an entrepreneurial class that had passed through the stage of primitive accumulation.

It was around the question of the tactics to be used in making the transition to capitalism that the first serious split appeared within the liberal camp. The moderates preferred an evolutionary transition. The well-known Hungarian economist Janos Kornai demonstrated that the complete privatization of state property would be "just as extreme and irresponsible a measure as the radical abolition of private property." Instead, Kornai argued, it was necessary to create the conditions for the embourgeoisement of society, and "to wait five, ten or perhaps twenty years until private enterprise finally triumphs."[19]

The naïveté of this approach is striking. If the state sector is supposed to maintain a significant role in society throughout the five to twenty years allotted to it, while simultaneously disintegrating and decaying, this cannot help but have catastrophic results for the economy as a whole, including private enterprise. This much is clear from the experience of the Soviet Union during the years from 1989 to 1991. If radical changes are introduced to the state sector (something of which Kornai is particularly fearful, issuing a special warning against self-management and other socialist experiments), the new private sector, consisting mainly of small and middle-sized firms, will turn into a subcontractor and junior partner of the growing and dynamic state sector. In this case the national bourgeoisie, instead of building capitalism, will become embedded in socialism; that is, the outcome will be the reverse of that desired by the liberals.

A different, more radical point of view was put by Democratic Russia ideologue and first mayor of Moscow Gavriil Popov. The ruler of the Russian capital was forced to admit publicly that capitalism could only be implanted in our country through the same methods as Stalinist Communism. The new system, he declared, would not grow naturally out of the past. It would "have to be implanted artificially, from outside, on the recultivated field of the old order." Denationalization and desovietization would have to come from without. It was true, Popov continued, that there was a gigantic difference, since "socialism came as something artificial"; the market, on the other hand, would "return as something natural." Nevertheless, he insisted, the process in both cases was "one of implantation, not of simple growth."[20] Such a strategy would necessarily require "a firm hand" and "strong authority."

It is amusing to reflect that the polemic between moderate and radical proponents of capitalism in Eastern Europe has resembled a sort of grotesque caricature of the polemic between bolsheviks and mensheviks during the Russian Revolution. Once again the bolshevik position, for all its superficial extremism, has turned out the be the only realistic one, since it has rested on a correct grasp of reality. Unlike the radicals, the moderate, reasonable liberals (like the mensheviks before them) have lacked a social base. In the concrete historical situation, the turn to capitalism could not have been carried out except through radical and extremist methods. It could not fail to be accompanied by social upheavals, bloodshed, and economic catastrophe. The pious hopes of a soft transition remained pious hopes, for the simple reason that neither the social, economic, nor political conditions existed for such a transition. The demand that society be spared the numerous sacrifices that would be involved if the shining capitalist future were pursued in earnest automatically presumed a rejection of capitalism itself.

In all the countries of the former Communist bloc, implementing privatization proved in practice to be a formidable task. The fight to ensure the triumph of private property invariably began with the emergence of a new bureaucracy. In Warsaw, following the adoption on July 13, 1990, of a special law on privatization which the Russian liberal press characterized as "a historic event in the development of Poland,"[21] the corresponding new ministry was established as well. The "democratic" administration that came to power in the Moscow Soviet acted in the same fashion. By the end of 1992, there were more state functionaries than there had been in the entire Soviet Union a year earlier. A large section of the new bureaucracy was concerned with questions of property.[22] In East Germany a special department concerned with the sale of state property was established—the *Treuhandanstalt*. Western businessmen who were confronted with its activity complained that the *Treuhandanstalt* was just as bureaucratic and impenetrable as the Communists had been earlier.[23]

Everywhere, the redistribution of property became a source of corruption. The Moscow economist Tatyana Koryagina, whom no one could suspect of harboring sympathies for Marxism, observed that the economic reforms had been transformed into "a testing-ground for dirty economic games with the people," and that in these circumstances, entrepreneurship would inevitably be overlaid with "a criminal ethic."[24]

In the autumn of 1990, summing up the results of two years of reforms in Poland, the well-known economist Jan Drewnowski stated that privatization remained on the periphery of reform and on the periphery of legality. There have been many examples of national assets being appropriated by the *nomenklatura*, using the foulest methods. Fortunes have been made through every conceivable type of swindle. Cases were reported in which the former owners of land and buildings lay claim to this property, but this was not a typical phenomenon. Basic changes to the structure of property ownership have not yet occurred, but this process has already become deformed.[25] Even in the former East Germany, data issued by the prosecutor's office show that about a third of private investment in 1991–1992 consisted of money-laundering operations by organized crime.[26] If the criminal bourgeoisie has become one of the moving forces of privatization, then another, no less important force has become the old party-state *nomenklatura*. The liberal Moscow journal *Panorama* complained that at the head of numerous conglomerates, joint ventures, and commercial associations formed on the basis of the former state sector, "hardened party cadres are often to be found."[27] As early as 1989 the London *Times* noted that in Poland apparatchiks were making haste to go into private firms, or in the worst case, to buy shares in the newly privatized state firms they used to run.[28] The same thing has happened in Hungary and Czechoslovakia, Latvia and Bulgaria.

At times property has been returned to its former owners and their heirs—that is, to representatives of the pre-war East European oligarchies, who were directly responsible for the region's economic backwardness and which, as a rule, collaborated closely with Nazi Germany during the years of World War II.[29] However, most of the productive capital that is subject to privatization was created during the post-war period.

The fact that throughout all of Eastern Europe the old *nomenklatura* played a key role in the dividing up of state property was quite natural. The nomenklatura, which had long since forged links with various mafia groups, was the only social group that really possessed the knowledge, means and contacts that were essential to the creation of a new class of property-owners. Ultimately, the decisive factor in the creation of new oligarchies was not the assets that the party elites had acquired through their totalitarian exploitation of society, but their system of personal contacts. In countries where private entrepreneurial capital had traditionally been lacking, these links were the main guarantee of success. The old ruling elites were reconstructed, and transformed into genuine ruling classes, conscious of their interests. Corruption, which was an inevitable accompaniment and important ingredient in this process, was transformed from the shadow of the system into one of its bases.

The unexpected bent shown by the nomenklatura for business activity aroused some confusion among liberal ideologues. They comforted themselves by arguing that this was a temporary phenomenon. "The origins of the new entrepreneurs are not important. Nothing terrible is going to happen if the party or the mafia invest their money in industry. Under market conditions these enterprises will either be forced to operate according to the principles of the market, or will fail, and will be sold to people who do know how to work in a market system."[30] In fact, the links between the new elites and the old bureaucracies have determined the type of market which is taking shape, and the type of capitalism which is being established in the East. As in developing countries, power has been exchanged for property and converted into property.[31] Power and property have remained indivisible, even though the system of political and economic relations in society and the methods of rule have changed substantially.

"It is difficult to express too much irritation with people who have imbibed the moral code and 'rules of the game' of the Brezhnevist epoch," wrote the noted economist Andrei Kolganov. "Earlier they had elbowed their way through to the feed troughs using slogans that were alien to their nature. Now the possibility has opened up to exercise fully their long-polished skills in manipulating the people, through proclaiming goals close to their true nature. Now their right to satisfy their unrestrained thirst for wealth, and to rigorously exclude the working masses from any influence on economic matters, are declared to be the main conditions for any progress or freedom. On this point there exists a complete unity of spirit between the 'heroes' of stagnation—zealous champions of the authoritarian-bureaucratic exploitation of the people under Communist slogans—and the fathers of privatization, champions of a return to the bosom of 'civilized society'."[32]

The Yugoslav sociologist Bogdan Denitch notes that decades of Communist power "have given birth to a very specific, warped, antisocial, semicrooked class of entrepreneurs, whose skills at cutting legal corners and finding ways through bureaucratic mazes have been sharply honed. These people are used to quick profits and corruption, and are not about to invest, even if they had the means, in the kind of dynamic and innovative private sector the economic reformers hope to encourage."[33]

In this respect Russia has continuously lagged behind the other countries of the former Eastern bloc, but the Russian ruling elites now have the opportunity to catch up with and overtake their colleagues in neighboring countries. The critical turning point came on August 19, 1991, when part of the central leadership in the Soviet Union tried to introduce a state of emergency. The organizers of the August putsch hoped that by imposing order on the country, they could achieve a new political compromise that would definitively secure new conditions for the dividing up of power and property. No one even tried to take any steps against Democratic Russia, its leader Boris Yeltsin, or other leaders of the government of the Russian Federation. Yeltsin used the events of August 19 finally to banish the Soviet leadership from power and to abolish the union. The actions of the putchists, the State Committee on the Emergency Situation, were declared to have amounted to a "coup d'etat" and a "conspiracy," and the members of the committee were arrested. Power passed into the hands of the Russian government and its political organizations. Gorbachev, having lost his post as the country's leader, quit the Communist Party and gave his blessing to its abolition. A few months later he was similarly to reconcile himself to the abolition of the union. The assets of the Communist Party were confiscated, and Communist newspapers were shut down. Matters were not confined to the dissolution of the Communist Party. On August 28 Yeltsin issued his Decree No. 96, which effectively abolished the law on local self-government. An offensive was unleashed against the organs of representative authority, against workers, and against left organizations. A country which had still not come to terms with the fall of the Communist regime was confronted with the threat of a new dictatorship.

In Russia, a frenzy of administrative measures began. The new leaders showed so little respect for elementary democratic procedures that they could not help but arouse resistance from the deputies in the soviets. Democratic Russia back-benchers accused their former idols of apparatus manipulation, of trying to create bureaucratic capitalism on the Chinese model, of using bolshevik methods, and of attempting to "drive people by force into the shining capitalist future."[34]

The ruling circles realized that they needed a broader social base. In the countries of Eastern Europe every possible device was used in order to lower the price of privatized property and to maximize the number of future shareholders. This was justified using references to social justice that were completely in line with the traditions of Communist propaganda. In Czechoslovakia and Russia the population were issued with vouchers—that is, privatization checks. The Yeltsin government assessed the share of each citizen in the general social property at a value of ten thousand rubles—thirty dollars at the exchange rate applying at the time. In Poland, privatization bonds were issued and distributed free of charge among the adult population. These bonds and vouchers were supposed to help workers obtain shares, but they could not take the place of money. Because workers rarely had significant savings, the population were issued with credits.[35] In Russia and Poland, the labor collectives of enterprises were formally able to obtain specified shares in the joint stock firms that were being established.

Despite the propaganda of people's privatization, these measures did not win mass support.[36] Large numbers of new shareholders, living on the verge of hunger, handed over their securities for the equivalent of a few dollars. The logic of capitalism demands that society should be divided into property-owners and proletarians. If everyone were a property-owner, no one would sell their labor power, the labor market could not function, and the system of capitalist relations could not exist. "Voucherization" turned out to be extremely advantageous to the elite of society. A system of collective responsibility was created, similar to that established by Communist governments. It was necessary to enlist as many people as possible in the process of dividing up public property. In the view of the elites, this was supposed to guarantee the irreversibility of the reforms. What was involved was the principle which applies in a gang of criminals when it is necessary to divide up the loot in order to ensure that everyone remains loyal. Meanwhile, the possibility of buying up vouchers for next to nothing, and the sale of enterprises at reduced prices, allowed the new rich to obtain property for almost nothing. By the most modest assessments, the price put on enterprises due for privatization in Russia was understated by ten times, while vouchers were sold for 30 percent of their nominal value.[37] Although privatization was justified by references to the need to increase the efficiency of the economy, the only firms that could successfully be sold were those which already were relatively efficient.[38] No one sought to take over unprofitable enterprises; only the state was prepared to make this kind of acquisition.

The buyers of shares were by no means guaranteed high profits and a comfortable life. On the contrary, they were in danger of finding themselves in a trap—of becoming debtors for many years to the state and to the banks, which had provided credits while promising profits which did not, and sometimes could not, exist. The widely publicized transfer of property rights to the labor collectives in most cases turned into a catastrophic form of bondage. The labor collectives were now dependent on the state, on commercial banks, on private investment funds, and on commercial intermediaries; meanwhile, their members lost the rights and guarantees they had enjoyed as hired workers.

The cut-rate prices at which property was sold off meant that the state was deprived of sorely needed funds. At the same time, the economy suffered from a shortage of the capital investments needed for its restructuring. The constant scandals that accompanied the privatization process forced even some anticommunist ideologues to doubt the correctness of the chosen path. Tatyana Koryagina spoke of the formation in Russia of a "mafia-tinged market economy."[39] Larisa Piyasheva, the first person to speak out openly in favor of capitalism in the Soviet press, was stating by the end of 1990: "Under our conditions, the idea of selling state property into private hands is mistaken." Continuing with this policy could mean only "a war of all against all."[40]

The battle of principles, ideas, and classes seemed finally to have retreated into the past, to be replaced by the clash of personalities and groups dividing up jobs and power. For all the diversity of political labels, the measures undertaken by all the governments of Eastern Europe were strikingly similar. Meanwhile, the approach which the governments were unanimously proclaiming as the only correct and, indeed, the only possible one, was not yielding the promised results. The economic position rapidly deteriorated in all the countries without exception.

The failure of market theories in Eastern Europe had two causes. First, these theories were totally unsuited to Eastern European conditions, and second, they were wrong in themselves. Either of these causes would have been fully sufficient to bring about a collapse.

The market makes it possible to maintain economic equilibrium, but it does not guarantee either the growth of output, or the introduction of new technology, or social progress. If enterprises find outdated technology more profitable, they are not going to replace it with new, and if equilibrium of supply and demand on the market is ensured through limiting demand, one cannot even talk of a rise in living standards. "An unregulated market under conditions of structural disproportion," wrote the noted Soviet economist V. Danilov-Danilyan, "leads to galloping inflation, which cannot under any circumstances be regarded as a means of correcting the disproportions. A furious price spiral is testimony to the powerlessness of the market to correct factors over which it has no control, since the entire point of the market as a regulator (here one must beware of confusing the market as a regulator with regulating influences that affect the market) consists in its power of returning the system relatively quickly to equilibrium, to stability. However the market, as is indicated by mathematical theory and confirmed in practice, is only a small-scale regulator. By itself, it can only cope with relatively small deviations from equilibrium."[41]

When extramarket mechanisms are at work in society, serving as stimuli to the growth of production, to a rise in living standards, to the acceleration of technical progress, or to the ecologization of the economy, the market helps attain these goals while simultaneously maintaining economic equilibrium. What happened in Eastern Europe after the collapse of Communism was just the reverse. The market proved incapable even of ensuring equilibrium of supply and demand. The monopolized and centralized structure of these economies meant there was no hope of competition developing. Privatization and free prices allowed complete freedom of action to the monopolists. Production fell, and prices rose.

The societies of Eastern Europe plunged into chaos. Growing unemployment was accompanied everywhere, except perhaps in Poland, by unrestrained inflation. Living standards fell, but enterprises did not become competitive. The victims of the reforms included not only workers, but also small entrepreneurs and individual peasant farmers. The abolition of state subsidies for agricultural production in Poland and Hungary, together with rising prices for machinery and fertilizer, dealt a blow to the rural population. Smallholders began falling into ruin, and unemployment rose among the peasantry; at the same time, the contraction of output in the cities ruled out any possibility of the growing number of idle hands finding work in industry and services. A mass slaughter of stock began, unparalleled since the time of collectivization in Russia. After decollectivization in Lithuania, the number of cattle fell by 25 percent, of pigs by 43 percent, and of chickens by 36 percent. Meanwhile, the prices of agricultural produce rose by 738 percent in the space of a year.[42] "A paradoxical situation has arisen...." the newspaper *Izvestiia* stated in the winter of 1991. "If the world price of a liter of milk today is about fourteen forints, in Hungary the cost of production is some six to nine forints dearer. So if Hungarian producers are to have any possibility of competing on the world market, Hungarian producers need subsidies of these same six to nine forints per liter. The most interesting thing is that this does not by any means signify that foreign competitors, say, Western European farmers, work much more efficiently than Hungarian stock farmers on their family plots or in agribusiness firms. The point is simply that in the supposed market economy of the West ... state subsidies to farmers cover from 60 to 100 percent of their costs of production!!"[43]

The mass ruin of the peasantry recalls the destruction of the traditional sector in the countries of the third world; the modern sector has failed to grow fast enough to digest the masses of superfluous people who are ready to leave the countryside. Countries which managed to avoid the horrors of Stalinist collectivization are now subject to analogous problems—thanks to free market policies. The Polish economist T. Kovalik noted that in 1992, after two years of liberal reforms, it was only in the state sector that "some weak signs of increasing efficiency" were in evidence.[44] In the private sector stagnation reigned, and productivity in the economy as a whole remained extremely low.

The outcome of the reforms in Hungary was no less deplorable. "At the same time as Western tourists enjoy Hungarian cuisine and music in first-class hotels, most families in Budapest have fallen into poverty," stated a correspondent for the West German *Die Welt*—a newspaper which cannot, in any way, be suspected of having left-wing sympathies.[45]

Even in the former East Germany, where, it might seem, the transition to the free market has been taking place under ideal conditions (the federal government spent substantial sums on unification, and the Western currency has been introduced, while the initial level of development was comparable with some developed capitalist countries), the process has not gone well. A correspondent for *Izvestiia* stated in

February 1991 that the optimistic prognoses had not been borne out. Production had declined, and unemployment was "growing at a desperate pace"; hundreds of thousands of people "employed in what were only recently modern and prestigious forms of production" were now "on the borderline."[46]

It was the advanced sectors that found themselves in the most difficult situation. This was not because their technological potential turned out to be lower than had been supposed. These enterprises were simply not ready to compete on the open market, even with their best products. They had yet to learn that the quality of production and its competitiveness are far from being identical. Success depends on a multitude of factors. In order to achieve success under new conditions, even enterprises with the best products required additional funds for reorganization. It was necessary to solve new problems that had been unknown earlier.

The funds were not to be had. In the absence of large public programs to ensure the modernization of the economy as a whole, investing capital in modernizing individual enterprises was too risky for private entrepreneurs. Factories shut down, and millions of people found themselves on the street. Meanwhile, the general technological level declined, and the country was less and less able to permit itself to produce complex modern items. Eastern Europe grew ever closer to the third world.

As has been explained, the political changes occurring in Eastern Europe were by no means favorable to economic recovery. The reunification of Germany dealt a heavy blow to the whole system of Eastern European integration. The British scholar of Eastern European problems Neil Asherson noted that the market for industrial goods in East Germany was shut off because firms there were shifting their orders to West Germany. At the same time, West German customers who formerly bought industrial products in Poland, Czechoslovakia, and Hungary have found cheaper suppliers in their own eastern territories. But the worst development has concerned Soviet oil. Eastern Europe now had to buy Soviet oil for hard currency and at world prices. These prices, meanwhile, were rising fast, and the conflict in the Persian Gulf made the search for alternative suppliers pointless. In a sense, Eastern Europe has seen a repeat of the catastrophe of the 1970s, when the rise in oil prices undermined attempts at economic liberalization in the region and helped to swell a huge foreign debt, especially in Poland and Hungary. This debt is still continuing to grow.[47] The dissolution of the Council for Mutual Economic Assistance and the shift to reciprocal accounts in hard currency have led to a sharp fall in trade between the former "brother" countries, at the same time, finding new markets has been impossible because of the world crisis. The disintegration of the USSR and Yugoslavia, and the enlistment of the Eastern European countries and Russia in the trade blockade declared by the United Nations against Serbia, have complicated the situation still further.

No one doubted that during the transition period a certain fall in output was inevitable. Nevertheless, the depression has exceeded the expectations of the most hardened pessimists. "In order to undo the damage wrought by forty years of Communism, much more painful measures may be required than many people are ready to digest," the *Economist* stated impassively.[48] However, not even the most painful measures from the arsenal of the neoliberal economic school were of any use. Production of consumer goods accounted for a large part of the fall in output, despite the fact that in Eastern Europe this sector had been inadequately developed even earlier. The old disproportions were not overcome, but became still more pronounced. The "cannibal" economy, in which producing metal for machines to extract ore in order to produce metal was more important than producing goods for the population, continued to nourish itself. Meanwhile, the sectors serving the public suffered as a result of people's lack of buying power.

Privatization reinforced the old economic structure. It not only failed to resolve the central problems of the economy, but also acted as a brake on structural change. No free competition arose between blocs of capital, or even between goods. The liberal press was forced to admit that monopolism was "rejuvenating itself," while in place of the illegal shadow economy, "a completely legal 'savage capitalism'" was rising up.[49] A new class of property owners had appeared, who were extracting monopoly profits and who had a vital interest in preserving the old centralized structure with all its disproportions. Under these conditions, whether an enterprise was profitable ran at a profit or at a loss indicated nothing about its efficiency. The rise in prices was accompanied by a fall in output, the fall in output increased the profits of the monopolists, and the growth of unemployment was accompanied by catastrophic inflation. The new oligarchy had no interest whatever in structural renovation or the modernization of the economy.

The same social preconditions of underdevelopment that were characteristic of most backward countries—the hegemony of conservative property-owners, and the intertwining of capitalist and pre-capitalist relations—began to reproduce themselves. The objective need to do away with these social barriers to development has been the main cause of most of the revolutions in backward countries, beginning with the Russian Revolution of 1917. It was the changes to the structure of society in Russia that ensured, though at the cost of great sacrifices, the rapid modernization of the 1930s. The collapse of Communism led to the old problems being reborn on a new level. The bureaucratic oligarchy, consolidating its control over the economy from above, also blocked the development of entrepreneurship from below. As Kolganov noted, in the system that had come into being, independent entrepreneurs and even foreign business interests that ventured onto the Eastern European market would "be crushed by the monopolists, who have fused with the corrupt bureaucratic elite." These new interests had "either to accept the 'rules of the game' of this system"—and a section of them were already prepared to do this—or to "violate the collective responsibility of 'nomenklatura capitalism.'"[50] In the latter case, Kolganov added, they could sooner or later turn into allies of the socialist forces.

As was to be expected, in the course of privatization an acute shortage of capital investments appeared. In both the West and the East, supporters of liberal reforms were united in the hope that private capital investments might come from abroad or through the acquisition by workers of shares and property on the Western model.[51] In fact, the population simply did not have money, and private capital was being invested not in production, but in trade and in real estate speculation, since the profits there were substantially higher.

"In the conditions of the transitional period," wrote the Soviet economist L. Freinkman, "the degree of risk involved in any capital investment is extraordinarily high. The system of centralized supply is disintegrating, while market trade in resources has not yet become established. To privatize enterprises in such circumstances is to consciously deprive most of them of supplies and sales. The political instability in the country aggravates the risk factor, turning private investment into an unwinnable lottery, into Russian roulette. In these circumstances, not only experienced shareholders but also our economically illiterate population have had the sense to refrain from buying securities."[52]

Where attracting private investment was concerned, a few cases in which Western firms bought shares in large companies, mainly in Hungary and Czechoslovakia, could not change the overall dismal picture. Trying to attract investors, governments sold off the national wealth for trivial sums. Privatization not only failed to yield substantial returns to the treasury, but in many cases was directly or indirectly subsidized from public funds.[53]

The liberals considered private investments to be the main precondition for stabilization. But what happened was the precise opposite: private capital held back, waiting for the state to ensure stability. It was a Catch-22 situation: if the efficiency of the public sector could not be raised, and the economy dragged out of crisis on this basis, private capital would not begin to operate. If, however, the public sector managed to cope with this task, private capital would no longer be vitally necessary.

Particular hopes were placed in the International Monetary Fund and transnational corporations, to which it was proposed to hand over part of the state sector. Moderate economists sought in vain to remind the politicians that Western capitalists "do not invest out of the goodness of their hearts, but above all in order to obtain profits," and that the widespread sale of state enterprises to foreigners could easily turn into "selling off the national estate."[54] Such warnings were not and could not be heeded. An adviser to Gorbachev, N. Petrakov, stressed that the demands of the IMF and the plans of the ruling circles "practically coincide." This could, Petrakov added, be called "selling off the Fatherland," but it was necessary to "say *nyet* to the nay-sayers."[55]

The government of the Hungarian Democratic Forum, despite its nationalist rhetoric, made attracting Western investment its main priority, while the opposition Free Democrats insisted that the Hungarian market be even more open to foreign firms. As the Hungarian sociologist Ivan Szelinyi observed, "an entrepreneur in Hungary now gets on better if he or she is a foreigner."[56] In Szelinyi's view these policies were fatal for the country, since only by encouraging local entrepreneurship and developing a national bourgeoisie would it be possible for Hungary, like South Korea and Taiwan, to make a success of capitalist development. The generally painful experience of third world countries which "collaborated" with the International Monetary Fund taught the Eastern European politicians nothing.

In 1989 and 1990 Western business executives showed great interest in Eastern Europe. But as scholars have noted, the Western companies that initially showed interest often quickly lost it. Discovering that Poland and other countries were far from being on the brink of an entrepreneurial revolution, and that patience and a knowledge of local conditions were required in order to conduct business there, firms scrapped their original plans.[57] Western observers noted the unimpressive results achieved by Poland despite the liberalization of the market and the encouragement given to Western capital investments. "It is surprising," reported the trade union expert Denis MacShane, "that very few Western firms have gone into Eastern Europe in a serious way. The United States, for example, is investing five times more in Mexico than in the entire Soviet bloc. Half of the joint ventures in Poland have an initial capital of less than ten thousand dollars."[58]

The Soviet government, which at the very beginning of perestroika adopted a law on joint ventures, was forced to acknowledge the total failure of this policy. By the end of 1989 only a third of the registered firms were actually functioning. Only an insignificant number of them were engaged in industrial production. Joint ventures made use of their numerous privileges to import goods duty-free. Meanwhile, despite the nonconvertible ruble, a clear tendency to capital flight was evident as early as mid-1990. Official spokespeople promised that by 1990–1991 the activity of foreign entrepreneurs in the Soviet Union "would also become noticeable on the internal market, including the consumer market."[59] By the time these promises fell due, Gorbachev had already been ousted from power, and chaos reigned in the Russian economy.

Western entrepreneurs quickly discovered that without links to the local bureaucracy and the local mafia, conducting business was practically impossible. The internal markets of Eastern Europe were ruled by the worst sector of international capital, which was also the best adapted to local conditions. This was primarily companies which had extensive experience of applying analogous methods in analogous circumstances in underdeveloped countries.

The liberal theoreticians honestly believed that the cheapness of labor power in Eastern Europe would make it possible to attract substantial capital investments from developed capitalist countries, and would stimulate the growth of export production within the country along the lines of the South Korean or Chinese models. In fact, the cheapness of labor power in Eastern Europe was a myth, since the calculations did not include the sector of the price of labor power that in Soviet-type societies used to be hidden.

In these societies, living standards that were comparatively high by comparison with the third world were ensured through a system of state subsidies and social consumption funds. Cheap housing, transport, and child care, together with subsidized food prices, made it possible to pay workers comparatively low wages. But maintaining equilibrium was possible only under certain circumstances. The most important of these was the existence in the country of only one proprietor, the state. This allowed the government extensive latitude for redistributing incomes. Funds that were spent on social welfare and services could be made up through low wages and high rates of profit in the state sector. Stable prices for basic consumer goods and low, stable wages made it possible to maintain fixed prices for industrial production, while preventing inflation and facilitating bureaucratic accounting and control. Unlike the situation in the Scandinavian countries, social welfare benefits were provided to the bulk of the population without the need for a complex system of taxation. The system was straightforward and comparatively stable.

As the role played by market factors increased, and bureaucratic administration became less effective, maintaining equilibrium grew more and more difficult. The Eastern European governments were already regarding the subsidies as burdensome, and were trying to reduce them. Meanwhile, popular dissatisfaction at the inability of the governments to maintain equilibrium and guarantee low-paid workers the promised minimum of social benefits led to growing opposition. The protesters themselves, even while demanding a quick transition to the market, were by no means ready to sacrifice these social guarantees. Social welfare benefits were perceived as an inalienable and natural right.

From the point of view of traditional market economics, Eastern Europe was always a sort of Alice-in-Wonderland place where the usual explanations did not apply, and where normal chains of cause and effect were absent. Western experts who studied the example of Hungary stated with surprise that "despite falling real wages, per capita consumption continued to rise in most of the 1980s, though at a slower pace than in the 1960s."[60] This is partly explained by the growth of the second economy, including the development of the black and grey markets, work in garden plots, and so forth. But none of this would have been possible had the system of traditional social guarantees not functioned more or less normally.

Privatization brought dramatic new problems. The closed circuit was broken, and the state could no longer compensate itself for its expenses out of the profits of enterprises. Maintaining social equilibrium was now possible only through high taxation, which would spur the growth of bureaucracy and discourage entrepreneurial activity, or through rapid wage increases. People were now forced to earn several times more simply in order to maintain their previous standard of living. This in turn led either to galloping inflation, or to the impoverishment of the population and the collapse of the internal market.

The example of the free economic zones and foreign entrepreneurship in China was incorrectly understood. The dissemination of capitalist elements into the Chinese economy was a success because the state system ensured social services for the private sector as well. So long as the bulk of enterprises and of the population live according to the old rules, a small number of firms can, with the agreement of the authorities, live under their own laws. So long as transport, a substantial part of the housing stock, and the system of social services remain part of a unified totalitarian state sector, private and foreign entrepreneurship is indirectly subsidized.[61] This is why foreign corporations and local private firms have had no need for a full and consistent transformation of the Communist regime in China. It is also the reason why China and Vietnam, with their Communist regimes, remain more attractive to foreign investors than countries which have proclaimed the goal of building capitalism.

As they integrate themselves into the world system, the former Communist countries have increasingly become part of the periphery. Their debt dependency has not diminished, and their technological backwardness has become more pronounced. In terms of per capita income as well, the populations of Eastern Europe by the early 1990s had also become much closer to the countries of the poor South than of the rich West. Average per capita income in Poland in 1988 was $1,860; in Mexico $1,760; in Hungary $2,460; and in Brazil $2,160. "We are now closer to the periphery and further from the center than at any time in the past hundred years," stated Ivan Szelenyi.[62]

Of course, to set Eastern Europe on the same plane as most of the countries of the third world would be incorrect. "People who describe the USSR as 'Upper Volta with missiles,'" writes Sergei Kara-Murza, "simply don't know Upper Volta. And if they do know it, they're acting unscrupulously."[63] Eastern Europe does not have to contend with a population explosion. With educated populations used to urban life and to European living standards, the former Communist countries differ dramatically from most of the third world. Even the republics of Soviet Central Asia clearly surpassed the majority of Islamic states in their indices of social development.

The countries of the former Eastern bloc might better be described as the semiperiphery of the new world order established at the beginning of the 1990s. Semiperipheral countries display many features linking them to the advanced states, but also other traits characteristic of backward countries. "Semi-peripheral states," writes Wallerstein, "are the ones that usually decline and ascend." Orienting toward the achievements of the advanced countries, they strive to emulate them, but rarely achieve this goal. "Many may try, but only a few succeed in significantly transforming the rank of their state in the world division of labor. This is because the very success of one eliminates opportunities and alternatives for others."[64] In Wallerstein's view, a great deal depends here on intelligent state policies.

As examples of the decline of semiperipheral countries in the seventeenth and eighteenth centuries, Wallerstein cites Spain and Portugal, and as areas on the rise he singles out Northern Europe and the British colonies in North America. Twentieth-century examples of the rising semiperiphery include Taiwan and South Korea. Eastern Europe is falling into decline.

The hopes of many politicians and economists in the East that their countries will become second Taiwans are fated to be dashed. The world market does not have a place for two Taiwans. The success of the Asian tigers, which occupy a specific place in the world division of labor, rules out the possibility of this model being repeated in other countries.

In Central Europe shifts are now taking place which are dramatically changing the relationship of forces between states. The efforts of reunited Germany to integrate the economy of the former German Democratic Republic into the capitalist center are undermining the chances of Czechoslovakia, the most developed country of the region; to invest capital there is less profitable and less safe than in the East German *Länder*. The policies of the Eastern European rulers have merely worsened the situation, condemning these countries, in Szelinyi's words, at best to the role of "the economic periphery of the new Germany."[65]

The clear and general failure of the liberal reforms has provoked a new ideological crisis in Eastern Europe. The ruling groups and parties have been splitting, engaging in fierce struggles with one another. A divide has opened up between populists and liberals. In Poland these forces are the populist Centrist Alliance, supporting President Walesa, and the liberal Democratic Action Movement (ROAD), headed by former prime minister Tadeusz Mazowiecki. In Hungary the populists of the Hungarian Democratic Front have waged a furious struggle against the Westernizers of the Party of Free Democrats. Insults have been exchanged, slanders have been circulated, and anti-Semitic attacks have become commonplace. In such a struggle the inevitable losers are the people and groups who have retained even a shred of honesty. Bogdan Denitch described this aptly as the Mexicanization of politics, in which elements of real democracy are included in an essentially undemocratic system.[66]

In criticizing one another, the numerous right-wing groups have tried to use the failure of the reforms to their own advantage, taking over ministerial posts and privileges from their rivals. This competition of political elites, warring with one another but supporting the same economic program, has allowed the parliamentary system, up to a point, to act as a social lightning rod. Popular dissatisfaction has been directed not against the ruling circles in general, but directly against the government currently in office.

The first victim of the new system was Polish Premier Mazowiecki, who in the presidential elections of November 1990 won only about 18 percent of the votes. Disappointed by the outcome of the reforms, the electors voted *en masse* against him, even though the other side was proclaiming exactly the same policies. A major sensation of the elections was the result gained in the second round by the émigre entrepreneur Stanislaw Tyminski. His pre-election campaign was a parody of the campaigns of the neoliberal candidates. Tyminski acted in effect as a parodic double of Mazowiecki. Preferring the grotesque copy to the original, Poles expressed their attitude to the government even better than if they had simply voted against the prime minister. Tyminski's success, however, also showed something else: the crisis of neoliberal policies was not being accompanied by the appearance of a healthy and convincing alternative. This was not simply for the reason that no such alternative was on offer, but also because society itself was not ready for it.

In these circumstances the historic leader of Solidarnosc, Lech Walesa, easily won the second round of the elections, and in December 1990 became the first non-Communist president of Poland in forty years. Mazowiecki resigned, and in his place Walesa appointed Jan Belecki, who immediately declared that for him, the main principles of the reforms carried out by the preceding cabinet remained fundamental.[67] Additional funds were assigned to support peasant farmers, but this did not solve the main problems of the countryside. The funds were obtained by reducing unemployment benefits. Simultaneously, a ban placed by Mazowiecki on leaders of the central administration engaging in free entrepreneurship was lifted. The spontaneous process through which bureaucratic capitalism was coming into being thus won official blessing at the highest level.

Such a cat and mouse game with society cannot continue indefinitely. The conflict between the elites who control the political system and the masses who are deprived of real representation must inevitably lead to open clashes. Even the ultraliberal newspaper *Moskovskie Novosti* noted after the election of Walesa that for the labor movement, "conflict with the president is inevitable, since the core of his program is accelerated privatization, with an unavoidable rise in the number of strikes, and a new spiral of inflation."[68] The president's proletarian origins and heroic past might postpone the conflict, but could not do away with the inevitable contradictions.

The wave of strikes was not long in coming. The first such actions began in the summer of 1990. They were halted thanks to Walesa's personal authority and to the trust that still remained in the government. The presidential elections reduced social tensions somewhat, arousing the hope among workers that by electing a former trade union leader as president, they could obtain a government more responsive to their interests. It quickly became clear that these hopes were illusory. As early as February 1991 coal miners, traditionally among the main bases of support for Solidarnosc, were protesting against the government.

By early 1991 it had become clear that the multiparty system that had been established on the ruins of the old political order was not working. "In this sense the example of Romania is particularly instructive," notes the French scholar Edith Lhomel. "Apart from members of the Hungarian minority, who support the Hungarian Democratic Union, almost no one identifies with the political parties seated in the parliament. This has made the street protests by workers and students, organized by the trade unions, still more important."[69]

A similar situation has arisen from Mongolia to Czechoslovakia, from Albania to Estonia. The crisis of the political parties has not been the result solely of ideological factors. As the political scientist M. Duverger wrote in the 1950s, if living standards are low and the masses cannot directly influence the political process, "parties take on a formal character; warring groups argue over power, using votes as soft dough out of which they mold whatever they want." To demonstrate this thesis Duverger drew on examples from Asia, Africa, and South America, but it would now be perfectly possible to add Eastern Europe to this list. In Western Europe itself during the nineteenth century, when only the dominant economic and financial groups "had at their disposal the press, the media of information and propaganda, and the apparatus needed for mobilizing voters, democracy did not exist; only the growth of parties, and above all of workers' parties, made it possible for the whole people to collaborate actively with political institutions."[70]

At the beginning of the 1990s, the new and old oligarchies held a complete monopoly on political life. Just as politics in Britain during the nineteenth and even the early twentieth centuries was a pursuit for gentlemen, in post-Communist Eastern Europe it remains a luxury for the elite.

Most of the new parties both in Eastern Europe and in Russia were oriented primarily toward the middle layers. Paradoxically, the vanguard role of the middle class was extolled both by the Centrist Union and ROAD in Poland, and by the populists and liberals in Hungary. It is difficult to think of any group in Russia that would have doubted this principle. When former Communists, abandoning the sinking ship of the old regime, announced the founding of the Republican Party, they declared that it was to be "a party of the intelligentsia, of the middle layers."[71] The same role was claimed by the Social Democrats, who affirmed that their party was aimed "at the formation in our society of the middle layers that traditionally have provided the basis for social democratic organizations in other countries(!)," and by liberal groups that promised to give birth to "a traditional class of entrepreneurs—an upper middle class."[72] In Poland the former Solidarnosc activist Zbigniew Bujak stated that power in his country had to lie with the middle layers, while workers and peasants, unless they wanted to lose their identity in the new conditions, had to seek opportunities for private entrepreneurship and small business activity.[73] People who could not enter the middle class had only themselves to blame.

The official ideologues of the new Eastern European regimes acknowledged that in reality the middle layers did not exist. They had been annihilated under Communism, and had now to be re-established, but no one was disconcerted by this. Politicians who attempted to speak in the name of this mythical class enjoyed near-complete ideological freedom. In the interests of a class that had still to be created, but to which, they considered, the future belonged, they were entitled to crush the resistance of the backward masses. Of the masses, that is, who had borne on their shoulders the whole burden of the struggle against the old regime, and who had brought the new leaders to power.

"The official propaganda speaks of 'normality', or of a 'return to Europe,'" wrote T. Kowalik, "as if prior to the 'Communist deviation' Poland had been a typical European country with market structures and an economy based on private property. But this was not the case. The bulk of the population lived and worked in the countryside, under conditions close to a subsistence economy. The modern capitalist sector was not only small, but also closely tied to the state. Polish capitalism was by nature state capitalism. Under Communist rule major demographic and social-professional shifts took place. But this modernization of the population cannot in any sense be regarded as instruction in the rules of conduct that apply in a market economy, or as developing the capacities for a quick and easy mastering of these rules."[74]

The middle layers that came into being under the Communist regimes differed sharply from those in the West. They were made up of groups that were formerly quite real, including the intellectual elite, the mafia, and a section of the administrative and party apparatus. These groups were united more by a common type and standard of consumption than by anything else.[75] Their orientation to Western European patterns of consumption also formed the subtext for the Westernizing ideology that held sway in the East. The hope that the changes in society would provide particular social layers with easier access to goods in short supply was not, perhaps, altogether false. But the price of the changes turned out to be the destruction of society, dealing a heavy blow to important sectors of the middle layers themselves.

In the front line of the changes were the "new lumpens"—the lumpenized middle layers. The heterogeneity of the middle layers meant that they found it more difficult than others to unite in defence of their interests. Their semiprivileged position under the old regimes, together with their access to knowledge and information, allowed them to become a more organized and influential political force just at the moment when the old order began to crack. This situation did not seem in the least paradoxical to the members of the middle layers, since they not only failed to take account of their own weakness, but with their lack of unifying interests, readily confused their own momentary advantage with the long-term tasks of society as a whole, or at least of their own social group. Joining with the mafia and the old nomenklatura in dividing up the plunder, many of them sincerely believed that they were becoming entrepreneurs and vehicles of social progress. A bloc formed between the old oligarchy and a section of the middle layers, and this became the dominant force in society. However, this by no means signified that the middle layers had come to power. On the contrary, the middle layers—like the proletariat during the Civil War in Russia—are now quickly becoming de-classed. Some have become upwardly mobile, filling out the ranks of the oligarchy, while others can no longer make ends meet. In other words, despite the forecasts of liberal economists that a new middle class was being formed, precisely the opposite process was taking place.[76]

This new lumpen elite is becoming the dominant force in political life.[77] The members of this elite accuse the bolsheviks of having created a myth of the proletariat, and in the absence of a real proletariat, of then turning for support to lumpen elements. But a similar charge can be levelled at the Polish and Russian liberals. While proclaiming the rebirth of the great democratic values of the West, the builders of capitalism in Eastern Europe have revived some of the worst aspects of bolshevik tradition.

The Polish sociologist Radislawa Gortat has described the situation that arose after the fall of the Communist regimes as "freedom without democracy."[78] The old mechanisms of totalitarian control have collapsed, but democratic institutions are not functioning. The increasing political chaos suits the people who are trying, amid the confusion, to seize the greatest possible share of power and state property. However, this cannot continue for long; the lack of genuine democracy creates the danger that the newly-won freedoms will be lost. In September 1993 the Russian democratic experiment was ended by a bloody coup staged by President Yeltsin. The parliament and local Soviets were dissolved, censorship reimposed, opposition parties outlawed, hundreds of people killed, thousands arrested. However this was not just something that happened in Russia. Yeltsin's coup was a turning point for the whole of Eastern Europe. As an extreme case of neoliberal reform, Russia once again has shown a general tendency: it became clear that any continuation of such reforms is incompatible with democratic institutions and respect for human rights.

Western democracy took shape under relatively favorable conditions. But while extolling civil society, many writers have failed to note that what has become established in the East is a civil society for the elite. Unlike the civil society of the West, this has not grown out of the lives of the majority of citizens.[79] A conflict has inevitably arisen between civil society and "real" society. Civil society, which has become transformed into the field of activity of professional political oligarchies and lumpen elites, has become increasingly antagonistic to real society, and as a result, has become openly antidemocratic.[80] It is as if the authoritarian evolution of the political systems in the East were genetically determined. The discrepancy between Western parliamentary models and the real conditions of social life of the masses in the East has transformed parliamentary institutions from organs of popular power into bodies hostile to any popular initiative.

The efforts by this civil society to find a bond with the masses and to root itself have led in two directions. They have usually amounted either to appeals for a return to the pre-Communist past, or to the encouragement by politicians of the most repellent chauvinism, of the most reactionary prejudices of the masses. The political circles that have now risen to power are simply a marginal elite torn from its social roots. The lumpens at the top have been able to find a mass social base only in the lumpen layers and moods at the bottom.

Apart from the Czech lands, not one of the Eastern European countries could boast of rich democratic traditions and significant economic achievements during the pre-Communist period. After the events of 1989 the most perceptive Western observers warned that "there is no reassuring past into which Eastern Europe can now slip back, no ancient formulas for peace and prosperity that can be dug out and dusted off."[81] It is not surprising that the ideological vacuum has been filled by old, seemingly long-discredited ideas. An unprecedented rise of nationalism has begun. At first the hatred was directed against the Soviet Union, but as the Soviet bloc disintegrated, internal conflicts emerged onto the surface. In Lithuania, not only Russians were abhorrent to the new authorities, but also the majority of Poles, who were refused the right to self-determination. In Romania the conflict between Romanians and Hungarians led to bloody clashes. In Czechoslovakia, which prided itself on its civilized, Western ways, the federation could not be saved from falling apart.[82] Yugoslavia disintegrated into warring regions. In Georgia the democratically elected government of Zviad Gamsakhurdia displayed monstrous cruelty toward the national minorities in Abkhazia and South Ossetia. In Tskhinvali, the capital of South Ossetia, Georgian militia members fired on peaceful residents, killing children and old people. During the winter they cut off heating and electricity. Newborn babies died in the maternity hospitals. President Gamsakhurdia was accused of violating democratic rights and overthrown, but under the government of Eduard Shevaradnadze the position of national minorities became still worse. Barbaric wars were fought in Abkhazia and South Ossetia, costing thousands of lives.

Despite the growth of anti-Semitism, the first victims of chauvinism were not Jews but Gypsies (Romany). The ideology of the new united Europe provided a wonderful justification for everyday racism. In the new Europe, there was no place for "barbaric" peoples, for Muslims or Semites. "'Eastern' populations such as Gypsies, Turks and Albanians," writes the American scholar John Feffer, "are singled out: for not being civilized, for producing too many children, for polluting the Mother-land. For those with long memories, the epithets applied to these populations will call to mind characterizations of Jews in this part of the world in the inter-war period."[83]

The Hungarian scholar Peter Bihari writes of "striking manifesta-tions of racism, of hatred for foreigners. The Stalinist thesis of the 'besieged fortress' has been replaced by arguments about the 'besieged nation.' The pseudo-internationalism of the past has now been re-placed by the use of nationalism as the main force cementing together a mass social base for the conservative government. Implicit in this, of course, is the 'preservation' of totalitarianism. The social victims of the restoration of capitalism are offered up as sacrifices on the altar of the nation. 'Who is not with us is not a Hungarian....'"[84]

The link between nationalism and authoritarianism, demonstrated tragically in the third world, is emerging once again in Eastern Europe. Nationalist groups have grown stronger as hopes for Western-style democracy have melted away. "If the economic crisis cannot be man-aged," Western experts warned in 1990, "then the multiparty system will be put under considerable strain. While privatization and liberal-ization as an ideology attracts Hungarian intellectuals and managers, for the masses it is nationalism combined with religious sentiment which seems to have stronger appeal."[85] Like all grim prophecies, this was fulfilled quickly and completely. In the spring of 1991, the first non-Communist president of Hungary, A. Gyonc, acknowledged that "bitterness and fear" were prevailing in the country. "People consider that just as before, developments are controlled from behind the scenes," Gyonc stated. "The country has been seized by a wave of fear—fear of a new pluralist dictatorship."[86]

As befitted model pupils of the Communist system, the new rulers of Eastern Europe were ready to perform heroic feats in order to overcome the problems they had themselves created. The only ques-tion was how long the people could endure this process. The less faith the population had in the official ideology, the less the ruling groups made use of democratic procedures. Despite massive propaganda campaigns in support of free enterprise, by the end of 1990 opinion polls in most Eastern European countries had shown that most of the people did not support privatization. If petty privatization (small enterprises, services, consumer goods production, and so forth) generally met with approval, most of those polled took a negative attitude to the formation of large private or joint-stock companies, and to the sale of major industrial enterprises.[87]

The ideologues of the new regimes insisted that reforms that were essential to the country should be introduced even against the will of the citizens. In the pages of *Literaturnaia Gazeta*, for example, V. Sirotkin declared that if the majority of the population were to resist privatization and the "100 percent" introduction of private property, these measures should be "introduced by decree."[88]

Millions of people discovered that life had been better under the old order. Then there had at least been stability and a certain confidence in the future; everything had been preordained. There was work, and people's basic physical survival was guaranteed. After the first year of changes in Czechoslovakia, Milos Rejchrt, who had earlier been an activist in the democratic opposition, stated: "The overwhelming majority of people now feel a strong nostalgia."[89] If things were that bad in Czechoslovakia, the most prosperous and stable of the former Communist countries, what were they like in impoverished Romania? In Poland, according to press reports, three-quarters of respondents in an opinion survey considered that life was better under the old Stalinist system.[90]

The public, following the political debates on television, came gradually to the conclusion that arguments in favor of private property and the free market were the invariable calling card of every corrupt demagogue. In millions of people in Eastern Europe, disillusionment with liberalism at first brought only feelings of apathy and hopelessness, but as in other countries, workers began little by little to realize that they needed their own organizations and their own policies.

CHAPTER 8

IN SEARCH OF A VANGUARD

To speak of alternatives is pointless so long as there is no force on the political scene that is capable of putting them into practice. Following the collapse of the Communist system democratic leftists succeeded in winning positions in parliaments, local councils, and state instrumentalities, but found that without strong organizations they had no impact on the course of events. The groupings of the democratic left were small, with high moral authority but negligible political influence.[1] In Czechoslovakia the left wing of the Civic Forum was represented in parliament, but lacked base-level structures and a clear program of action. The Left Alternative group in Hungary was an association of intellectuals, belonging to three distinct parties and without links to the labor movement. In Russia, the Socialist Party was described by journalists as a "vanguard without an army."[2] Labor Solidarity in Poland retained some ties with the trade unions, but also remained primarily a group of politicians and ideologues without a mass base. Activists of the Polish Socialist Party (PPS) found that their youth and decisiveness could not make up for their lack of cadres and political experience.

The problem was not in a shortage of attractive ideas. The leftists failed to become the expression of concrete social interests. Often, they were simply unable to clarify the question of what type of party and which policies were needed in the struggle for the principles which they proclaimed. Things went no better for the social democrats than for the radical left. In the early stages of democratization, social democratic parties sprang up like mushrooms throughout the countries of the Communist bloc. Their ideologues hoped that the populations of Eastern Europe, trying to attain Western living standards without sacrificing social guarantees, would turn in their direction. As the Bulgarian social democrat Petar Dertliev put it, they wanted a market economy, but more like the one under Mitterand than under Thatcher.[3]

The East German social democrats, aided by their Western brother party, did in fact register certain successes. However, these were far fewer than party leaders had expected. In Hungary the social democratic party failed completely to win representation in parliament, and in Romania it finished up the weakest of the opposition parties, receiving even fewer votes than the Socialist Workers Party that had been established by former Communists. The few social democrats who won election to the parliaments in Czechoslovakia, Bulgaria, and Russia acted there as part of the democratic bloc. The success of social democrats who stood as candidates of the Civic Forum in Czechoslovakia was in sharp contrast to the failure of the Social Democratic Party.

As a political current, social democracy arose in wealthy and developed capitalist countries with profound democratic traditions. Efforts to implant social democracy in the third world have either failed, or have served as ideological justification for quite different policies. Here there were neither abundant resources which the rulers of society might share with the labor movement, nor a competent officialdom, nor a socially responsible bourgeoisie with a traditional Protestant ethic. A socialism of distribution is possible only where there are no special problems in organizing modern production.

The slogan of the social democrats in Eastern Europe was "a market economy while retaining social guarantees." This sounded very attractive, but everyday reality showed the emptiness of such formulas. The old social support mechanisms that had existed under the Communist regimes were visibly disintegrating, while the methods of Western social democracy were failing to work in the impoverished Eastern European countries. The Western rulers were ready to finance the integration of Eastern Europe into the world capitalist economy as a new periphery or semiperiphery, but not to pay for the maintenance of social welfare systems. Discussing the prospect of mass unemployment and impoverishment in Eastern Europe, an observer for the *Economist* stated with categorical harshness: "This is painful, but inevitable. In the Eastern European countries where unemployment is not rising significantly, reforms are still not going ahead in earnest."[4]

As in the countries of Latin America, the dismantling of social welfare provisions has become a sort of guarantee for the International Monetary Fund and the Western banks that the Eastern European governments intend to implement real changes. Western experts, including right-wing social democrats, have spoken seriously of the need for Eastern Europe to follow a Latin American path.[5] There is a certain logic to this. "Carrying through a transition to the capitalist market while maintaining social guarantees for the population is a well-known impossibility," wrote the prominent Soviet sociologist Sergei Kara-Murza, "since the market and entrepreneurship are based on personal risk and personal responsibility, and on primordial forces; you might win, but you might also suffer total disaster.... Everyone now places his or her labor power on the market as a commodity (we are not talking here about the buyers of this commodity, the entrepreneurs; they are not worried about social welfare). Naturally, there can be no guarantee that this commodity will be purchased. Moreover, a certain proportion of the commodities on offer must inevitably be rejected. And of course, the price of labor power as a commodity is determined not by the work itself, but by the relationship between demand and supply, and also by threat to do harm to the entrepreneur (this may take the civilized form of strikes, or the more elemental forms of murder, robbery, poisoning the water supply, and so on)."[6]

It is obvious that one of the key factors deciding the real level of social security in a society living by the laws of the free market is the strength and degree of organization of the labor movement. But the poorer the country, the more difficult it is to extract concessions from the ruling class, and consequently, the more radical the labor movement is compelled to be. In such circumstances, social democratic concepts of class peace fail to work. Prescriptions which might be suitable for Sweden or Austria have turned out to be impossible to apply in North Africa, Romania, or Russia. An efficient, modern capitalism is a prerequisite without which social democracy simply cannot exist. However Karl Kautsky or Eduard Bernstein might have perceived the role of this movement, social democracy historically has not proven to be an alternative to capitalism, but its socialist satellite.

Social democracy has only succeeded in carrying out reforms when the economic conjuncture has been favorable. The weakening of the movement in Western Europe during the 1980s was linked to its inability to advance a convincing anticrisis program. In these circumstances, Eastern European social democracy has been unable to offer its supporters anything apart from appeals for the restoration of capitalism; in this respect it has differed little from more conventional right-wing forces. Hungarian Socialist Party leader Gyula Horn acknowledged that social democracy in Hungary and other countries of Eastern Europe "hasn't been able to put forward its own workable solution yet" to the problems of the region; thus it was essential to join forces with the liberals.[7] Gyorgy Markus, an ideologue of the party's right wing, was even more forthright on this point. Since the consolidation of democratic capitalism in Markus's view represented the only possible road to social progress in Eastern Europe, social democracy had to use every possible means to aid privatization, to expedite the redistribution of property and incomes in favor of the rich, and to end state regulation of the economy—in short, to advance the cause of capitalization. There was no need to be especially perturbed by the fact that these policies would "differ substantially from those of most Western social democrats, being more reminiscent of social-liberalism, or perhaps, 'right-wing' social democracy."[8]

Oleg Rumyantsev, the founder of the Social Democratic Party of the Russian Federation (SDPR), admitted openly that his party and the right-wing liberal groups in essence made up two sections of one big party.[9] Rumyantsev argued that his party "could prove attractive for its healthy opportunism, by which I understand not adaptationism, unprincipled behavior, or the pursuit of short-term advantage, but an ability to make use of the available possibilities in order to implement real policies on a principled basis. Another attraction might become a culture of rational analysis and foresight, of participation in practical work and compromise."[10] Meanwhile, the main question remained unanswered: policies in whose interests, serving what goals? The ideologues of the SDPR, as of most other parties in Russia, preferred not to trouble their minds with such issues. Politics for them was a kind of sport, in which it was necessary simply to rise from the amateur to the professional league. What kind of social compromise can one speak of in Russia today? For compromise to be possible between workers and capitalists, there must at least be something to divide up. Russian admirers of the Swedish model soon discovered that at its basis lay capitalism. Dreaming of a social democratic future, they called first for the dominance of capital to be consolidated, and then for the workers to be defended against it. Property was to be privatized first, then a mixed economy established. First it was necessary to destroy the united trade unions that posed an obstacle to entrepreneurial freedom, then to organize trade unions all over again. Such a program, however, could far better be implemented by right-wing liberals than by social democrats.

The SDPR did not have serious rivals, claimants to the same label, since Gorbachev's dream of creating social democracy on the basis of the Communist Party had collapsed in 1991. But the SDPR lacked loyal supporters, ready to back it in any circumstances. The party reached its peak in 1990, when it had about five thousand members. A year and a half later no more than half remained. Western sponsors lost interest in their fraternal organizations in the East. In the SDPR leadership, squabbles broke out that had nothing to do with political disagreements. In 1992 the crisis in the party led to Rumyantsev being removed. The fallen leader publicly accused his colleagues of envy, ambitiousness, and "infantilism."[11]

The Communist parties also tried to overcome their problems with the help of social democratization. In Poland, the PUWP after its crushing election defeat declared itself a social democratic party.[12] A left-wing split-off proclaimed itself the Social Democratic Union. The Hungarian and Bulgarian Communist parties, which had refashioned themselves as Socialist, began citing Mitterand and Craxi. The social democratic turn of the Communist politicians greatly complicated the positions of other parties and groups that laid claim to the status of genuine social democrats. The catastrophic failure of the social democratic party in Hungary can be explained as reflecting the superior electoral appeal of the former Communists. The same phenomenon was to be observed in the Baltic states. The Romanian Front for National Salvation, headed by former Communist functionaries, also used social democratic slogans, forcing the real social democrats onto the sidelines. As a Western observer noted, if the FNS were to succeed in appropriating the social democratic label, the development of social democracy in the country would be delayed "perhaps for another decade."[13]

Aleksandr Lilov, who headed the Bulgarian Socialist Party, spoke of a "social market economy," and of the need to "repeat the experience of the German Social Democratic Party."[14] The Bulgarian socialists maintained a studious silence about their Communist past. The Party of Labor of Albania, long the main bastion of Stalinism in Europe, made a similarly abrupt turn to social democracy, renaming itself the Socialist Party. The party ideologue Dritero Agolli, who in the past had been a close friend of Stalinist dictator Enver Hoxha, called for a decisive break with the past: "We must now leave the road mapped out over the past forty-seven years. The theories of Marx, Lenin, and Hoxha have led to misery, poverty, and despair. . . ."[15] In Czechoslovakia the Communist Party recast its program in a liberal spirit.[16] During a discussion of a program of action for the Communist Party in independent Estonia, "the word 'socialism' was heard from the conference podium only once—during a speech by a representative of the Swedish Left Party."[17] In Lithuania and Latvia the Communist parties split into supporters and opponents of independence. The supporters of independence in Lithuania renamed their organization the Democratic Party of Labor, and declared their social democratic orientation.[18] The orthodox faction suffered defeat, and after the events of August 1991 was driven into clandestinity. As early as 1992, according to press reports, the Lithuanian Democratic Party of Labor made a noticeable "turn from a social democratic to a social-liberal orientation."[19] The party program devoted particular attention to the need for privatization, since this is "the only way to create the market."[20] The only difference between the Democratic Party of Labor and the rightists on this point was that, in the view of the former Communists, privatization ought to proceed gradually.

The Bulgarian Socialist Party followed the same course as the liberal opposition. "In essence," observed a Western Marxist journal, "both consider free entrepreneurship to be the only salvation for the collapsing Bulgarian economy, although their priorities and their relationships to the social processes differ. Both of these forces include right-wing groups which hope to benefit from the free market and which speak out against the independent unity of the workers. The leaders of both organizations are afraid of losing their popularity among Bulgarian nationalists, and avoid giving public support to the Turkish minority which is struggling for the restoration of the rights it lost under Zhivkov."[21] Dimitrina Petrov and Krasimir Kanev consider that the Bulgarian Socialist Party is pursuing a strategy in the interests of the former Communist elite, concealing this behind populist appeals to rural or recently urbanized voters.[22] These strata made important gains in the course of Communist modernization, and are now justly afraid that their position will deteriorate. Meanwhile, as a result of cultural backwardness and paternalistic links with the traditional bosses, it has been hard for these groups to create their own independent social and political organizations. They have thus come to count on being defended by the old nomenklatura.

The social democratization of the post-Communist parties was the result not only of attempts to retain political influence in the new circumstances. The more the party elites have been drawn into business, the more these parties have been inclined to support privatization and private entrepreneurship. Even in Vietnam, where the ideological bases of the party have remained unshaken, the official press has admitted that the market reforms have led to the growth of unemployment and to the impoverishment of the lower strata of society, "against a background of the strikingly luxurious lives and declining moral character" of the old party leadership.[23] During its final years the Communist Party of the Soviet Union was preoccupied not so much with the struggle against right-wing forces, as with developing its own business activities. The party's officially declared property holdings were valued at ten billion rubles in 1990 prices. Experts of the Moscow Higher Party School noted that this figure was understated by roughly ten times—that is, if a free market were introduced, "the Communist Party would be the wealthiest property-owner, with capital exceeding 100 billion."[24]

By the autumn of 1990 the party bureaucracy was acting openly as a collective capitalist. "The Communist Party's entrepreneurial activity is gathering pace," reported the country's largest-circulation weekly, *Argumenty i Fakty.* " . . . An intensive process has begun of depositing party funds in the banks, and of transfering print-shops, publishing houses, and resort establishments to a commercial basis."[25] Following instructions from the leadership, and often the dictates of their own party consciences as well, functionaries at all levels applied themselves actively to making money.

In 1991 the property of the Communist Party of the Soviet Union was confiscated, and the party itself was banned.[26] In the Baltic republics the property of the independent Communist parties was nationalized. In Bulgaria the property of the Socialist Party was expropriated. However, this could not prevent the flourishing of many party functionaries who had established their own firms with the help of party funds.

Gorbachev's efforts to renew the Communist Party led to its political collapse. As the noted Soviet political scientist V. Viunitsky noted as early as 1990, all party members had previously acted in one and the same all-national organization. But as soon as ideological discipline ceased to be enforced, it became apparent that the party had no unifying character; among its members could be found liberals, Stalinists, social democrats, fascists, and large numbers of quite apolitical people: "It is clear that such diverse forces cannot coexist under one roof. In essence, the party takes a variety of approaches to vital social questions. Because diverse tendencies are included within the present 'one size fits all' organization, these differences are not fought out in interparty struggles, but within the framework of 'internal' party discussions. Meanwhile, the irreconcilability of the positions expressed means that this debate cannot lead to practical results." In this situation, Viunitsky reasoned, the "decay and political downfall of the party" was a completely natural development.[27]

In fact, two neocommunist projects existed side by side in Russia and Eastern Europe at the beginning of the 1990s. On the one side was a conservative-reformist project advanced primarily by the leadership of the old parties, and on the other, a project of fundamentalist renewal. The former sought to preserve as much as possible of the old apparatus, and to stabilize the bureaucratic organizational structures with the help of a new social democratic or social-liberal ideology. The supporters of the latter project were ready to make many sacrifices, but in order to restore ideological purity and to recreate the original Bolshevik party.

Despite the incompatibility of these views, it was extremely difficult to draw a dividing line between the currents involved, especially since each of them consisted not of a single organization or ideological platform, but of a conglomerate.[28] Both currents sought ultimately to resolve the internal problems of the unwieldy Communist organization, and not the problems of the workers. Not just for the bureaucrat-reformists, but also for the renovators, the question of the material or ideological heritage of the party was therefore much more important than uniting the workers in struggle for their real interests. Protesting against the triumph of the "criminal" bourgeoisie in the Eastern European societies, the remnants of the ideological Communists in Russia call for the revival of the great faith, repeating like an incantation: "We consider it necessary to do everything possible to reform the 'red church', and to create in its votaries a resemblance to those who with their selfless devotion gave the social doctrine the status of a new world religion."

While not denying the Stalinist savagery, the corruption, the suppression of democracy, and even the antipopular essence of the party's power, they add that "the symbols, the martyrs, and the Faith itself are no more responsible for this than was Christ for the actions of the Holy Inquisition."[29] Indeed, Christ was not responsible for the Inquisition, but those who deified Christ with this very act made the Inquisition essential. Communist tradition in the form which it has assumed in the late twentieth century is unacceptable for precisely this reason: that, even in the hands of the best of its present-day adherents, it transforms socialism into religion. Replacing critical theory with a religious faith in ideology, idolizing the symbols and prophets of the faith, such Communism inevitably destroys any possibility of human liberation. The party serving the interests of the workers is replaced by the party which puts the workers at the service of an idea. When the demands of the masses fail to coincide with the schemas of the ideologues, these demands are declared revisionist, opportunist, immature, and so forth.

Marx, as is well known, observed at one point that ideas which are not based on interests invariably finish up being disgraced. The experience of the Communist parties, on the other hand, has shown that organizations which are created for the sake of serving ideas quickly acquire their own interests, which ultimately are hostile to the interests of the masses.

The concern shown by the theoreticians of revolutionary Marxism for the creation of a reliable proletarian leadership is quite natural; a centralized party of the Leninist type, based on rigid subordination and iron discipline, is an ideal weapon for manipulating activists, and is completely incapable of defending itself against betrayal by its leaders. For this reason, the hopes placed in genuine proletarian leadership always turn out to be vain as well. In such an organization the most revolutionary, most proletarian, leadership will inevitably either be corrupted or swallowed by the apparatus without whose aid it cannot pursue its line under conditions of consistent centralization.

No organization can get by without an apparatus and a bureaucracy, but the role and tasks of the apparatus can differ greatly. Under the conditions of a vanguard party, in which unity is achieved through harsh discipline, the apparatus inevitably begins to control first the political behavior of activists, then their thoughts, and then the leadership of the party as well. By the early 1990s in Eastern Europe, it was possible to speak only of one more or less successful attempt to create a modern left organization on the basis of a Communist Party. This was the Party of Democratic Socialism (PDS) in Germany. In two years the party's leader, the lawyer Gregor Gysi, succeeded in transforming this decrepit organization into a viable and dynamic body with its own political face. The PDS declared that it would pursue its goals "both through extraparliamentary movements and through parliamentary action."[30] Unlike other leaders of post-Communist parties, Gysi did not set out to prove his moderation and adherence to Western values. The PDS pledged to struggle for "radical changes in the structure of power in society," for the "institutionalization of democratic alternative power" (*gegenmächten*), and for "the real socialization of large-scale production" (*den grossen Produktionseinheiten*).[31]

While the party of the Greens underwent a serious crisis, torn apart by contradictions between pure ecologists and ecosocialists, realists, and fundamentalists, proponents of a party of protest and those who would have turned the Greens into a respectable party of practical politics, the Party of Democratic Socialism increasingly assumed the role of parliamentary representative of the new social movements.

As might have been expected, the left radicals in most cases regarded the PDS with distrust and even hostility. In the theoretical journal *Quatrième Internationale,* the Trotskyist H.-J. Schultz wrote that although the PDS could in no sense be considered a continuation of the old Stalinist party, its reformist turn was irreversible: the PDS would never succeed in proving that its reformism was better and deserving of greater trust than that of others, and thus would never move into a struggle for power.[32]

Using general concepts such as *reformism* or *the socialist perspective,* Western "revolutionists without revolutions" did not take into account the fact that the West German social democrats, having become part of the country's everyday system of rule, had long since ceased to act as a reformist force. Nor did these left radicals see the specific role which the PDS was to play in the society of eastern Germany.

The local nomenklatura was unable to play any substantial role in eastern Germany's transition to capitalism. The country was simply seized by the West German ruling class, effectively colonized. The western bosses did not leave the old bureaucrats any chance to secure their privileges. Even the functionaries of the eastern Christian Democracy were given no more than minor roles. This social rout of the nomenklatura made any struggle by it to preserve its political positions quite pointless. The old rulers simply dropped out of the game, leaving the party structures in the hands of the renovators.

The collapse of the old nomenklatura also rendered capitalist development in eastern Germany extremely unstable. Although annexation by one of the most powerful capitalist states might at first glance have seemed to guarantee the former German Democratic Republic a successful transition to capitalism, this did not occur. In removing the nomenklatura, Western capital destroyed the very social layer on which it might have based itself.

The relative stability of the PDS in the east and the failure of its attempts to win votes in the west spoke for themselves. Despite unification, the societies of eastern and western Germany have remained totally distinct. Moreover, between 1989 and 1992 the gulf widened. Anger at the peripheralization and effective colonization of the former GDR pushed thousands of eastern Germans onto the side of the PDS. But the very fact that this party was rooted in the society of the eastern regions, and its ability to respond to the problems of this society, made it impossible for the party to grow in the totally different sociocultural milieu of the west.

One of the party's supporters wrote that the efforts of the PDS to develop its activity in the West were "naked stupidity."[33] The role of the PDS in German national politics depended on its ability to consolidate itself in the East. "The members of the PDS," Gysi noted, "brought with them important, though often negative, experience accumulated during the forty years when the GDR existed. Unlike other parties, the PDS did not unite with one of the large parties of the Federal Republic. Its distinctively East German experience was thus preserved. This experience will naturally be enriched thanks to collaboration with leftists from West Germany."[34] The PDS thus acquired another important task: as a result of its unique position, it could act as a bridge between East and West.

The temporary triumph of the right-wing liberal ideologies that filled the ideological vacuum after Communism caused confusion and even panic in many left-wing Western intellectuals. They failed to grasp that socialist ideas—unlike the "religion" of communism—reflect not just certain values dear to intellectuals, but the objective interests of the mass of workers.[35] In this sense as well, socialism cannot be excluded or replaced so long as the workers themselves exist.

As society develops, socialist ideas change their form. The Russian Revolution of 1917 could not fail to exert an enormous influence on socialists throughout the world. The success which the bolsheviks seemed at first glance to have achieved made their model of the party attractive. Even those such as Trotsky who criticized Lenin, and who later differentiated themselves sharply from Stalinism, continued to see in the Bolshevik party a universal model, guaranteeing success under any circumstances. However, the political experience which leftists have now acquired places on the agenda the question of a new conception of the party.

Attempts to establish vanguard parties in the West and in the countries of the third world have led to a series of catastrophic failures. Revolutionary regimes headed by parties of the bolshevik type have invariably degenerated, while opposition parties have turned into sects.

In Turkey during the 1960s and 1970s Marxist groups of various tendencies were operating. "While it was true that the masses did not regard the Turkish left as mature enough to be a candidate for power, in either of these two decades" writes the Turkish socialist Mehmet Salah, "because of its influence on mass organizations and its leading role in mass struggles, at least it had been regarded as a serious political force." By the time of the military coup of September 12, 1980, however, the leftists completely lost the confidence of society, a result of sectarian clashes between themselves and of their political ambitions. "The Turkish left," Salah continues, "was wholly unsuccessful in convincing the masses of the credibility of its leadership. First and foremost, the left was unable to put forward a coherent political program. . . . Dreaming that problems could only be solved with slogans like 'the only way is revolution,' 'people's war,' or 'power comes from the barrel of a gun' together with hundreds of others, the left could neither politically orient nor politically educate the masses."[36]

Events in the Arab world developed in an analogous fashion. Anti-imperialist slogans not only failed to provide a substitute for strategy, but also had lamentable consequences for the revolutionaries themselves. A Trotskyist journal wrote that leftists in the Near East vacillated between uncritical collaboration with various fundamentalist or nationalist currents and support for the most reactionary regimes.[37] The Trotskyist scholars, of course, blamed everything on the Stalinist leadership of the workers' and Communist parties. But the very principle of the vanguard party, uniting orthodox Trotskyists with Stalinists and Maoists, made such tragedies inevitable. Between 1989 and 1991 numerous Trotskyist sects sent their representatives to the countries of Eastern Europe, as they had earlier sent them to the countries of the third world. Although none of these groups could boast of political successes, all of them claimed the right to lead the proletariat, since "they alone remained faithful to the revolutionary socialist program."[38]

The attempts by small Trotskyist groups to be consistently revolutionary in the far from revolutionary conditions of the West dooms them to chronic failure. But even when a serious political crisis erupts, they are rarely able to play a substantial role in the struggle. The French used to joke that their generals always prepared the army to fight the previous war. It could be said that the vanguard party is always being readied for the previous revolution.

During the 1980s disillusionment with vanguardism, together with the rise of new social movements in the West and in the countries of the third world, opened up new possibilities for leftists. At the same time new illusions were created. Many writers argued that parties in general had become outmoded and unnecessary, and that in the modern-day world only spontaneous movements could mount successful struggles for change. "The social movements of the 1960s and 1970s," wrote James Petras and Morris Morley, "presented a special problem to Latin America's military and capitalist rulers. Unlike earlier populist movements which were tied to and dependent on a personal *caudillo*, these new movements were largely autonomous; based on rank-and-file leaders who were easily replaceable. Nor were these organizations dependent on a bureaucracy or ministry. They were self-generating and sustaining; every member was a potential organizer or leader." Most of the movements of the 1970s were crushed, but in the second half of the 1980s they revived. The experience of the Latin American movements, Petras and Morley consider, not only places in doubt the need for a revolutionary party, but to a significant degree shows the unfitness of political parties as instruments of a successful struggle for change. There has not been a single case in which victory has been achieved by a workers' party of the traditional European type, resting on the trade unions. "The movement form of organization provides the flexibility, inclusiveness and decentralized structure that facilitates entry into political action from the various sites of social action in a way that trade unions and electoral parties cannot. The movement's openness to influence and control from below, its capacity to act directly on concrete problems of everyday life and its face-to-face debates and non-hierarchical structures provide it with a capacity to mobilize sectors of the working class that the electoral parties cannot activate. Movement organization is the form most compatible with the real existing process of working-class formation in Latin America."[39]

The idea of the movement has seized even authors who had earlier been enthralled by the bolshevik experience. Andre Gunder Frank, for example, wrote in 1990 that social movements, to a much greater degree than parties or the state were now emerging as a force capable of bringing socialism nearer. Frank acknowledges the instability of mass movements, and does not deny the danger of their degeneration, but nevertheless sees that this "is less a mark of their weakness, irrelevance, or self-negation" than a sign of their "vitality."[40]

In reality, such new ideas are only the mirror image of old illusions. Authoritarian structures often grow out of mass spontaneous movements. Without formal institutions or democratic procedures, such movements provide an ideal setting for manipulation, intrigue, and for the appearance of uncontrolled and irresponsible leadership. The experience of Eastern Europe during the 1980s showed that the internal decision-making mechanisms in spontaneous mass movements and vanguard parties are strikingly similar. A democratically organized party is essential as the core of a mass movement. This is not merely the movement's parliamentary wing or political instrument, but a guarantee of political responsibility, and of the accountability and controllability of the leadership; it is a factor serving to stabilize the movement. In this sense the party and the movement are equally necessary to one another. They have to collaborate, and they have to be independent. Movements must not be run by the party along bolshevik lines, but neither should the party be subordinate to the movement.

The collapse of the bolshevik myth of the party does not mean that discussion on the political vanguard has once and for all come to an end. It is essential to ponder the meaning of the word *vanguard*. It refers to a detachment which moves ahead of an army, but which does not lead the army after itself. Clearly, the vanguard may be only a part serving the general interests of the forces as a whole. This has nothing in common with the bolshevik tradition of the vanguard party. The Leninist theory of the vanguard has often been criticized by liberal, Marxist, anarcho-syndicalist, and social democratic theoreticians. But without recognizing it, most of these critics have shared Lenin's main initial preconceptions. Samuel Farber rightly notes that Lenin was in fact neither the creator nor the inventor of this concept of the party. At the heart of his views lay an uncritical endorsement of the Jacobin experience.[41]

Jacobin ideology has not only been an important element in the bourgeois-democratic tradition; it represents the most extreme and consistent political expression of the ideas of the European enlightenment, which in one degree or another have inspired all the modernizing projects in Russia and the countries of the third world. For all its attractiveness, the ideology of the enlightenment has provided moral justification for numerous tyrants and dictators who have oppressed their backward peoples "for their peoples' good." The eighteenth-century enlighteners firmly believed that they possessed a ready and comparatively full knowledge of the perfect society. They knew for certain that progress was identical with the development of industry and the growth of well-being, and the perfect state was embodied for them in the existing forms of the most progressive European democracy and of the equally progressive bureaucracy. Power had to reside with those who possessed knowledge, and a concentration of knowledge signified a concentration of power. Society had to be transformed from above by enlightened rulers.

Faith in the ready-made model of development, which existed either in practice or in the minds of the ideologues, was inculcated forcibly in societies which could not be squeezed into this model. Some bearers of true enlightenment accepted responsibility for disseminating true knowledge among the unenlightened masses, while considering their social ideas to be just as final and indisputable as their concepts of the order of the universe.

It was only natural that the ideology of the enlightenment, even though it advocated tolerance and human rights, was eurocentric and authoritarian. Not surprisingly, the ideas of the enlightenment gave birth as early as the eighteenth century to a right-wing variant embodied in the theory of enlightened absolutism and in the practice of Catherine II and Friedrich the Great, and to a left-wing variant— Jacobin dictatorship.

Rousseau and Marx, each in their own way, tried to overcome the narrowness of the enlightenment tradition. But in the conditions of Russia, as later in the countries of the third world, Marxist ideas were perceived as a more modern and radical variant of the enlightenment. Lenin's constant references in his later works to the enlightening role of the bolsheviks were by no means accidental. An enlightened majority, possessing true knowledge, became a revolutionary party armed with progressive theory. Bolshevism became the Jacobinism of the twentieth century.[42]

The tragic consequences of this course were easily foreseen from the very beginning. Those who spoke out against it included not just right-wing social democrats, but also such revolutionists as Rosa Luxemburg and Leon Trotsky. In the words of P. Broue, one of today's most authoritative scholars, Trotsky regarded Lenin's Jacobinism as a tendency no less dangerous than the revisionism of Bernstein, and in the period from 1903 to 1905 even described Lenin and the Bolsheviks as the party's reactionary wing.[43] After the beginning of World War I both Trotsky and Luxemburg chose in favor of bolshevism, the latter with substantial reservations. Knowing what they did not and could not have known, we can now conclude that in renouncing their original views in favor of Lenin's concept of the party they made a fatal mistake.

Lenin set out to reproduce the Jacobin experience, while avoiding a repetition of the mistakes that had caused the downfall of the Jacobin dictatorship. The result was the creation of a repressive apparatus whose power, in Farber's words, exceeded many times over everything that even the most extreme Jacobin might have imagined.[44] A democratic perspective demands not only the rejection of centralism in the party and of Leninism in ideology. It is essential to reject the Jacobin-enlightenment conception itself. In place of transformations from above, embodied in the ready-made model of European industrial society, socialists have to promote changes from below. The prime task of the revolutionary party must become not the seizure of power in the center, but helping workers to organize themselves at the local level in order to solve current social problems. This concrete work does not mean renouncing the struggle for power. But the significance of the struggle is altered radically. The challenge issued to the authorities takes on the form of growing pressure from below. Instead of turning "bad" people out of their armchairs and seating themselves in these armchairs instead, the forces of the left must aim to redistribute power within society. The new power will then arise not simply as the result of elections or an uprising, but will be formed spontaneously by the masses themselves. This does not exclude struggling for a majority in parliament or for the formation of a left government. But such struggles become inseparable from the transformations from below.

The failure of the bolshevik experiment has not taken the question of the vanguard off the agenda, but it forces us to pose this question quite differently. What is needed to transform society—a vanguard party or a social vanguard? Despite all the efforts of left ideologues, the slogan of workers' power will remain an abstraction—not because the popular masses are incapable of becoming the dominant force in society as liberal thinkers suppose, but because the world of labor is itself heterogeneous. Only a government built and supported by the most skilled and educated strata of workers can oust the old and new oligarchies from power, and replace the rule of elites with a democracy of mass participation. Often, these strata are not the most radical in their demands, but they are unquestionably the most consistent in their actions. The more educated strata become the vanguard of change not because of their correct ideology, but because of their role in production. The advantage possessed by these educated strata is that they have the indispensable knowledge, social experience, and capacity for self-organization that allow them to grasp key decisions and get them right. While the poorest strata of the urban and rural populations in the countries of the periphery are often declassed, and fall readily under the influence of reactionary utopias, more skilled and experienced workers understand their interests far better. Only if the new power has a base among workers such as these will it be able to avoid the revival on a new basis of authoritarianism and of bureaucratic control over the masses—the blights that have appeared repeatedly in the history of numerous revolutions.

These better qualified workers are relatively few in number, and, like any social stratum, have their own weaknesses and narrow-minded prejudices. They will never really manage to take power unless they find a common language with the broad mass of workers and take the lead in the mass popular movement. This hegemony of the organized skilled workers is inconceivable unless the interests of all the participants in the new social bloc—and above all, of unskilled workers—are taken genuinely into account. In certain conditions a section of independent entrepreneurs and managers, trying to overcome backwardness and dependency, may join in this bloc.

The tasks which the ideologues of modernization posed but proved unable to fulfill must be carried out on a new basis. Overcoming backwardness will become possible only when the main goal of the changes becomes surmounting the gap between the modern and traditional sectors, between advanced and backward enterprises, between the capital cities and the hinterland. It will only become possible when intermediate technologies and the social policies that correspond to them help to build a bridge between the modern and underdeveloped strata. Only policies aimed at achieving these goals will allow the creation of a genuine unity between qualified and untrained workers.

An alliance between more and less skilled workers will not come spontaneously. In periods of expansion, the skilled and educated strata can see more concrete benefit in allying with modernizing elites. But the overall period of unlimited expansion is over, and skilled workers are discovering that the only way they can expand as a social group and do better individually is to change the model of development. Thus the very measures that benefit poorer workers—education programs, infrastructural development, introduction of intermediate technology, etc.—are needed by qualified workers to create new jobs and opportunities for both the skilled and traditional workforce. Moreover, implementing such measures would require a confrontation with the elites, who tend to see all this as a waste of money in periods of capital shortage.

The strategy of the emerging left forces thus amounts to overcoming the structural gaps within the economy and society.[45] This is a real prospect for the world of skilled and educated labor, since overcoming backwardness simultaneously involves the growth of these skilled strata. They gradually begin to incorporate all of society, ultimately overcoming the division of labor as well. In essence this is a problem of democratization: undermining the rule of elites in order to turn the actual majority of the population into the political majority.

Of course, this is a relatively distant prospect, and perhaps a utopian one. The present-day task is to ensure that parties based on the more skilled and educated strata also express the interests of all of the oppressed. The ability of the new social vanguard to win political power depends on its readiness and ability to ensure a new social compromise—one that takes into account the diverse interests of the broader masses while simultaneously bolstering the hegemony of the skilled and educated workers. The compromise must be based on real discussion within and between the diverse sections of the population to determine what people really want. These demands would serve as the basis for a program of structural reform.

If the forces of the left are really to implement such a project, they will have to overcome many of their own traditions and prejudices. They will have to reject their present common ground of bolshevik-Jacobin concepts in favor of Antonio Gramsci's ideas of hegemony, which, despite being cited just as often, are poorly understood.[46] And the left will also have to change its way of political thinking: it can no longer base its arguments on why people's demands cannot be attained under capitalism, but rather on what it will take to realize them.

Socialist parties, like other parties, will have to lead their supporters, but not in military fashion, not mechanistically, not through orders, instructions, slogans, and demagogy. Their task is to rally the masses to the organized efforts of the most advanced strata, and to reconcile the different or differently perceived interests of various groups of workers. What we need is not a consistently revolutionary leadership in the spirit of romantic Marxism, but cadres who possess the art of compromise—compromise, that is, between the diverse strata of workers, not with the ruling oligarchs. Only then will the hegemony of the social vanguard become a political reality.

A revolutionary-reformist project cannot be worked out without the left intelligentsia, but it has to be worked out on the basis of the interests of hired labor. The demands which are raised spontaneously by workers in the modern sector have to be taken very seriously, and not abandoned as quickly as possible in favor of "higher" forms of revolutionary consciousness. Instead of subordinating the proletariat to more advanced parties and more radical social strata, it is essential to create political organizations that allow the proletariat itself to become the force deciding the direction and speed of the political process, not in words but in actual fact. This can only be achieved if authoritarianism is ended, and if attempts to create centralized parties are rejected. Whether they win or lose, the left parties must keep changing, experimenting, developing more political alternatives from grassroots movements.

The program of the left needs to be relatively broad, reflecting the spontaneous demands of the masses. As a rule, the left forces in Eastern Europe and the third world are as heterogeneous as the worker masses themselves. This creates both additional problems and new opportunities. "The obstacle to victory is not the multiplicity of revolutionary forces," noted the participants in a theoretical conference of Latin American leftists, "The obstacle is the divisions between them."[47] Mass left-wing organizations in the third world often take the form of blocs uniting several parties and currents, none of which can claim a monopoly on the leading role. The real pluralism within such organizations allows workers to speak their own minds even when each group or current, taken in isolation, continues to believe in its role as the revolutionary vanguard.

During the mid-1980s attempts to unite the left were made in many countries. These efforts included the Broad Front in Uruguay and the United Left in Peru. In 1985 Argentinian leftists organized the Popular Front, which was recognized by journalists as "the first manifestation of unity in many years."[48] The participants in these blocs also included Communists, who had acknowledged that their parties were not the only organizations capable of fighting for socialism, and who accepted that minorities had to retain the right to participate in discussion and to publish their views in the party press. Recognizing that the right to dissent should not be a privilege solely of the leadership, the leaders of the Latin American parties began to speak of a broad internal party democracy, to include "the existence of currents and tendencies, disseminating their ideas, projects, and alternatives, not only in vertical, but also horizontal fashion."[49] Since the mid-1980s Latin American leftists have proclaimed their goal to be radical reforms and the transition from formal democracy of the Western type to a political system in which traditional political freedoms were combined with direct participation by the masses in government. The leaders of the United Left in Peru declared that their task was "not just to win elections, but also to organize the people for democracy."[50]

This has involved attempts to go beyond the bounds of the liberal state and elite politics, struggling for an authentic popular power in which the political mobilization of the masses proceeds not from above, by order of the revolutionary authorities, but from below, in the process of finding democratic solutions to everyday problems. There is no place here for the traditional enlightening authoritarianism, but at times the political struggle demands authoritarian methods. It is possible to ensure a certain degree of democracy even under conditions of clandestinity, but a consistently democratic organization can only be created when there is a measure of legality. The example of the Sandinistas shows that in between the overthrow of a dictatorship and the beginning of broad social reforms there must be a period during which institutions of political democracy can take shape and the forces of the left themselves can ripen, reconstructing their organizations and preparing to tackle new tasks. Otherwise, the forced radicalization and Cubanization of the regime—which began occurring in Nicaragua— cannot be avoided.

When, on the other hand, the forces of the left concentrate their attention on restoring and strengthening political freedoms or on defending the everyday interests of workers, they risk losing their strategic perspectives. They will be doomed for a lengthy period to playing the role of a permanent opposition, or to acting as radical allies of a centrist government.

The tasks of revolutionary reformism were formulated with particular clarity by the United Left in Peru in the mid-1980s. Nevertheless the victor in the 1985 presidential elections was not the United Left candidate, Lima Mayor Alfonso Barrantes, but APRA leader Alan García. Declaring itself a social democratic organization, APRA set out to combine traditional Latin American populism with the experience of Western European reformism. During the revolutionary period of

1968 to 1975, and later when they were in opposition to the right-wing government of Fernando Belaúnde Terry from 1980 to 1985, the Apristas absorbed many ideas from the radical left. APRA, a Peruvian socialist noted, was "an inalienable part of the popular-national bloc," and also expressed "the leftward shift of society."[51] García, who in Europe was described as "a Latin American Felipe Gonzalez,"[52] represented a new type of leader. "At once more worldly in its outlook and less vehement in its anticommunism, this young, foreign-educated generation sought to develop APRA as a democratic, left-of-center alternative to the Marxist Left. As a deputy to Congress, García stood out with his eloquent speeches against the IMF and Belaúnde's policies and in support of the Sandinista government of Nicaragua. . . . At the same time, he cultivated personal relations with important businessmen and technocrats, many of whom would later be invited to participate in formulating APRA's governmental plan, a blueprint for which had been drawn up in García's own book, *A Different Future*."[53] This Europeanized radical technocrat managed to sense the mood of the public better than any of the Marxist leaders. APRA appeared at once to be serious, radical, and realistic. Against this background the leaders of the United Left, by their own admission, found themselves in a disadvantageous position.[54] García gained 48 percent of the votes, while Barrantes, who took second place, attracted only 23.5 percent.

Even this still represented a success. For Latin America, wrote the Peruvian sociologist Guillermo Rochabrun, the United Left was "a unique phenomenon in terms of its relationship to the masses, the breadth and variety of its activity, its relative unity, and its intellectual level."[55]

The success of 1985, however, was not consolidated. Differences arose among leftists on their relationship to the García government. The traditions of vanguard politics made themselves felt at all levels. Despite their own rhetoric, the leftists based their relations with the masses who supported them "more on mobilization than on real participation."[56]

The left-wing leaders lacked a clear strategy, and often preferred to remain in opposition. Activists in left parties often confessed that they were scared of winning the elections. If the Apristas set out to win the support of the broadest possible range of social layers, the Marxists confined themselves to mobilizing their traditional social base. Differences between various groups, though often insignificant in themselves, quickly emerged into the open. "The real contradiction within the left," wrote the Peruvian political scientist R. Roncagliolo, was "not between Marxists and non-Marxists, not between true believers and heretics, but between centripetal and centrifugal forces." The inability of leftists to overcome their weakness created a situation in which the United Left would always suffer defeat, at least until they managed "to become something more than simply leftists, transcending the boundaries of their own narrow-mindedness."[57] Most activists managed to console themselves with the thought that the country had not yet matured sufficiently for a radical left government, but in fact it was the radical leftists themselves who were not mature enough to become the government, easily yielding the initiative to the Apristas. This cost both the leftists and Peruvian society dearly.

The first steps taken by the government of Alan García were comparatively resolute. The new president refused to make full interest payments on the foreign debt so long as the country was unable to guarantee subsistence minimum incomes to its millions of poor citizens. He promised to change the priorities of development, stressed the significance of the traditional sector and of agriculture, limited the privileges of North American capital, began a struggle against bureaucracy and corruption, reduced military spending, and conducted a purge of the army command. The state sector began to be reorganized. Thanks to price controls, inflation by the end of 1985 was cut from 11 percent to 2.7 percent. The government nationalized the transnational firm Belco Petroleum, and forced other foreign corporations to accept conditions of operation that were more advantageous for the country. In carrying out these measures, García rested not only on his own party, but also on the support of the left opposition. However, Peru needed more radical changes if its problems were to be solved. The nationalization of the banks and other radical steps were not part of a strategic plan, but rather, defensive reactions to growing economic difficulties. The García government gradually lost control of the situation. Attempting in any way possible to weaken the leftists who were its main rivals, the regime undermined its own positions. For their part, the leftists were unable to define where they stood in relation to García's reforms, at times opposing them and at other times declaring their solidarity. The government's contradictory policies exacerbated the disagreements within the socialist camp. The coalition of left forces split into the Socialist Left and United Left.

Although the disagreements between leftists were very serious, most observers consider that a still more pernicious role was played by the "undemocratic practices characterizing the left as a whole."[58] Left-wing leaders at first accepted a series of moves to ensure broader participation by the masses in political decision-making, but then began to backtrack. In 1989 delegates to the congress of the United Left were elected without any interference from the party bureaucracies, and in the early 1990s the United Left held primary elections on the U.S. model to select candidates for municipal and parliamentary elections. But when it came to presidential elections, the leaders of the movement reverted to traditional practices. The results of the primaries were overturned, and candidacies were decided in behind-the-scenes discussions between the groups. This demoralized activists and helped turn large numbers of voters away from the leftists.

The crisis of the left opposition did not make life easy for the Aprista government. The promised new approaches to development remained empty slogans. An economic upturn during 1986 and 1987 was achieved mainly through well-tried Keynesian methods of pumping up demand, and through using state regulation to stimulate the market. All of this affected mainly the modern, urban economy. As before, the country remained oriented toward expanding exports, rather than toward the internal market. By 1988 this strategy had totally exhausted itself, and nothing remained for the government except to hope for a rise in foreign investment. The popularity of the president and his party fell catastrophically. As early as 1988 experts were warning that despite all the efforts by the authorities, living standards were doomed to fall, or at best to stagnate.[59]

In the elections of April 1990 APRA suffered a crushing defeat, but neither left coalition scored any notable successes. Another failure at the polls was that of the coalition of liberal rightists who had put their stake on the writer Mario Vargas Llosa, a former left radical who had become a liberal ideologue. The independent candidate Alberto Fujimori won thanks to the support of leftists and Apristas who regarded him as a lesser evil. Once installed in the presidential palace, Fujimori began implementing the policies of the right. This development decisively demoralized the socialists. While criticizing Fujimori, they could not deny that most leaders of the left had given the new government *carte blanche*, and that some had even agreed to accept ministerial posts. Prominent leftists were forced to speak of numerous difficulties, of "internal differences and a weakening of links with the masses."[60]

The crisis of confidence in the government, and the loss by the masses of any hopes of successful reforms, aided only the extremists of the Sendero Luminoso terrorist group. Seeking to defeat the terrorists through purely military methods, the authorities heightened the tensions still more. The lack of real change in the countryside guaranteed that the repression would be ineffective. The country was plunged into chaos. The Fujimori government dissolved the congress and suspended the constitution. The majority of the population looked on passively as these events unfolded.[61]

The Fujimorization of Peru and the successes of *Sendero Luminoso* would have been impossible had the democratic left become a real alternative. As we read in the Marxist journal *Margenes*, "Sendero Luminoso has been able to survive and develop because it has a real social base. No one can argue that it receives significant support from abroad. The repression aimed against it has been ruthless. Its vitality in such circumstances is explained simply by the fact that there are layers in society whose interests it expresses, or who believe that it expresses their interests. These are the layers that have been forgotten by the other political forces, the layers that oppose the existing order, and whose problems no one except the Senderistas has cared to address."[62]

Both APRA and the leftists have oriented primarily to workers in the modern sector, giving little thought to the interests of the unmodernized masses, who remain on an equal social footing with the Senderistas. During election campaigns the left has often drawn the unmodernized masses over to its side (as, indeed, has APRA), but no one has sought to develop a strategy of change corresponding to their real needs. Until this is done, the layers remaining outside the modernization process will not simply oppose the policies of the ruling classes, but depending on the cultural peculiarities of each country, will also inevitably give their support to fundamentalist, Stalinist, or left-extremist movements. The vitality of Stalinist groups in Russia in the 1990s is a phenomenon of the same variety as the successes of Sendero Luminoso.

The antisocial protest spawned by an inhuman society has enormous destructive potential. Democratic leftists have a huge responsibility. Without a strategy of development that takes into account the interests of the most dispossessed and forgotten layers, it is impossible to bring about change within a framework of democracy. A base among the educated workforce is essential, but it is not enough. The backward, unmodernized layers cannot simply be led. It is necessary to enter into dialogue with them, to reach compromises with them, and above all, to allow them genuinely to enlist in the process of change.

This will be impossible unless the economic thinking of socialists changes substantially. If the theoreticians of alternative development, the proponents of ecological harmony, and the critics of industrial civilization are gradually coming to an understanding of the need for political action, then socialists should be driven by the logic of their own political struggle to re-examine their own concepts, and to re-evaluate alternative theories which just recently seemed to be no more than utopian distractions.

The Peruvian sociologist J. Martínez Alier, referring to Schumacher, speaks of the "ecological heterogeneity" which needs to become a component part of "contemporary Marxism."[63] Unless the character of development changes, it will be impossible either to establish a stable democracy or to ensure greater justice in society. Conversely, without democratic institutions it will be impossible to bring about changes in the interests of the majority. Anyone who sacrifices democracy for the sake of socialism, even temporarily, is in reality sacrificing socialism.

While not renouncing extraparliamentary struggle, radical leftists are again discovering parliament. As has been explained, they are capable of winning significant successes in this field. When the Colombian insurgent organization M-19 halted its armed struggle and nominated candidates in parliamentary elections, it promptly emerged as one of the leading political forces in the country. For the organization's leaders, the shift to peaceful political struggle was a historic chance to open up "discussion of social and political reforms," in order to "go into a new century with a new nation."[64] M-19 leader Antonio Navarro Wolff became one of the most popular public figures in the country, while the movement established by the former guerrillas became a serious force, recognized by Latin American politicians as capable of playing a very important role not only in Colombia, but also in the development of the entire continent.[65] The former guerrillas were showered with accusations of opportunism. "It is logical," wrote a Trotskyist journal, "that the masses, on rejecting the bourgeois parties, should turn initially to opportunist organizations which present themselves as democratic, since the masses currently possess a democratic consciousness."[66] These democratic moods of the masses, of course, do not suit the kind of revolutionaries who regard the democratic movement merely as a transitional phase in the process of permanent revolution. Meanwhile, the successes of M-19 and of the Brazilian Workers Party have stemmed precisely from the fact that they have become the decisive forces in the struggle to democratize society.

The idea of combining parliamentarism with extraparliamentary struggle is far from new. But today it is acquiring a new meaning, as a party of the left forces, combining various methods of exerting pressure on the authorities, becomes the parliamentary expression of the will of extraparliamentary mass movements. The party has, in effect, opened up the walls of the parliament. The street is no longer counterposed to the parliamentary chamber, and is not a substitute for it; the voices of the street and of the factory burst into parliament thanks to the presence there of socialists. Thus dialogue with the mass movements becomes a part of the normal processes of decision-making, of administration, and of implementing change. As the Soviet political scientist Kiva Maidanik notes, the left parties in Latin America during the 1990s have aimed "at broad collaboration on an equal basis with mass social movements," and have rejected the idolizing of centralized organization. Just as important is the fact that for the first time they have begun seriously to address the interests and problems of workers in the traditional sector, the "marginal masses," and have recognized the significance of "their values and culture."[67]

An example of this new approach is provided by the Brazilian Workers Party (PT). This party was founded in 1979, and nine years later had emerged into the forefront of political life, winning majorities in municipal elections in the largest industrial centers, São Paulo, Santos, Vitória and Porto Alegre, as well as in thirty other cities. In the 1989 presidential elections, PT candidate Luís Ignácio da Silva, known to Brazilians as Lula, took second place with 31 million votes. The vote in 1989 was hotly contested, and his opponent, a wealthy populist, was later impeached in the biggest political scandal in Brazil's history. In

1994 Lula was outflanked by Fernando Henriques Cardoso, a moderate social democratic academic, who capitalized on the early success of an anti-inflation monetary plan he helped devise.

However, from the first run to the second, the PT expanded its base, moved much of its following from support for Lula as a charismatic leader to acceptance of its program, and increased its number of regional and local elected offices by a considerable margin. The strength of the Workers Party has consisted in the fact that it is a relatively young organization, not burdened with the traditions and errors of the past. The Communist Party and the radical left groups were smashed in the 1970s,[68] and the Workers Party grew directly out of the trade union movement of the late 1970s. The party is not a populist, but a class organization. It arose in the industrial south, and went on to become the most reliable voice for the interests of the backward north.[69]

Leftists everywhere looked hopefully to the Brazilian phenomenon; against the background of defeats for socialists throughout the world and the discrediting of Marxist terminology, the PT was making gains while using radical socialist slogans. This party showed that it was possible to combine organizational and ideological pluralism, reflecting the heterogeneity of the social base, with effectiveness in practical work. The presence of numerous currents and the decentralization of power within the party did not prevent it from winning elections, and the coexistence of reformist and revolutionary tendencies was not transformed into factional warfare.

The Workers Party resembles neither a Leninist party nor the Western social democratic parties with their well-oiled, soulless administrative machines. This is a party-movement, based on the trade unions and local initiative groups. The alliance of reformist with revolutionary currents makes ideological pluralism not only desirable, but also inevitable. "We are the result of the synthesis of various currents, believing in freedom and united in our diversity," states a PT document. "We include Social Christians, representatives of various Marxist traditions, non-Marxist socialists, secular and radical democrats, and so on. But the party's program cannot be identified exclusively with any of these currents. The Workers Party does not have an official philosophy. Various positions co-exist within the party, in dialectical interdependence, allowing us to find a dynamic synthesis in the process of working out concrete policies. We are all united by a belief in freedom, and by a desire to create a new society free from exploitation and oppression."[70]

"The decentralized structure of the Workers Party corresponds to the principles of democratic socialism, in as much as the means are just as important as the end," writes the Brazilian sociologist Maria Helena Moreira Alves. "It is impossible to build a democratic and socialist society on authoritarian structures of organization."[71] In these circumstances the most difficult problem is that of party discipline. After the majority adopts a decision, all tendencies are obliged in theory to carry it out. In fact, some groups have followed their own line, creating numerous problems for the PT and its elected representatives. Lula lamented at one point that intraparty democracy at times degenerated into complete anarchy. "In that case, why have a party at all?" he wondered. "I consider that individual freedom has to end where the collective will begins. But one must have guarantees that collective freedom will be realized in the most democratic manner, with a maximum of discussion and with complete openness."[72]

In many cities where the PT has won elections, this intraparty organizational freedom has led to the municipal administration encountering fierce opposition from its own party. In São Paulo this led to defeat, but in other cities the party's experience in municipal politics has been more successful. The party has shown that it can govern effectively, while overcoming disagreements and conflicts within its own camp.[73] The PT has shown itself to be a remarkably stable organization. Its internal pluralism has proved to be a good safeguard against splits. The Brazilian experience has been so inspiring that calls for repeating it have been heard in many countries. Achieving this, however, has turned out to be far more difficult than the enthusiasts have supposed.

In Turkey the liberalization of the regime following the military coup d'etat of 1980 gave the socialist groups the chance to establish a mass legal party. Left-wing ideologues declared that as a result of the extreme weakness of the bourgeois opposition, democratic freedoms could be won only by the workers movement. The mass protests by miners in 1991 showed that this prospect is entirely real. "The ability of the workers to construct a political alternative depends, however, on their establishing a workers party, which must become the decisive force in this struggle."[74] Nevertheless, the attempts to unite the left in Turkey have failed. Defending ideological positions inherited from the 1970s, the revolutionary groups have been incapable either of working together or of drawing worker activists onto their side.

Much more successful has been the unification of the left in Mexico, where no one has tried to copy the experience of the Brazilian Workers Party. For the first time in decades, the opposition in 1988 succeeded in mounting a challenge to the Institutional Revolutionary Party (PRI), which has become firmly intertwined with the state and which exercises monopoly control over the country's political life. The opposition candidate, who almost won the election, was Cuauhtémoc Cárdenas, the son of a founder of the ruling party and previously a member of its leadership. The ruling circles found a reliable means of insuring themselves against defeat, falsifying the election results. "Computers conveniently 'failed' on election night, and results from half the voting booths have never been made public. The PRI 'won' with 50.4 percent, a far cry from its usual 75 percent and up."[75]

The success of Cárdenas not only placed the dominance of the PRI in question, but also changed the relationship of forces in the opposition. The right-wing Party of National Action (PAN) was forced into the background, especially since under new president Carlos Salinas de Gortari the PRI's nationalist slogans were replaced by liberal-technocratic ones. His policies, aimed at privatization and at subordinating the country to the demands of Western capital, were justly dubbed "salinastroika."

The Socialist Party of Mexico (PSM) and the Trotskyist Revolutionary Workers Party (PRT), which traditionally had enjoyed a significant influence in society, hoped vainly for a growth in their ranks. "The PRI was not the only party defeated in the electoral contest," notes the Mexican socialist A. Anguiano. "The strongest of the traditional left, the PSM and the PRT, suffered great losses in this rebellion of the masses." The old left organizations, which had inherited the structures and psychology of the revolutionary vanguard, were proving unable to head the movement. "The crisis of the left is in part due to its inability to go beyond itself and establish social roots. But the left also finds itself in crisis because of the loss of long-term political perspectives in favor of short-term partisan, self-interested needs."[76] In just the same fashion the old left have not appreciated the depth of the political break which

Cárdenas and the democratic current he headed have made with the PRI.

A part of the Mexican socialist movement, choosing to side with Cárdenas, united in the Movement for Socialism (MAS). It was their decision to take part in the presidential campaign of the opposition candidate that gave this campaign its radicalism. The Socialist Party attached itself to Cárdenas at the last moment. Analyzing the reasons for its lack of success, the PSM immediately after the elections supported the idea of establishing a united mass left party on the basis of the pre-election coalition. This new formation took the name Party of the Democratic Revolution (PRD).

The rise of the PRD sharply altered the country's political landscape. This party, which clearly stood outside the traditional political framework, was promptly condemned by many radical theoreticians. "The PRD lacks ideological coherence," wrote the American James Cockroft, "and has no program beyond a vague nationalist populism. It champions popular causes, new elections and the 'abolition of the one-party state and corporatism,' but it offers little to assure skeptical Mexicans that their lives will improve."[77]

By the beginning of the 1990s the problems the PRD was encountering were in fact common to all serious left parties, including the Brazilian Workers Party. Lula, who, thanks to the successes of his party, had become one of the most authoritative left-wing leaders not only in Latin America but throughout the world, admitted freely that the Workers Party had still to define what type of socialism it had in view.[78] The socialist perspective, he argued, ought to be ensured not through the ideological directives of a revolutionary proletarian leadership, but through the self-organization of the masses in struggle for their own interests. "Leftists have to understand that it is the masses who have to develop the socialist project. They have to appreciate that it is impossible to create a vanguard party unless the masses themselves become the vanguard."[79] The PT program advanced a series of reforms aimed at ensuring greater economic independence, more democracy in the taking of major decisions, and a more just distribution of wealth. The program spoke in a relatively general way about socializing property as far as possible without state ownership, and also about social control over the economy.

The moderate nature of the party's documents allowed both supporters and critics to speak of a resemblance between its ideas and those of social democracy.[80] PT ideologues in turn declared that theirs was a party of a qualitatively new type, which was "an alternative to social democracy, but which at the same time will not take the Communist path."[81] The PT was not preparing to administer the capitalist system; it aimed at overcoming capitalism. Despite the obvious influence of social democratic ideas, moderate reformist forms of Western socialism had no prospects in the conditions of Latin America.[82] The Workers Party was doomed to radicalism. But it was also required to be pragmatic and efficient. "The right wing might be able to afford mistakes, but the left can't," Lula stated. "People who have nothing to eat can't wait."[83]

The millions of people who voted for the PT demanded simultaneously that the party make radical changes to society and successfully administer it. This is not just a problem of the Workers Party, but a contradiction of reality itself, a contradiction which any radical party coming to power by the democratic path must inevitably confront. Whatever the constructs of party ideologues, this problem can only be resolved in practice.

The PT program was scarcely more radical than that of the Mexican PRD or of the Colombian leftists. Even as critics were counterposing the Mexican PRD, with its populist style, reformist slogans, and questionable leader, to the Brazilian PT as an example of a class party, these organizations were developing their collaboration. Cuauhtémoc Cárdenas noted that although there were substantial differences between the Workers Party, the PRD, and other mass left-wing organizations in Latin America, they were kindred in the sense of being pluralist movements of a new type. In his view, these forces made up a joint liberation front, able through their united efforts to lead the people of these countries out of their oppressed and dependent condition. "These movements, both the PRD and others which rest on the mobilization of the masses and on popular action, see in Latin American integration a means of strengthening democratic and social rights, and of winning national independence."[84]

Despite its defeats in the 1994 elections, the PRD, along with the right-wing National Action Party (PAN), has punctured the monopoly on government power previously held by the PRI. However, the balance of Mexican politics had already been completely upset by the

Chiapas rebellion led by the Zapatista Army of National Liberation (EZLN). The Zapatistas—"armed reformists," as Jorge Castañeda described them at a Columbia University lecture in March 1994—presented a combination of traditional Latin guerrilla strategies with the experience of social movements. This challenge, which filled a gap left by the PRD and others of the more qualified strata, polarized Mexican society in general and the forces of the left in particular. The EZLN brought a new agenda, representing the poorest in Mexico, linking democratization, education, infrastructural development, civil rights, respect for local majorities, and the people's daily needs; the PRD failed to respond to the new agenda—and was forced to rethink its entire project.

The new strategy of the left forces in Latin America was quick to bear fruit. Soon after the rise of the Brazilian Workers Party, the Venezuelan radical party Causa R announced its formation, and in Uruguay the Broad Front strengthened its positions. In both countries in 1993 leftists were administering the capital city, and had transformed themselves into serious contenders for power.

In South Korea as well, the democratization of the regime was followed by a marked increase in the strength of the left. As a Western journalist observed, following the near-complete abolition of censorship at the end of the 1980s "it was possible to find in the bookshops Korean editions of practically any strain of Marxist thought from Marx to Trotsky, from Rosa Luxemburg to Lukacs, from Gramsci to Marcuse, from the Frankfurt School to the *New Left Review*, from Althusser to Mandel."[85] Although it was still too soon in the early 1990s to speak of the South Korean left as a real force, in 1990 the People's Party appeared on the scene, emerging like the Brazilian Workers Party out of struggles by the labor movement.

The only country in which democratization and the growth of the left movement were accompanied during the 1990s by a strengthening of the traditional Communist Party was South Africa. Thanks to the authority won in the course of the antiracist struggle by Communists in the African National Congress (ANC), their party became a mass force. Emerging from clandestinity, the Communist Party tried to prove its respectability through an extremely moderate program and declarations of support for perestroika in the USSR. Gorbachev's new thinking was seized upon here at the very moment when Gorbachevism was finally collapsing in its homeland. This "new thinking" could not compete with a real liberal capitalist approach, argued a journal published by South African socialists. Such ideas do not provide suitable options either for capital, or for the working class.[86]

It is not surprising that in South Africa as well, the need is being felt for new ideas and for independent left organizations able to achieve not just a compromise between black and white oligarchies, but radical democratic reforms. One such group is the Workers Organization for Socialist Action, which to Stalinism and capitalism counterposes workers' self-management and direct democracy. Now, however, slogans are no longer enough.

The American left-wing philosopher Ronald Aronson, who visited the country in 1992, observed that "even though South Africa remains largely unripe for a socialist transformation in traditional Marxian terms, redistributive concerns (quasi-socialist at least) are a fundamental part of the agenda."[87] As Aronson notes, South Africa's numerous problems cannot be solved by capitalist methods, but socialist measures will not necessarily be successful either. What is needed is a complex multilevel strategy which includes substantial elements of socialism. In such circumstances the success of the left forces will depend on the degree to which they can counterpose to the compromise of the elites—supported by the general efforts of liberals, Stalinists, and moderate black and white nationalists—a *compromise of the masses*, opening the way for real economic democracy and political freedom. Such a compromise must be based on real discussion among the popular sectors, including unions, civic organizations, and grassroots social movements, to ascertain what people really want. The current debates among anti-apartheid forces suggest that a program of structural reform should be based on these demands, rather than goals set by isolated leadership groups, however respected.

New political winds have also been blowing in Eastern Europe. The fall in living standards, the growth of unemployment, and the collapse of social welfare systems whose existence had not been thought to require justifying, could not fail to arouse protests. In the autumn of 1990 Jan Drewnowski noted that it was impossible not to admire the patience of the workers, who have almost never resorted to strikes. They never showed such impressive patience under the old regime. Nevertheless, the fact that in the first year of transition there have been virtually no strikes was not to the credit of the reformers. It is no more than natural that time should be needed to restore order to the economy, and no one will argue that living standards can be raised in a matter of days. However, such a position cannot last long.[88]

In Hungary in the autumn of 1990 taxi drivers went on strike. By general agreement, the strikers were expressing the mood of broad layers of the population. "This kind of reaction from the population— open and bitter discontent—might have been expected," noted Hungary's largest newspaper, *Nepszabadsag*, "After all, people's patience is not limitless." But to the authorities, however strange it might seem, the "autumn tempest" came as a surprise. A fierce conflict broke out between the state and society. "The obstinacy of the government, which is insisting on new gasoline prices, and also its weak links with the public, have provided a sharp contrast with the mobilized population. The government has failed to notice how confidence in it has fallen sharply during the course of the crisis. Millions of people have seen how the government is unable to solve the problems that have arisen. At the same time, the crisis has brought people into activity, tearing them out of the accustomed routines of their everyday lives, and at the first chance that has appeared for active protest, it has become clear that the bulk of the population are by no means apathetic or apolitical. The 'little revolution' that is emerging on the popular level, and of which there has been too little during the present transition period, smacks of nostalgia and of the mood of 1956. The halting of street traffic, and the masses of people pouring into the streets, have provided a reminder of this."[89] It remains only to recall that the revolution in Hungary in 1956 took place under socialist slogans. In 1994, the Hungarian Socialist Party was voted into office, showing that even the worst of Socialists were gaining on the liberals.

In the spring of 1991 a wave of strikes swept across eastern Germany. As a correspondent for *Izvestiia* noted aptly, workers who had earlier studied class war from hated communist textbooks were now "beginning actively to assimilate it in practice."[90]

In Lithuania in 1991 the policies of the government of Kazimiera Prunskiene were calling forth resistance not only from the Russian and Polish minorities, but also from Lithuanian workers. After sudden price rises in January 1991, strikes broke out at Lithuanian Airlines, the Vilnius railway depot, a plant producing radio measuring equipment, and then in many other enterprises. "The usually very restrained Lithuanians were outraged, and began cursing the government. They were especially appalled by the prices of cheese and of 'wet' sausage; Lithuania from time immemorial has been a land of sausage-eaters. The prices of taxis and of private cartage also rose sharply, though unofficially. And that is not to speak of cigarettes on the black market."[91]

The wave of protests forced the authorities to revoke the price rises, and the Prunskeine government resigned. For a brief period, the Stalinist "Communist Party of Lithuania on the platform of the CPSU" stepped into the political limelight, calling for the strikes to be continued "until the introduction of presidential rule."[92] Responding to the appeals of his supporters, the president of the USSR promptly sent military units into Lithuania. The troops received instructions to fire on an unarmed crowd. But on meeting with popular resistance, Gorbachev retreated; everything in Lithuania remained as before.[93] Several months later the Communist Party of Lithuania was banned, and the government turned with fresh enthusiasm to privatizing property. The lack of a strong, independent organization of workers made such an outcome inevitable. The Union of Workers of Lithuania, headed by right-wing social democrats, was not ready to act as an alternative political force. The strikes in Hungary, Poland, and the Soviet Union showed the strength of the workers' movement and its determination to resist the liberal reforms. But for the moment, this strength was not accompanied by a corresponding consciousness.

Everywhere, there was a lack of active, genuinely independent trade unions. Even in Poland, where in 1980 the slogan "Free Trade Unions!" had roused millions of workers to struggle against the old regime, the union organizations were very weak. Solidarnosc was never a real trade union. During its best period, in 1980 and 1981, it was a mass popular movement. By 1991 no more than a quarter of the original membership remained under its banner, and even its own activists doubted its ability to act as an effective labor leadership.

During the years of martial law the Solidarnosc leaders managed to create a strong underground organization, but they lost contact with the masses. For the movement's leaders, foreign aid and the donations of private entrepreneurs sympathetic to democracy became more important than the support of rank-and-file workers. This predetermined the right-wing course that Solidarnosc was to follow after 1989. The veteran of the democratic movement Karol Modzelewski noted that in introducing martial law, General Jaruzelski "did in Poland what Pinochet did in Chile. Without Jaruzelski there would have been no Balcerowicz. If Jaruzelski hadn't broken the back of the Solidarity mass movement, it would have been impossible to implement the Balcerowicz economic program. No one would have dared to even suggest such a program. It was the destruction of Solidarity as a mass movement that made the transition to a liberal-monetary economic policy possible."[94]

The old trade unions, that workers in Eastern Europe had received as an inheritance from the old regime, were ineffective and bureaucratized. But in 1991 and 1992 important changes began taking place within them. They had retained most of their members and assets. Thanks to leadership changes and democratic reforms, they succeeded in substantially increasing their authority within society. The traditional trade unions, notes the Hungarian sociologist Gyorgy Markus, "are now the only trade unions with real mass membership."[95] Events unfolded in analogous fashion in Russia, in other republics of the former USSR, and even in Poland and Bulgaria, where there were strong anticommunist union federations. In the summer of 1992, when Poland was gripped by strikes, the traditional unions played the decisive role in them. Activists of Solidarnosc and of its split-off Solidarnosc-80 combined with members of the pro-Communist All-Polish Federation of Trade Unions (OPZZ) to mount joint actions.[96] During the strikes the workers not only fought for higher wages and improved working conditions, but also demanded "an end to chaotic privatization."[97]

As the press acknowledged, the leadership of Solidarnosc was in an exceptionally difficult position, trying to retain good relations with the government and simultaneously "fearing a loss of influence among the workers."[98] The ruling circles in turn saw the trade unions as a real threat: "in all the Eastern countries the most conservative powers are concentrated in the old trade unions," the Hungarian sociologist Julia Szalai warned her readers, "they're quite active in trying to block the whole transformation process."[99] Following mass demonstrations and meetings organized by the Russian trade unions in October 1992, the liberal *Moscow News* wrote that "after a long vacation, the trade union 'school of communism' has once again thrown open its doors."[100]

Under cover of demagogic propaganda, the authorities have everywhere introduced anti-union measures. The rights of labor unions have been restricted, and their property seized. This in turn has forced the unions onto the road of political involvement. In late 1991 growing discontent with the authoritarian policies of the Russian rulers made the slogan of "a Party of Labor" popular among the country's union leaders. This idea also aroused warm support among activists of the largest non-Communist left groups, the Socialist Party and the Confederation of Anarcho-Syndicalists. Many Communist-democrats were attracted to the concept as well. The Appeal of the Party of Labor, adopted on August 28, 1991 (the same day as Yeltsin's Decree no. 96), spoke of the formation of a broad "party-movement" based on "initiatives from below."[101]

For a long time, leftists in Eastern Europe remained in a political vacuum. The overwhelming majority of the intelligentsia stood firmly on the side of the neoliberals, turning their backs on the bulk of the population. It was essential to overcome the new ideological hegemony of liberalism, and to win even just a section of the intelligentsia over to the side of the socialist project.

In 1989 and 1990, the majority of commentators in both East and West agreed that in Eastern Europe the word "socialism" had been hopelessly compromised, and that forces acting under socialist slogans had no chance of success. This seemed so obvious that few people even bothered to study the results of opinion surveys.

In fact, the term socialism was perceived in negative terms only in the uppermost strata of society—among the administrative bureaucracy, the oligarchy, the mafia, and the intellectual elite. To a certain degree these groups, which dominated society and controlled the mass media, were capable of imposing the hegemony of their ideas. But among workers, and even among significant groups of managers, different feelings prevailed. Surveys conducted in Russia between 1989 and 1991 showed clearly that among workers and even engineers, socialist ideas enjoyed considerable popularity, though the majority of the creative intelligentsia and of students decisively rejected them.[102] The left, in other words, was not in fact socially isolated; what had really occurred was that the intellectual elite had placed itself in opposition to the masses.

The discontent among working people could not fail to affect the balance of political forces. In the first free elections for the Polish Sejm, the Union of the Democratic Left, founded by social-democratized Communists, scored a major success, falling only one percent short of becoming the largest single party. The well-known Polish political observer David Warszawski noted that many former supporters of Solidarnosc had voted for the Union of the Democratic Left because Solidarnosc itself had renounced its original ideas and values. The left wing of Solidarnosc had been too weak. People had voted for the former Communists "because they had no other choice."[103]

In 1992 the Union of Labor was established, uniting former members of Solidarnosc with a section of the Communist reformers. The decisive role in the founding of the new party was played by Labor Solidarnosc, a group of left-leaning intellectuals from the original Solidarnosc. Other groups to join in the process included the Democratic Social Movement, headed by the veteran of the underground Solidarnosc movement of the 1980s Zbigniew Bujak, and also the Social Democratic Union and the July 8 Movement, which had split from the Polish United Workers Party. The new organization was more radical than the Union of the Democratic Left, but also significantly weaker. Despite their harsh criticisms of neoliberalism and of attempts at the "bureaucratic construction of capitalism," the leaders of the Union of Labor, like many other left activists in Eastern Europe, continued to idolize Western social democracy.[104] Nevertheless, the rise of the Union of Labor and the success of the Union of Democratic Forces bore witness to important changes in Polish political life. The forces of the left, despite their internal problems, were beginning to play a serious role.

In Czechoslovakia the Communists did not change their name; in 1968 their party had headed the Prague Spring, and still earlier had been the main strength of the antifascist resistance. In local elections in November 1990 the Czechoslovak Communists achieved important successes.[105] The professional politicians who remained in the ranks of the Communist and post-Communist parties had learned a great deal in 1989. In the elections of 1992 the Left Bloc, established by the Czech Communist Party, showed itself to be an influential social force. Several former dissidents were elected to parliament on the same list with Communists. The old division into democrats and Communists was giving way to a demarcation between right and left. In Slovakia the 1992 elections were won by the Movement for a Democratic Slovakia, which united leftists and moderate nationalists. In the municipal elections in eastern Berlin in the spring of 1992 the outstanding successes were those of the Party of Democratic Socialism.

The ideological packaging in which the program of the left parties was presented was not regarded by voters as particularly important. The Polish Communist-reformists tried their utmost to social democratize themselves. The Czech Communists, on the other hand, stressed their fidelity to the traditions of the party. The PDS in Germany presented itself as a party with a completely new, original ideology. And all these parties made progress.

People were not supporting the post-Communist parties because they believed the new ideas these parties were presenting. Millions of citizens of the former Eastern bloc countries had simply discovered that the politicians had deceived them by promising them prosperity under capitalism. In response, people voted for the largest party of the left opposition, or for the most familiar and serious of the left parties.

The outcome of the 1992 elections in Lithuania was a real sensation. An absolute majority of the seats in the Sejm went to the Democratic Party of Labor (DPL), headed by Algirdas Brazauskas. For the first time in Eastern Europe, free elections had been won by a party of the left. For the first time, an opposition had turned a government out of office by democratic means.

On the eve of the elections the right-wing press had unleashed a furious propaganda campaign against the DPL. The leader of the ruling Sajudis movement, Vitautas Landsbergis, spoke of a "pack of dogs" said to be "preparing a creeping coup."[106] The newspapers constantly reminded their readers of the Communist history of Brazauskas and the Laborites. However, this campaign had unexpected results. Immediately before the elections, the left-centrist newspaper *Respublika* published a long list of prominent Sajudis members with details of their former posts and titles. The list was headed by Laureate of the State Prize of the Lithuanian SSR and Merited Artist of the Lithuanian SSR Vitautas Landsbergis. "These people," the newspaper commented bitterly, "are patriots twice over, selflessly serving both Lithuanias, the Soviet and the independent. Up to this point they have not renounced either the titles or the prizes."[107]

The nationalist leaders of Sajudis were certain that voters would support them simply because Sajudis had led the country to indepen-dence. But life in independent Lithuania was nowhere near so beauti-ful as expected. The country's population saw a deepening economic crisis, pointless conflicts with Russia and Belarus, authoritarianism, and the oppression of national minorities.

Those who voted for the DPL included a majority of youth and even some entrepreneurs, trying to preserve the market for their goods in the countries of the former Soviet Union. "People today are more concerned about whether there is heating and hot water in their buildings, than about the ghost of communism that is supposedly looming up behind the backs of the neocommunists," admitted the liberal *Moscow News.* "Society has grown tired of the extremism of the right, and is looking for reconciliation."[108]

The success of Brazauskas was repeated in September 1993 by the Polish left. While ex-Communist Social Democrats and the Peasant Party became the majority in the Sejm, the Union of Labor emerged from the elections as another important political force with forty-five deputies. This triumph of the post-Communist left in Poland as well as in Lithuania didn't mean a dramatic change in the strategy of eco-nomic development. Ex-Communist technocrats proved to be much less radical then the new left and much less interested in noncapitalist alternatives.

The triumph of liberalism proved to be short-lived. In 1989 and 1990 capitalism scored a victory of global scope, but the consequences of this victory turned against the capitalist world system itself. The neoliberal reforms in Eastern Europe and Latin America synchronized the devel-opment of these regions. Events in one country have had a powerful political resonance in others, placing the whole system of dependent capitalism under threat. After 1989 it seemed to many people that decades would have to pass before left-wing parties would manage to adapt to the new conditions and seize the initiative. By the mid-1990s, however, the picture is already completely different. Neoliberal gov-ernments have had trouble holding off the wave of popular discontent, while mass movements have been advancing radical slogans, and the ideology of the free market has lost its attractiveness.

The revival of the left forces in Eastern Europe and their growth in the more developed countries of the third world contrast sharply with the continuing crisis of Western social democracy. Once again, new ideas and new political forces have arisen on the periphery of the capitalist system, throwing out a challenge to the old order. This is not a repetition of the past, however, but a new stage in a historic struggle.

NOTES

Preface

1. M. Brie and E. Boelke, *Russland wieder in Dunkeln* (Berlin, 1992), p. 45.
2. Robert Kurz, *Der Kollaps der Modernisierung* (Frankfurt am Main, 1991), p. 272.

Chapter 1: The Third World in a Labyrinth of Problems

1. For many people in the countries of the North, it is as though the problems of the South did not exist. With sickening European arrogance, the French writer J. Freund writes that on the whole there is no crisis in the third world, that these countries have not yet reached the necessary stage of development for their people to understand a European crisis, "since they live in such poverty that the very idea of a crisis is beyond their comprehension. What significance does all this have for the hungry of Bangladesh or Calcutta? What is involved is exclusively a European crisis, and only Europeans are conscious of it as such" (J. Freund, *La fin de la Renaissance* [Paris, 1980], p. 8). Indeed, a well-fed French bourgeois perceives the crisis differently than do the inhabitants of the developing countries. For the bourgeois, a crisis means a 5 percent cut in real income, while for millions of people in the third world it means death from starvation. Freind considers that what is involved is not a crisis at all, but the sunset of Europe. The idea is far from new. But when Oswald Spengler in 1918 advanced this hypothesis, his *Decline of the West*, unlike Freind's book, represented a major philosophical development. He laid the basis for the modern theory of civilization. Nevertheless, Spengler failed to see the difference between the open European civilization and the closed civilizations of the East. (For a more detailed treatment, see Boris Kagarlitsky, *Dialektika Nadezhdy* [Paris, 1988].) In reality, the East has not known crises; it has known only the degeneration or collapse of civilizations. A crisis is associated with the possibility of renewal and of the reconstruction of the basis of a society and a civilization. In the twentieth century all humanity in one degree or another has perceived the features of European civilization, but this civilization is itself in crisis. Evidence of this is provided both by the appearance in considerable quantities of books such as Freind's, and the serious attention paid to them. The crisis

can and must be overcome, on the scale of humanity as a whole. The spiritual and political resources of the West are relatively great, but they are clearly insufficient to solve present-day world problems even on the theoretical level. During the 1980s theoretical discussions in the third world were both deeper and more concrete than in the West. The teachers would now do well to accept instruction from the pupils.

2. *Ideologicheskie protsessy i massovoe soznanie v razvivaiushchikhsia stranakh Azii i Afriki* (Moscow, 1984), p. 9.

3. *New Left Review* (London), no. 180 (1990): 13.

4. *Marxism Today* (London), no. 1 (1983): 46.

5. L. Ratinov in *Elites in Latin America*, edited by S. M. Lipset and A. Solari (London and New York, 1967), p. 81.

6. *Kur'er UNESCO*, November 1981, p. 6.

7. A. Frondizi, *Estrategia y táctica del movimiento nacional* (Buenos Aires, 1964), p. 164.

8. A. Brewer, *Marxist Theories of Imperialism: A Critical Survey* (London and New York, 1990), p. 284.

9. V. V. Mikheev, *V poiskakh al'ternativy. Aziatskie modeli pazvitiia: sotsialisticheskie i "novye industrial'nye strany"* (Moscow, 1990), pp. 73, 93.

10. *Monthly Review* (New York), vol. 37, no. 5 (October 1985): 29–30.

11. Mikheev, *V poiskakh al'ternativy*, pp. 101, 102.

12. *New Left Review*, no. 182 (1990): 29.

13. *Left Business Observer* (New York), no. 42 (1990): 5.

14. *Strukturnye sdvigi v ekonomike i evoliutsiia politicheskikh sistem v stranakh Azii i Afriki v 70-e gody* (Moscow, 1982), p. 157. (Below: *Strukturnye sdvigi.*)

15. Samir Amin, *L'Economie arabe contemporaine* (Paris, 1980), p. 58.

16. Venezuela provides a typical example of a country eating its way through its national accumulation funds. Only an insignificant proportion of Venezuela's oil dollars were invested in the development of science. According to calculations by experts, in 1984 the number of scientists in the country was only 3,500, instead of the 16,000 needed to solve the main problems standing in the way of economic progress; see *Izvestiia* (Moscow), 2 September 1984.

17. *British Book News*, February 1983, p. 73.

18. *Latinskaia Amerika* (Moscow), no. 10 (1983): 68.

19. *Dialog* (Moscow), no. 17 (1990): 80.

20. *Socialist Organiser* (London), no. 472 (1991): 7.

21. *Correo Internacional* (Buenos Aires), no. 11 (January 1991): 31.

22. *Workers Power* (London), no. 134 (September 1990): 10.

23. *Le Monde*, 22 January 1991, p. 11.

24. *Za rubezhom* (Moscow), no. 8 (1991): 7.

25. *Socialist Organiser*, no. 472 (1991): 7.

26. *Voprosy ekonomiki* (Moscow), no. 6 (1984): 122. Developing countries were forced to acquire complex, expensive, and often ineffective modern armaments. Recent Western research has shown convincingly that increases in the prices charged for armaments have often been accompa-

nied by declines in the military capabilities of these weapons. See Mary Kaldor, *The Baroque Arsenal* (London, 1981); Andrew Cockburn, *The Threat* (London, Melbourne, etc., 1983). For a discussion of the general problems of the arms race in the third world, see "Disarmament—Development," in *Links* (London), no. 18 (1983). It is noteworthy that during the war in the Persian Gulf, the greatest losses suffered by the Western forces resulted not from ultramodern French and Soviet-built combat aircraft, but from the ability of the Iraqis to organize effective defence using traditional methods tested during World War I.

27. P. Adams, *Odious Debts* (London and Toronto, 1991), p. 184.
28. *The Observer* (London), 1 July 1984, p. 11. The *Times* (London), 27 February 1984, even declared in a lead article that the bankers ought to admit publicly that "their earlier decisions were wrong."
29. *Révolution africaine* (Paris), no. 1041 (1984): 28. It should be recognized that the overaccumulation of capital which could not be invested on advantageous terms, either in the West or in many cases in the third world, made the providing of loans an economic necessity for the countries of the center. Latin America was transformed into a gigantic precipitation tank of international capital. However, the inefficiency of the dependent economies placed this policy in doubt. A critical threshold of indebtedness was very quickly reached.
30. *Moscow Tribune*, 21 October 1992. By the end of 1992 an analogous agreement had also been reached with Ukraine. For a discussion of the policies of the IMF see Andrei Kolganov, "'Vostochnyi pokhod' Mezhdunarodnogo Valiutnogo Fonda," *Solidarnost* (Moscow), no. 5 (1992).
31. *Al'ternativy* (Moscow), no. 2 (1992): 8. English edition: *Socialist Alternatives* (Montreal), no. 2 (1992).
32. Susan George, *A Fate Worse than Debt* (London, 1990), p. 263.
33. *Time*, 2 July 1984, p. 4.
34. *The Times* (London), 3 March 1984, p. 9.
35. *Against the Current* (Detroit), no. 27 (July-August 1990): 27.
36. *Finance and Development*, December 1979, pp. 8-9.
37. Thomas Malthus, *Opyt o zakone narodonaseleniia*, vol. 1. (St. Petersburg, 1868), p. 96.
38. W. McNeill, *Population and Politics since 1750* (Charlottesville and London, 1990), p. 2.
39. Ibid., pp. 13–15.
40. *Razvivaiushchiesia strany: demograficheskaia situatsiia i ekonomicheskii rost* (Moscow, 1981), p. 51.
41. A. Sauvy, *Malthus et les deux Marx* (Paris, 1964), p. 111. The use of child labor brings about a worsening of the position on the labor market. The children force adults out of work.
42. Muammar al-Kaddafi, *Zelenaia kniga* B.m., b.g., vol. 3, pp. 67–68.
43. *Population Bulletin*, no. 2 (1976): 28.
44. *Strukturnye sdvigi*, p. 62.

45. *Razvivaiushchiesia strany,* p. 65.
46. A Soviet demographer observed: "The familiar saying 'I don't care whether or not I'm fat, I'm just concerned about staying alive,' applies literally to the bulk of the population in these countries. In other words, the key question is not why, let us say, the Indians are mainly vegetarians, or how the lack of animal protein affects their health, but why they receive inadequate quantities even of vegetarian foods, and why even the national average calorie intake is below the required level" (*Razvivaiushchiesia strany,* p. 69). Among those who die of hunger, a third (18 million a year!) are children below the age of five. The real number of victims of hunger is even greater, since people are weakened by malnutrition. "People die because they cannot resist illnesses," says E. Sauma, the head of the Food and Agriculture Organization; "Even the cold can kill a child, a woman or a man" (*Newsweek,* 5 December 1983, p. 56).
47. E.F. Schumacher, *Small is Beautiful* (London, 1974), p. 71.
48. *Razvivaiushchiesia strany,* pp. 6–7. Rates of urbanization in Latin America have been especially high, almost twice those in Asia and Africa. As many as 40 percent of urban residents live in shantytowns.
49. A. Bose, *Studies in India's Urbanisation* (Delhi, 1966), p. 63.
50. Planirovka, *Stikhiino voznikaiushchie gorodskie poseleniia* Doklad OON (Geneva, 1967), p. 15.
51. T. S. Pokataeva, *Razvivaiushchiesia strany: problema urbanizatsii* (Moscow 1977), p. 41. In the USSR the internal passport system, for all its obvious injustices, nevertheless helped prevent urban crises during the process of industrialization.
52. *Voprosy Filosofii* (Moscow), no. 9 (1976): 102.
53. A. I. Goryacheva and M. G. Makarov, *Obshchestvennaia psikhologiia* (Leningrad, 1979), p. 75.
54. E. Primakov, *Vostok posle krakka kolonial'noi sistemy* (Moscow, 1983), p. 5.
55. *Strukturnye sdvigi,* p. 38.
56. K. Marx and F. Engels, *Sochineniia,* vol. 19, p. 416. See also pp. 116–121. Some Marxists try to be more royalist than the king himself; the French Communist J.L. Gombeau, for example, calls on his readers to "reach an understanding of the problems now confronting underdeveloped countries" through studying Marx's writings on the industrial revolution in the West (*Economie et politique,* no. 75–76 [July-August 1983]: 52).
57. Marx and Engels, ibid., vol. 4, p. 428.
58. Ibid., vol. 9, pp. 135–136.
59. *Développement et socialisme* (Dakar, 1963), p. 24.
60. Marx and Engels, *Sochineniia,* vol 9. p. 225.
61. Ibid., p. 230.
62. V.I. Lenin, *Polnoe Sobranie Sochinenii,* vol. 21, pp. 400–406; vol. 23, pp. 1–4.
63. T. Dos Santos, *Dependencia y cambio social,* (Caracas, 1977), p. 40. See also: T. Dos Santos, *Lucha de clases y dependencia en America Latina* (Bogotá, 1970), p. 222. Dos Santos's views aroused objections from Soviet scholars. A. V. Shestopal declared that Dos Santos showed a biased attitude to

Levoradikal'naia sotsiologiia v Latinskoi Amerike [Moscow, 1981], p. 144). In fact, Lenin considered that the export of capital has an impact on the development of capitalism in the countries to which it is exported, greatly accelerating this process (Lenin, *Polnoi*, vol. 27, p. 362). Lenin agreed with Marx's original hypothesis that in backward countries imperialism continued to play a progressive role, though the social price exacted for this progress was excessively high. Countries that were drawn into the world capitalist economy had of necessity to be capitalized.

64. Rosa Luxemburg, *Nakoplenie kapitala*, vol. 1–2 (Moscow and Leningrad, 1934), pp. 258, 259. A biographer of Rosa Luxemburg describes this work (*The Accumulation of Capital*) as "a little-read, and for most of the human race unreadable Marxist classic" (R. Abraham, *Rosa Luxemburg* [Oxford, New York, and Munich, 1989], p. 109). For a discussion of the contemporary significance of Luxemburg's ideas see Joan Robinson, *Collected Economic Papers*, vol. 2 (Oxford, 1960), and also Boris Kagarlitsky, *Dialektika nadezhdy*, pp. 21, 22.

65. A. Cordova, *Marxismo y subdesarrollo* (Caracas, 1975), p. 28.

66. André Gunder Frank, *Latin America: Underdevelopment or Revolution* (New York and London, 1969), p. 9.

67. Luxemburg, *Nakoplenii* (Moscow), pp. 259–60.

68. Pokataeva, *Razvivaiushchiesia strany: problema urbanizatsii*, p. 30.

69. Lenin, *Selected Works*, vol. IX (New York, 1937), p. 166. Lenin's original term is *mnogoukladnost'*.

70. A. I. Levkovsky, *Sotsial'naia struktura razvivaiushchikhsia stran* (Moscow, 1978), pp. 12–13. From the point of view of Marxist theory a multisystem society is one in which several modes of production coexist, each of them giving rise to their own social superstructure. If we examine this phenomenon using the categories of Western economics, a multisystem society is distinguished by "a substantial difference between the productivity of labor in various groups of enterprises"; see A. di Fillippo, *Desarrollo y disigualidád en la America Latina* (Mexico, 1981), p. 246.

71. *Razvivaiushchiesia strany v sovremennom mire: edinstvo i mnogoobrazie* (Moscow, 1983), p. 11.

72. *Ekonomika razvivaiushchikhsia stran: teorii i metody issledovaniia* (Moscow, 1979), p. 156. (Below: *Ekonomika razvivaiushchikhsia stran.*)

73. *Ideologicheskie protsessy*, p. 9.

74. Marx and Engels, *Sochineniia*, vol. 9, p. 132.

75. Ibid., vol. 12, p. 724.

76. *The Development of Underdevelopment in China: a Symposium* (White Plains, NY, 1980), p. 103.

77. T. Szentes, *Nekapitalisticheskii put' razvitiia i razvivaiushchiesia strany* (Budapest, 1966), pp. 4–5.

78. T. Dos Santos, *Lucha de clases y dependencia en America Latina*, p. 234.

79. I. Bognar, *Ekonomicheskaia politika i planirovanie v razvivaiushchikhsia stranakh* (Budapest, 1966), p. 15.

80. *Kur'er UNESCO*, November 1981, p. 28.

81. *Ideologicheskie protsessy*, p. 32.
82. A. V. Shestopal, *Mirazhi El'dorado v XX veke* (Moscow, 1974), p. 34. Shestopal bases his arguments on the ideas of Frank, Dos Santos, and other left radical Western scholars, but does not acknowledge this.
83. Some regions of the periphery such as the southern United States, Ireland, southern Italy, Spain, and Portugal may be integrated into the economic system of the center, so long as extensive growth takes place in the center itself. As this occurs, the burden on the remaining areas of the periphery increases, and the exploitation to which they are subject is intensified. The shift by the center to an intensive model of growth and to new generation labor-saving technologies—in itself a huge progressive development—simultaneously reduces the chances for backward societies of making the breakthrough into the group of industrialized states. There have also been instances in which countries at a medium level of development have seen this level degraded. In the early years of the twentieth century, Argentina and Uruguay were ranked with Australia and Canada as relatively developed societies, but they have gradually drawn closer to the developing countries. For a more detailed treatment of relations between the center, the periphery, and the semiperiphery in the world capitalist system see Imanuel Wallerstein, *The Modern World-System I* (San Diego etc. 1974). One may disagree with Wallerstein's views, but it is hardly possible to dispute the fact that a world system exists, or that the roles played by particular countries within this system have changed.
84. *L'Espresso*, 6 March 1983, no. 9, p. 166.
85. Celso Furtado, *El mito del desarrollo económico y el futuro del Tercer Mundo* (Buenos Aires, 1974), p. 28.
86. Ibid., p. 27. Using the principle of "follow the leader," individual states might achieve the ranking of developed countries, but the overall problems of the third world will not be solved in this fashion. Even countries such as Brazil which have made advances along this road cannot manage the final burst without encountering a serious social crisis which puts the whole endeavor under threat.
87. *Les socialistes et le Tiers Monde* (Nancy, 1977), p. 27.
88. J. Silva Colmenares, *Tras la máscara del subdesarrollo: dependéncia y monopolios* (Bogota, 1983), p. 87.
89. *Revue français de science politique* 1979, no. 4–5, pp. 614–15.

Chapter 2: The Illusions of National Independence

1. *Les socialistes et le Tiers Monde* p. 101.
2. *Socialist Affairs* (Amsterdam), no 1 (1977): 34–35.
3. C. Guelfi, *Metropoli e terzo mondo nella crisi* (Rome, 1979), p. 186.
4. *Common Crisis: North-South: Cooperation for World Recovery* The Brandt Commission, (London, 1983), pp. 8, 13.
5. *Monthly Review*, vol. 42, no. 5 (October 1990): 31.
6. *Socialist Review* (San Francisco), vol. 20, no. 3 (July-September 1990): 61.
7. *Mirovaia ekonomika i mezhdunarodnye otnosheniia*, no. 7 (1983): 66.

8. K. Griffin in *The Development of Underdevelopment in China*, p. 105.

9. K. Brutents, *Sovremennye natsional'no-osvoboditel'nye revoliutsii* (Moscow, 1974), p. 397.

10. *Latinskaia Amerika*, no. 8 (1983): 26.

11. In British and American writings the term *multinational corporations* is used along with the term *transnationals*, which is preferred by scholars from the former USSR and the countries of the third world. In my view the latter term better expresses the essence of this phenomenon.

12. *Révolution africaine, no. 1041 (1984): 34*.

13. *Vostok: rubezh 80-kh godov*, p. 38. If the unilateral nationalization of transnational capital proves impossible, this does not exclude the possibility of nationalization on the basis of agreements with the former owners. But such agreements will only be successful if the national state acts from a position of economic strength.

14. *Ibid.* p. 42. For a more detailed treatment of the discussion in the journal *Latinskaia Amerika* and of the positions taken by V. P. Lukin see V. Storozhevsky in *Detant*, no. 3 (1985). Following the collapse of the USSR, Lukin was for some time in charge of Russia's foreign policy, in which capacity he called for harsh measures against the former "fraternal republics," above all Ukraine. Later, he was banished from Moscow, becoming ambassador to the United States.

15. *Rabochii klass v mirovom revoliutsionnom protsesse* (1982), pp. 41, 44.

16. *Latinskaia Amerika*, no. 10 (1983): 65.

17. *Vostok: rubezh 80-kh godov*, p. 38.

18. In Ford plants in Mexico and Brazil, assembly workers on the conveyor belts received 42.5 percent and 9 percent, respectively, of the wages of their counterparts in the United States. For fitters, the corresponding figures were 42.4 percent and 15.3 percent. See Primakov, *Vostok posle krakka kolonial'noi sistemy*, p. 119.

19. *Latinskaia Amerika*, no. 9 (1983): 67.

20. *The Economist*, vol. 291, no. 7340 (5 May 1984): 106.

21. *Latinskaia Amerika*, no. 10 (1983): 79.

22. *Review of Radical Political Economics*, vol. 19, no. 1 (Spring 1987): 12.

23. J.D. Gould, *Economic Growth in History* (London, 1972), pp. 1–3.

24. *Za rubezhom*, no. 29 (1985).

25. G. Roustang, *Le travail autrement* (Paris, 1982), p. 150.

26. *Za rubezom*, no. 8 (1984): 15. The Brandt Commission noted that the wealthy countries transfered their problems to the developing world via a whole range of mechanisms (*Common Crisis: North-South*, p. 17). In other words, the higher the level of transnationalization of an economy and the greater the degree to which it is integrated into the world capitalist division of labor, the higher the risk that it will be infected with the social and economic illnesses of the West. The main Western illness that ravages the economies of developing countries is inflation. This is borne in various active zones, and as economists note, is then transmitted through channels of distribution into the remaining sectors, so that prices rise

everywhere, irrespective of the state of aggregate supply and demand and of whether the economy is growing or in recession (*Ekonomika razvivaiushchikhsia stran*, p. 75).

27. Furtado, *El mito del desarrollo económico*, p. 39.

28. *Razvivaiushchiesia strany v sovremennom mire*, p. 41.

29. Adams, *Odious Debts*, p. 192.

30. Summary document of the Second Latin American Meeting of Workers' Representatives in Defence of the Public Sector (ELASPE). Cited in *Tribune internationale*, no. 69 (September 1992): 5.

31. *El Trabajo*, no. 21 (1992).

32. *Que Hacer*, no. 35 (June 1985); *La Republica* (Lima), 6 June 1985. See also: *Wissenschaftliche Beitrage der Institut für Ökonomik der Entwicklungsländer der Hochschule für Ökonomik*, Jg. 10, Heft 1 (Berlin 1975).

33. Catharine Samay and I. Sheremet'ev, *Al'ternativy*, no. 2 (1992): 93.

34. R. Mauro Marini, *America Latina. Dependência e integração* (São Paulo), p. 146.

35. *Latinskaia Amerika*, no. 9 (1983): 68.

36. *Gosudarstvennyi sektor v stranakh Afriki*, (Moscow, 1976), p. 9.

37. *Institute of Development Studies Bulletin* (Brighton), vol. 3, no. 4 (1971): 27.

38. A. Graft-Johnson, *An Introduction to African Economy* (London, 1962), p. 100. See also *Obshchestvennye nauki*, no. 4 (1981): 128.

39. Max Weber, *Izbrannye proizvedeniia* (Moscow, 1990), pp. 49, 53. See also articles by Weber on Russia in *Sintaksis* (Paris), no. 22 (1988).

40. F.R. Sagasti and S. M. Guerrero, *El desarrollo científico y tecnológico de America Latina* (Buenos Aires, 1974), p. 56.

41. *Ethiopiques* (Dakar), no. 21 (1980): 97.

42. *Políticas económicas, desarrollo industrial y tecnología en Colombia: 1925-1975* (Bogotá, 1976), p. 37. The American scholars Michael Tanzer and S. Zorn note that the same is happening with respect to energy policy. Copying Western technology, the developing countries have made themselves dependent on the oil companies and OPEC, although they often have alternative sources of energy. "The only practical solution for this impasse for most developing countries is a strategy that focuses on the use of indigenous energy resources, whether these are oil, natural gas, coal, hydropower, or such newly important sources as solar energy or alcohol production from sugarcane" (Michael Tanzer, S. Zorn, *Energy Update* [New York, 1985], p. 105).

43. *Voprosy ekonomiki*, no. 5 (1984): 126.

44. For a more detailed treatment see *Kur'er UNESKO*, November 1981, p. 6.

45. *Argumenty i fakty*, no. 52 (1990): 5. During the 1990s the Russian ruling circles also began looking for ways to profit from earlier fraternal aid to the developing countries. In 1991 the Moscow newspaper *Kommersant* reported that "Vietnam, Mongolia, Jordan, and possibly other countries of the Third World are for a period of five or six years to furnish various types of fresh produce, processed foodstuffs and preserves to Russia as payment on their debt to the Soviet Union" (*Kommersant*, no. 26 [1991]:

1). The debtors were to purchase technology and equipment in the United States and Canada using hard currency earned from shipments of cheap raw materials. Becoming dependent on Western capital, the Soviet government imposed exploitative agreements with the West on its traditional partners in anti-imperialist struggle.

46. Marx and Engels, *Sochineniia*, vol. 9, p. 227.

47. F. R. Sagasti, *Tecnología, planificación y desarrollo autónomo* (Lima, 1977), p. 139.

48. Sagasti and Guerrero, *Desarrollo*, p. 16.

49. *Corriere della sera* (Rome), 6 October 1981, p. 9.

50. *Time*, 2 July 1984, p. 6.

51. *Le Monde*, 25 August 1983.

52. *Razvivaiushchiesia strany: nakoplenie i ekonomicheskii rost. Materialy konferentsii* (Moscow, 1974), p. 23. Sheinis argues that in most cases there has been no strategy of industrialization, but only a wish to undertake something in the spirit of the times (*Razvivaiushchiesia strany: ekonomicheskii rost i sotsial'nyi progress* [Moscow 1983], p. 14).

53. M. Bacha, *Révolution africaine*, no. 1041 (1984): 22.

54. O.K. Draier, B.V. Los', V.A. Los', *Ekologicheskie problemy razvivaiushchiesia stran* (Moscow, 1983), p. 55.

55. I. Kravchenko, *Ekologicheskaia problema v sovremennykh teoriiakh obshchestvennogo razvitiia.*

56. *Za rubezhom*, no. 5 (1984): 15.

57. M. Kalecki, *Essays on Developing Economies* (Hassocks, 1976), pp. 17, 23.

58. *Razvivaiushchiesia strany: demograficheskaia situatsiia i ekonomicheskii rost*, p. 204. An excavator that saves on the labor of ditch-diggers increases the use of the labor of engineers, assembly workers, and so on. This work, associated with modern technology, is carried on mainly in the center, and the increasing complexity of the technology renders it more expensive.

59. Draier, Los', and Los', *Ekologicheskie problemy*, p. 84.

60. *Le Monde*, 27 March 1984, p. 19.

61. J. de Castro, F. Perroux, and H. Jaguaribe, *America Latina y los problemas del desarrollo* (Caracas, 1974), p. 36.

62. For an example of how superficially many of Schumacher's admirers understood his ideas, see J. Porrit, *Seeing Green* (Oxford, 1984).

63. Schumacher, *Small is Beautiful*, p. 192.

64. Ibid., p. 154.

65. Leszak Kolakowski, *Main Currents of Marxism*, vol. 3 (London, 1978).

66. On the possibilities offered by airships, see *Angliia*, no. 90 (1984). In the USSR, several authors of the journal *EKO* defended the idea of airship construction as an important sphere of technological progress; see *EKO*, no. 8 (1983): 78. Airships could become a promising form of transport in the Russian North.

67. The German scholar Elmar Altvater notes a direct link between market relations and the development of technologies based on the consumption

of oil. The transition to solar energy will create other forms of organization of the economy. See Altvater, *Der Preis des Wohlstands* (Münster, 1992).

68. Shchelkin, *Razvivaiushchiesia strany: nakoplenie i ekonomicheskii rost*, p. 69. Soviet scholars were inclined to categorize this as a forced concession to the demands of the real world (ibid., p. 79).

69. *Latinskaia Amerika*, no. 2 (1984): 84. The Nicaraguan leaders attempted to work out their own method for combining the scientific and technical revolution with the economy of a developing country. Not tempted by "pharaonic" projects, they proclaimed their first task to be the development of small industry. See *Barricada*, 2 July 1984.

70. *Así es*, no 111 (29 June 1984): 18.

71. G. Dauncey, *After the Crash* (London, 1988), p. 130.

72. *Ideologichskie protsessy*, p. 64. The low productivity in the traditional sector is explained not only by the primitiveness of the tools, but also by the attitude to labor which is typical of seminatural economies and which was also present in medieval Europe. People "do not hurry about their work. There is not the slightest interest in ensuring that a particular task is carried out rapidly, or that a large quantity of goods is produced in a given period" (V. Zombart, *Burzhua* [Moscow 1925], p. 12; see also A.Ia. Gurevich, *Kategorii srednevekovoi kul'tury* [Moscow 1972]). According to accounts by Indian scholars, the transition from the sickle to the scythe takes six years. Modernizing the human individual can stimulate productivity, but it does not devalue the old tools of labor, since society cannot yet provide new ones in sufficient quantities.

73. V. Khoros, *Ideologicheskie protsessy*, p. 39.

74. *Populism: Its Meaning and National Characteristics* (London, 1969), p. 44.

75. *Ethiopiques*, no. 21 (1980): 10.

76. *Ethiopiques*, no. 14 (1978): 47.

77. *Daily News* (Dar es Salaam), 23 October 1982.

78. I. Wallerstein, *Africa and the Modern World* (Trenton, NJ, 1986), p. 71.

79. *Asien, Africa, Latein Amerika*, Heft 2, S. 306 (1984); *Il Messagero*, 2 November 1985.

80. *Socialist Affairs*, no. 1 (1979): 8.

81. *Natsionalizm v sovremennoi Afrike*, p. 135; L. Sadovskaia, *Sotsial-reformizm v Afrike* (Moscow, 1983), p. 38.

82. *Révolution africaine*, no. 1041 (1984).

83. J. Rous, *Tiers monde. Réforme et révolution* (Paris 1977), p. 245.

84. *Inprecor*, no. 319 (1990): 25.

85. African reformism has two variants: a more moderate variety in Kenya and Senegal, and a more radical one in Tanzania and Madagascar. Kenya is considered a model of the comparatively successful development of capitalist relations in Africa, with this development proceeding not so much from above as from below. But this is explained by the fact that the Kenyan path is based upon a social democratic model of capitalism. In the 1990s the general shift to the right by all African regimes has meant that the differences between them have become only minor.

86. See G. Arrighi and J.S. Saul, *Essays on the Political Economy of Africa* (New York and London, 1973), pp. 300, 337.
87. The policies of reformist regimes in Africa provoked acute crisis in the orthodox Communist parties. The Party of Independence and Labor of Senegal, as its own leaders admitted, found itself on the brink of catastrophe; see *Partii nauchnogo sotsializma v Asii i Afrike* (Prague, 1983), p. 38. A significant section of its membership quit to join other left-wing organizations. The Communists of Madagascar also suffered a split, after proving unable to define their relationship to the reforms. In Senegal the Party of Independence and Labor launched furious attacks on the government. In Madagascar the Communists collaborated with the authorities, while recognizing the existence of differences which cannot be hidden, since they are of a principled ideological character (Ibid., p. 79).
88. Colin Stoneman and Lionel Cliffe, *Zimbabwe* (London and New York, 1989), p. 192.
89. *Man and Development*, vol. IV, no. 4 (December 1982): 126.
90. *Against the Current*, vol. VII, no. 3 (July-August 1992): 36.
91. It is not by chance that social democracy has scored its greatest successes in the Protestant countries of Northern Europe. The Protestant ethic, which Max Weber considered so essential for the formation of an effective capitalism, made possible the rise of a bourgeoisie which was not just dynamic, but also socially responsible, and which was capable of making compromises and thinking in strategic terms. Nothing similar exists in any of the developing countries.
92. On the role of hereditary workers in the formation of left movements, see *Uzlovye problemy razvivaiushchikhsia stran* (Prague, 1980), p. 42. See also: *The Role of the State Sector in Developing Countries* (New Delhi, 1977).
94. Amin, *L'Economie arabe contemporaine*, pp. 61–62.
95. "The game is too risky. We cannot perform experiments on the earth since we have only one earth on which we can live" (J. Schell, *The Fate of the Earth* [London, 1982], p. 77). The struggle to force people to respect their own planet is not only a struggle against the arms race or environmental pollution, but also against the models of development which are the primary causes of both one and the other. Here the problems of the third world coincide directly with the problems of the industrialized countries. It is impossible to change the relations between people and nature without changing the relations between people. The environmental situation does not exist outside the social and economic context, and will change along with it. The service performed by Marx consists partly in the fact that he took a serious attitude to the idea of a return to nature. In this respect Marx was a direct successor to Rousseau, but Marxism contains a radical rethinking of Rousseau's ideas. Marx did not speak out against science. On the contrary, he believed that as industrial civilization progressed it would be science, which had given birth to the alienation of humanity from nature, that would help us to return to nature. Marx often spoke of the rebirth of primal, archaic forms of relations between

people. What seems archaic to bourgeois consciousness is by no means necessarily so. The archaicism of the Bible is its guarantee of immortality, since what we find there is not only humanity's past, but to a significant degree its essence. Archaic societies did not know alienation and exploitation; in this sense, but only in this sense, the past remains a model for the future and a reproach to the present.

Chapter 3: The Zigzags of Political Modernization

1. The following peculiarities of the transition from agrarian to industrial society may be noted: the transition from simple to extended reproduction; from noneconomic compulsion to hired labor; and from the natural economy to commodity production. The power of the ruling elite is based not on the possession of land as before, but on control over industrial production. A single internal market emerges, and a single standard of consumption. Science becomes a force of production. Horizontal mobility increases. The transition to industrial society is irreversible, since it is accompanied by the modernization of the individual personality and by changes in the quality of labor power. Even the destruction of German industry in World War II did not prevent Germany from renewing itself as an industrial power. So long as modernization remains incomplete, however, its results are in a certain sense reversible.

2. F.H. Cardoso, *On the Characterization of Authoritarian Regimes in Latin America* (Cambridge, England, 1978), p. 1.

3. R.F. Byrnes, ed., *After Brezhnev: Sources of Soviet Conduct in the 1980s* (Bloomington, IN, 1983), p. 363.

4. A. Vanaik, *The Painful Transition* (London and New York, 1990), p. 72.

5. B. Anderson, *Imagined Communities* (London and New York, 1989), p. 109.

6. S. Amin et al., *Transforming the Revolution: Social Movements and the World System* (New York, 1990), p. 108. (Below: *Transforming the Revolution.*)

7. When Indian Marxists analyse the system of British colonial rule, they often refer to Gramsci and his theory of hegemony. Mohit Sen notes that the colonial government rested not only on repression, but also on the definite consent of its subjects. In such circumstances an armed uprising had no chance of success, and the struggle for independence was transformed into a long and complex process of conquering political space for the opposition. See *Mainstream*, vol. XXXI, no. 6 (19 December 1992): 19.

8. *Marxism Today*, June 1985, p. 38.

9. *Congress Presidential Address from the Foundation to the Silver Jubilee* (Madras, 1935), p. 729.

10. *Vostok: rubezh 80-kh godov*, p. 134.

11. *The Times* (London), 16 June 1984.

12. For a more detailed treatment, see *Strukturnye sdvigi*, pp. 98–117.

13. Samuel Bowles and Herbert Gintis, *Democracy and Capitalism* (New York, 1986), p. 187.

14. Vanaik, *Transition*, p. 75.

15. *Mainstream*, vol. XXXI, no. 6 (19 December 1992): 5.
16. *Newsweek*, 12 November 1990, p. 4.
17. Vanaik, *Transition*, p. 67.
18. Tariq Ali, *The Nehrus and the Gandhis*, (London, 1985), p. 290.
19. *Mainstream*, vol. XXXI, no. 6 (19 December 1992): 32.
20. There was no political preparation for decolonization in Africa. The ease with which independence was won was in itself suspicious. Nowhere apart from Algeria and in the African possessions of backward Portugal was there a serious war. In Kenya the British crushed the Mau Mau rebellion without great difficulty, and then departed at a time when nothing was preventing them from staying. Decolonization held advantages above all for the former colonizers; it allowed the capitalist center to confirm and intensify the dependency of the periphery, while ceasing to take responsibility for solving its social and political problems.
21. *South*, October 1986, p. 93.
22. *Voprosy Istorii*, no. 8 (1973): 76. See also Chapter 1, note 69, above.
23. *Razvivaiushchiesia strany v sovremennom mire*, p. 71.
24. *Strukturnye sdvigi*, p. 115.
25. *Latinskaia Amerika*, 1984, no. 1, pp. 61, 63.
26. *Dipendenza e sottosviluppo in America Latina* (Turin, 1972), p. 297.
27. E. Stanley, *The Future of Underdeveloped Countries: Political Implications of Economic Development* (New York, 1961), pp. 223–24.
28. *The Methodology of Comparative Research* (London, 1970).
29. *After Brezhnev*, p. 364.
30. E. Ernesto Parra and T. Isabel Aguirrezal, "Suramerica 76: Modelos militares de desarrollo" *Controversia* (Bogotá), no. 46 (1976): 52.
31. *Latinskaia Amerika*, no. 4 (1984): 129.
32. J. Comblin, *El poder militar en America Latina* (Salamanca, 1978), p. 267.
33. Friedrich Nietzsche, *Werke*, Hrsg. von Nietzsche-Archiv (Leipzig, 1984), 1912, Bd. 3, S. 317.
34. G.G. Vodolazov, *Dialektika i revoliutsiia* (Moscow, 1975), p. 71. It is curious that Vodolazov managed to free himself of such thoughts, in 1991 joining the thoroughly technocratic People's Party of Free Russia.
35. Marx and Engels, *Sochineniia*, vol. 4, p. 306.
36. Martin Heidegger, *Die europäische Nihilismus* (Pfullingen, 1967), S. 312.
37. Heidegger, *Nietzsche* (Pfullingen, 1961), Bd. 2, S. 333.
38. *El Dia* (Mexico), 18 December 1980.
39. L. Senghor, *On African Socialism* (London, 1964), p. 132–33.
40. J.-P. Biondi. *Le tiers-socialisme. Essai sur le socialisme et le «tiers monde»* (Paris, 1976), p. 67.
41. D. Likhachev, *Zametki o russkom* (Moscow, 1981), p. 67.
42. Lenin, *Polnoe sobranie sochinenii*, vol. 45, p. 361, etc.
43. *Sovremennyi natsiolanizm i obshchestvennoe razvitie zarubezhnogo Vostoka* (Moscow, 1978), p. 129.
44. *The African Communist*, 1977, no. 68, p. 37. Among the black population of the Republic of South Africa the black nationalist Pan-Africanist

Congress enjoys a certain influence, though much less than the African National Congress, which calls for the creation of a multiracial democratic regime. For a more detailed treatment see T. Mazawai, "Black South Africa Divided", *New Socialist* (London), April 1985, no. 26. More moderate conceptions of African nationalism (Zambian humanism and so on) have often concealed pro-Western and unprincipled politics.

45. *Afrique action*, 30 July 1961.

46. *Der Spiegel*, 1983, no. 6, S. 113.

47. T. Dos Santos, *Lucha de clases y dependencia en America Latina*, p. 127. Along with creole nationalism in Latin America an Indianist current has traditionally existed, dreaming of a return to pre-Columbian and pre-Hispanic traditions. This current has never dominated ideological life. While polemicizing against the Indianists, the outstanding Peruvian Marxist José Carlos Mariátegui took a very serious attitude to the question of the emancipation of the Indians, writing that for Indo-America there is no salvation without European or Western science and thought; see J.C. Mariátegui, *Siete ensayos de interpretación de la realidad peruana* (La Habana, 1963), p. xiv.

48. *Oficina nacional de información*, no. 17/18 (Lima, 1972): 50.

49. Lenin, *Polnoe*, vol. 23, pp. 1–4.

50. *Natsionalizm v sovremennoi Afrike* (Moscow, 1983), p. 19.

51. Khamsin 11, *Modern Turkey: Development and Crisis* (London, 1984), pp. 65, 64.

52. A. V. Shestopal, *Mirazhi El'dorado v XX veke*, p. 175.

53. I. Horowitz, *Three Worlds of Development* (New York, 1970), p. 179.

54. F. Bonilla, I. Cothler, *La investigación sociológica y la formulación de políticas* (Caracas, 1967), p. 18. The British scholar Jack Woddis cites a curious statistic. In Africa during the years from 1963 to 1968 alone thirty-two military coups d'etat or attempted coups took place. In the seventeen countries of Francophone Africa, only seven leaders who had come to power at the time of achieving independence remained in power by 1970. In Asia, forty-two coups or attempted coups took place between 1945 and 1972. In the case of Latin America, Woddis refuses to give a precise figure, noting only that here military coups are becoming "almost a way of life, even often a subject to be laughed at, though it is in no sense a joke for the people concerned. " See J. Woddis, *Armies and Politics* (London, 1977), p. 9.

55. Cited in J. Abbott, *The Iranians: How they Live and Work*, (New York, 1977), p. 63.

56. *Rabochii klass v mirovom revoliutsionnom protsesse*, 1981, p. 51.

57. N.R. Keddie, with a section by Y. Richard, *Roots of Revolution* (New Haven and London, 1981), p. 35.

58. *Vostok: rubezh 80-kh godov*, p. 158.

59. *Iran Today* (Teheran, 1973), p. 35. Soviet experts declared that the ideology of the Shah possessed "a clearly expressed anti-feudal thrust" and "also was not without anti-imperialist tendencies; it posed the question of the need to nationalize foreign property." See *Sovremennyi*

natsionalizm i obshchestvennoe razvitie zarubezhnogo Vostoka (Moscow, 1978), pp. 101–102.
60. M. R. Pahlevi, *Die soziale Revolution Irans* (Düsseldorf-Köln, 1967), S. 23. Cited in W. Ritter, *Der Iran unter der Diktatur des Schah-Regimes* (Frankfurt am Main, 1979), p. 54.
61. Kagarlitsky, *Problems of Communism*, no. 2 (1983): 81.
62. Abbott, *Iranians*, p. 12.
63. *Vostok: rubezh 80-kh godov*, p. 159.
64. Ibid., p. 160. Something similar also occurred in the USSR during the years of forced industrialization. For a more detailed treatment see Kagarlitsky, *Dialektika nadezhdy.*
65. C.S. Prigmore, *Social Work in Iran since the White Revolution* (1976), pp. 171–72.
66. S.A. Agaev, *Iran v proshlom i nastoiashchem* (Moscow, 1981), p. 177.
67. Erich Fromm, *Escape from Freedom* (New York, 1961), p. 237.
68. *Asien, Afrika, Latein Amerika*, 1982, Bd. 10, Heft 2, S. 1031.
69. Ibid., S. 1033.
70. Ritter, *Der Iran unter der Diktatur des Schah-Regimes*, p. 166.
71. Ibid., p. 203.
72. Marx and Engels, *Sochineniia* , vol. 33, p. 55.
73. *Ideologicheskie protsessy*, p. 89.
74. I. Illich, V. Sanders, *ABC: the alphabetization of the popular mind* (New York, 1989), p. 67.
75. *Filosofiia epokhi rannikh burzhuaznykh revoliutsii* (Moscow, 1983), p. 556.
76. *Cambio 16*, 1984, no. 653, p. 139. Bani Sadr has in mind the fact that it was he who in 1971 advanced the idea of an Islamic republic.
77. Keddie, *Roots of Revolution*, p. 182.
78. B. Mey, *The Third World Calamity*, (London 1981), p. 3.
79. *Social Sciences—For What?*, (Oslo, etc., 1980), pp. 94–95.
80. *Le Monde diplomatique*, no. 297 (1978): 13.
81. Ritter, *Der Iran unter der Diktatur des Schah-Regimes*, p. 135.
82. V. Gurnitskii, *Pesochnye chasy* (Moscow, 1983), p. 205.

Chapter 4: The Neo-Archaic State

1. Even right-wing authors are forced to agree that the socialism put into effect by such governments "has nothing in common with the usual understanding of this term. 'Socialism' is no more than a foreign word borrowed for use in internal propaganda" (J. Freund, *La fin de la Renaissance*, p. 57).
2. *The Quarterly Journal of Economics*, November 1964, p. 573.
3. *Strukturnye sdvigi*, p. 39.
4. *Vostok: rubezh 80-kh godov*, p. 71.
5. *Panorama* (Moscow), no. 296 (16 January 1984): 60.
6. *Foreign Policy*, no. 43 (Summer 1981): 67.
7. The resemblance between the social systems in pro-Western and pro-Soviet states of the third world forced Soviet scholars to declare that the sole

criterion for judging the progressive or reactionary character of these states was their foreign policy, and in particular their relationship to the USSR. Hence even feudal and semifeudal states could be part of the progressive camp (see *Osnovy marksistsko-leninskoi filosofii* [Moscow, 1975], p. 352.)

8. *New Era,* July 1976, p. 26.
9. *The African Communist,* no. 68 (1977): 82.
10. *Le Monde,* 29 March 1984, p. 6.
11. *Time,* 30 May 1983, p. 20.
12. Kuznets, *Economics and Development* (London, 1960), p. 145.
13. Frank, *Latin America,* p. 11.
14. J.H. Mittelman, *Ideology and Politics in Uganda: from Obote to Amin* (Ithaca and London, 1975), p. 261.
15. Marx and Engels, *Sochineniia,* vol. 25, part 1, p. 364.
16. *Vostok: rubezh 80-kh godov,* p. 54.
17. Y. Craipeau, *Les pays que l'on dit socialistes* (Paris), p. 222.
18. P.L. Berger, B. Berger, and H. Keller, *The Homeless Mind* (London, 1981), p. 118.
19. *Ethiopiques,* no. 13 (1978): 25.
20. *Etumba,* no. 768 (23 October 1984): 2, quoted from an issue of the newspaper *La Semaine Africaine* (Congo) banned by censors.
21. *Gosudarstvo sotsialisticheskoi orientstsii* (Moscow, 1975), p. 9.
22. V.F. Volianskii, *Nekapitalisticheskii put' razvitiia* (Moscow, 1983), p. 50.
23. *Gosudarstvo sotsialisticheskoi orientatsii,* pp. 8–9.
24. *Afrika: kul'tura i obshchestvennoe razvitie* (Moscow, 1984), pp. 69–70.
25. S.L. Agaev, *Iran,* p. 155.
26. R. Anwar, *The Tragedy of Afghanistan* (London and New York, 1988), pp. 146, 147.
27. *Libération,* 12 September 1984, p. 24.
28. *The African Communist,* no. 69 (1977): 93.
29. *The Times* (London), 26 October 1984, p. 17.
30. *UNESCO Courier,* November 1981, pp. 11–12.
31. *Problems of Communism,* vol 34, no. 3 (May-June 1985): 56.
32. *Le Monde,* 19 October 1984, p. 5.
33. *Razvivaiushchiesia strany: demograficheskaia situatsiia i ekonomicheskii rost,* p. 124. wrote that the most striking aspect of the situation in Algeria was the great mass of people of working age who were completely or partly unemployed. See Y. Craipeau, *Les pays que l'on dit socialistes,* p. 219.
34. *Razvivaiushchiesia strany: demograficheskaia situatsiia i ekonomicheskii rost,* pp. 128, 130.
35. M. Löwy, *The Politics of Combined and Uneven Development* (London, 1981), p. 174.
36. *Panorama,* no. 926 (16 January 1984): 60, 63. The governments of Angola and Mozambique explained their economic difficulties as resulting from South African intervention. This point of view is shared by many Western leftists (see J. Saul, "Destabilization in Mozambique," *Studies in Political*

Economy [Ottawa], no. 23 [Summer 1987]). Meanwhile, as was noted by the Italian newspaper *La Repubblica* (6 November 1986), the insurgents in Mozambique and Angola were incapable of offering a political alternative. Their successes were simply the result of "the failure of the regime."

37. *Razvivaiushchiesia strany v sovremennom mire,* pp. 84-85.

38. *Le Monde,* 29 March 1984, p. 6. The situation in other African countries was somewhat better. But there as well, it rapidly became clear that, in the words of the official newspaper of the Republic of Burkina Faso (formerly Upper Volta), collaboration with big brother and other big ideological brothers was "not a guarantee of successful development" (quoted in *Le Monde,* 8 November 1984).

39. The developing country which tried longest to imitate the Soviet model was Mongolia. With Soviet help it achieved substantial successes, but failed nevertheless to enter the ranks of modern industrial societies. The education system is also relatively undeveloped; the country has only seven institutions of higher learning. Most of the industrial products and items of equipment used in the country are imported; at the end of the 1980s the USSR accounted for 87 percent of foreign trade. Between 1960 and 1976 the deficit in Mongolian-Soviet trade increased from 23.9 million rubles to 417.2 million. In 1976 the cost to the Soviet Union of one day of Mongolia's development stood at 1.1 million rubles. See E. Bavrin, *Mongolskaia Narodnaia Respublika* (Moscow, 1976), pp. 42, 46-47, etc.

40. C. Simon in *Le Monde,* 6-7 August 1989.

41. Some scholars argue that "the consequences of outside interference in Africa at whatever level is almost invariably disastrous", and events in Africa "only work when we leave it alone" (*British Book News,* February 1984, p. 73). This is an exaggeration. Collaboration with the United States, the USSR, or China has been neither a guarantee of success, nor a cause of failure.

42. See D.I. Steinberg, *Burma's Road toward Development: Growth and Ideology under Military Rule,* (Boulder, CO, 1981). On the economic crisis of the 1980s see *Far Eastern Economic Review,* 17 April 1986.

43. *Newsweek,* 13 December 1980, p. 37.

44. S. Amin, *Irak et Syrie: 1960-1980. Du Projet National à la Transnationalisation* (Paris, 1982), p. 148.

45. *Ekonomika razvivaiushchikhsia stran,* pp. 333-34.

46. Marx and Engels, *Sochineniia,* vol. 25, part 2, p. 354.

47. In the words of Soviet scholars, "since in the conditions of the transitional state social progress is attained in the course of class struggle (including in the area of the exercise of power), democratization is accompanied by, and cannot fail to be accompanied by, certain limitations on civil rights." It is considered inadmissible "that the revolution should sacrifice its social goals to abstract concepts of formal democracy" (*Gosudarstvo sotsialisticheskoi orientatsii,* p. 137). The implication is that in the West social progress was achieved without "acute class struggle."

48. *Ekonomika razvivaiushchikhsia stran*, p. 336.
49. *Razvivaiushchiesia strany: ekonomicheskii rost i sotsial'nyi progress*, p. 333.
50. Berger, Berger, and Keller, *The Homeless Mind*, p. 116.
51. Ibid., p. 117.
52. *Gosudarstvo sotsialisticheskoi orientatsii*, pp. 11, 147.
53. A.G. Walder, *Communist Neo-Traditionalism* (Berkeley, Los Angeles, London, 1988), p. 8.
54. *Gosudarstvo i agrarnaia evoliutsiia v razvivaiushchikhsia stranakh Azii i Afriki* (Moscow, 1980), p. 115.
55. *Revoliutsiia i demokratiia* (Prague, 1980), p. 89.
56. Soviet scholars recognized a link between the experience of our country and that of third world dictatorships in which the state also turned into an apparatus totally controlled by the ruling party (*Aziia i Afrika Segodnia*, no. 6 [1978]: 32).
57. *Gosudarstvo sotsialisticheskoi orientatsii*, p. 41.
58. *Le Point* (Paris), no. 585 (1983): 21.
59. *The Observer*, 1 July 1984, p. 12.
60. *Le Point*, no. 585 (1983): 21.
61. *Problems of Communism*, vol. 34, no. 3 (May-June 1985): 45.
62. V. Ponomarev (ed.), *Kirgiziia*, (Moscow, 1989), samizdat.
63. *Novoe Vremia*, no. 43 (1992): 8.
64. In November 1992 the forces of the Russian 201st Division effectively prevented the Kulyab faction from taking up strategic positions in the republican capital. These moves by the Russian forces were explained as the result of an unwillingness to allow "large-scale military actions" (*Moskovskie novosti*, no. 44 [1 November 1992]: 9). The soldiers themselves regarded events quite differently. The officers declared openly that their families could be safe only in areas controlled by the Kulyab group. The Russian population demanded that the military give them weapons with which to defend themselves against the Islamic forces, and among the Russian officers in Kurgan-Tiube "no one even tried to conceal the fact that their sympathies were on the side of the Kulyab faction. " (*Novoe vremia*, no. 43 [1992]: 10). Tadzhiks and Russians importuned Laktionov, the commander of the Kulyab regiment, saying: "Just like you, we don't want the Union to collapse, but you don't help us" (Ibid., p. 11). During the winter the Kulyab faction occupied the capital.
65. *Ideologicheskie protsessy*, p. 90.
66. Samir al-Khalil, *Republic of Fear* (New York, 1989), p. 68.
67. *Sovremennyi natsionalizm i obshchestvennoe razvitie zarubezhnogo Vostoka*, p. 190.
68. *Ideologicheskie protsessy*, p. 88.
69. *Filosofiia epokhi rannikh burzhuaznykh revoliutsii*, pp. 163, 167.
70. *Ideologicheskie protsessy*, p. 11.
71. *Gosudarstvo i agrarnaia evoliutsiia v razvivaiushchikhsia stranakh Azii i Afriki*, p. 119.
72. *Elima*, 11 August 1974.

73. *Le Point,* no. 586 (1983): 31.
74. *Natsionalizm v sovremennoi Afrike,* pp. 97–98.
75. *Le Monde,* 29 March 1984, p. 6.
76. *Religii mira* (Moscow, 1982), p. 137.
77. Cited in *Natsionalizm v sovremennoi Afrike,* p. 200.
78. I. Koval'skii, *Katolitsizm i mirovoe sotsial'noe razvitie,* (Moscow, 1974), p. 159.
79. *Le Monde,* 22–23 April 1984, p. 4.
80. Al-Qaddafi, *Kniga,* vol. 3, p. 43.
81. Ibid., pp. 44–45.
82. P. Kalck, *The Central African Republic* (New York and London, 1980).
83. J.J. Jrensen, *Uganda: A Modern History* (New York, 1981), p. 237.
84. T. and M. Melady, *Idi Amin Dada: Hitler in Africa* (Kansas City, 1977), p. 26.
85. *Gosudarstvo sotsialisticheskoi orientatsii,* p. 191.
86. In the early 1980s Colonel Qaddafi spoke openly of the forthcoming "physical liquidation of all enemies of the revolution. " See *Nouvelles Littéraires,* no. 2818 (1982): 10; *El País* (Madrid), 29 April 1984. Not limiting himself to threats, he created special detachments charged with carrying out reprisals against enemies of the regime who had fled abroad. In this way the Libyan emigrants M. Ramadan and M. Mafa were killed in Britain.
87. *Gosudarstvo sotsialisticheskoi orientatsii,* p. 98.
88. The British Marxist P. Keleman wrote that the new revolutionary leadership did not recognize the rights of nations to self-determination, including the right of peoples to secede from Ethiopia, and "did not aim at the destruction of the old state apparatus and its replacement by popular organs of power" (*Socialist Register* [London], 1982, p. 247). All that changed was the names of the organs involved.
89. *Mezhdunarodnaia zhizn',* no. 9 (1973): 43.
90. *Searchlight South Africa,* vol. 1, no. 4 (February 1990): 71.
91. Arrighi and Saul, *Essays on the Political Economy of Africa* (New York and London, 1973), p. 25; Arrighi, *Sviluppo economico e sovrastrutture in Africa* (Torino, 1969), p. 254. Soviet scholars noted that the gap between the incomes of proletarians and peasants was "rather substantial," but argued that this was the result of "the objective needs of the reproduction of labor power" (*Rabochii klass i rabochee dvizhenie v Afrike* [Moscow, 1979], p. 61).
92. *Ethiopian Herald,* 18 January 1977.
93. Amin, *Trois experiences africaines de développement. Le Mali, la Guinée et la Ghana* (Paris, 1965), p. 277.
94. *Libération,* 12 September 1984, p. 25.
95. Even supporters of the neo-archaic authorities acknowledge that law-breaking has become a constant practice. See F. Halliday and M. Molineux, *The Ethiopian Revolution* (London, 1981), p. 37.
96. *The African Communist,* no. 69 (1977): 90.
97. *Libération,* 12 September 1984, p. 24.
98. *Les Pays,* p. 239.

99. See *Socialist Register* 1982, p. 248.
100. *Za rubezhom*, no. 3 (1976): 21.
101. *Rabochii klass i rabochee dvizhenie v Afrike*, pp. 224–25.
102. *The Economist*, no. 7366 (3 November 1984): 15.
103. *Izvestiia*, 23 May 1991.
104. *Les Pays*, p. 234.
105. *The Economist*, no. 7319 (10 December 1983): 44. For further details of the repression against communists in Iraq see *Comment*, 1 December 1979, p. 422.
106. *Libération*, 12 September 1984, p. 22.
107. *Time*, 30 May 1983, p. 20.
108. *Le Monde*, 29 March 1984, p. 6.
109. Cited in *Le Monde*, 28 March 1986, p. 3.
110. *International Herald Tribune*, 4 April 1984, p. 1.
111. *Revoliutsiia i demokratiia*, pp. 89–90. The Communist Party of Iraq was forced to state that "the restriction of democratic freedoms, and the imposition of the concept of the "leading party" were inadmissible. The Iraqi communists stressed "the fundamental importance of political democracy as a tool for defending and deepening democracy in society" (Ibid., p. 88).
112. *Le Monde*, 7 November 1984, p. 6. For Guinea, the seizure of power by the armed forces was a step forward. The massive terror came to an end. *Le Monde* wrote: "It seems as though the armed forces have learnt from Amnesty International" (10 April 1984, p. 1).
113. See *The Guardian* (Manchester), 6 July 1984. As the Iranian Marxist Mansoor Hekmat notes, the collapse of the East and the "open door" policy followed there with regard to Western capital have inspired new hopes in all of those in Africa, Asia, and Latin America who believe in Western models of development. (*Komonist*, 1991, no. 61; English translation in *International*, July 1992, no. 1).
114. *Direct Action*, 4 December 1990, p. 12, reprinted from the *Guardian* (New York).
115. *Iran: istoriia i sovremennost'* (Moscow, 1983), p. 168.
116. *Problems of Communism*, no. 2 (1983): 83.
117. *Iran: istoriia i sovremennost'*, p. 155.
118. Cited in *Narody Afriki i Azii*, no. 4 (1970): 46–47.
119. A comparison of events in Iran with those in Nicaragua reveals not only differences in the cultural, political, and economic conditions in these countries, but also, unfortunately, a huge difference in the level of theoretical study of revolutionary questions by leftists.
120. One might even argue that the Stalinization of Iran would at least be no worse than Khomeini's Islamization. The result might be a national Stalinism of the Albanian type.
121. The Spanish journal *Cambio 16* noted that Khomeini's supporters and Stalinists have a very similar understanding of social struggle (*Cambio 16*,

no. 640 [5 March 1984]: 62). Some Western journalists described Khomeini as "an Islamic Stalin" (*L'Espresso*, no. 6 [12 February 1984]: 34).

122. *Iran: istoriia i sovremennost'*, p. 199.
123. Ibid., p. 215.
124. *Newsweek*, 15 June 1981, p. 19.
125. *Partii nauchnogo sotsializma v Azii i Afrike*, pp. 148, 150, 153.
126. *Mezhdunarodnyi ezhegodnik. Politika i ekonomika* (Moscow, 1982), p. 242.
127. *Materialy XXVI s'ezda KPSS* (Moscow, 1981), p. 13.
128. In 1982 one of the regime's functionaries told an American journalist that arrested members of the Mojahedeen still hoped for popular support. Prisoners were brought to the stadium and stood up against a wall. The crowd of onlookers had been given the right to order their execution or to remain silent. On the count of three, the mullah related, the people shouted "Fire!" (*Newsweek*, 8 March 1982, p. 34). According to official figures, more than 4,000 people were shot between 1979 and 1982 (*Za rubezhom*, no. 5 [1984]: 6). Between June 1981 and March 1984, according to calculations by the Mojahedeen, 7,755 people were shot (*Daily Telegraph* (London), 16 March 1984). In 1984 it was officially acknowledged that "at least 10,000 political oppositionists" had been killed; according to some accounts the figure was as high as 30,000 (*L'Espresso*, no. 6 [1984]: 33).
129. *Daily Telegraph*, 16 March 1984, p. 5.
130. *Financial Times*, 1 March 1984, p. 3.
131. Agaev, *Iran*, p. 236.
132. *Panorama*, no. 934 (12 March 1984): 101.
133. *Iran: istoriia i sovremennost'*, p. 174.
134. *L'Espresso*, no. 6 (12 February 1984): 32.
135. *New York Times*, 17 December 1979.
136. *Financial Times*, 1 March 1984.
137. The Italian left-wing paper *Il Manifesto* (29 August 1984) argued that the crucial moment was the visit to Teheran of West German Foreign Minister Hans-Dietrich Genscher. For more details of the privatizations carried out during the 1990s see *Labor Solidarity*, October 1992. The steps in the direction of the market were supposed to increase the efficiency of the economy, but they simultaneously exacerbated social problems. In the early 1990s the country was swept by a wave of strikes—the first since the overthrow of the Shah. This time the demands were economic. In the new situation as in the past, the Islamic regime has been unable to dispense with state-bureaucratic control over the economy. Something like a mixed economy has spontaneously formed: large industrial enterprises remain state-owned, while small and medium industry is in private hands (see *Cambio 16*, no. 640 [1984]: 62).
138. Agaev, *Iran*, p. 230.
139. After being forced to flee Iran, Bani-Sadr said he saw no great difference between the regimes of the Shah and Khomeini. "They are two sides of the same coin" (*Cambio 16*, no. 653 [1984]: 137). The collaboration

between the liberal modernizer Bani-Sadr and the Khomeini camp was no accident either.

Chapter 5: The Revolutionary Model: I

1. Ernesto Che Guevara, *Obras, 1957–1967,* vol. 2 (Havana, 1977), p. 111.
2. Vietnam proved a more problematic model. Here the war continued until 1975. The bureaucratic degeneration of the regime occurred not after, but during a prolonged revolutionary war. The French scholar P. Rousset stresses that the war was won by the forces of the Communist North; in the course of the struggle the popular movement was effectively smashed, the revolutionary cadres of the South were wiped out, the proletariat was declassed, and social structures were thrown into disarray. "If Vietnam had been victorious in 1968, or in 1965, 1954, or 1945, it would be a different Vietnam". See *Inprecor,* no. 196 (13 May 1985): 10; see also the article by P. Rousset in the Italian journal *Critica communista,* no. 1 (1979). Peace for the Vietnamese did not begin in 1975 either. The continuation of war in Indochina during the 1980s (this time against Vietnam's former allies, the Chinese and the Khmer Rouge) strengthened the militarization of society and impeded the carrying out of reforms. But the late 1980s saw the beginning of reforms similar to those in China.
3. A comparison between the results of the economic reforms in China and the consequences of the capitalist experiments in Russia and Eastern Europe is provided in a number of works by the British economist John Ross. See J. Ross, *Natsional'noe ili mezhdunarodnoe reshenie problem Rossii* (Moscow, 1992).
4. At the end of the 1970s a discussion took place in the USSR on the social nature of the ruling circles in China. This was, in fact, an attempt to grasp the essence of the bureaucratic state that existed in both countries. See the article by F. Burlatskii in the journal *Voprosy filosofii,* no. 2 (1980): 124. For a review of "the Chinese discussion" see B. Kagarlitsky, *The Thinking Reed* (London and New York, 1988), pp. 301–303. See also M. Stepanov, *Plenniki drakona (Moscow, 1980), and Kagarlitsky, Dialektika,* pp. 275–82.
5. "The alternation of periods of radical socioeconomic restructuring in the spirit of "barracks communism" with periods in which the results of these experiments have been wiped out. . . has become a sort of "norm" of the life of Chinese society during the past fifteen years" (*Ekonomika KNR: vozmozhnosti i real'nost'* [Moscow, 1976], p. 31). In 1980 I assessed the situation in much the same fashion. B. Shragin in *Problemy Vostochnoi Evropy,* no. 11–12 (1985): 150–152 describes how skeptically Soviet dissidents regarded the changes in China.
6. Quoted in G. A. Ganshin, *Ocherk ekonomiki sovremennogo Kitaia* (Moscow, 1982), p. 89.
7. *El País,* 12 October 1984, p. 8.
8. The theoretician of reform Su Shaozhi referred directly to the link between the changes in China and the "Hungarian road." See Su Shaozhi, *Democratization and Reform* (Nottingham, 1988), p. 174.

9. According to the *Financial Times*, capital investments by Western firms in joint venture enterprises more than doubled in 1983 alone (24 February 1984, p. 4).

10. See *Izvestiia*, 20 July 1984. A significant proportion of the funds belonged to overseas Chinese.

11. The private sector acted as an important means for increasing employment. American economists enthused over the way in which people who had been unemployed the day before, and who had virtually no capital, began to establish commercial enterprises and workshops, offering the consumer goods that were "fashionable", and "in the Western spirit." (See *International Herald Tribune*, 25 July 1984.) Although the volume of production by private enterprise in the mid-1980s was a mere 0.6 percent of gross industrial product, the number of individual entrepreneurs reached 1.47 million people.

12. *The Economist*, no. 7365 (27 October 1984): 15. *Problemy Dal'nego Vostoka*, no. 1 (1984): 63.

13. *Problemy Dal'nego Vostoka*, no. 3 (1984): 101.

14. O. Vladimirov and M. Il'in, *Evoliutsiia politiki i ideologii maoizma v 70-kh, nachale 80-kh godov* (Moscow, 1980), p. 151.

15. See, for example, *World Health Forum*, vol. 2, no. 1 (1981): 117.

16. D. Barac, *Deng Hsiao-ping* (Moscow, 1989), p. 240.

17. T. Sommer, *Die Chinesische Karte* (Munich, 1979), p. 328.

18. The Chinese dissident Liu Binyan notes that the impressive rise in living standards has been the main reason for the stability of the country's Communist regime (*New Left Review*, no. 194 [July-August 1992]: 6). Meanwhile, Soviet scholars in the early 1980s stated that China had begun "to develop in a more stable fashion"; see *Problemy Dal'nego Vostoka*, no. 3 (1984): 32. The reforms were described as advisable, and it was said that they might "in certain circumstances help accelerate economic development." However, these measures were held to contradict socialism, and to lead "to estrangement from it" (*Maoizm bez Mao* [Moscow, 1980], p. 99).

19. *Vorwärts* (Basel), 11 December 1980, p. 9.

20. *Za rubezhom*, no. 50 (1984): 6.

21. *The Economist*, no. 7365 (27 October 1984): 15.

22. *Socialist Register* 1982, p. 189.

23. *New Left Review*, no. 124 (1980): 19.

24. Leung Wangyue, *Smashing the Iron Rice Pot* (Hong Kong, 1988), p. 194. It should be noted that the real cost of labor power in China is significantly higher than appears at first glance, since the government requires entrepreneurs to contribute to social funds that are used to subsidize cheap housing, food, and so forth. Such payments, however, are not always demanded. See ibid., p. 195, and below, chapter 7.

25. *Left Business Observer*, no. 42 (1990): 4.

26. *Asahi Evening News*, 31 October 1990.

27. A.G. Walder, *Communist Neo-Traditionalism*, p. 34.

28. Leung Wangyue, *Smashing*, p. 187.

29. Orville Schell, *Discos and Democracy* (New York, London, etc., 1989), p. 53. The question is asked as to why no significant privatization of state property has been undertaken in China. Obviously, the reasons include not only factors of an ideological character, but also the continuing need of the statocracy to hold itself together; bureaucratic solidarity has prevailed over the desire for personal enrichment and the urge to seize property.
30. See S. Ishikawa, *China's Food and Agriculture: Performance and Prospects* (Tokyo, 1982), Hitosubashi University Reprint Series, no. 108, p. 143.
31. *Ekonomika KNR: vozmozhnosti i real'nost'*, p. 75.
32. *Peking Review*, no. 14 (1970): 12.
33. Ishikawa, *China's Food and Agriculture*, p. 93.
34. *American Economic Review*, May 1983, p. 320.
35. *Voprosy ekonomiki*, no. 2 (1982): 124.
36. *The Guardian*, 27 July 1984.
37. *Marxism Today*, vol. 28, no. 12 (December 1984): 17.
38. O. Borisov, *Vnutrenniaia i vneshniaia politika Kitaia v 70-e gody* (Moscow, 1982), p. 287.
39. *KNR v 1976* (Moscow, 1978), pp. 62–63.
40. *Le Monde*, 9 July 1977.
41. See *Socialist Register* 1982, p. 201.
42. *International Herald Tribune*, 30 October 1981.
43. *El País* (Madrid), 4 June 1984.
44. , *Les Pays*, p. 177.
45. *Problems of Communism*, no. 2 (1982): 61.
46. , *Les Pays*, p. 176.
47. *Problems of Communism*, no. 2 (1982): 61.
48. Cited in *Problemy Dal'nego Vostoka*, no. 1 (1984): 153, 157, 154. In Chinese society of the 1980s a real spiritual crisis was to be observed; the ideology of consumption was pressing hard upon Maoist ideas. The success of the reforms was accompanied by the demoralization of broad layers of the population. The technocrats could not provide the masses with anything better than the slogan "Enrich yourselves!" The Czechoslovak reforms of 1968, which expanded political freedoms, differed qualitatively from Deng's reforms, in which there was no mass struggle and the development of the political process was determined by factional combinations within the elite. In China, as earlier in Hungary, a new opposition began to form. Many critics of the government sought to counterpose humanistic principles to the ideology of consumption, while nevertheless accusing the authorities of being unable to construct an authentic consumer society on the Western model.
49. *International Herald Tribune*, 25 July 1984.
50. Quoted in *Problemy Dal'nego Vostoka*, no. 4 (1984): 124. See also Su Shaozhi, *Democratization*, p. 160.
51. *Dao i daosizm v Kitae* (Moscow, 1982), p. 5.
52. *Voprosy filosofii*, no. 10 (1975): 62.

53. *Problemy Dal'nego Vostoka*, no. 2 (1984): 113. For a discussion of tradition and modernism in old Chinese culture, see Z.G. Lapina, *Uchenie ob upravlenii gosudarstvom v srednevekovom Kitae* (Moscow 1985), pp. 224, 230–31, and elsewhere. Chinese modernism grows out of traditional thinking and its values. As Lapina notes, theoreticians in medieval China already adopted an eclectic approach to tradition, renewing it through changes of accent and through excluding the most antiquated principles. When Chinese military experts after Mao's death declared that their new doctrine would combine modern and traditional methods, they were acting totally within the spirit of their historical culture.

54. *Kitai: gosudarstvo i obshchestvo* (Moscow, 1977), p. 147.

55. *Problemy Dal'nego Vostoka*, no. 2 (1984): 147.

56. D. Robinson, *No Man is Alien: Essays on the Unity of Mankind* (Leiden, 1971), p. 157.

57. *Against the Current*, no. 22 (September-October 1989): 31–32.

58. *October Review* 1990, no. 3–4; *Selections from October Review, 1980–1990* (Hong Kong, 1990), p. 24.

59. *Telos*, no. 80 (1989): 22.

60. *October Review* 1990, no. 3–4.

61. *Telos*, no. 80 (1989): 25.

62. Liu Binyan, *New Left Review*, no. 194 (July-August 1992): 7.

63. Ibid.., p. 16.

64. Che Guevara, *Obras*, vol. 2. See also , *Les Pays*, p. 189. Many thinkers in other Latin American countries agreed fully with this. See Emir Sader in *Historia do Marxismo no Brasil*, I (Rio de Janeiro, 1991); Sader, *Cuba, Chile, Nicaragua. Socialismo na America Latina*, (São Paulo, 1992); J. Pearce, *Under the Eagle: U.S. Intervention in Central America and the Caribbean* (London, 1982), p. 32.

65. W.A. Williams, *The United States, Cuba and Castro* (New York, 1962), p. 73.

66. M. Aguirre and A. Montes, *De Bolivar al Frente Sandinista* (Madrid, 1979), p. 44. Even historians sympathetic to the Communist Party recognize that it remained basically alien to the revolutionary process (*Storia delle rivolusioni del XX secolo*, vol. 3 (Rome, 1968): 1457.

67. *Estudios*, no. 83 (1982): 15. The American sociologist Horowitz noted maliciously that Castro has done more to destroy Marxist orthodoxy than a whole century of anti-Marxist criticism. The Cuban revolution did not appear to be a result of the historical process, but a triumph of the will over history. See I.L. Horowitz, *Ideology and Utopia in the United States, 1956–1976* (London and Oxford, 1977), p. 182.

68. Che Guevara, *Obras*, vol. 1, p. 31.

69. *Cambio 16*, no. 653 (1984): 127.

70. Régis Debray, *La critique d'armes* (Paris, 1974), p. 213. Even in this work, Debray essentially remains true to his old approach. As the Trotskyist Adolfo Gilly remarks, he "did not discuss a program," and sought to reduce theoretical questions "to a simple discussion of the tactic of armed struggle" (*Critica comunista*, no. 1 [1979]: 65, 64; *Nexos*, no. 10 [1978]).

71. Che Guevara, *Obras*, vol. 2, pp. 12, 14.
72. Ibid., vol. 1, p. 61.
73. *Piat' let kubinskoi revoliutsii* (Moscow, 1963), p. 125.
74. A. Gramsci, *Sochineniia*, vol. 3, pp. 406, 408.
75. Frank, *Latin America*, p. 350.
76. Dos Santos declares that unless socialism is victorious, then as in Europe in the 1930s, the crisis of capitalism will give birth to fascism. Socialism or fascism—there is no other choice (Dos Santos, *Socialismo o fascismo* [Buenos Aires, 1972], p. 114). Fascism in Europe was born of the crisis not of backward, but of developed, capitalism. Dictatorship and reaction are not always fascism.
77. Frank, *Latin America*, p. xv.
78. Ibid., p. 409.
79. Gary W. Wynia, *The Politics of Latin American Development* (Cambridge, New York, etc., 1990), pp. 165, 207.
80. *Cambio 16*, no. 653 (1984): 127.
81. *Dos tendencias en la revolución colombiana* (no date or publication cite listed), p. 65. Debray declares that revolutionaries "should not fight on alien territory," that is, on the "territory" of representative democracy. Social-reformism with its demagogy and half-measures opens the way to a fascism which can be called "demofascism" (*Diez años de la revista "Casa de las Americas"* [La Habana, 1970], pp. 22, 30). This is similar to the "social-fascism" thesis of the Stalinists in the 1930s.
82. *Cambio 16*, no. 653 (1984): 125, 127.
83. *The Times* (London), 3 March 1984. The negative consequences of guerrilla warfare included the annihilation of the best part of the left intelligentsia. As a Soviet historian wrote, to throw the revolutionary vanguard into struggle without waiting for a revolutionary situation "is not only stupid, but criminal as well" (B. Koval', *Latinskaia Amerika: revoliutsiia i sovremennost'* [Moscow, 1981], p. 59).
84. Alain Touraine, *Vie et mort du Chile populaire* (Paris, 1973), p. 73.
85. Williams, *U.S., Cuba*, p. 51.
86. A. Silverman, *Ideology and Social Change in Latin America* (New York, 1977), p. 237.
87. Che Guevara, *Obras* vol. 2, p. 299.
88. *Piat' let kubinskoi revoliutsii*, p. 130.
89. *Desiat' let kubinskoi revoliutsii* (Moscow, 1968), p. 156.
90. M. Sales, *Kontinent*, no 22 (1980): 233.
91. *Ideology and Social Change in Latin America*, p. 252.
92. See Sales, op. cit. Castro, like Mao, combined in himself traits of Lenin, Trotsky, and Stalin. Che Guevara was saved by his departure for Bolivia from the need to make a choice between the roles of executioner and victim.
93. Alekseev, *Latinskaia Amerika*, no. 5 (1984): 111, 112, 113.
94. Edward Crankshaw, *The Observer*, 1 July 1984.
95. Alekseev, *Latinskaia Amerika*, no. 7 (1984): 78.

96. Samuel Farber, *Revolution and Reaction in Cuba, 1933–1960* (Middletown, CT, 1976), p. 223.

97. K. I. Mikul'skii, *Ekonomicheskii rost pri sotsializme* (Moscow, 1983), p. 201.

98. *Newsweek*, 7 November 1983, p. 26. For a Marxist analysis of Castroism and its crisis see J. Habel, *Ruptures en Cuba* (Montreuil, 1991).

99. See *Historia do Marxismo no Brasil* I, p. 183; Sader, *Cuba, Chile, Nicaragua. Socialismo na America Latina*, p. 32.

100. From this point of view, it is interesting to consider the experience of Israel. The founders of the Jewish state dreamed of a national and socialist revolution. Even Soviet authors recognized that the founders of Zionism sought "to escape from national and social oppression by uniting their efforts in a single current of collective labour" (*Gosudarstvo Izrail'* [Moscow, 1982], p. 109). The first Jewish settlers in Palestine were under the strong influence of the first Russian revolution of 1905. But incessant conflicts with their Arab neighbors resulted in the militarization of society, the centralization of rule, and the supplanting of revolutionary ideas by nationalism. Among European Jews since the nineteenth century there have been many critical-minded intellectuals whose Jewish origins have allowed them to differentiate themselves from official society. Among such people have been Marx, Trotsky, and Freud. Even bourgeois Jews felt a certain alienation from their class. In Israel the left intellectuals were forced aside by dogmatists and pragmatists. The conditions which gave rise to the critical consciousness of Marx and Freud were lost once Jews were in their own land. As Jewish writer Clive Sinkler argued, Israel is no longer simply involved in a struggle for its existence; what is in question is its soul (see *Sunday Times* [London], 6 November 1983).

Chapter 6: The Revolutionary Model: II

1. A. Shul'govskii, *Armiia i politika v Latinskoi Amerike* (Moscow, 1979), p. 269.

2. R. Einaudi, *Dipendenza e sottosviluppo in America Latina*, p. 321.

3. E.E. Parra and T.I. Aguirrezabal, *Modeles*, p. 12.

4. Ibid., p. 6.

5. *El Peruano*, 26 February 1975.

6. *Margenes*, vol. 2, no. 3 (1988): 81.

7. Parra and Aguirrezabal, *Modeles*, p. 10. The search for an individual road is not always a sign of nationalism or isolationism. Theories devised in Europe on the basis of the conditions applying in industrialized societies cannot be applied mechanically in developing countries. European ideas have value for the third world so long as they concern general principles.

8. Frank, *Lumpenburguesia: lumpendesarrollo* (Barcelona, 1972), p. 189.

9. Einaudu, *Dipendenza e sottosviluppo in America Latina*, p. 320.

10. *Latinskaia Amerika*, no. 4 (1984): 10.

11. G. Pasquino, *Militari e potere in America Latina* (Bologna, 1974), p. 108.

12. *Panorama*, no. 923/924 (2 January 1984): 134–35.

13. Soviet scholars complained that the Velasco Alvarado regime was unable

to raise itself to a higher level, and could not ensure the transition to socialism (*Latinskaia Amerika*, no. 4 [1984]: 9).

14. Among the countries of Latin America, Peru is distinguished by its rich history of social thought. At the sources both of APRA and of the Marxist parties stood theoreticians who were known far beyond the borders of the country—Haya de la Torre and Mariátegui. In a polemic with one another during the 1920s, they laid the groundwork in one case for radical anti-imperialist nationalism, and in the other for Latin American Marxism. These two tendencies were to struggle and coexist over the decades, and not only in Peru. Although Mariátegui and Haya de la Torre gave different answers to the questions of development, it should not be forgotten, as a Peruvian historian notes, that "the polemicists had earlier been friends for many years, and shared a preoccupation with the same problems" (A. Flores Galindo, *La agonía de Mariátegui* [Lima, 1989], p. 110). It could be said that a posthumous polemic between Mariátegui and Haya de la Torre continues in Latin America today.

15. *Que Hacer*, no. 35 (June 1985): 50, 65. Before his death, General Velasco forecast a new upsurge of the left movement in 1984 and 1985, and a softening of the differences between Apristas and Marxists. See ibid., p. 51.

16. *Latinskaia Amerika*, no. 2 (1984): 61. The peculiarities of the "Latino-European" Chilean society made the experience of this revolution equally valuable for Europe and for the third world. Some writers have tried to show that the Chilean revolution was no more than a formalistic concept employed by Enrico Berlinguer and other leaders of the Italian Communist Party in the devising of their moderate policies (see *New Left Review*, no. 153 [1985].) However, it cannot be denied that in many respects the policies of the Italian Communists prior to 1973 were oriented toward the same strategic goals as those of the Chilean leftists.

17. *Conferencia teórica internacional. Características generales y particulares de los procesos revolucionarios en America Latina y el Caribe* (Havana, 1983). See also *Latinskaia Amerika*, no. 4 (1984).

18. In practice, the orthodox Communist Parties avoided armed struggle even during periods of military dictatorship. The Argentinian Communists described the guerrillas fighting against the military regime as "terrorists."

19. *Panorama*, no. 923–24 (1984): 143.

20. Quoted in *Sovremennye ideologicheskie techeniia v Latinskoi Amerike*, p. 212.

21. Y. Craipeau, *Les pays que l'on dit socialistes*, p. 189.

22. O. Fals Borda, *Las revoluciónes inconclusas en America Latina* (Mexico, 1970), p. 82.

23. *Dipendenza e sottosviluppo in America Latina*, pp. 296–304.

24. Mariátegui, *Siete ensayos de interpretación de la realidad peruana*, p. 21.

25. Dos Santos, *Lucha de clases y dependéncia en America Latina*, p. 114.

26. Arismendi, *Problemas de una revolución continental* (Montevideo, 1963), p. 56.

27. *Latinskaia Amerika*, no. 4 (1984): 15.
28. Ibid., p. 375.
29. *Latinskaia Amerika*, no. 4 (1984): 58. During the late 1970s, Eurocommunist tendencies were in evidence in several parties. The Argentinian Communist E. Agosti spoke of the need for a period of transition which would see the appearance of forms of economic and political organization which were "not yet socialist, but no longer capitalist" (Agosti, *Revoliutsiia, intelligentsiia, kul'tura* [Moscow, 1984] p. 330).
30. *Conferencia teórica internacional*, p. 8.
31. Ibid., pp. 11, 199.
32. Marx and Engels, *Sochineniia*, vol. 7, p. 432 (*The Peasant War in Germany*, Chapter VI).
33. Astesano, *Historia socialista de America* (Buenos Aires, 1973), p. 119. Some Cuban emigrants consider that responsibility for events in Cuba should not be assigned to the Russians or Americans, but to the Latin American cult of the strong leader: "When Franco died, Castro proclaimed three days of mourning" (*International Herald Tribune*, 29 August 1984).
34. *Marxism Today*, January 1985, p. 9.
35. Nigel Harris, *Of Bread and Guns* (London, 1983), p. 271.
36. B.I. Koval', *Latinskaia Amerika: revoliutsiia i sovremennost'*, pp. 147–48. The Sandinistas' initial program consisted of fifteen points. It demanded the destruction of "the reactionary state structure created out of electoral farces and military coups," the restoration of democratic liberties, and the creation of "a system which will provide the people with the opportunity for full participation both on the national and on the local level." In addition, the revolution would "put an end to the scourge of unemployment," would implement a "just" tax policy, and so forth: see *America Latina en armas* (Buenos Aires, 1971), pp. 52–54. While listing the goals, the program said virtually nothing about the means to be employed. Some writers later accused the Sandinistas of secretiveness, emphasizing that the heirs of Sandino knew more about the perspectives of the revolution than they were prepared to reveal. The adherents of this viewpoint clearly underestimate the revolutionary naïveté of the Latin American radicals of the 1960s.
37. *Mao Tsze-dun. Izbrannye proizvedeniia po voennym voprosam* (Moscow, 1958), pp. 72–73.
38. *Latinskaia Amerika*, no. 6 (1984): 13. It is curious that the socioeconomic dynamic in the years from 1978 to 1980 was similar in Iran, Poland, and Nicaragua. In each case the world upsurge and the world crisis played a role.
39. Sader, *Cuba, Chile, Nicaragua*, p. 66.
40. E.M. Farinas, *Nicaragua. Lucha, llora y muerte. Para ser libre!!* (Barcelona, 1970), pp. 186–87.
41. *Barricada* (Managua), 10 July 1984, p. 4.
42. *New Socialist*, no. 21 (November 1984): 20. Rodney Arismendi shares this view. The Sandinistas, he argued, combined the military and tactical experience of the Cuban revolution with the political strategy of the Chilean.

Hence their victory did not "devalue the Chilean experience," but on the contrary, confirmed that it was necessary to advance toward socialism "by way of a variety of democratic forms" (Arismendi, *Primavera popular en Nicaragua*, no publication site listed, 1979, p. 30).

43. P. Cannabrava, *Tras los pasos de Sandino* (Madrid, 1978), p. 164.
44. *Centroamerica en crisis* (Mexico, 1980), p. 120.
45. *La Prensa* (Managua), 3 October, 1978.
46. R. Gauger, *Nicaragua in Jahr der Befreiung* (Hamburg, 1981), pp. 26–27.
47. *The Times* (London), 6 March 1984, p. 8.
48. *Latinskaia Amerika*, no. 9 (1984): 16.
49. *Revolution*, no. 189 (14 October 1983): 20.
50. *Paese sera*, 23 October 1984.
51. *Za rubezhom*, no. 19 (1984): 4.
52. *END Journal*, no. 13 (December 1984-January 1985): 11.
53. E. Cardenal, *La Paz mundial y la Revolución de Nicaragua* (Managua, 1981), p. 7.
54. Gauger, *Nicaragua in Jahr der Befreiung*, pp. 30, 29, 31.
55. Pearce, *Under the Eagle*, p. 128.
56. In 1974 Burnham declared his People's National Congress of Guyana "a Marxist-Leninist party." This created the paradoxical situation in which both the government and the opposition used the language of Marxism. This did not prevent them from waging an irreconcileable struggle against one another, a struggle behind which ethnic rivalries were concealed.
57. *Latinskaia Amerika*, no. 6 (1983): 35.
58. J. Luna, *Grenada: La nueva joya del Caribe* (La Habana, 1982), p. 77.
59. *Sunday Times*, 6 November 1983, p. 16.
60. *The Times*, 27 February 1984. The right-wing Daily Telegraph (18 September 1984) notes that Bishop did not conceal "his Marxist program," but "took a cautious attitude toward the bourgeoisie."
61. *New Left Review*, no. 141 (September-October 1983): 16.
62. *Sunday Times*, 6 November 1983.
63. *The Observer*, 6 November 1983, p. 7.
64. *New Left Review*, no. 141 (1983): 17.
65. *Sunday Times*, 6 November 1983.
66. After the collapse of the revolution, one of Bishop's surviving colleagues, Kendrick Radix, explained the restricted freedoms by refering to "the difficulty of the revolutionary process" (*L'Espresso*, 11 December 1983, p. 34).
67. According to the *Daily Telegraph* (18 September 1984), Bishop stressed that there was no need to "annoy the imperialists too much." The Reagan administration, however, was not prepared to show restraint.
68. *The Observer*, 4 March 1984, p. 18.
69. *Revolution*, no. 189 (1983): 20.
70. *Grenada: Whose Freedom?* (London, 1984), p. 56. Similar situations arose in other countries as well. In Angola, the regime of Agostinho Neto came under attack from groups that demanded a more consistent Cubaniza-

tion. The country's leaders were declared to be "rightist," inclined to "social democracy," and even "anti-Soviet" (*African Communist*, no. 71 [1977]: 39). The government of Jerry Rawlings in Ghana split in analogous fashion.

71. *L'Espresso*, no. 49 (1983): 34.

72. *Sunday Times*, 6 November 1983, p. 11.

73. *Izvestiia*, 16 November 1983.

74. *The Times*, 26 October 1983.

75. *Newsweek*, 7 November 1983, p. 24.

76. *Latinskaia Amerika*, no. 5 (1982): 137.

77. *The Guardian*, 25 October 1984.

78. *Latinskaia Amerika*, no. 4 (1992): 37.

79. Quoted in *Barricada*, 30 October 1983.

80. *Barricada*, 3 July 1984. The Sandinista press stressed that in Nicaragua there was "such a degree of ideological pluralism" that at times it even represented "an obstacle" (*Barricada*, 29 September 1984; *Ventana* no. 174, p. 6). Such declarations served on the one hand to justify repression, and on the other, were needed in order to convince Nicaraguans that although the FSLN was forced to use repressive measures, it retained its commitment to pluralism.

81. *Peace News*, 30 November 1984, p. 12.

82. The Sandinistas' position with regard to democratic liberties was at first contradictory. Culture Minister Ernesto Cardenal declared: "Never in history has there been such a thing as a revolution with freedom of the press, but we promised to do this" (E. Cardenal, *La Paz mundial y la Revolución de Nicaragua*, p. 7). Cardenal regarded democratic rights as a sort of luxury which the Sandinistas could allow themselves. The maintenance of press freedom, in his view, depended on the good will of the government. The editor of the newspaper *El Nuevo Diario* declared in an interview with a Soviet correspondent that it would be desirable to eliminate the opposition press as a "source of disinformation," but that the majority of the leadership did not share this view (*Literaturnaia gazeta*, 9 January 1985, p. 15). The contradictory nature of the positions held by the Nicaraguan revolutionaries created a constant danger that the Cuban road would be repeated. This time, however, the situation turned out differently. In 1962–1963 (three years after Castro's victory), the USSR already accounted for about 50 percent of Cuba's foreign trade turnover. In Nicaragua in 1984, five years after the revolution, Western nations remained the country's main trading partners, far outstripping Cuba and the countries of the Eastern bloc. Castro in 1959 also promised elections, then postponed them, and finally, cancelled them altogether. The Sandinistas, by contrast, kept their promise.

83. *International Herald Tribune*, 25 July 1984, p. 4.

84. Even before the Sandinistas came to power, the Socialist International established close links with them, as well as with the New Jewel Movement and the Revolutionary Democratic Front of El Salvador. The leaders of

the Socialist International recognized the need for social democrats to unite with more radical groups that were leading armed struggles against dictatorships. The international actively aided these organizations, while at the same time trying to strengthen its influence within them.

85. *International Herald Tribune*, 24 October 1984.
86. *Cambio 16*, no. 647 (23 April 1984): 53. The Reagan administration and its propagandists tried to depict the democratization in Nicaragua as a tactical move. The Sandinistas were described in Washington as a monolithic "Marxist-Leninist party." In fact the Sandinistas, like the New Jewel Movement, were a coalition of various groups. The Argentinian scholar C. M. Vilas notes that Sandinismo was "a socially heterogeneous and contradictory force, united politically by the dynamic of the revolution" (C.M. Vilas, *Perfiles de la revolución sandinista* [Havana, 1984], p. 396). Revolutionary practice, however, while capable of smoothing over contradictions, is also liable to exacerbate them.
87. *El País*, 25 October 1984. In the Western press it was reported that the Democratic Coordinating Committee called for a boycott of the elections because the Reagan administration "did not want the right-wing leader Arturo Cruz to finish up in first place" (*END Journal*, no. 13, p. 11; *New York Times*, 31 October 1984). According to a Peruvian sociologist, Nicaragua's enemies were afraid that the country would become a second Cuba, but were still more afraid that it would not become a second Cuba. Nicaragua was dangerous to them because of its originality (*Que Hacer*, no. 35 [June 1985]: 67).
88. *Le Monde*, 7 November 1984.
89. *Le Monde*, 3 November 1984; *The Economist*, no. 7365 (27 October 1984): 52.
90. *Problems of Communism*, September-October 1985, p. 17; *Le Monde*, 3 November 1984.
91. *El País*, 15 January 1985. The experience of Latin America and Eastern Europe shows that elections alone do not create democracy. The whole system of state and social institutions has to guarantee social freedoms.
92. *Cambio 16*, no. 727 (4 November 1985): 112. The leader of the Nicaraguan Liberals, Virgilio Godoy, declared that the state of emergency was directed not so much against the contras as against the opposition parties and trade unions. As a British left-wing journalist observed, the decision to impose the state of emergency was provoked by rumors of a general strike in Managua, in protest against the low level of wages (*New Internationalist*, no. 156, [February 1986]: 26).
93. *Centroamerica en crisis*, p. 124.
94. Gauger, *Nicaragua in Jahr der Befreiung*, p. 135.
95. *America Latina en armas*, p. 53.
96. During the 1980s the relatively moderate left-wing government in Bolivia tried without particular success to introduce elements of workers' democracy to the state sector. Self-management also failed in Yugoslavia, where for the first time this slogan was proclaimed as official policy. Neverthe-

less, it should not be concluded that participation by workers in management is impossible. It is essential to make a clear distinction between
questions which can and should be decided by the labor collectives, and
questions which should be decided by organs of management. It also has
to be recognized that industrial democracy involves not just taking into
account the interests of the labor collectives, but also defending the
interests of consumers, of the region, and of society. Workers' participation in management has to be part of an integrated democratic system.

97. F. Perroux, *Masse et classe* (Paris, 1972), pp. 65–66.
98. *Mao Tsze-dun. O novoi demokratii (i drugie raboty)* (Moscow, 1960), p. 21.
Che Guevara reiterated Mao's idea, declaring that it was in the countryside that "ideal conditions for the struggle" were to be found (Che
Guevara, *Obras*, vol. 1, p. 61).
99. *Dipendenza e sottosviluppo in America Latina*, p. 303. Sociological studies
have shown that in its composition, the Sandinista Front differed little
from other insurgent organizations. See C.M. Vilas, *Perfiles de la revolución
sandinista*, pp. 164–98; *Casa de las Americas*, 1986, no. 154, p. 162, etc.
100. *Storia delle rivolusione del XX secolo*, vol. 3, p. 1457.
101. Che Guevara, *Obras*, vol. 1, p. 77.
102. This is confirmed not only by the experience of Latin America. During
the guerrilla war in Namibia the insurgents of SWAPO created a repressive apparatus to which dissidents within the movement fell victim.
According to Paul Trewhela, this transformed SWAPO into a de facto
accomplice of the South African regime. The insurgent leaders and the
colonizers were united by "a common methodology of rule" (*Searchlight
South Africa*, vol. 2, no. 6 [January 1991]: 56). Analyzing the Vietnamese
experience, a Trotskyist scholar came to the following conclusion: "When
a revolutionary war is drawn-out, its negative aspects prejudice the revolutionary mobilization of the masses" (*Inprecor*, no. 196 [13 May 1985]:
12). In particular circumstances, arguments about the advantages of the
armed road can turn out to be anti-revolutionary. It is significant that the
insurgents of the Revolutionary Armed Forces of Colombia rejected
armed actions, sensing that the masses "were conscious of goals which it
was possible and necessary to attain through legal struggle, with the help
of elections, parliament, councils, and assemblies" (*Prisma
latinoamericano*, no. 6 [1986]: 5).
103. *Marxism and the Science of War* (London, 1981), p. 272.
104. A. Blanco Muños, *Latinoamerica: la historia violentada* (Caracas, 1977), p.
27.
105. Harris, *Of Bread and Guns*, p. 271.
106. *The Diliman Review*, November-December 1984, p. 6.
107. *Guardian Weekly*, 15 September 1985. To the very last, the official Moscow
newspapers spoke sympathetically of Marcos, counterposing him to "the
U.S. dictatorship" (*Izvestiia*, 12 January 1986). The pro-Soviet Communists in the Philippines declared their critical support for the regime
(*Mezhdunarodnoe rabochee dvizhenie* [Moscow 1980], p. 309).

108. *Guardian Weekly*, 1 September 1985.
109. *The Diliman Review*, November-December 1984, pp. 8–9.
110. M. Löwy, *The Politics of Combined and Uneven Development* (London, 1981), p. 231.
111. Latin American leftists throughout the 1970s already spoke of the danger of becoming "pawns in the political game of the great powers" (*Nueva sociedad*, no. 48 [1980]: 122).
112. *Forward Motion* (Boston), May 1990, p. 12.
113. *Against the Current*, no. 26 (May-June 1990): 12.
114. *Against the Current*, no. 29 (November-December 1990): 38.
115. *Dissent*, Winter 1991, p. 121.
116. Sader, *Cuba, Chile, Nicaragua*, p. 74.
117. As an example, one can cite the left-wing government in the Indian state of Kerala. Under the leftists, a radical agrarian reform was carried out, infant mortality was reduced to a third of the national average, life expectancy rose substantially, and the rate of literacy was increased to three-quarters of the population, compared with a national average of no more than half. As scholars have noted, these successes were registered because the leftists in Kerala, excluded from power in the center, did not have to try to deal with the difficult questions of international economic and political relations: trade, the deficit, the long-standing military-political pressure from the United States, and so on (*Monthly Review*, vol. 42, no. 8 [January 1991]: 36–37). Any attempt to implement analogous reforms on a national scale would have aroused far sharper conflicts. The reforms in Kerala, which as successful examples of "social democratic" measures are almost unique in the third world, were not achieved by social democrats, but by radical Marxist groups and mass movements.
118. *Barricada* 10–11 April 1991; *Inprecor*, no. 332 (1991): 20.
119. M. Quandt, *Against the Current*, no. 29 (November-December 1990); P. Berman, *Dissent*, Winter 1991.

Chapter 7: Eastern Europe: Another Road to the Third World

1. *Economic Transition in Eastern-Central Europe and the Role of Social Democracy* (Budapest, 1992), p. 51.
2. J.A. Zammit, D. Ghai, N. Tiruchelvam, B. Turner, *Hungary in Transition: From Socialism to Capitalism?* (Geneva, 1990) p. 16.
3. *International Spectator*, vol. XXV, no. 4 (October-December 1990): 264.
4. Ibid., p. 314.
5. Zammit et al., *Hungary in Transition*, p. 43.
6. *Liudi i steny. Vostochnaia Evropa: shtrikhi k portretu peremen* (Moscow, 1990), p. 15.
7. *L'Espresso*, no. 26 (1 July 1990): 109.
8. *Inprecor*, no. 323 (1991): 17. In 1991 a campaign of slander began against Jan Kavan, a veteran of the dissident movement and activist in the left wing of the Civic Forum. On the basis of unconfirmed statements he was accused of having collaborated with the state security apparatus. It was

demanded that he resign from his position as deputy. The attacks on Kavan aroused indignation throughout the world. The Czechoslovak leadership became the target of dozens of protest letters from human rights defence organizations.

9. *International Viewpoint*, no. 195 (26 November 1991): 13.

10. *International Viewpoint*, no. 236 (12 October 1992): 28.

11. *East European Reporter*, vol. 4, no. 3 (Autumn-Winter 1990): 23.

12. *New Politics* (New York), vol. 4, no. 13 (1) (1992): 90.

13. *Pravda*, 4 February 1991.

14. When the activity of the security services was investigated in East Germany, it was learned that informers had included leading figures from both the Christian Democrats and the Social Democrats. The country's first and only non-Communist prime minister, Lothar de Maizière was forced to resign after details of his past were revealed.

15. *New Politics*, no. 13 (1992): 97.

16. Ibid., pp. 98–102.

17. *Nezavisimaia Gazeta*, 14 February 1991.

18. *Literator*, no. 44 (23 Novermber 1990).

19. Janos Kornai, *Put' k svobodnoi ekonomike* (Moscow, 1990), pp. 124–25 (English translation: *The Road to a Free Economy* [New York, 1990]).

20. *Ogonek*, no. 51 (1990): 5.

21. *Argumenty i fakty*, no. 52 (1990): 4.

22. According to data published by the Russian trade unions, the number of state functionaries in the USSR almost doubled during the years of perestroika, which was supposed to be accompanied by an uncompromising struggle against bureaucratism.

23. *The Economist*, vol. 317, no. 7677 (20 October 1990): 90.

24. *Literator*, no. 44 (23 November 1990).

25. *East European Reporter*, vol. 4, no. 3 (Autumn-Winter 1990): 16.

26. *International Viewpoint*, no. 236 (12 October 1992): 14.

27. *Panorama*, no. 11 (September 1990): 3.

28. *The Times*, 12 September 1989.

29. In most of the countries of Eastern Europe the social democrats supported the return of property to its former owners, sometimes with certain conditions attached. The Social Democratic Party of Estonia declared that in order to minimize the level of new social injustice and ensure a successfully functioning society, various flexible mechanisms of compensation should be used when property is returned to its former owners and their heirs. (See *Program of the Social Democratic Party of Estonia* [Tallinn, 1992], p. 11.) For obvious reasons, the neocommunist parties objected to this. However, they objected very cautiously, reluctant to cast doubt on the sacred principle of private property itself. The Lithuanian Democratic Labor Party, for example, referred to the need to ensure the efficiency of the privatization process. If this principle is not observed, the whole population will suffer, including people who are receiving compensation

for past injustices (*Programme of the Democratic Labour Party of Lithuania* [Vilnius, 1991], p. 5).

30. *Panorama*, no. 15 (January 1991): 2. This particular statement came from I. Korovikov, one of the leaders of the Party of Free Labor. Despite its name, this party had declared its intention to devote itself exclusively to defending the rights of entrepreneurs (ibid.). Analogous statements can be found on the pages of official bulletins. Noting that primitive accumulation has everywhere been accompanied by theft, violence, and the ruination of the masses, the ideologues of liberalism appealed to the people not to be get nervous, and to wait while the new bourgeoisie accumulated its capital. The question was, of course, whether a generally modern society could allow itself to pass once again through the stage of primitive accumulation. In sixteenth-century Europe the primitive accumulation of capital was accompanied by economic crisis and by the devastation of production in the noncapitalist sector from which the wealth needed by the bourgeoisie was being extracted. In its level of technological development and social organization the capitalist sector was far more advanced than the precapitalist sector of the time. In Eastern Europe today everything is the reverse. The business sector is at a very low level of development—technologically, culturally, and socially. Meanwhile, developed state industry is being destroyed for the business sector's benefit. Enterprises with modern technology are shutting down, and highly skilled workers are losing their jobs.

31. The new owners were not prepared to hand over power, but were no longer willing or able to rule in the old way. The Communist state with its monolithic structures and its ideology of universal equality no longer suited them.

32. *Dialog*, no. 17 (1991): 45. Max Weber demonstrated the role of the Protestant ethic in the formation of capitalism. In Russia, such cultural preconditions for capitalism did not exist. The German scholar Frank Hoffer notes that during the period of the establishment of capitalism in Southeast Asia, patriarchal Confucian traditions provided a substitute for the Protestant ethic. "In Soviet society, where all moral categories are now completely devalued, such a symbiosis of traditional values and modern technology is completely impossible" (F. Hoffer, *Perestroika* [Marburg, 1992], p. 224). Nor have things gone well in the Protestant Baltic countries.

33. Bogdan Denitch, *The End of the Cold War* (London and New York, 1990), pp. 54–55.

34. *Kommersant*, no. 7 (1991): 12. Mistrust of democracy is characteristic of the new elites not only in the Soviet Union and the most backward countries of the former Eastern bloc. For a discussion of the situation in Hungary, for example, see E. Szallai, "The New Elite," *Across Frontiers*, vol. 5, no. 3 (Fall-Winter 1989–1990).

35. In Poland it was announced that only from 30 to 40 percent of shares would be sold for cash, and that the remainder would be sold on an

installment basis. The buyers formally became co-owners of the enterprises after the first cash payment. The remaining part of the capital was considered a debt, and had to be paid off out of the future profits of the company involved—assuming, that is, that the company made profits at all. The workers in each enterprise were given the right to acquire 20 percent of the shares at a discount, but the overall value of these discounts could not exceed the average annual wage in the public sector. Steps were thus taken immediately to ensure that the labor collectives would not be allowed to control the property.

36. See G.V. Osipov, ed., *Sotsial'naia i politicheskaia situatsiia v Rossii: sostoianie i prognoz (1992)* (Moscow, 1993), pp. 71–73.

37. For details of the real relationship between the value of the assets to be privatized and the effective demand for property in the former USSR see *Al'ternativy,* no. 2 (1992).

38. In the West as well, only profitable state companies have as a rule been easy to privatize.

39. *Voprosy ekonomiki,* no. 3 (1990): 119.

40. *Komsomol'skaia pravda,* 6 October 1990.

41. *Novyi mir,* no. 5 (1990): 195.

42. *New York Times* (weekly Russian-language review), no. 8 (1993): 1.

43. *Izvestiia,* 4 February 1991.

44. *Al'ternativy,* no. 2 (1992): 23.

45. *Die Welt,* 6 November 1990.

46. *Izvestiia,* 18 February 1991.

47. *Marxism Today,* December 1990, p. 25.

48. *The Economist, The World in 1991* (London, 1990), p. 40.

49. *Moskovskii komsomolets,* 28 December 1990.

50. *Dialog,* no. 17 (1990): 47.

51. *Chartist,* October-December 1990, p. 33.

52. L. M. Freinkman, *Za 500 dnei ili za 600 sekund?* M. G. Deliagin, *Tovarishch pravitel'stvo, pozhalei moiu mamu* (Zelenograd, 1990), pp. 6–7. In 1992 the lack of interest shown by potential investors in the Russian government's privatization checks fully confirmed this forecast. The price of vouchers fell constantly despite all the efforts of the government to prop it up.

53. In the case of Moscow, it was possible to observe a certain increase in the effectiveness of the privatization program following the resignation of Gavriil Popov from the post of mayor and his replacement by the pragmatic Iuri Luzhkov. The Luzhkov administration accompanied its privatization with constant threats that new property-owners who did not do the mayor's bidding would be expropriated. Some of Luzhkov's successes were gained precisely through the use, or threatened use, of old command methods.

54. Kornai, *The Road to a Free Economy,* p. 53.

55. *Moskovskie novosti,* no. 2 (13 January 1991): 8. *Nezavisimaia gazeta* economic observer M. Leont'ev argued explicitly in favor of using harsh political measures to strengthen the confidence of international capital: "Substan-

tial quantities of capital began flowing into Chile and South Korea only after appropriate political and economic conditions were established."

56. *Links* (London), December 1990/January 1991.
57. *The Times/European Business*, 6 November 1990, p. 9.
58. *Peace & Democracy News*, vol. V, no. 1, p. 6.
59. *Argumenty i fakty*, no. 32 (1989): 2.
60. Zammit et al., *Hungary*, p. 22.
61. The state has levied additional taxes on private and foreign entrepreneurs to maintain the system of social guarantees, but as a rule these payments have not covered the outlays by the state on social welfare for workers of private and transnational companies. See Leung Wangyue, *Smashing the Iron Rice Pot.*
62. *Links*, no. 247/248 (December 1990/January 1991): 32.
63. *Dialog*, no. 10 (1990): 45.
64. I. Wallerstein, *The Modern World-System II: Mercantilism and the Consolidation of the European World-Economy, 1600–1750* (New York, London, etc., 1980), p. 179.
65. *Links*, no. 247/248 (December 1990/January 1991): 32.
66. Denitch, *The End of the Cold War*, p. 55.
67. *Pravda*, 4 February 1991.
68. *Moskovskie novosti*, no. 2 (13 January 1991): 12.
69. *Inprecor*, no. 323 (1991): 19.
70. M. Duverger, *Les partis politiques* (Paris, 1958), pp. 465–66. Ken Livingstone noted that the guarantee of democracy in the West is not private property (which can exist perfectly well under a fascist regime), but the activity of workers' organizations and of political parties, above all those of the left. The weaker the trade unions and leftists, the more likely it is that the former Communist countries will be faced with a "transition from dictatorship with a welfare state to dictatorship without one" (*New Statesman*, 13 September 1991, p. 14).
71. *Gospodin narod*, no. 1 (1990): 2.
72. *Dialog*, no. 17 (1990): 30.
73. *East European Reporter*, vol. 4, no. 3 (Autumn-Winter 1990): 10.
74. *Al'ternativy*, 1992, no. 2, p. 23.
75. It is significant that in the West, consumption (and imitating the life style of the elites) played an important role in the formation of the middle layers. See S. Ewen, *All-Consuming Images* (New York, 1988), pp. 65–67. For a more detailed discussion of the middle layers in Eastern Europe, see B. Kagarlitsky, *The Disintegration of the Monolith* (London and New York, 1992).
76. Throughout the world, the 1980s and 1990s have not only been the era of neoliberalism, but also the period when the position of the middle layers has begun to weaken. The American sociologist Steven Rose notes that in the course of the 1980s the U.S. middle class shrank, and that in two-thirds of cases the people leaving it passed into groups with lower incomes. If, in 1978, 52. 3 percent of Americans could be considered

middle-class, the corresponding figure in 1986 was only 44. 3 percent (S.J. Rose, *The American Profile Poster* [New York, 1986], p. 9).

77. In the 1970s the Hungarian sociologist Ivan Szelinyi spoke of the Eastern European intelligentsia as being "on the road to class power." In the 1990s he stated that the intellectual elite could not hold the dominant position in society; its members were destined either to join the bourgeoisie, or to serve the interests of the new elite. See Robin Blackburn, ed., *After the Fall* (London, 1992). The turbulent process of lumpenization of the middle layers, however, excluded even the possibility of bourgeoisification. The intellectual elite turned out to be capable of adopting a bourgeois style of consumption, but became infected with a lumpen, not a bourgeois, psychology.

78. *Przeglad Spoleczny*, no. 2 (May 1992): 27.

79. Numerous theories of global civil society achieved particularly wide currency among Western leftists during the late 1980s. This was linked not only with the crisis of traditional Marxism, but also with the efforts of a section of the left intelligentsia that had entered politics on the crest of the radical wave of 1968 to adapt to capitalist society. Post-modernist theories of political struggle (not only global civil society, but also various forms of identity politics and "new-times-ism," as elaborated in the British publications *Marxism Today* and *New Times*) have allowed the intellectual elite to retain some autonomy with regard to the bourgeois establishment, while reducing conflict to a minimum, and ridding itself completely of any obligations with regard to workers and their organizations. If the radicalism of 1968 counterposed the more left-wing intellectuals to the "insufficiently revolutionary" workers, then in the 1980s the former radicals were once again counterposed to the workers, trade unions and "old" left parties, once again accusing them of being ossified and so forth. Only this time, it was the former radicals who were occupying positions to the right of the labor movement. Earlier, social democratic reformism had been rejected as insufficiently radical; now, any consistent and integrated program of reform is rejected simply on the grounds that society does not need complex social and economic reforms. Post-modernist writers have preferred not to admit that civil society itself is in severe crisis not only in the East, but also in the West. The ineffectiveness of parliaments, the powerlessness of the free press to act as the initiator of change, the growth of fascist and nationalist movements, voter apathy, and the weakness of political parties have contrasted sharply with the stability and dependability of bureaucracy, which has taken on an international character within the framework of the European Community and the United Nations. In a certain sense, the relationship of forces both in the East and in the West has changed perceptibly in favor of the traditional centralized state apparatus, not of civil society.

80. Among the first to recognize this was a Yugoslav dissident, Tomaz Mastnak, a Slovene. Analysing the events that had led to the break-up of Yugoslavia and the civil war in Bosnia, he noted that "civil society is not

necessarily a democratic concept in itself, and therefore should not be seen as a panacea." In the former Yugoslavia, in Mastnak's view, "civil societies are waging the war, so it would not seem wise to place much hope in them to make peace" (*Yugoslav War Report*, November-December 1992, p. 7).

81. N. Hawkes, ed., *Tearing Down The Curtain: The People's Revolution in Eastern Europe* (London, Sydney, etc., 1990), p. 154.

82. The disintegration of Czechoslovakia was not simply the result of the nationalist ambitions of political leaders. Industrial developments in Slovakia, which before 1939 had represented the agrarian periphery of the Czech republic, took a course quite different from that in the Czech lands. The liberal policies of Klaus hit especially hard at Slovakia. The old contradiction between the backward East and the developed West sharpened to the point where they tore the federation apart. See *East European Reporter*, vol. 5, no. 5 (September-October 1992).

83. John Feffer, *New Politics*, vol. III, no. 2 (10) (Winter 1991): 117.

84. *Alternativy*, 1992, no. 2, p. 2.

85. Zammit et al., *Hungary*, p. 45. The durability of democracy depends both on national traditions and on the peculiarities of each individual country. In this case the chances of Czechoslovakia could be said to be better than those of, say, Romania. For an analysis of the formation of civil society, see the corresponding section of J. Keane, *Civil Society and the State* (London and New York, 1988). For a study of the political culture of Poland, see A. Moscato, *Chiesa, partito e masse nella crisi polacca (1939-81)* (Maduria, Bari, and Rome, 1988). On Romania, see G. Kligman, "Reclaiming the Public: A Reflection on Creating Civil Society in Romania," *East European Politics and Societies*, vol. IV, no. 3 (Fall 1990). A comparative study of the political situation and of the state of civil society in the countries of Eastern Europe at the initial stage of the changes can be found in *Telos*, no. 79 (Spring 1989), special issue on Eastern Europe.

86. *Izvestiia*, 5 March 1991.

87. For data from surveys in the USSR, see *Voprosy ekonomiki*, no. 2 (1990): 67–69; from Russia under Yeltsin, *Sotsial'naia i politicheskaia situatsiia v Rossii: sostoiania i prognoz*; from Czechoslovakia, *Inprecor*, no. 319, (1990): 5; from Poland, *Zycie Warszawy*, 27 November 1990, and *International Viewpoint*, no. 198 (21 January 1991): 15.

88. *Literaturnaia gazeta*, 13 February 1991.

89. *Le Monde Diplomatique*, January 1991, p. 3.

90. *Green Left Weekly* (Sydney), 12 August 1992, p. 17.

Chapter 8: In Seach of a Vanguard

1. In the GDR in November 1989 New Forum and other left groups dominated the streets, while several months later they no longer played any particular role in public life. The positions of noncommunist leftists in the GDR have been formulated most successfully in Wolfgang Ullmann: *Demokratie jetzt oder nie!* (Munich 1990). The differences between the left radicals united in Union-90 (*Bündnis-90*) and the Party of Democratic

Socialism are clearly evident in a joint interview by Ullmann and Gregor Gysi. See Gregor Gysi, *Einspruch!* (Berlin 1992).

2. *Vecherniaia Moskva*, 11 September 1990; *Nezavisimaia gazeta*, 23 March 1991.

3. *East European Reporter*, vol. 4, no. 3 (Autumn-Winter 1990): 26.

4. *The Economist, The World in 1991*, p. 38.

5. D. Meissner and J. Meyer-Stamer, "Lateinamerikanische Schwellenländer: Vorbild für Osteuropa?" *Vierteljahres Berichte*, no. 129 (September 1992): 253. In the winter of 1991 the leader of the Moscow Communist Party organization, Iu.N. Prokof'ev, pointed to South Korea and Chile under Pinochet as models for the future of Russia.

6. *Dialog*, no. 10 (1990): 46–47.

7. *Social Democracy and Transition in Eastern-Central Europe* (Budapest, 1992), p. 13.

8. *Vierteljahres Berichte*, no. 129 (September 1992): 253.

9. *Nezavisimaia gazeta* 14 February 1991. As one of the leaders of the Leningrad section of the Social Democratic Party noted, Russian social democracy was characterized by "right-wing positions, bordering on liberalism"; Russian social democrats were distinguished from liberal democrats only by a greater readiness "for dialogue with Communists"; *Panorama*, no. 11 (September 1990): 6.

10. *Nezavisimaia gazeta*, 1 October 1992.

11. Ibid. The efforts by the party to create its own distinctive public face were just as fruitless after the removal of Rumyantsev as they had been under the former leadership. The social democrats spoke of the need to support the strategies of the government, and at the same time saw potential allies in the Party of Labor and the Socialist Party of Workers, both of which opposed these strategies. An appeal for active collaboration with the trade unions was accompanied by a qualification: only trade unions outside the Federation of Independent Trade Unions of Russia, which unites more than 85 per cent of hired workers. After the Sixteenth Plenum of the SDPR leadership, Yurii Khavkin, representing the party's commission on collaboration with the government, acknowledged openly on the pages of *Nezavisimaia gazeta* that the government was rejecting practically all the suggestions it received from the social democrats. Nevertheless, he maintained, the effort at cooperation had to be continued. The SDPR's suggestions were not rejected from political motives. This is clear from Khavkin's revelation that the party's principal demand was for "the opportunity to purchase one share for one voucher" (*Nezavisimaia gazeta*, 7 October 1992). It did not even occur to the "experts" of the SDPR that while the vouchers have a nominal worth of ten thousand rubles, shares can be issued with any face value.

12. The change of name was accompanied by a review of programmatic aims. The former Communists became unexpectedly amenable to the market and to private entrepreneurship. In practice, this party had pursued neoliberal policies long before 1990. "All or almost all of the right-wing

groups in the country are calling for a pact with the government," one of the leaders of the Polish socialists, Petr Ikonowicz, observed in 1990. "Why is this? For the simple reason that the economic reform urged by the Communists coincides with the program of the rightists" (cited in *Socialismo o Barbarie*, Winter 1991, p. 79).

13. *New Politics*, vol. III, no. 2 (Winter 1991): 159.

14. Aleksandr Lilov, *Bolgarskata Sotsialisticheska Partiia triabva da stane nova partiia* (Sofia, 1991), p. 35.

15. *East European Reporter*, vol. V, no. 1 (January-February 1992): 54.

16. *Le Monde Diplomatique*, no. 442 (January 1991): 3.

17. A. Glubotskii, *Estoniia, Latviia, Litva, Belorussiia. Politicheskie partiia i organizatsii* (Moscow, 1992), p. 11.

18. *Programme of the Democratic Labour Party of Lithuania* (Vilnius 1991), p. 3. The Democratic Labor Party of Latvia characterizes itself as a left party of the parliamentary type, and also stresses its social democratic orientation (see Glubotskii, *Estonia*, p. 34). As usual in Eastern Europe, alongside the Democratic Labour Party of Lithuania a "real" social democratic party was operating; this stood on even more right-wing positions. The leaders of this party stressed that "social democrats involve themselves in a constant search for compromises, for reconciliation between opposing sides. They know that there will always be the unfortunate, the poor, the homeless, the unemployed, but they believe that these people cannot be allowed to remain in destitution, without elementary support from the state. Humanity—there is the key to understanding the actions of this party"; see *Respublika* (Vilnius), no. 41 (1992): 3). The principle here is no longer social reform, but mere social philanthropy.

19. Glubotskii, *Estonia*, p. 57.

20. *Programme of the Democratic Labour Party of Lithuania*, p. 5.

21. *Inprecor*, no. 320 (1990): 9.

22. *New Politics*, no. 13 (1992): 90.

23. *Pravda*, 4 June 1990.

24. *Gorizont*, no. 11 (1990): 19. It is curious that the building of the Moscow Higher Party School where this research was carried on was officially valued, with its hotel and hostels, at 12 million rubles. Thirty-three buildings, the property of the regional party organs in Moscow, were assigned a value of approximately 30 million.

25. *Argumenty i fakty*, no. 40 (1990): 2.

26. The events of August 1991 are discussed in more detail in my article "*Strannyi perevorot*", which was published in the journals *New Statesman, Vek XX i mir*, etc., and an edited version of which was also included in B. Kagarlitsky, *The Disintegration of the Monolith* (London & New York, 1993).

27. *Dialog*, no. 17 (1990): 35.

28. In Hungary a partial differentiation occurred when the party split into the Socialist Party and the Socialist Workers Party. In Russia the reformist conservatives were represented simultaneously by three groups corresponding to M.S. Gorbachev, A.N. Yakovlev, and E.A. Shevardnadze, and

Iu.N. Prokof'ev. Also in this camp were the opposition Democratic Movement of Communists, a large part of which later helped to found the People's Party of Free Russia. Meanwhile, the radicals were grouped around the Russian Initiative Congress led by S. Kurginian, as well as including part of the Marxist Platform. After the August 1991 coup attempt, moderates united in the Socialist Party of Workers, and orthodox Communists and Stalinists in the Russian Communist Workers Party (RKRP). After the ban was lifted from the Communist Party in 1993, a large group of moderates went over to the Communist Party of the Russian Federation, headed by Gennadii Ziuganov.

29. S.E. Kurginian, B.R. Autenshlius, P.S. Goncharov, Iu.V. Gromyko, I.Iu. Sundiev and V.S. Ovchinskii, *Postperestroika: kontseptual'naia model' razvitiia nashego obshchestva, politicheskikh partii i obshchestvennikh organizatsii* (Moscow, 1990), pp. 69, 67. After the events of August 1991 the ideologue of the "Post-perestroika" group, S. Kurginian, switched from neocommunist to "patriotic" positions, proclaiming the need to overcome the contradiction between left and right to form a national movement.

30. *PDS Pressedienst*, no. 23 (7 June 1991): 7.

31. Gysi, *Einspruch!*, p. 261.

32. *Quatrième Internationale*, no. 39 (December 1990-January 1991): 52. Replying to this criticism, the PDS ideologue André Brie stressed that an anticapitalist perspective was inconceivable without a "radical reformist project" resting on concrete interests. The social democrats lacked such a project, but the PDS was working towards it; see *Utopie-Kreativ*, vol. 16 (December 1991): 109.

33. *Arbeiterkampf*, no. 328 (11 March 1991): 41.

34. Gysi (ed.), *Wir brauchen einen dritten Weg* (Hamburg, 1990), p. 19.

35. A reservation must be made here: in this case the word "communism" is used to refer to "existing communism," the ideology and practice of the Communist movement, rather than "classless society," the sense in which Marx understood the term.

36. *Khamsin 11*, pp. 110–11.

37. *Socialist Worker Review* (London), March 1991, p. 13.

38. *Permanentnaia revoliutsiia* (publication of the Committee for the Soviet Section of the Fourth International), no. 1 (1991): 1. Ernest Mandel and various other representatives of Western Trotskyism should be given their due for rejecting attempts to found their own sections in Eastern Europe.

39. James Petras and Morris Morley, *U. S. Hegemony Under Siege*, (London and New York, 1990), pp. 161, 157, 167.

40. Andre Gunder Frank and M. Fuentes in *Transforming the Revolution*, p. 179.

41. Samuel Farber, *Before Stalinism: The Rise and Fall of Soviet Democracy* (London and New York, 1990), p. 213.

42. This was not denied by Lenin himself, who spoke repeatedly of the Jacobinism of the Bolsheviks. The German scholar Robert Kurz notes that this Jacobin strain in the Bolsheviks' thinking was closely connected with

their role as a radical modernizing party (see Kurz, *Der Kollaps der Modernisierung* pp. 46–47). Kurz, however, depicts the Bolsheviks as a petty-bourgeois party basing themselves on an incorrect understanding of Marxist theory. This interpretation is in conflict with historical facts. The Bolsheviks were a genuinely working-class party, and the revolution of 1917 was carried out by many millions of people who rejected bourgeois modernization, but who ended up in the prison of bureaucratic modernization. The tragedy of Russian history consists precisely in this. It is curious that while criticizing Jacobinism, some left radical writers still try to preserve the idea of a vanguard party. See, for example, *Per una nuova idea della rivoluzione e del socialismo* (Rome, 1990).

43. P. Broue, *Trotsky* (Paris, 1988), p. 88.

44. Farber, *Before Stalinism*, p. 115–24. See also Kagarlitsky, *Dialektika nadezhdy* (Paris, 1988).

45. The ideologues of perestroika in the Soviet Union proclaimed "multi-structuralism" as the supreme virtue, confusing it with a mixed economy.

46. A. Vanaik, calling for the creation in India of a radical left movement uniting revolutionaries and reformists, considers that this "Gramscian" project does not in any way contradict Leninist vanguardism (A. Vanaik, *The Painful Transition*, p. 271). In fact, two approaches are in conflict here.

47. *Conferencia teórica internacional*, p. 453.

48. *Prisma latinoamericano*, no. 1 (1986): 3.

49. *Latinskaia Amerika*, no. 3 (1984): 56.

50. *Que Hacer, 34*, June 1985, p. 20.

51. *Que Hacer, 35*, June 1985, p. 65.

52. *La Reppubblica*, 16 April 1985.

53. Poole and Renique, *Peru: Time of Fear* (London, 1992), p. 126–27.

54. *Unidad* (Lima), 24 October 1985. Comparing the social bases of the United Left and APRA, scholars noted that the Apristas in 1985 succeeded in "mobilizing the overwhelming majority of the marginal population of the city and of the country's interior regions" (*Latinskaia Amerika*, no. 8 [1986]: 46). Barrantes and the United Left received backing from the working class and from members of peasant unions. On this basis, rightists argued that Peruvian Marxists were defending the interests of the most prosperous sectors of the working population (*Russkaya mysl'*, 13 June 1986, p. 16). The majority of Lima slumdwellers, who had supported Barrantes as mayor of the Peruvian capital, voted for García in the presidential elections.

55. Guillermo Rochabrun, *Margenes*, vol. 2, no. 3 (1988): 95.

56. *Movimientos sociales y democracia: la fundación de un nuevo orden* (Lima, 1986), p. 35.

57. *Que Hacer* no. 35, p. 53.

58. Poole and Renique, *Peru*, p. 136.

59. *South*, January 1988, p. 28.

60. *Inprecor*, no. 333 (1991): 18.

61. "Dominated by self-interested politicians from established parties, this Congress has so far failed to generate popular support" (*Green Left Weekly/Venceremos,* Winter 1992, p. 3). According to *Latin America Weekly Report,* as many as 96 percent of Peruvians supported Fujimori's coup. Even if this figure is greatly exaggerated, there is clearly deep disappointment among Peruvians with the institutions of liberal democracy. Compared to this, Yeltsin's 1993 coup looks much less successful and the record of the Russian Congress, itself not very good, at least looks better.
62. Margenes, vol. 1, no. 2 (1987): 150–151.
63. J. Martínez Alier, ibid., p. 71.
64. *Hoy X hoy* (Bogotá), 28 March 1989, p. 28.
65. Cuauhtémoc Cárdenas in *Sous le drapeau de Socialisme,* no. 118–119 (1991): 21.
66. *Correo internacional,* no. 13 (March 1991): 41.
67. *Latinskaia Amerika,* no. 4 (1992): 37.
68. E. Sader and K. Silverstein, *Without the Fear of Being Happy* (London, 1991), p. 105.
69. *Journal M,* no. 42 (December 1990): 7.
70. *Inprecor,* no. 317 (1991): 23.
71. Maria Helena Moreira Alves, *Monthly Review,* vol. 42, no. 4 (September 1990): 14.
72. *Inprecor,* no. 331 (1991): 18.
73. On the experience of the Workers Party in the field of municipal administration, see Jorge Bittar (ed.), *O modo petista de governar. Caderno especial de Teória y Debate,* Emir Sader, *Gobernar para todos* (São Paulo, 1992).
74. *Correo internacional,* no. 13 (March 1991): 16.
75. *Monthly Review,* vol. 42, no. 7 (1990): 43.
76. *Against the Current,* no. 17 (November-December 1988): 35.
77. *Monthly Review,* vol. 42, no. 7 (1990): p. 46.
78. *Journal M,* no. 42 (December 1990): 11.
79. *Inprecor,* no. 331 (1991): 19.
80. *Socialismo: impasses e perspectivas* (São Paulo, 1992), p. 187.
81. J. Genoino, *Repensando o socialismo* (São Paulo, 1991), p. 25.
82. For an example of the renewed appeal of Social Democratic thinking in the Latin American left, see J.G. Castañeda, *Utopia Unarmed: The Latin American Left After the Cold War* (New York: 1993).
83. *Veja,* 21 April 1993, p. 37.
84. Cárdenas, *Sous le drapeau de Socialisme,* no. 118-119 (1991): 21.
85. *Inprecor,* no. 334 (1991): 7.
86. *Workers Voice* (London), no. 2 (March 1991): 23.
87. *Socialist Review* (San Francisco), no. 2 (1992): 115.
88. *East European Reporter,* vol. 4, no. 3 (Autumn-Winter 1990): 16.
89. *Za rubezhom,* no. 50 (1990): 11. Reprinted from *Nepszabadzsag.*
90. *Izvestiia,* 6 March 1991.
91. *Moskovskii komsomolets,* 16 January 1991.
92. *Izvestiia,* 11 January 1991, p. 2.

93. The leaders of the Lithuanian Communists stated that Gorbachev promised them in advance his support and the introduction of presidential rule in the republic. See Glubotskii, *Estonia, etc.*, p. 54.
94. *Labour Focus on Eastern Europe*, no. 42 (1992): 40.
95. *Vierteljahres Berichte*, no. 129 (September 1992): 253.
96. *International Viewpoint*, no. 235 (September 1992): 9-11.
97. *Inprecor*, no. 359 (1992): 18.
98. *Gazeta Wyborcza*, 24 July 1992, no. 173.
99. Julia Szalai in H. Wainwright et al. (eds.), *After the Wall: Democracy and Politics in the New Europe* (Amsterdam, 1992), p. 78.
100. *Moskovskie novosti*, 1 November 1992.
101. *Moskovskaia pravda*, 31 August 1991.
102. *Dialog*, no. 17 (1990); *Demokraticheskaia Rossiia*, no. 5 (1990). Public opinion surveys commissioned in 1992 by the Russian television program *Vesti* yielded results that were staggering from the point of view of the official propagandists. A total of 67 percent of respondents acknowledged the advantages of socialism, and only 18 percent considered that socialism had no advantages.
103. *East European Reporter*, vol. 5, no. 1 (January-February 1992): 20.
104. *Przeglad Spoleczny*, no. 4 (1992): 41. Documents of the Union of Labor, and articles and materials by its ideologues, were published in English in *Labour Focus on Eastern Europe*, nos. 41 and 42 (1992).
105. *Inprecor*, no. 319 (1990): 5.
106. *Respublika*, no. 41 (1992): 1.
107. Ibid., p. 2.
108. *Moskovskie novosti*, no. 44 (1 November 1992): 9.

INDEX

317